STUDY GUIDE

to accompany

MACROECONOMICS

DAVID N. HYMAN

Prepared by

DONALD P. MAXWELL
Central State University

1989

IRWIN

Homewood, IL 60430
Boston, MA 02116

Contents

Preface

1 Economics: What It's All About, 1

Basic Tools for Analyzing Economic Relationships, 9

2 The Economic Way of Reasoning: Models and Marginal Analysis, 28

3 Production Possibilities and Opportunity Cost, 36

4 Market Transactions: Basic Supply and Demand Analysis, 52

5 Using Supply and Demand Analysis, 70

6 The Price System: How It Functions and When It Fails, 83

7 Elasticity of Supply and Demand, 98

8 Gross National Product and the Performance of the National Economy, 111

9 Business Cycles and Unemployment, 125

10 Inflation and Its Consequences, 138

11 The Forces of Aggregate Supply and Demand: Investigating the Causes of Cyclical Unemployment and Inflation, 148

12 The Components of Aggregate Demand: Consumption, Investment, Government Purchases, and Net Exports, 162

13 Aggregate Demand and Keynesian Analysis of Macroeconomic Equilibrium, 181

A Complete Keynesian Model, 195

14 Aggregate Supply: Its Influence on Macroeconomic Equilibrium and Economic Growth, 198

15 The Functions of Money, 211

16 The Banking System, 226

17 The Federal Reserve System and Its Influence on Money and Credit, 238

18 Stabilization of the Economy Through Monetary Policy, 250

19 Stabilization of the Economy Through Fiscal Policy: Effects on Aggregate Demand and Aggregate Supply, 266

20 The Federal Budget Deficit and the National Debt, 280

21 Tradeoffs Between Inflation and Unemployment and the Theory of Rational Expectations, 291

22 International Trade, Productivity, and the Economics of Less Developed Countries, 306

23 The Economics of Foreign Exchange and the Balance of International Trade, 320

24 Economics and Ideology: Socialism vs. Capitalism, 333

TO THE STUDENT

This Study Guide to accompany Hyman, Economics is designed as a set of interactive modules covering the key concepts developed in the textbook chapters and appendices. These modules will help you understand and apply the concepts you need to know. The Study Guide is based on my experiences teaching university economics for over a decade.

Each chapter of the Study Guide begins with **Chapter Challenges**, which give you the important learning objectives of the corresponding textbook chapter. This is followed by **In Brief: Chapter Summary**, which asks you to complete the summary, and in doing so review key concepts. The **Vocabulary Review** that follows is a fill-in exercise that will reinforce your understanding of the key terms in David Hyman's Economics glossary. Next comes a set of problems and exercises, **Skills Review**, selected to reinforce the main learning objectives of the chapter. These questions are presented in the same order as the concepts appear in the textbook. Each block of questions in the Skills Review section is subtitled according to the learning concept to which it applies, so that you can concentrate on areas that require extra study. These problems and exercises involve graphing, filling in tables, completing sentences, matching, listing, and discussion. For most chapters, advanced questions are included. These offer additional challenges and the opportunity to apply more advanced analysis, such as algebraic analysis, to certain problems.

After the Skills Review, a minitest of 15 to 20 multiple choice questions, like those you will encounter on exams, is included in the **Self-Test for Mastery**. These questions will give you feedback to determine how well you have mastered the important concepts of the chapter. The self-test is followed by 3 to 5 discussion questions that ask you to apply the concepts of the chapter to issues and problems. Following this **Discussion** section, 20 chapters of the Study Guide include a **Pop Quiz**. This exercise asks you to read a recent Wall Street Journal news article and answer one or two discussion questions. At the end of each chapter or appendix is an answer key. **Chapter Answers** include answers to all sections of the Study Guide, including discussion questions, so that you can check your progress.

In using this Study Guide, I suggest you first read the textbook chapter, paying particular attention to the introductory statement of learning objectives for the chapter and the concept checks that appear throughout the chapter. Next, complete the fill-in summary section of the Study Guide. Go back to the textbook and read and study the section for any parts of the summary that you answered incorrectly. Answer the vocabulary exercise next, after you review the glossary terms in the margins of the text chapter.

The problems and exercises in the Skills Review correspond closely to the examples used by David Hyman in the textbook. Try to answer the questions in the Skills Review and go back to the text for additional study if you have difficulty understanding how to answer a question. You can use the answer key for help, but you will get the most benefit by first studying the text and then working the problems in the Study Guide, rather than by going directly to the answer key.

After completing the Skills Review, take the self-test of multiple choice questions and compare your answers to those in the answer key to see where you need to spend additional study time. Review the concepts in the text and Study Guide that you have not yet mastered. Now try to answer the discussion questions from the Discussion and Pop Quiz sections. Read the answers to the discussion questions in the answer section. If there are discussion questions that you do not understand, go back to the corresponding sections of the text and Study Guide for additional study.

ACKNOWLEDGMENTS

I would like to thank the editors and staff at Times Mirror/Mosby and Irwin for suggesting this project and providing advice and support throughout the preparation of the manuscript. In particular, I would like to thank Jean Babrick, Developmental editor for Supplements, and Denise Clinton, Sponsoring Editor, for their encouragement and assistance. I would like to thank David Hyman for making this possible. I also want to thank the copy editors, Elisabeth Heitzeberg and Sandy Gilfillan for their work on the manuscript. Finally, thanks to Kathy Lumpkin, Production Editor, and her staff for bringing the Study Guide to you.

The Study Guide was reviewed by an expert in the design of of educational supplements and by several experienced university economics instructors for general content, appropriateness, and accuracy. Special thanks go to the technical reviewers of the manuscript, Kathy Gillespie of St. Louis University and Ben Childers of the University of Missouri, Columbia. Additional and very sincere thanks go to **Irwin Feller**, Penn State University, **James Kahn**, State University of New York, Binghamton, **William Witter**, University of North Texas, and **Richard Spivack** of Bryant College for reviewing the entire manuscript and providing valuable feedback and suggestions.

Don Maxwell
Central State University

1

Economics: What It's All About

CHAPTER CHALLENGES

After studying your text, attending class, and completing this chapter, you should be able to:

1. Describe the mechanism of the economy and the discipline of economics.
2. Understand the concepts of scarcity and opportunity costs.
3. Discuss major branches of economic inquiry: microeconomics, macroeconomics, positive analysis, and normative analysis.

IN BRIEF: CHAPTER SUMMARY

Fill in the blanks to summarize chapter content.

Economics is a study concerned with the use society makes of its
(1)_____ (scarce, abundant) resources in attempting to satisfy the
(2)_____ (normal, unlimited) desires of its members. The economy
represents the mechanism or structure that organizes scarce resources for the
purpose of producing the goods and services desired by society.
(3)_____ (Inflation, Scarcity) is the fundamental problem facing all
economies. It is also the reason decisions or choices involve
(4)_____ (opportunity costs, production costs).

The real cost or opportunity cost of any choice is the value of the sacrifice
required in making that decision. That sacrifice represents the foregone
opportunity to pursue the (5)_____ (next best, any) decision. A
fundamental problem confronting an economy is how to best meet the desires of
individuals in a world of scarcity. Economies do this by addressing several
basic questions: (a) What will be produced? (b) How will goods and services be
produced? (c) To whom will goods and services be distributed? An economy's
answers to the first two questions reveal the (6)_____ (fairness,
efficiency) with which resources are used to satisfy the desires of society.
The third question requires that society make value judgments regarding the
distribution of income.

The two major branches of economic analysis are macroeconomics and
microeconomics. (7)_____ (Macroeconomics, Microeconomics) is concerned
with the economic behavior of individual decision-making units in the economy.
(8)_____ (Macroeconomics, Microeconomics) is concerned with the
effects of the aggregate economic behavior of all individuals, firms, and
institutions. Inflation and unemployment are two topics that are studied in
(9)_____ (macroeconomics, microeconomics), whereas the determination of
prices and an analysis of markets are subjects dealt with in
(10)_____ (macroeconomics, microeconomics).

Positive economic analysis seeks to determine (11)_____ ("what ought to be", "what is"). (12)_____ (Positive, Normative) economic analysis emphasizes the "should" or "ought to" approach. Positive analysis tries to uncover cause-and-effect relationships that are subject to empirical observation and verification. In contrast, normative analysis depends upon the analyst's (13)_____ (value judgment, mathematical skills). Disagreements arise among practitioners in any discipline. With positive analysis, it is possible to resolve disagreements empirically. With normative analysis, disagreements stem from different value systems and must be resolved in ways other than looking at the "facts."

VOCABULARY REVIEW

Write the key term from the list below next to its definition.

Key Terms

Economy	Macroeconomics
Economics	Unemployment rate
Scarcity	Inflation
Opportunity cost	Positive analysis
Microeconomics	Normative analysis

Definitions

1. _____: the cost of choosing to use resources for one purpose measured by the sacrifice of the next best alternative for using those resources.

2. _____: economic analysis concerned with the individual choices made by participants in the economy--also called price theory.

3. _____: the rate of upward movement in the price level for an aggregate of goods and services.

4. _____: seeks to forecast the impact of changes in economic policies or conditions on observable items, such as production, sales, prices, and personal incomes, and then tries to determine who gains and who loses as a result of the changes.

5. _____: the mechanism through which the use of labor, land, structures, vehicles, equipment, and natural resources is organized to satisfy the desires of those who live in a society.

6. _____: the imbalance between the desires of society and the means with which those desires are satisfied.

7. _____: evaluates the desirability of alternative outcomes according to underlying value judgments about what is good or bad.

8. _____: a study of society's use of scarce resources in the satisfaction of the unlimited desires of its members.

9. _____: economic analysis that considers the overall

performance of the economy with respect to total national production, consumption, average prices, and employment levels.

10. _____: measures the ratio of the number of people classified as unemployed to the total labor force.

SKILLS REVIEW

Concept: Describe the mechanism of the economy

1. List the three basic questions that all economies must answer:

   a. _____
   b. _____
   c. _____

Concept: Opportunity cost

2. Identify the likely opportunity costs associated with the following decisions.

   Hint: Think in terms of what would likely be sacrificed in pursuing a decision. In other words, what would have been the next best use of your time, money, or resources?

   a. You decide to attend a university full time.
   b. Your decision to purchase a new home results in a larger portion of your income committed to mortgage payments.
   c. You are having such a good time in the Caribbean, that you decide to extend your vacation by taking an additional week of vacation at no pay.
   d. As a manager, you decide to commit some of the corporation's resources to a plant expansion project.

3. Advanced Problem. Suppose that you are a farmer capable of producing corn or soybeans. Over the years you have maintained records regarding your total production of both crops. Assume that you have made full and efficient use of your resources throughout this period. Furthermore, assume that the only reason corn relative to soy production has changed is because of your desire to grow the combination of crops that produce the highest net farm income. Referring to your production data below, determine the opportunity cost of producing an additional bushel of soybeans. If the current price of a bushel of corn is $7, what is the dollar value of that opportunity cost?

Production Data
(000s of bushels)

	Soy	Corn
1981	100	20
1982	50	40
1983	25	50
1984	0	60
1985	75	30
1986	150	0
1987	125	10

a. Opportunity cost measured in bushels of corn: _____ bushels

b. Opportunity cost measured in dollars: $ _____

Concept: Positive and normative analysis

4. In the blanks provided, indicate whether the following statements involve positive (P) or normative (N) analysis:

    a. _____ Fred ought to get his act together.
    b. _____ My professor arrives for class late every morning.
    c. _____ The drought in the Midwest is increasing corn prices.
    d. _____ Government is too obtrusive and therefore its power should be reduced.
    e. _____ Lower state income tax rates are always preferable to higher rates.
    f. _____ Poverty is a serious problem in the United States.

5. Monitor your own statements as you interact with friends, family members, or fellow students and try to determine if your statements are based upon fact or observation or value judgments. For one day, carry a sheet of paper divided into two columns--label one column "fact" and the other "value judgment." Record your interactions with others and think about whether positive or normative statements are being made.

SELF-TEST FOR MASTERY

Select the best answer.

1. Which of the following best describes the study of economics?

    a. A study concerned with how to make money
    b. A fuzzy combination of Wall Street and insurance
    c. A study of how society uses its goods and services in determining the proper distribution of income
    d. A study of how society uses its scarce economic resources in satisfying the unlimited desires of society

2. The mechanism through which resources are organized in order to satisfy the desires of society is known as:

    a. A corporation.
    b. Government.
    c. An economy.
    d. A factory.

3. Scarcity means that:

    a. Resources are in finite supply.
    b. Poverty takes its toll on those with limited means.
    c. Choices are unnecessary.
    d. An imbalance exists between desires and the means by which those desires are satisfied.

4. The real cost of a choice or decision is its opportunity cost. Which of the following best defines opportunity cost?

    a. The actual dollar outlay required to produce a good or service
    b. The value of the forgone next best alternative
    c. The value to the resources required to implement the decision

4

d. The value of the loss that occurs when a speculative investment does not meet profit expectations

5. If a state government had a limited amount of tax and other revenue but decided to substantially increase the amount of appropriations to public education, appropriations to other functions such as corrections, health, and welfare would diminish. What concept is represented by this statement?

a. Opportunity costs
b. Normative analysis
c. Efficiency
d. None of the above

6. Microeconomics is a branch of economics that:

a. Studies the impact of inflation on the unemployment rate.
b. Studies the behavior of individual decision-making units in the economy.
c. Studies the effects and consequences of the aggregate behavior of all decision-making units.
d. Is only concerned with the determination of income.

7. Macroeconomics is a branch of economics that:

a. Studies the effects and consequences of the aggregate behavior of all decision-making units in the economy.
b. Is only concerned with the determination of individual market prices.
c. Studies the behavior of individual decision-making units in the economy.
d. Studies neither inflation nor unemployment.

8. Topics such as business cycles, unemployment, and inflation are studied in _____, whereas the determination of prices and the study of individual markets are studied in _____.

a. Positive analysis/normative analysis
b. Normative analysis/positive analysis
c. Microeconomics/macroeconomics
d. Macroeconomics/microeconomics

9. The rate of unemployment is defined as:

a. The number of job seekers.
b. The number of individuals who have been laid off or are unemployed but seeking work.
c. The number of job seekers as a percentage of total employment.
d. The number of individuals who have been laid off or are unemployed but seeking work expressed as a percentage of the labor force.

10. With respect to inflation, which of the following is true?

a. A one-time price increase of bananas constitutes inflation.
b. Inflation represents a widespread and continuing increase in prices.
c. Inflation represents the main or fundamental problem faced by all economies.
d. Inflation is studied in microeconomics.

11. Which of the following involves value judgments?

a. Normative analysis
b. Positive analysis

c. The search for a superconducting material operable at room temperature

d. The decision to install lifeline (discount) electric utility rates for the elderly

e. A and d

12. _____ makes "ought to" or "should" statements, whereas _____ makes statements based upon observable events and therefore can be subjected to empirical verification.

a. Positive analysis/normative analysis
b. Normative analysis/positive analysis
c. Macroeconomics/microeconomics
d. Microeconomics/macroeconomics

THINK IT THROUGH

1. Define economics, including its branches, microeconomics and macroeconomics. What are some topics typically addressed by each of these branches?

2. Explain why scarcity and opportunity costs are related. Give an example from your personal or business experiences of the opportunity cost of a decision.

3. As you will discover later in the text, under certain assumptions it can be shown theoretically that a perfectly competitive economy will produce a distribution of income where labor receives an income based upon its productive contribution to the enterprise. This is consistent with the protestant ethic which states that hard work and reward should go hand in hand. This statement involves both positive and normative analysis. Discuss.

CHAPTER ANSWERS

In Brief: Chapter Summary

1. Scarce   2. Unlimited   3. Scarcity   4. Opportunity cost   5. Next best
6. Efficiency   7. Microeconomics   8. Macroeconomics   9. Macroeconomics   10.
Microeconomics   11. "What is"   12. Normative   13. Value judgments

Vocabulary Review

1. Opportunity costs 2. Microeconomics   3. Inflation   4. Positive analysis
5. Economy   6. Scarcity   7. Normative analysis   8. Economics   9.
Macroeconomics   10. Unemployment rate

Skills Review

1. a. What will be produced?
   b. How will goods and services be produced?
   c. To whom will goods and services be distributed?

2. a. If you attend a university full time, there are a number of potential sacrifices all of which have value. The most obvious sacrifice is the potential income you could have earned had you been employed full

time. You may have less time to spend with your family and friends, as well as less leisure time. Direct outlays on tuition, room, and board could have been invested or saved.

b. As recently as the early 1970s it was not uncommon for homeowners to allocate only 15% of their incomes to mortgage payments. Today it is more common for families to spend as much as 25% to 35% of their incomes for housing. If you commit a much larger share of your income to housing, given scarcity (or a limited income), you must cut your spending elsewhere. The reduction in the value of goods and services consumed as a result of purchasing a more expensive home represents the opportunity cost of your decision.

c. If you choose to take a week of vacation without pay, you obviously sacrifice the income you would have earned otherwise. That extra week, as a result, is much more costly to you than the previous week of vacation.

d. If corporate funds are to be used for a specific project, they cannot be used for alternative investment projects. Depending on the needs of the firm, the funds could be invested in financial assets generating an interest income. The funds could be used for other investment projects yielding income. Businesses interested in achieving the highest level of profit will usually allocate funds to the projects yielding the highest return because to do otherwise would mean that the firm would be sacrificing opportunities to earn profit.

3. a. Two fifths of a bushel of corn. Historical production data reveal that for every 10,000-bushel increase in corn production, there is a 25,000-bushel decrease in soy output. Because the farmer is fully using his or her resources and employing these resources efficiently, the only way soy production can be increased is by withdrawing resources from corn production and employing those resources in soy production. Consequently, for every bushel increase in corn production, there is a 2.5-bushel decrease in soy production. In other words, for every additional bushel of soy produced, corn production must be reduced by two fifths of a bushel.

b. Two fifths of a bushel times $7 per bushel = $2.80. The opportunity cost of producing a bushel of soy measured in dollars represents the dollar value of that sacrificed output of corn.

4. a. N   b. P   c. P   d. N   e. N   f. N

Self-Test for Mastery

1. d   2. c   3. d   4. b   5. a   6. b   7. a   8. d   9. d   10. b   11. e
12. b

Think it Through

1. Economics is a study of how society uses its scarce resources to satisfy the unlimited wants of its members. Macroeconomics is a study of the effects of the aggregate economic behavior of all decision-making units in the economy, whereas microeconomics is concerned with an analysis of the decision making of individual firms, households, or other decision-making units. Business cycles, inflation, and unemployment are topics covered in macroeconomics. Microeconomics, also known as price theory, analyzes among other things individual markets and the determination of prices.

2.   If there were no scarcity, the opportunity costs of decisions requiring the use of resources would be zero. There would be such a thing as a "free lunch." If resources were available everywhere and in unlimited supply, the farmer in the above example could at any time produce more soy or corn without having to sacrifice the output of the other.

3.   The first statement regarding a competitive economy's ability to reward labor on the basis of labor's productive contribution is deduced from economic theory, which itself is a collection of postulates based upon empirically verifiable observations. In this sense, this statement involves positive analysis. The second statement declares that this method of income distribution is "good." But this is based upon a value system consistent with the protestant ethic, which is only one of many possible value systems. It is therefore a normative statement.

Basic Tools for Analyzing Economic Relationships

IN BRIEF: APPENDIX SUMMARY

Fill in the blanks to summarize appendix content.

Describing data graphically requires a number of considerations. Does the variable take on positive values only or does it also take on negative values? What is the unit of measurement? For what purpose are the data to be plotted? If you want to present a cause-and-effect relationship between two variables, a plot of the variables on a (1)_____ (set of axes, bar graph) would be appropriate. If you are interested in the cause-and-effect relationship of a third variable, a (2)_____ (bar graph, set of axes) cannot be used. If you are only interested in presenting the fluctuation in a variable over time, a plot on a set of axes is usually all that is required, although a bar graph can be employed.

Because most economic variables take on positive values, a set of axes having an origin in the extreme (3)_____ (northeast, southwest) corner is required. As you read vertically upward or horizontally rightward from the origin, units of measurement become increasingly positive. Each axis is defined in terms of a unit of measurement. Units of measurement can be discrete or continuous. A (4)_____ (discrete, continuous) variable is expressed in units that are indivisible. A (5)_____ (discrete, continuous) variable is divisible into fractions of a whole.

A plot of a specific set of values or (6)_____ (coordinates, intersections) of two variables on a set of axes produces a curve when the points are connected by a line. The curve can reveal important information regarding the association among the two variables plotted. If the variable on the vertical axis increases when the variable plotted on the horizontal axis increases, there is a (7)_____ (positive, negative) relationship between the two variables. If the variable on the vertical axis decreases when the variable plotted on the horizontal axis increases, the relationship is a (8)_____ (positive, negative) one. If there is no change in the variable plotted on the vertical axis when the variable on the horizontal axis changes, there is no relationship between the variables.

The (9)_____ (intersection, slope) of a curve describes the rate of change in the variable on the vertical axis given a change in the variable on the horizontal axis. A curve describing a positive relationship between variables has a (10)_____ (positive, negative) slope. A curve describing a negative relationship has a (11)_____ (positive, negative) slope, and a curve indicating no relationship between the two variables has a slope of zero. On a bowl-shaped or inverted bowl-shaped curve, a slope of zero represents the point at which the curve (or the value of the variable plotted on the vertical axis) reaches a maximum or minimum value. Two curves that just touch each other but do not intersect have (12)_____ (unequal, equal) slopes at that point of tangency. If two curves (13)_____ (intersect, are tangent), the two slopes at that point can both be positive or negative or one can be positive and the other negative, but they cannot be equal to each other as is the case with (14)_____ (an intersection, a tangency).

VOCABULARY REVIEW

Write the key term from the list below next to its definition.

Key Terms

Origin   Coordinate
Curve   Positive relationship
Slope   Negative relationship
Bar graph   Discrete variable
Intersection   Continuous variable
Tangency   Time series data

Definitions

1. _____: Measures the rate at which the variable on the vertical axis rises or falls as the variable on the horizontal axis increases.

2. _____: Data that show fluctuations in a variable over time.

3. _____: The point on a set of axes at which both variables, X and Y, take on a value of zero.

4. _____: A graph that shows that value of Y as the height of a bar for each corresponding value of X.

5. _____: The point at which two curves cross on a set of axes.

6. _____: Variable Y increases whenever variable X decreases and vice versa.

7. _____: Variable Y increases whenever variable X increases and vice versa.

8. _____: A variable that can realistically and meaningfully take on minute fractions of a variable.

9. _____: A point at which two curves just touch but do not intersect.

10. _____: A pair of numbers that corresponds to a pair of values for variables X and Y when plotted on a set of axes.

11. _____: A variable that cannot vary by fractions of units.

12. _____: A straight or curved line drawn to connect points plotted on a set of axes.

SKILLS REVIEW

1. a. Using the production data from question 3 in the Skills Review
        section in Chapter 1, construct the following bar charts:

Production Data

	Soybeans (000s of bushels)	Corn (000s of bushels)
1981	100	20
1982	50	40
1983	25	50
1984	0	60
1985	75	30
1986	150	0
1987	125	10

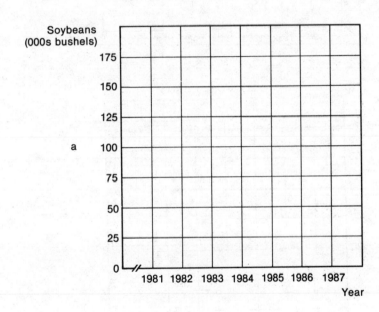

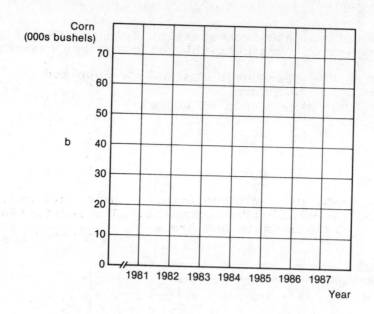

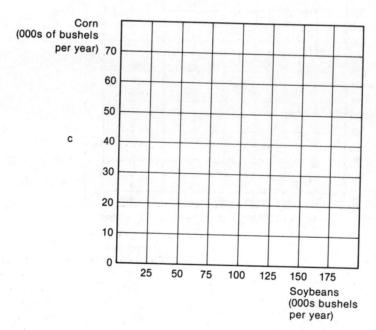

b.   Which of the above bar charts depict time series data and which depict a functional relationship representing the concept of opportunity costs?

    1.   Figure A _____
    2.   Figure B _____
    3.   Figure C _____

2. The following data represent quantities of tennis rackets demanded by consumers and supplied by producers at various prices:

Tennis Rackets
(000s per month)

Price per Racket	Quantity Demanded	Quantity Supplied
$10	75	15
20	65	20
30	55	25
40	45	30
50	35	35
60	25	40
70	15	45

a. In the figure below, plot a curve showing the relationship between price and quantity demanded by consumers. The relationship is a _____ relationship and has a _____ slope.

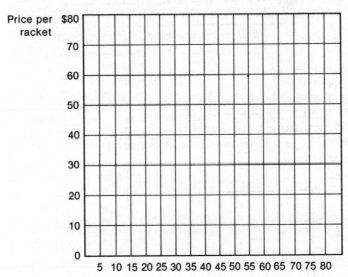

Price per racket

Quantity of rackets
demanded
(000s per month)

b. In the figure below, plot a curve showing the relationship between price and quantity supplied by producers. The relationship is a _____ relationship and has a _____ slope.

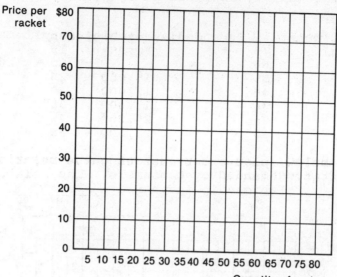

Price per $80
racket

70

60

50

40

30

20

10

0

5 10 15 20 25 30 35 40 45 50 55 60 65 70 75 80

Quantity of rackets
supplied
(000s per month)

c. In the figure below, plot both curves from parts a and b above. The coordinate at which the two curves cross is called a/an _____. At what price and quantity supplied and demanded do the two curves cross? Price_____, quantity demanded_____, quantity supplied_____.

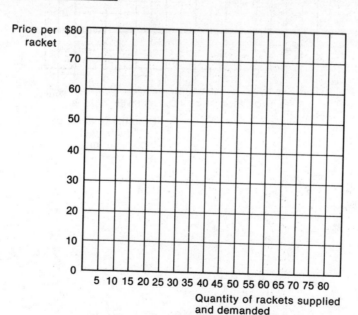

Price per $80
racket

70

60

50

40

30

20

10

0

5 10 15 20 25 30 35 40 45 50 55 60 65 70 75 80

Quantity of rackets supplied
and demanded
(000s per month)

3. Suppose that you are a manager for a producer of business forms and you have noticed that over time your sales of business forms appear to increase as the rate of growth in the nation's output or GNP increases. That observed relationship is depicted in the table below:

	Rate of Growth in GNP (%)	Sales of Business Forms
Year 1	3.0	15,000
2	3.5	17,000
3	2.0	11,000
4	5.5	25,000
5	6.0	27,000

a. In the figure below, plot a time series curve describing the behavior of the rate of growth in GNP.

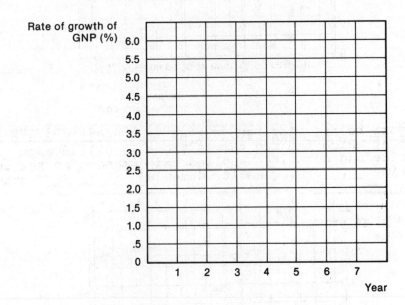

b. In the figure below, plot a time series curve describing the behavior of business forms sales.

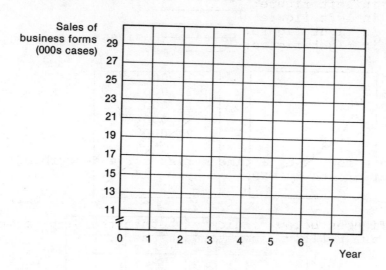

c. In the figure below, plot the functional relationship between the rate of growth in GNP and sales of business forms.

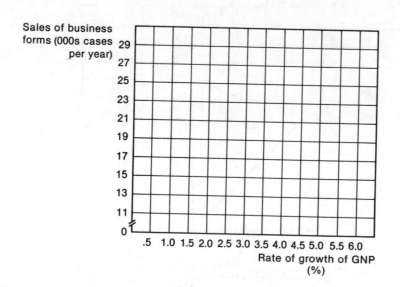

d. Advanced Question. If the rate of growth in GNP is expected to be 4.5% in year 6, what would you predict to happen to business form sales?

4. a. For the figures below, indicate whether a tangency exists or an intersection occurs at:

Point A in left figure: _____
Point B in right figure: _____

16

b. For the figures below, indicate whether the curves at the point of tangency or intersection have a positive or negative slope.

```
Curve 1 in left figure:  _____
Curve 2 in left figure:  _____
Curve 1 in right figure: _____
Curve 2 in right figure: _____
```

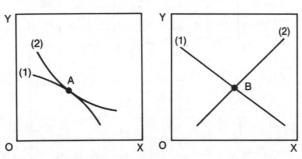

5. Referring to the figures below, indicate whether the slope at the designated points are positive, negative, or zero.

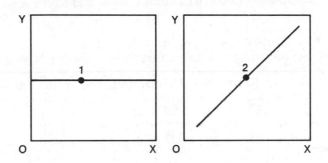

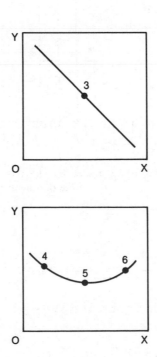

17

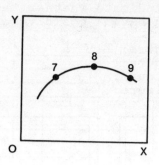

1. _____
2. _____
3. _____
4. _____
5. _____
6. _____
7. _____
8. _____
9. _____

6. __Advanced Problem__. Suppose two variables are related to each other by the following equation:

$$Y = a + bX, \quad \text{where } a = 10 \text{ and } b = 1/2$$

a. Complete the table. (Use the Y1 column for the case where a = 10.)

X	Y1	Y2
100		
200		
300		
400		
500		
600		
700		
800		

18

b.   Plot the relationship between X and Y1 in the figure below.
     (1)   The slope =_____.
     (2)   The intercept (value of Y1 at X = 0) =_____.

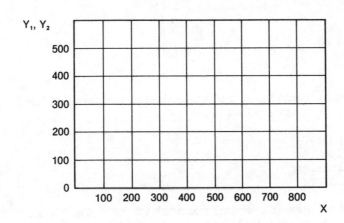

c.   Assume that the constant term a in the above equation increases from
     10 to 60. Complete column Y2 above and plot the new relationship in
     the figure in part b. The curve has shifted _____. The
     slope =_____ and the intercept = _____.

SELF-TEST FOR MASTERY

Select the best answer.

1.   Which of the following does not indicate a functional relationship between
     variables X and Y?

     a.   As X increases, Y increases
     b.   As X decreases, Y increases
     c.   As X increases, Y remains unchanged
     d.   As X decreases, Y decreases

2.   When a value for X is paired with a value for Y on a set of axes, this
     combination of values is known as:

     a.   A tangency.
     b.   An intersection.
     c.   A coordinate.
     d.   The origin, if at least one value is zero.

3.   A curve represents a set of coordinates that are connected by a line.
     Which of the following statements is true?

     a.   A curve by definition cannot be a straight line.
     b.   A curve must have either a positive or negative slope.
     c.   A line of zero slope is not a function and therefore is not a curve.

19

d. A curve may be a straight or a curved line. If it is a curved line, it is possible to have a positive, negative, or zero slope at different points on that curve.

4. If Y increases as X is increased, there is a _____ relationship between X and Y. If Y decreases as X is increased, the functional relationship is said to be a _____ one.

    a. Adverse, positive
    b. Negative, positive
    c. Obtuse, negative
    d. Positive, negative

5. A function exhibiting a positive relationship between X and Y has a _____ slope and a curve that is _____.

    a. Positive, upsloping
    b. Negative, downsloping
    c. Positive, downsloping
    d. Negative, upsloping

6. A function exhibiting a negative relationship between X and Y has a _____ slope and a curve which is _____.

    a. Positive, upsloping
    b. Negative, downsloping
    c. Positive, downsloping
    d. Negative, upsloping

7. Which of the following defines the origin?

    a. The origin is the beginning of a set of time series data.
    b. The origin is the coordinate on a set of axes where the value of variables X and Y are both zero.
    c. The origin is the coordinate on a set of axes where the values of variables X and Y represent the initial values of the data plotted.
    d. The origin is that point on the northeast corner of a set of positive axes.

8. The slope can be defined as the:

    a. Change in Y/change in X.
    b. Rate of change in Y over time.
    c. Rate of change in X over time.
    d. None of the above.

9. A _____ variable is indivisible into fractions of a unit, whereas a _____ variable is divisible into fractions of a whole.

    a. Continuous, discrete
    b. Discrete, continuous
    c. Positive, negative
    d. Time series, constant

10. Which of the following variables have discrete units of measurement?

    a. Automobiles
    b. Gasoline
    c. Coffee beans
    d. The nation's money supply

11. Of the following variables, which one is a continuous variable?

    a.   Computer
    b.   House
    c.   Basketball
    d.   Natural gas

12. When two curves just touch each other, they have _____ slopes.

    a.   Equal
    b.   Unequal
    c.   Positive and negative
    d.   Only zero

13. The point at which two curves just touch each other is called:

    a.   A tangency.
    b.   The origin.
    c.   A data point.
    d.   An intersection.

14. The point at which two curve cross is called:

    a.   A tangency.
    b.   The origin.
    c.   A data point.
    d.   An intersection.

15. The values of X and Y at an intersection:

    a.   Will be the same on both curves.
    b.   Will be the same on both curves for the X variable only.
    c.   Will not be the same on both curves.
    d.   Depend upon the placement of the origin.

THINK IT THROUGH

1. Referring to the data below, plot the price and quantity demanded data on the axes below. On the same set of axes, plot the price and quantity supplied data and interpret the meaning of the intersection. Suppose a third variable changes, such as the introduction of VCRs, and as a result the quantity of movie tickets demanded at each price level declines by 20,000 tickets per week. What happens to the curve representing the demand data? What happens to the intersection?

Price per Ticket	Quantity Demanded	Quantity Supplied
	(000s per week)	
$2	80	20
3	70	30
4	60	40
5	50	50
6	40	60
7	30	70

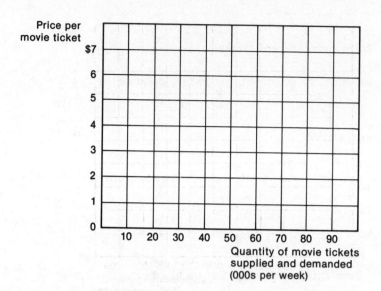

Price per
movie ticket

Quantity of movie tickets
supplied and demanded
(000s per week)

2.   The following data represent the relationship between interest rates and building permits issued for new residential construction in a local housing market. Plot the relationship on the axes below and determine if a positive or negative relationship exits. Because of a regional recession, assume that local incomes decline and outmigration of people reduce the demand for new housing and thus reduce building permits issued by 100 permits per month at each mortgage rate. Plot the new relationship on the same set of axes and compare the position and slope of the new curve to the one that you previously plotted.

Mortgage Rate %	Permits Issued (000s per month)
8.5	1050
9.0	1000
9.5	950
10.0	900
10.5	850
11.0	800
11.5	750

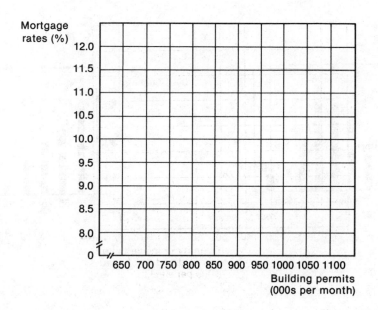

Mortgage rates (%)

Building permits (000s per month)

ANSWERS TO CHAPTER APPENDIX

In Brief: Appendix Summary

1. A set of axes or a bar graph 2. Bar graph 3. Southwest 4. Discrete 5. Continuous 6. Coordinates 7. Positive 8. Negative 9. Slope 10. Positive 11. Negative 12. Equal 13. Intersect 14. Tangency

Vocabulary Review

1. Slope 2. Time series data 3. Origin 4. Bar graph 5. Intersection 6. Negative relationship 7. Positive relationship 8. Continuous variable 9. Tangency 10. Coordinate 11. Discrete variable 12. Curve

Skills Review

1.   a.

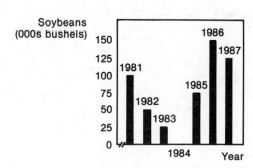

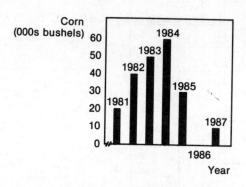

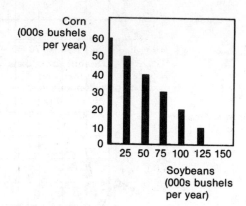

b.   (1)   Time series
         (2)   Time series
         (3)   Functional relationship

2.

a.

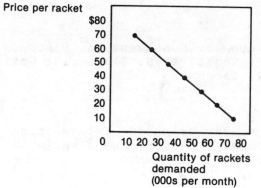

Negative, negative

b.

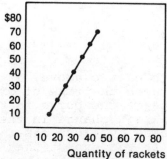

Positive, positive

24

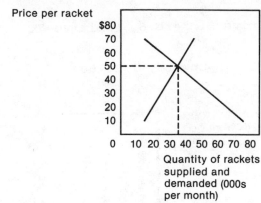

Price per racket

c.

Intersection, $50, 35, 35

3.

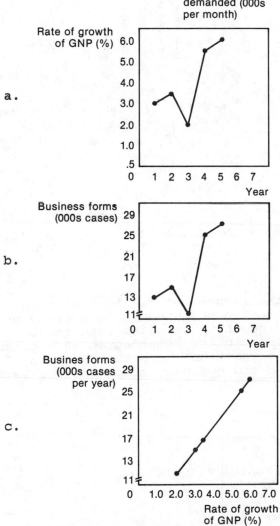

a.

b.

c.

d. From the functional relationship in part c above, it can be seen that a positive relationship exists between the rate of growth in GNP and sales of business forms. The slope of the curve is the change in business form sales for each percentage change in the rate of growth of GNP. Business form sales increase by 4,000 cases for each 1% increase in the GNP growth rate. If you expect that the growth rate of GNP will be 4.5% in year 6, then sales of business forms can be predicted to fall from 27,000 to 21,000 cases.

4. a. Tangency, intersection
   b. Negative, negative, positive, positive

5. 1. Zero 2. Positive 3. Negative 4. Negative 5. Zero 6. Positive 7. Positive 8. Zero 9. Negative

6. a. Y1
        60
       110
       160
       210
       260
       310
       360
       410

    c. Y2   Upward, 1/2. 60
        110
        160
        210
        260
        310
        360
        410
        460

    b.

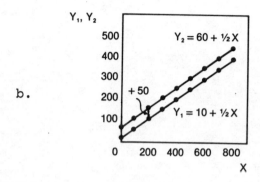

(1) 1/2   (2) 10

Self-Test for Mastery

1. c 2. c 3. d 4. a 5. a 6. b 7. b 8. a 9. b 10. a 11. d 12. a 13. a 14. d 15. a

Think It Through

1. The two curves intersect at point A in the figure below. At that point, the values for price and quantity are the same on both curves. At a price per movie ticket of $5, the quantity demanded and quantity supplied both equal 50,000 tickets per week. A reduction of 20,000 tickets demanded at each price shifts the demand curve leftward. The new intersection shows that a price of $4 is now required to equate quantity demanded and quantity supplied at a level of 40,000 tickets per week.

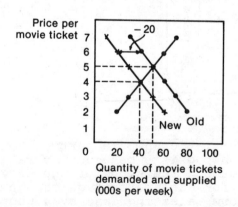

2. The relationship between mortgage rates and new building permits issued is a negative one. If building permits issued decline at each mortgage rate by 100 permits per month, the new curve lies to the left of the old curve but has the same slope.

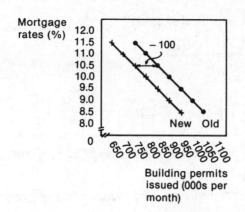

2

The Economic Way of Reasoning: Models and Marginal Analysis

CHAPTER CHALLENGES

After studying your text, attending class, and completing this chapter, you should be able to:

1. Understand the purpose of theory and the concept of an economic model and its uses.
2. Develop the notion of rational behavior and a general method of analyzing the way individuals make decisions, which is called marginal analysis.

IN BRIEF: CHAPTER SUMMARY

Fill in the blanks to summarize chapter content.

Economic analysis helps us understand the world around us. It helps us understand the functioning of the various sectors in the economy and the choices made by individual decision-making units. (1)_____ (Assumptions, Economic theories) simplify reality so that the underlying cause-and-effect relationships among variables can be understood. (2)_____ (Economic variables, Data) are quantities or dollar amounts that have more than one value. Theories are necessary in order to better understand the complexities of reality.

(3)_____ (A bar graph, An economic model) is a simplified way of expressing a theory. It can be expressed verbally, graphically, in tables, or mathematically. Assumptions underlie a theory because theories are (4)_____ (depictions of, abstractions from) reality, and it is necessary to establish the environment and motivation of people for which the theory holds. Economic models can be used to develop hypotheses. (5)_____ (An assumption, A hypothesis) is a statement of relationship between two variables that can be tested by empirical verification. Deductive reasoning is used when taking a general body of knowledge or theory and using implications of the theory to construct hypotheses. Hypotheses that have been subjected to repeated empirical verification and have withstood the test of time become (6)_____ (hypotheses, economic principles or laws). A good model is one that can generate accurate predictions. But even a model that does not predict perfectly can still be useful in helping us understand the causal relationships among variables and the consequence of the assumptions underlying the model. The causal relationships that we want to understand are difficult to isolate unless we make the assumption of (7)_____ (ceteris paribus, the invisible hand). Otherwise, we cannot be sure that we have identified the exact relationship between the two variables of interest.

Economic analysis makes the assumption of rationality. Rationality means that most people behave as if they are comparing the additional gains or benefits from a choice or decision to the sacrifices or opportunity costs associated with that decision. The opportunity cost of a decision is known as its marginal (8)_____(benefit, cost). If the marginal benefits of a decision exceed the marginal costs, the individual's net gain or benefit (9)_____(increases, decreases). If the marginal cost of a decision exceeds the marginal benefits, the decision would not be undertaken because the individual would experience a net (10)_____(loss, gain). If a choice or decision is pursued to the point where marginal benefits and marginal costs are equal, the individual achieves the (11)_____(maximum, minimum) net gain.

VOCABULARY REVIEW

Write the key term from the list below next to its definition.

Key Terms

Marginal analysis	Ceteris paribus
Theory	Behavioral assumptions
Variable	Rational behavior
Economic model	Marginal benefit
Hypothesis	Marginal cost

Definitions

1. _____: a quantity or dollar amount that can have more than one value.

2. _____: "other things being equal"--used to acknowledge that other influences aside from the one whose effect is being analyzed must be controlled for in testing a hypothesis.

3. _____: establishes the motivation of persons for the purpose of understanding cause-and-effect relationships among economic variables.

4. _____: a decision-making technique involving a systematic comparison of benefits and costs of actions.

5. _____: the additional benefit obtained when one extra unit of an item is obtained.

6. _____: the sacrifice made to obtain an additional unit of an item.

7. _____: an abstraction or simplification of actual relationships; establishes cause-and-effect relationships.

8. _____: statement of a relationship between two or more variables.

9. _____: seeking to gain by choosing to undertake actions for which the extra benefit exceeds the associated extra cost.

10. _____: a simplified way of expressing economic behavior or how some sector of the economy functions.

SKILLS REVIEW

Concept: Economic models and uses

1. Develop a hypothesis regarding the level of family spending on goods and services and the level of family income. Describe that hypothesized relationship by setting up two columns of data reflecting the variables in your hypothesis. Is the hypothesized relationship a positive or negative relationship? Suppose that you gathered actual data on your variables and for some families your hypothesized relationship did not hold. Of what use is the _ceteris paribus_ assumption in trying to isolate the relationship between family spending and income?

Family Spending on Goods and Services ($)	Family Income ($)

2. Suppose that you want to investigate the relationship between prices of restaurant meals and the quantity of meals demanded by local area households. Economic theory implies that there is a negative relationship between price and quantity demanded but that income, tastes, preferences, and other variables also influence quantity demanded. Clearly state your hypothesis and its underlying assumptions.

Concept: Marginal analysis

3. During the presidential campaign, Republican George Bush recommended that his party's platform include a proposal for child care payments of up to $1,000 to low-income working families and a tax credit for other families with children under age 4 in which at least one parent works. Assume that you are a single parent with young children. Using marginal analysis, assess the impact of such a program on your decision to work or to work additional hours.

4. Assume that the price you are willing to pay for an additional unit of a good measures the marginal benefit received. How could you measure the marginal cost of the decision to consume that extra unit?

5. A rational decision maker comparing the extra gains and losses of a decision will _____ net gains if the decision or choice is pursued to the point where _____ equals _____. Explain the logic of this statement.

6. _Advanced Question._ You are an administrator of the Environmental Protection Agency concerned with allocating cleanup funds from the agency's Superfund for the removal of toxic wastes. The following data represent the marginal benefits and costs associated with removing units of pollution from a polluted river. Your task is to decide if there is a net gain to society from cleaning the river and what level of pollution reduction would maximize that net gain.

Units of Pollution Reduction	Marginal Benefits	Marginal Costs
	(millions of dollars)	
0	$ 0	$ 0
1	10	2
2	8	4
3	6	6
4	4	8
5	2	10

a. Is there a net gain to society from cleaning the river? Discuss.

b. Nets gains are maximized at a level of pollution reduction of _____, where marginal benefits and marginal costs are _____.

SELF-TEST FOR MASTERY

1. The decision-making technique involving a systematic comparison of the benefits and costs of actions is known as:

   a. Deductive reasoning.
   b. Total gains analysis.
   c. Marginal analysis.
   d. Ceteris paribus.

2. A/An _____ is a simplification of reality seeking to uncover the underlying cause-and-effect relationships among economic _____.

   a. Assumptions/variables
   b. Economic theory/assumptions
   c. Hypothesis/theories
   d. Economic theory/variables

3. Which of the following is true regarding economic variables?

   a. Economic variables have more than one value.
   b. Economic variables are quantities or dollar amounts.
   c. Economic variables are necessary to economic theories and models.
   d. All of the above.

4. A/An _____ is a simplified way of expressing an economic theory.

   a. Economic model
   b. Assumption
   c. Abstraction
   d. Economic principle

5. Which of the following assumptions is necessary in order to isolate the relationship between two variables?

   a. "All things allowed to vary"
   b. "All things held constant"
   c. "Ceteris paribus"
   d. B and c

6. If gasoline prices rise, the quantity of gasoline demanded will fall. This statement is a/an:

   a. Assumption.
   b. Theory.
   c. Abstraction.
   d. Hypothesis.

7. Economic hypotheses that have been subjected to repeated empirical investigation over time and have not been rejected, become:

   a. Economic policy
   b. Assumptions

31

c. Economic principles or laws
d. None of the above

8. If household purchases of automobiles are determined by both the level of household income and the interest rate and you want to isolate the relationship between interest rates and auto sales, you must assume:

a. That the interest rate remains unchanged.
b. That auto sales remain unchanged.
c. That household income remains unchanged.
d. None of the above because you would want to know both the effect of interest rates and income on auto sales.

9. Which of the following best defines rational behavior?

a. Seeking to gain by choosing to undertake actions for which the marginal benefits exceed the associated marginal costs
b. A comparison of the total gains and losses from a decision
c. Decisions that avoid habit or impulse purchases
d. Improving net gain by pursuing decisions in which the marginal costs of a decision exceed the marginal benefits

10. _____ can be defined as the extra benefit received from undertaking some action.

a. Total benefit
b. Total gain
c. Marginal benefit
d. Total net gain

11. _____ can be defined as the extra cost associated with some action.

a. Total cost
b. Marginal cost
c. Total loss
d. Total net loss

12. The total net gain from a decision or action reaches a _____ when a decision or action is pursued to the point where _____ equals _____ .

a. Maximum,total cost,total benefit
b. Minimum, marginal benefit,marginal cost
c. Minimum, total benefit, marginal benefit
d. Maximum, marginal benefit, marginal cost

13. The sacrifice made to obtain an additional unit of an item is known as:

a. Opportunity cost.
b. The maximum tradeoff.
c. Marginal cost.
d. A and c.
e. B and c.

THINK IT THROUGH

1. Define the concepts of economic theory and economic models. Discuss the importance of assumptions underlying models and theories.

2. Pollution is harmful to society, and the reduction of pollution levels increase society's total benefits. But if a 50% reduction in the pollution level resulted in an equality between the marginal benefits and marginal costs associated with pollution reduction, society would be better off if pollution were not eliminated completely. Reconcile the two statements.

3. A rational person would never engage in habit or impulse buying. Discuss.

4. A hypothesis requires the use of the ceteris paribus assumption. Why? Give an example.

5. A theory must depict reality. Do you agree? Explain.

CHAPTER ANSWERS

In Brief: Chapter Summary

1. Economic theories 2. Economic variables 3. Economic model 4. Abstractions from 5. Hypothesis 6. Economic principles or laws 7. Ceteris paribus 8. cost 9. Increase 10. Loss 11. Maximum

Vocabulary Review

1. Variable 2. Ceteris paribus 3. Behavioral assumptions 4. Marginal analysis 5. Marginal benefit 6. Marginal cost 7. Theory 8. Hypothesis 9. Rational behavior 10. Economic model

Skills Review

1. Hypothesis: Other things held constant, family spending on goods and services is expected to be positively related to family income.

   If upon gathering data on family spending and income it is found that the relationship between spending and income is not positive, that does not mean that your hypothesis is invalid. To determine the validity of your hypothesis, you must isolate the relationship you are interested in from all other variables that might influence family spending. If you do not, you cannot be sure that an increase in family spending is the result of increases in income or some third variable.

2. Hypothesis: Other things being the same, the price of restaurant meals and the quantity of restaurant meals demanded are expected to be inversely (negatively) related.

   The ceteris paribus assumption is necessary to control for other factors that influence quantity demanded, such as income and tastes and preferences. For instance, prices could be falling but incomes could fall as well. A family might dine out less often even at lower prices if their income has fallen.

3. As a working parent and particularly a single working parent, one of the major costs associated with work is child care. If you worked full time

at the minimum wage of $3.35 per hour and paid $450 per month for child care for two children, you would have $86 dollars left over to support you and your family. There is little incentive to work full time for a month just to bring home $86. But suppose that as a result of new legislation, $100 of that monthly child care bill is paid for by the government. You are now left with $186 per month. This amount, although insufficient to meet the minimum needs of a family of three, is nevertheless still very important. If you were deterred from working before the new law, publicly subsidized child care payments increase the net gain to you from work and might induce you to seek employment. If you are already working, these payments might induce you to work additional hours because now the net gains from work are higher.

The marginal benefits from working an additional hour include among other things the value of goods and services that can be purchased with the income earned from that hour of work. The marginal cost of work involves the sacrifices incurred in order to work. These sacrifices include the loss of leisure time, the loss of time spent with family and friends, and the resources spent on such things as child care and transportation that could have otherwise been spent on goods and services.

Child care subsidies can be viewed as reducing the marginal cost of an hour of work or as increasing the marginal benefits realized from work. A reduction in day care costs increases the amount of the hourly wage available for non-day care expenditures. In this sense, the marginal benefit of an hour of work increases. Regardless of how the problem is viewed, total net gains from work increase. This will likely increase employment among single parents.

4. The marginal cost of a decision to consume a unit of a good is the sacrificed next-preferred goods that could have been consumed. The dollar value of this forgone consumption is a measure of marginal cost.

5. Maximize, marginal costs, marginal benefits

If marginal benefits exceed marginal costs from some action, a person can add more to his or her total benefits than total costs by undertaking the action. In other words, net benefit or gain increases. As long as marginal benefits exceed marginal costs, total net gains can be increased by pursuing an activity. When an activity has been pursued to the point where marginal benefits and costs are equal, no further increases to net benefits can be realized because the addition to total benefits would just be offset by the addition to total costs of the action.

6. a. Yes, because marginal benefits from pollution reduction up to a point exceed the sacrifice incurred in reducing pollution.

b. 3, equal at $6 million. At this point, society's total benefits and costs equal $24 million and $12 million, respectively. Society's net gain is therefore $12 million. No other level of pollution reduction will result in as large of a net gain.

Self-Test for Mastery

1. c 2. d 3. d 4. a 5. d 6. d 7. c 8. c 9. a 10. c 11. b 12. d 13. d

Think it Through

1. Economic theory is a simplification of reality seeking to establish and explain important cause-and-effect relationships in the economy. An economic

model is a simplified way of expressing a theory. A model can be presented verbally, in tables, in graphs, or mathematically. Assumptions are necessary for both theories and models because they outline the environment or motivation of people for which the theory and model hold.

2. If pollution reduction were undertaken to the point where marginal benefit and marginal cost were equal and that happened to be at a 50% level of pollution reduction, then no further net gains to society could be realized by additional reductions in pollution. In fact, if additional pollution reduction beyond the 50% level resulted in marginal costs exceeding marginal benefits, society would experience a net loss and be worse off than when there was more pollution.

3. In fact it might be quite rational for a person to engage in habit or impulse buying if that person experiences psychic loss, dissatisfaction, or stress associated with certain actions or choices. A person may buy the first used car he or she sees but may be doing so in part because of a distaste for bargaining and haggling. A person may shop only locally because of an aversion to driving in traffic.

4. A hypothesis is a statement of relationship between two economic variables. To be certain that you have isolated the cause-and-effect relationship between the two variables, it is necessary to hold the effect of other influencing variables constant. Otherwise, you cannot be sure that the relationship you have hypothesized is valid or instead results from some third variable that you have not considered.

5. A good theory yields accurate predictions, but even a theory that predicts inaccurately is of value in establishing cause-and-effect relationships and determining the significance of assumptions.

3
Production Possibilities and Opportunity Cost

After studying your text, attending class, and completing this chapter, you should be able to:

1. Show how limited available technology and scarce resources imply limited production possibilities over a period.
2. Demonstrate that the use of productive capacity to make more of any one good or service available involves sacrificing the opportunity to make more of other items available.
3. Discuss the basic determinants of a nation's production possibilities and how these can expand over time.
4. Understand the concept of productive efficiency and discuss its significance.
5. Demonstrate that when you use income over a period to buy more of one item, you sacrifice the opportunity to buy more of some other item over the period.

IN BRIEF: CHAPTER SUMMARY

Fill in the blanks to summarize chapter content.

(1)_____(Economy, Production) is the process of using economic resources or inputs in order to produce output. Economic resources consist of labor, (2)_____(capital, money), natural resources, and entrepreneurship. The quantity and productivity of economic resources and the extent and efficiency with which they are employed determine the output potential of a nation during a given period of time. Constraints in the availability or use of resources represent the (3)_____ (opportunity costs, scarcity) confronting nations. (4)_____(Technology, A larger labor force) allows us to delay the sacrifices implied by scarce resources by increasing the productivity of resources. Improvements in resource productivity mean that a nation can produce more output with a given endowment of resources.

A (5)_____(marginal benefit, production possibilities) curve is a convenient tool for showing the implications of scarce resources. Assuming (a) a given quantity and productivity of resources, as well as a given state of the art with respect to technology and (b) full and efficient employment of resources, it can be shown that a nation can produce more of one class of goods only by (6)_____(sacrificing, increasing) the production of other goods. That sacrifice is a nation's (7)_____ (dollar outlay, opportunity cost) of producing more of a given good. As a nation produces more of a good, the opportunity cost (8)_____(rises, falls) because resources that are increasingly (9)_____(less, more) productive must be transferred from the production of other goods. This implies that a given increase in the production of one good will require ever (10)_____(smaller, larger) reductions in output of other goods. The law of increasing costs exists because resources (11)_____(are, are not) equally adaptable to all employments.

A point on the production possibilities curve represents a combination of the two classes of goods in question where output is at a maximum. A point inside the curve implies either (12)_____(unemployed, fully employed) resources or (13)_____(efficiently, inefficiently) employed resources. A point outside the curve represents a combination of goods that is (14)_____(attainable, unattainable) in the short run. But with an increase over time in the quantity and productivity of resources, together with improvements in technology, a point outside the curve is attainable in the long run.

Maximum production is attainable in the short run when resources are employed fully and efficiently. Productive efficiency means that a nation (15)_____(can, cannot) reallocate resources among the production of goods and services and achieve a gain in the output of one good only by causing a reduction in the output of another. Specialization and the division of labor are critical for the attainment of maximum productive efficiency.

The process of economic growth can be shown as (16)_____(inward, outward) shifts over time in the production possibilities curve. A nation can generally produce more of all goods over time as long as it experiences resource growth and an improvement in the quality of resources and technology. A nation's growth is influenced by its willingness to forgo some (17)_____(future, current) production of consumable output so that resources can be used for the production of (18)_____(consumable outputs, capital). Production of capital today increases the production possibilities in the future not only by increasing the quantity of capital but also by increasing the productivity of other resources.

The problem of scarcity confronting nations also confronts the individual. An individual has a limited amount of income per time period with which to consume and save. Given the prices of goods and services, that limited income can purchase, at a maximum, those combinations of goods and services which require the full expenditure of income. A curve representing these various combinations of goods and services is known as a (19)_____(budget line, production possibilities curve). An increase in income over time allows the individual to consume more of all goods. This is shown by an (20)_____ (inward, outward) shift of the budget line. Holding income constant but allowing prices to fall likewise (21)_____(increases, decreases) the quantities that can be purchased. This too shifts the budget line (22)_____(inward, outward). Rising prices or inflation will shift the budget line (23)_____(inward, outward) if income remains constant. Finally, given a limited income and constant prices, the only way an individual can consume more of one good is by reducing consumption of other goods. The opportunity cost of consuming more of one good is the (24)_____(increase, reduction) in consumption of quantities of other goods.

VOCABULARY REVIEW

Write the key term from the list below next to its definition.

Key Terms

Economic resources   Production possibilities curve
Labor   Law of increasing costs
Capital   Productive efficiency
Natural resources   Division of labor
Entrepreneurship   Economic growth
Technology   Budget line

Definitions

1. _____: the inputs used in the process of production.

2. _____: the specialization of workers in particular tasks that are part of a larger undertaking to accomplish a given objective.

3. _____: shows an individual's opportunities to purchase two goods if he or she spends an entire month's income on these two goods at their current prices.

4. _____: the equipment, tools, structures, machinery, vehicles, materials, and skills created to help produce goods and services.

5. _____: shows the maximum possible output of one good that can be produced with available resources given the output of the alternative good over a period.

6. _____: the talent to develop products and processes and to organize production of goods and services.

7. _____: the expansion in production possibilities that results from increased availability and increased productivity of economic resources.

8. _____: the knowledge of how to produce goods and services.

9. _____: the physical and mental efforts of human beings in the production of goods and services.

10. _____: attained when the maximum possible output of any one good is produced given the output of the other goods. At this point it is not possible to reallocate economic resources to increase the output of any single good or service without decreasing the output of some other good or service.

11. _____: acreage and the physical terrain to locate structures, ports, and other facilities; also, natural resources that are used in crude form in production.

12. _____: the opportunity costs of extra production of any one good in an economy will increase as more and more specialized resources best suited for the production of other goods are reallocated away from their best use.

Concept: Scarce resources and limited production possibilities

1. List four economic resources:

    a. _____
    b. _____
    c. _____
    d. _____

2. Which of the following uses of resources will likely increase labor productivity? (+, Increase; 0, No change.)

    a. _____ Expenditures on capital
    b. _____ Expenditures on more fashionable clothes
    c. _____ Expenditures on health care
    d. _____ Expenditures on education and training
    e. _____ Expenditures on military goods

Concept: **Production possibilities and opportunity cost**

3. The data in the table below represent the production possibilities for a nation producing two classes of goods.

Production Possibilities	Consumer Goods	Capital Goods
	(millions of units)	
A	0	90
B	20	80
C	40	65
D	60	47
E	80	26
F	100	0

   a. On the axes below, plot a production possibilities curve from the data in the table above.

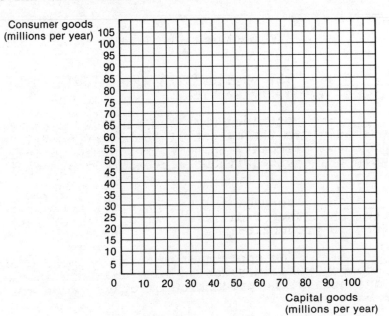

39

b.   What is the meaning of a point <u>on</u> the production possibilities curve?
c.   What is the opportunity cost associated with an increase in the production of consumer goods by 20 million units?
      (1) From point B to C? _____ units of capital
      (2) From point C to D? _____ units of capital
      (3) From point D to E? _____ units of capital
      (4) From point E to F? _____ units of capital
d.   Do opportunity costs rise or fall as additional units of consumer goods are produced? Explain.

4.   Referring to the figure below:

a.   Interpret the meaning of point A.
b.   Interpret the meaning of point B.

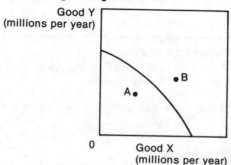

Concept: Determinants of a nation's production possibilities

5.   Indicate whether the following events would cause the production possibilities curve to shift outward (O) or would leave it unchanged (U):

a.   _____ Increased production of houses at full employment
b.   _____ Increases in the quantity of resources
c.   _____ Improvements in the quality and productivity of economic resources
d.   _____ A reduction in prices
e.   _____ Increases in income
f.   _____ Improvements in technology

6. a. On the axes below, draw a production possibilities curve for a
        nation. Now assume that economic growth is taking place. Draw a new
        production possibilities curve on the same axes reflecting this
        growth.

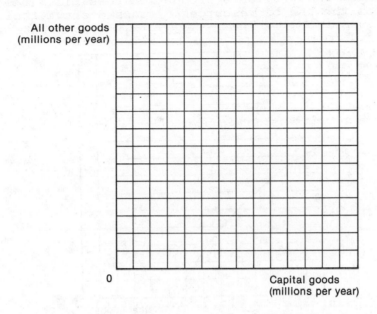

All other goods
(millions per year)

0

Capital goods
(millions per year)

    b. On the axes below, draw a production possibilities curve for a
        nation. Assume as above that the nation is experiencing growth, but
        also assume that the economy is investing more heavily in capital and
        technology than the economy shown above in part a. Draw a new
        production possibilities curve reflecting this.

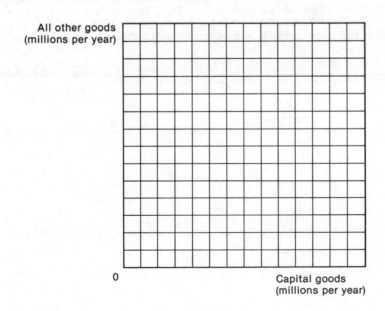

All other goods
(millions per year)

0

Capital goods
(millions per year)

7. a. If a nation used resources for capital or technological improvements for a specific industry, such as the aircraft industry, what are the implications regarding future levels of production not only in the aircraft industry but for other industries as well?

    b. Show the shift in a nation's production possibilities curve that results from the use of resources discussed above.

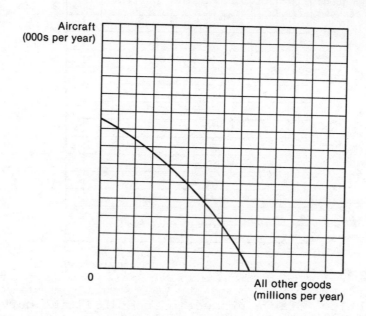

Aircraft
(000s per year)

0

All other goods
(millions per year)

Concept: Limited income and opportunity cost

8. Suppose that as a university student you receive $50 per month from your parents to be used as spending money. You spend all of your money each month on beer or compact discs (CDs). Assume that the price per six-pack of beer is $2.50 and the price of a CD is $10.

    a. Determine six combinations of beer and CDs that cost a total of $50. List the combinations in the table below.

Combination	Beer (six packs)	CDs (units)
A	_____	_____
B	_____	_____
C	_____	_____
D	_____	_____
E	_____	_____

    b. Plot these combinations below. The curve that you have plotted is called a _____.

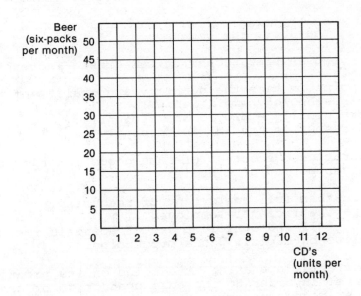

Beer (six-packs per month)

CD's (units per month)

c. On the figure in part b, show what would happen to the curve if:
    (1) your parents began to send $100 per month
    (2) your total funds are still $50, but the price of beer increases to $5 and the price of CDs decreases to $5.

9. Advanced Question

    a. Derive the equation for the budget line in Question 8, part b.
    b. In question 8, part c1 alters the equation for the budget line in what way? Part c2 alters the equation in what way?

SELF-TEST FOR MASTERY

Select the best answer.

1. Which of the following can be defined as the process of using economic resources to produce outputs?

    a. Economics
    b. Production
    c. Economy
    d. Technology

2. Economic resources consist of:

    a. Money, credit, and capital
    b. Labor, capital, and money
    c. Labor, capital, natural resources, and money
    d. Labor, capital, natural resources, and entrepreneurship

3. Which of the following best defines capital?

    a. Money
    b. Plant and tools

c. Investment funds available for speculative financial outlays
d. Goods or skills that are produced in order to produce goods and
    services

4. Scarcity exists in the short run because:

a. At a given point in time technological growth increases at a constant
    rate.
b. At a given point in time the quantity and quality of resources and
    the state of technology are fixed.
c. Resources are usually employed inefficiently.
d. The world's resources are in finite supply.

5. A nation must sacrifice the output of some goods in order to produce other
    goods during a given period of time if:

a. There is less than full employment of resources.
b. Resources are inefficiently employed.
c. There is both full and efficient use of economic resources.
d. A nation relies on capital goods production.

6. If a nation is currently operating at a point on its production
    possibilities curve, in order to increase production of one good, the
    production of other goods must be:

a. Held constant.
b. Increased.
c. Decreased.
d. None of the above.

7. If a nation is currently operating at a point inside its production
    possibilities curve, it:

a. Has full employment.
b. Has unemployed and/or inefficiently employed resources.
c. Is operating at full potential.
d. Must reduce the output of one good in order to produce more of
    another good.

8. The law of increasing costs states that:

a. Opportunity costs rise as more of a good is produced.
b. Opportunity costs fall as more of a good is produced.
c. Rising resource prices are inevitable because of scarcity.
d. Economic growth is always associated with inflation.

9. The law of increasing costs is the result of the fact that:

a. Resources can be easily adapted to the production of any good.
b. Scarcity reduces supply and increases costs.
c. Resources are not equally adaptable to all employments.
d. People reach a point of satiation at which they no longer purchase
    goods.

10. Economic growth is the process whereby the production possibilities curve
    shifts:

a. Inward
b. Outward
c. Either inward or outward
d. Outward, then inward

11. Points outside of the production possibilities curve are _____ in the _____.

    a.   Attainable/short run
    b.   Unattainable/short run
    c.   Attainable/long run
    d.   Unattainable/long run
    e.   B and c

12. Production efficiency is achieved:

    a.   If resources are reallocated among the production of goods and services and the output of one good can be increased without decreasing the output of other goods.
    b.   If there is no waste in the production process.
    c.   If resources are reallocated among the production of goods and services and the output of one good can be increased only by reducing the output of other goods.
    d.   At a point within the production possibilities curve.

13. If nation A commits a larger share of its resources to capital and technological improvements than nation B, then over time _____ will realize _____ outward shifts in its production possibilities curve.

    a.   Nation B/larger
    b.   Nation A/smaller
    c.   Nations A and B/the same
    d.   Nation B/smaller

14. An individual's ability to consume goods and services depends upon:

    a.   Income only.
    b.   The rate of inflation.
    c.   The individual's income and the prices of the goods and services consumed.
    d.   Tastes.

15. A/An _____ is a curve indicating an individual's ability to consume various combinations of two goods or services over a period of time.

    a.   Production possibilities curve
    b.   Income curve
    c.   Price line
    d.   Budget line

16. The budget line shifts _____ when there is a/an _____ in income.

    a.   Inward/increase
    b.   Outward/decrease
    c.   Inward/decrease
    d.   Outward/decrease or increase

17. An individual's ability to increase the consumption of goods and services is _____ when the price of one or both goods _____.

    a.   Increased/decrease
    b.   Decreased/decrease
    c.   Increased/increase
    d.   Unchanged/increase unless income decreases

18. The sacrifice or opportunity cost associated with an individual's consumption of an additional good :

   a. Is the reduction in other goods consumed when the individual does not spend all of his or her income.
   b. Is the increase in other goods consumed when unused income is spent.
   c. Is the reduction in other goods consumed when an individual has no additional income.
   d. None of the above

THINK IT THROUGH

1. Explain why a nation's endowment of economic resources necessitates choices between current and future uses of resources.

2. Explain under what conditions a nation incurs an opportunity cost as it produces more of a good. How does the law of increasing cost fit into your discussion?

3. How do technology and capital expenditures improve the quality or productivity of "other" economic resources?

4. Assume that the United States contributes disproportionately more resources to the defense of Western Europe than do the other NATO allies, and as a consequence these other countries can invest a larger share of their resources in capital and other goods and services. Use production possibility curves to show both the short- and long-run consequences regarding the economies of the United States and Western Europe.

POP QUIZ   Read the news brief at the end of this chapter and answer the questions below.

1. Explain the nature of the short-run opportunity cost associated with the housing boom of the 1970s.

2. What are some of the long-run consequences of the housing boom? In other words, short-run choices affect long-run choices. Explain.

CHAPTER ANSWERS

In Brief: Chapter Summary

1. Production 2. Capital 3. Scarcity 4. Technology 5. Production possibilities curve 6. Sacrificing 7. Opportunity cost 8. Rises 9. Less 10. Larger 11. Are not 12. Unemployed 13. Inefficiently 14. Unattainable 15. Can 16. Outward 17. Current 18. Capital 19. Budget line 20. Outward 21. Increases 22. Outward 23. Inward 24. Reduction

Vocabulary Review

1. Economic resources 2. Division of labor 3. Budget line 4. Capital 5. Production possibilities curve 6. Entrepreneurship 7. Economic growth 8.

Technology 9. Labor 10. Productive efficiency 11. Natural resources 12. Law of increasing costs

Skills Review

1. a. Labor b. Capital c. Natural resources d. Entrepreneurship

2. a. + b. 0 c. + d. + e. 0

3. a.

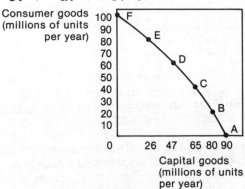

   b. A point on the production possibilities curve represents a maximum level of production over a period of time for consumer and capital goods. At this level of production, resources are fully and efficiently employed.
   c. (1) 15 (2) 18 (3) 21 (4) 26
   d. Rise. Opportunity costs rise because in order to produce more and more consumer goods, increasing quantities of resources have to be reallocated from the capital goods industry to the consumer goods industry, and these resources are increasingly less adaptable to consumer goods production.

4. a. A point inside the curve represents a level of production involving unemployed resources or inefficient production or both.
   b. A point outside the curve is unattainable in the short run because of resource constraints. In the long run, however, it is possible to reach point B if the productivity and quantity of resources increase.

5. a. U b. O c. O d. U e. U f. O

6. a.

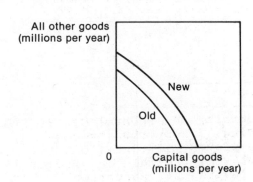

b.

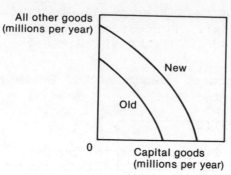

7. a. Even if capital or technological improvements were made only in the aircraft industry, the levels of production in other industries would likely increase. The capacity to produce in the aircraft industry has increased, which means that more aircraft <u>can</u> be produced than before. Since capital increases the productivity of other resources, more aircraft could be produced with the same quantity of resources previously employed in the aircraft industry, or the same number of aircraft could be produced as before but now with fewer resources. These resources, therefore, could be used elsewhere in producing other goods and services.

b.

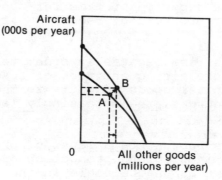

8. a.

Combination	Beer	CDs
A	20	0
B	16	1
C	12	2
D	8	3
E	4	4
F	0	5

b. Budget line

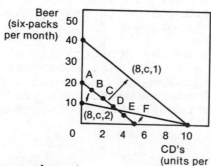

c. (1) (on figure above)
   (2) (on figure above)

9.　a.　Assume that the student's income (I) is spent in its entirety on beer (B) and compact discs (CDs). Furthermore, assume the price of beer (PB) and the price of a CD (PCD) are $2.50 and $10, respectively.

$$I = (PB)(B) + (PCD)(CD)$$

Solve the above equation for (B).

$$B = I/PB - (PCD/PB)(CD)$$

Notice that the vertical intercept of the budget line is the level of income divided by the price of beer. Also notice that the slope of the budget line is negative and equals the ratio of prices of the two goods.

　b.　(1)　An increase in income will increase the intercept term or constant term in the above equation. The budget line will shift upward.

　　　(2)　A decrease in the price of CDs and an increase in the price of beer will make the slope less negative and will decrease the intercept term. The budget line becomes flatter, with the vertical intercept decreasing.

Self-Test for Mastery

1. b　2. d　3. d　4. b　5. c　6. c　7. b　8. a　9. c　10. b　11. e　12. c　13. d　14. c　15. d　16. c　17. a　18. c

Think it Through

1.　A nation's endowment of resources, whether plentiful or limited, is a constraint to future growth. With full and efficient use of resources, a nation can produce only so much over a given period of time. Using resources today for capital means giving up the consumption of other goods today. But capital increases the future capacity to produce and also increases the productivity of economic resources. Because of this, a nation that forgoes consumption today and invests in capital will be able to consume more tomorrow.

2.　A nation incurs a sacrifice or opportunity cost associated with the use of resources when (a) there is full employment of resources and (b) efficient production of output. If this were not the case, a nation could produce more of one good without necessarily reducing the consumption of other goods by either employing its resources more fully or by more efficiently producing its output.

　　At full employment and efficient production, a nation incurs rising opportunity costs if it produces more and more of a given good because of the law of increasing costs. Because resources are not completely adaptable to all uses, they must be withdrawn in increasing amounts from other industries in order to produce given quantities of the good.

3.　Both capital and technology increase the productivity of the production process. More output can be produced with the same amount of resources. A farmer with a tractor is far more productive than one with a digging stick. This is the story of American agriculture. The enormous productivity increases in the U.S. farm sector have been made possible by the mechanization of agriculture.

4.   The United States not only sacrifices output of consumer goods and
services in the short run but also sacrifices a higher rate of future economic
growth and living standards.

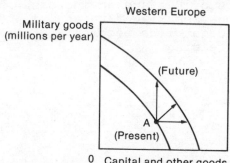

United States

Military goods
(millions per year)

(Future)

A
(Present)

0 Capital and other goods
(millions per year)

        Western Europe, in contrast, is able to consume both more capital and
other goods in the short run and because of greater capital investments will
realize a faster rate of GNP growth in the future.

Western Europe

Military goods
(millions per year)

(Future)

A
(Present)

0 Capital and other goods
(millions per year)

Pop Quiz

1.   The housing market boomed in the 1970s because of distortions caused by
high marginal tax rates and inflation. It was not uncommon for a homeowner in
the 1970s to face a negative real rate of mortgage interest. Even though
family size and real median family income were falling and energy costs were
rising significantly, these distortions were significant enough relative to
these demographic and economic factors to result in not only a large increase
in the quantity of housing, but also an increase in the average size per home.
A sizable portion of the nation's savings went into housing rather than into
business capital investment. Inflation had the effect of reducing the private
after-tax return on business investment. In the short run, the additional
housing was acquired at the expense of less business investment.

2.   The short-run choice of more housing and less business investment implies
long-run consequences. A nation that underinvests in productive capital will
experience a slower rate of economic growth and lower living standards in the
future. Edwin Mills estimated the socially-optimal combination of investment
funds and concluded that the housing stock is 25% too large and other forms of
capital stock need to be increased by 12%. If the economy operated with the
socially-optimal composition of investment, Mills estimates that GNP would be
$3.606 trillion in 1983 rather than $3.278 trillion--a difference of $4,410 per
family. Thus, long-run living standards were sacrificed for short-run
consumption of additional housing.

50

More Costly Housing No Cause for Alarm

By Dwight R. Lee

Home ownership is the American dream, and a vibrant housing industry is associated with a healthy economy. Yet concern has been expressed recently that this dream is increasingly out of reach for many young Americans. A study cited in Housing Affairs Letter in March finds the homeownership rate among households in the 25-29 age bracket fell 17% between 1980 and 1987, and "finds [the] less affluent paying an increasing percentage of income for a dwindling supply of affordable housing." Yesterday, Michael Dukakis, campaigning at a housing redevelopment project in Cincinnati, spoke of "the problem of home ownership for young families."

But is less affordable housing a problem that warrants concern? Before concluding that it is, consider that homeownership was more affordable in the 1970s for reasons that were harmful to the economy then and for which we are still paying a price today. There are reasons for applauding the fact that homeownership has become a more costly dream and that the housing industry is not as robust as it was in the '70s.

Record in Housing Starts

The 1970s saw both a record number of housing starts and a steady increase in the size of houses. This occurred despite the fact that after-tax real income actually declined for the family of median income during the '70s and average family size was decreasing.

On the basis of sound economic decision-making, fewer new houses would have been constructed and those that were constructed would have been smaller. But economic circumstances in the 1970s were not conducive to sound decision-making. The housing boom can be explained by two factors that spelled gloom for the overall performance of the economy: high marginal tax rates and inflation.

Both distort economic decisions and by doing so make the economy less productive. High marginal tax rates reduce the private cost of consumption while at the same time reducing the private return on productive activities. Inflation, in addition to creating noise in the crucial allocative signals of changing relative prices, discourages commitments to long-term investments by increasing the uncertainty in future price levels. During the '70s, while reducing overall economic performance, high marginal tax rates in combination with inflation gave an artificial boost to the housing industry.

Consider being faced with a 40% marginal income-tax rate (common in the '70s), an inflation rate of 10% (exceeded at times during that decade), and a new mortgage. The interest rate on the mortgage will be about 14% (a 4% real rate plus 10% to account for inflation), and the after-tax interest rate will be 60% of that, or 8.4%. But since inflation is decreasing the value of money by 10% a year, the real after-tax interest rate is not 8.4%, but negative 1.6%. This negative interest rate serves as a tremendous subsidy to the purchase of a new house. And it is a subsidy that increases with both the inflation rate and the marginal tax rate.

During the '70s, this subsidy not only increased artificially the number of houses demanded, it also had a perverse effect on the size of houses. By any realistic standard, the size of newly constructed houses should have decreased. The average family size declined from 3.24 people in 1970 to 2.76 in 1980. The cost of home heating and cooling skyrocketed with the price of energy. And median family income, after adjusting for inflation and taxes, was $436 less in 1980 than in 1970. Nonetheless, during the 1970s the size of the average new house increased to 1,760 square feet from 1,510 square feet. Rather than expanding the nation's productive capital, Americans were putting their savings into larger houses for smaller families to be heated and cooled by increasingly costly energy.

These 1970 distortions in the housing industry are of more than just historical interest. The 1970s may be history, but we are still paying dearly for the distortions just described.

The housing industry attracts a significant percentage of the nation's saving in direct competition with other capital goods such as new plants and equipment. And while inflation and high marginal tax rates were increasing the private after-tax return on housing investment in the 1970s, they were decreasing the private after-tax return on business capital investment.

Since business capital is carried on the books at its historical cost, depreciation expense always understates the real replacement cost of capital during inflation, and therefore taxable profits are overstated. Also, the capital gains tax is assessed against increases in the nominal value of capital stock, which is always greater than increases in the real value during inflation. Again, taxable profits are overstated and investment in business capital is discouraged. So the success of the housing industry in the 1970s came at the expense of the type of investment that would have increased the productivity of the economy and meant higher incomes in the 1980s.

In a study published earlier this year, economist Edwin S. Mills estimated that if investment funds had been allocated between housing and other forms of capital investment in the proportion that maximized their combined social return, then the housing stock would have been approximately 25% smaller, and other forms of capital stock about 12% larger, than was the case in 1983. Mr. Mills also estimated that had we benefited from such an investment mix, gross national product would have been $3.606 trillion in 1983 (in 1983 dollars) instead of the $3.278 trillion actually achieved. This is a difference of about $4,410 for each family in the U.S.

It should be pointed out that Mr. Mills's study considers the effect of the distortion in investment not only over the 1970s, but also over several previous decades. But because of the high inflation rates and high marginal tax rates during the 1970s, a significant proportion of the distortion—and its adverse consequences for our current GNP—occurred in the 1970s.

Fortunately for the future productivity of the economy and for our incomes, the inflation rate was down to a little less than 5% in 1987 and marginal tax rates have been reduced significantly by the 1986 tax reform. A bias in favor of housing still exists because mortgage-interest payments remain fully deductible against taxable income. But this bias is now far less than it was in the 1970s.

Misplaced Concern

While good for the economy, lower inflation and reduced marginal tax rates have indeed increased the private cost of homeownership. This higher cost affects all home buyers, but since marginal tax rates declined more at higher income levels than at lower income levels, the increased cost is greater for higher-income families. According to a study published earlier this year by economist Theodore Crone, tax reform (assuming a 5% inflation rate and a 10.4% mortgage-interest rate) has increased the first-year cost of homeownership by 6.9% for a family with a $20,000 annual income and by 23.1% for a family with a $40,000 annual income.

It is more difficult for all young families to purchase their first home now than it was in the '70s. And when they are able to buy a home, it is more likely to be a smaller home than their counterparts were buying a decade ago. Considered in isolation this may appear to be cause for concern. But such concern is seen to be misplaced when the changes in economy that explain the higher cost of homeownership are considered. Indeed, young families are better off today than they were 10 years ago for the same reason it is more costly for them to buy that first home.

Mr. Lee is Ramsey professor of economics at the University of Georgia and a visiting professor at the Center for the Study of American Business at Washington University in St. Louis.

4

Market Transactions: Basic Supply and Demand Analysis

CHAPTER CHALLENGES

After studying your text, attending class, and completing this chapter, you should be able to:

1. Discuss the purposes and functions of markets.
2. Explain how a demand curve illustrates the law of demand and distinguish between a change in demand and a change in quantity demanded.
3. Show how a supply curve illustrates the law of supply and distinguish between a change in supply and a change in quantity supplied.
4. Describe the conditions required for market equilibrium and locate the equilibrium point on a supply and demand diagram.
5. Explain the consequences of shortages and surpluses in markets and how prices adjust in a free and unregulated competitive market to eliminate shortages or surpluses.
6. Show how changes in supply and demand affect market equilibrium.

IN BRIEF: CHAPTER SUMMARY

Fill in the blanks to summarize chapter content.

Understanding the concept of a market and the role it plays in the allocation of resources and the distribution of output is critical to an understanding of how economies function. (1)_____ (Markets, Trade publications) communicate information to buyers and sellers alike. The forces of supply and demand, which are basic to every market, interact to produce a (2)_____ (market quantity, market price) that acts as a vehicle for communicating the wants of buyers to sellers. (3)_____(Cost-benefit analysis, Supply and demand analysis) is a method of isolating the forces of supply and demand so that the factors determining market prices can be understood. This allows us to better understand the communication and rationing functions of the price system.

Demand constitutes amounts of goods and services that buyers are willing and able to buy at a given price during a given period. A (4)_____(demand schedule, demand curve) is a table of data showing the relationship between the prices of a good and the associated quantities demanded, holding all other influencing factors unchanged. A (5)_____(demand curve, demand schedule) is a plot of the price-quantity demanded coordinates. The demand schedule and its demand curve show that price and quantity demanded are negatively related. This relationship is known as the law of (6)_____(increasing returns, demand). When there is a change in price, quantity demanded changes. This is called a (7)_____(change in demand, change in quantity demanded). A change in demand determinants other than the price of the good will shift the demand curve. A shift in the demand curve means that, at a given price, quantity demanded will either increase or decrease. This is called a (8)_____(change in demand, change in quantity demanded). Changes in

52

demand are caused by changes in (a) income, (b) wealth, (c) the prices of related goods, (d) price expectations, (e) tastes, and (f) the number of buyers in the market.

Supply represents the quantities that sellers are willing and able to produce and make available to the market at a given price during a given period. A (9)_____(supply schedule, supply curve) is a table of data showing the relationship between the prices of a good and the associated quantities supplied by sellers, all other influences on supply remaining the same. A (10)_____(supply curve, supply schedule) is a plot of the price-quantity supplied coordinates. The relationship between price and quantity supplied is a positive one and is called the law of (11)_____ (monetary incentives, supply). A (12)_____(change in quantity supplied,change in supply) is caused by a price change. This is shown by a movement along a given supply curve. A (13)_____(change in quantity supplied, change in supply) is the result of influences other than price, such as (a) the price of inputs, (b) prices of other goods, (c) technology, (d) price expectations, and (e) the number of sellers in a market. These nonprice influences shift the supply curve.

The forces of supply and demand interact to produce a market (14)_____ (outcome, equilibrium), or state of balance, where the quantities demanded by buyers are just equal to the quantities supplied by sellers. In a state of equilibrium, buyers and sellers have no incentive to alter levels of consumption or production. It is the market (15)_____(price, quantity) that equates the quantities supplied and demanded.

A price above a market equilibrium price results in a (16)_____(shortage, surplus) because the quantity supplied at this price exceeds the quantity demanded. A price below the equilibrium price causes a (17)_____(shortage, surplus) because the quantity demanded exceeds the quantity supplied. In a competitive market, a seller tries to get rid of surpluses by (18)_____(increasing inventories, cutting prices). Falling prices will reduce surpluses. When the price falls enough to equal the market equilibrium price, the (19)_____ (shortage, surplus) is eliminated completely.

Shortages require some form of rationing. Sellers ration the limited supply of goods among competing buyers by (20)_____(increasing, decreasing) prices. But price increases reduce the quantities demanded and increase the quantities supplied, which in turn reduce the shortage. Shortages are completely eliminated when the price has risen (21)_____(above, equal to) the market equilibrium price. Market prices remain unchanged in a competitive market unless the underlying forces of supply or demand change. A change in demand, a change in supply, or a change in both supply and demand (22)_____ (can, cannot) alter the market equilibrium price and quantity.

VOCABULARY REVIEW

Write the key term from the list below next to its definition.

Key Terms

Market	Market equilibrium
Change in quantity demanded	Quantity supplied
	Demand
Supply and demand analysis	Supply
	Law of supply

53

Quantity demanded
Demand schedule
Law of demand
Complements
Demand curve
Surplus
Change in relative
  price
Change in demand

Supply schedule
Supply curve
Change in quantity
  supplied
Substitutes
Change in supply
Shortage
Equilibrium

Definitions

1. _____: an increase or decrease in the price of a good relative to an average of the prices of all goods.

2. _____: a graph that shows how quantity demanded varies with the price of a good.

3. _____: a table that shows how the quantity supplied of a good is related to the price.

4. _____: the quantity of a good sellers are willing and able to make available in the market over a given period at a certain price, other things being equal.

5. _____: a relationship between the price of an item and the quantity supplied by sellers.

6. _____: other things being equal, the higher the price of a good, the greater the quantity of that good sellers are willing and able to make available over a given period.

7. _____: an arrangement through which buyers and sellers meet or communicate for the purpose of trading goods or services.

8. _____: explains how prices are established in markets through competition among many buyers and sellers, and how those prices affect the quantities traded.

9. _____: attained when the price of a good adjusts so that the quantity buyers are willing and able to buy at that price is just equal to the quantity sellers are willing and able to supply.

10. _____: exists if the quantity demanded exceeds the quantity supplied of a good over a period of time.

11. _____: prevails when economic forces balance so that economic variables neither increase nor decrease.

12. _____: exists if the quantity supplied exceeds the quantity demanded of a good over a period of time.

13. _____: a change in the relationship between the price of a good and the quantity supplied in response to a supply determinant other than the price of the good.

14. _____: a change in the amount of a good buyers are willing and able to buy in response to a change in the price of the good.

15. _____: a change in the relationship between the price of
a good and the quantity demanded caused by a change in a demand
determinant other than the price of the good.

16. _____: goods whose use together enhances the
satisfaction a consumer obtains from each.

17. _____: goods that serve a purpose similar to that of a
given good.

18. _____: a graph that shows how the quantity supplied
varies with the price of a good.

19. _____: other things being equal, the lower the price of
a good, the greater the quantity of that good buyers are willing and able
to purchase over a given period.

20. _____: a change in the amount of a good sellers are
willing to sell in response to a change in the price of the good.

21. _____: a relationship between the price of an item and
the quantity demanded.

22. _____: a table that shows how the quantity demanded of a
good would vary with price, given all other demand determinants.

23. _____: the amount of an item the buyers are willing and
able to purchase over a period at a certain price, given all other
influences on their decision to buy.

SKILLS REVIEW

Concept: Demand, law of demand, changes in demand and quantity demanded

1.   The following is a demand schedule for corn:

Price per Bushel	Quantity Demanded (000s bushels per week)	
	(a)	(b)
$4.00	850	_____
3.75	900	_____
3.50	950	_____
3.25	1,000	_____
3.00	1,050	_____
2.75	1,100	_____
2.50	1,150	_____

a.   Plot the demand curve on the diagram below.

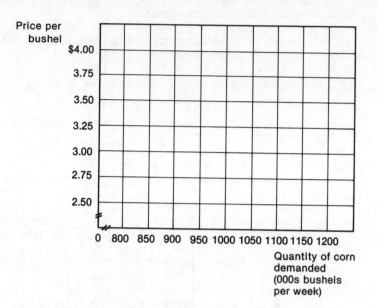

Price per bushel

Quantity of corn demanded (000s bushels per week)

b.   What kind of relationship exists between the price per bushel of corn and the quantity of corn demanded?

c.   Assume that the prices of other vegetables are falling relative to the price of corn. Will this cause the demand curve to shift? Why?

d.   Assume that the quantity of corn demanded decreases by 50,000 bushels at every price level. Show the impact of this by completing column b above.

e.   Show the impact from part d on the demand curve that you plotted in part a.

2.   List six nonprice determinants of demand:

a.   _____
b.   _____
c.   _____
d.   _____
e.   _____
f.   _____

3.   Indicate for each of the following if a demand curve for automobiles will shift to the right (R), left (L), or remain unchanged (U):

a.   _____ Auto prices fall
b.   _____ Price of gasoline triples
c.   _____ Incomes decrease
d.   _____ Stock market gains increase wealth
e.   _____ Public transit fares fall to zero
f.   _____ Auto price increase expected

Concept: Supply, law of supply, changes in supply and quantity supplied

4.   The following is a supply schedule for corn:

Price per Bushel	Quantity Supplied (000s of bushels per week)	
	(a)	(b)
$4.00	1600	_____
3.75	1400	_____
3.50	1200	_____
3.25	1000	_____
3.00	800	_____
2.75	600	_____
2.50	400	_____

   a.   Plot the supply curve on the diagram below.

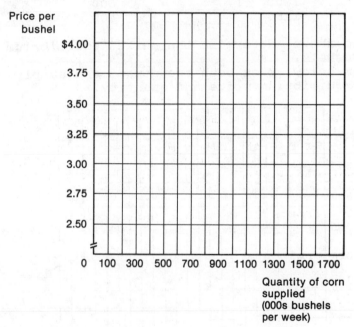

Price per bushel

Quantity of corn supplied (000s bushels per week)

   b.   Is there a positive or negative relationship between the price of corn and the quantity of corn supplied? Explain.
   c.   Suppose a serious drought reduces corn output at each price by 100,000 bushels. Show the impact in column b above by completing the table.
   d.   Plot the new supply curve from column b on the diagram from part a.

5.   List five nonprice determinants of supply:

   a.   _____
   b.   _____
   c.   _____
   d.   _____
   e.   _____

6.   Which of the following will cause the supply curve for hamburgers to shift to the right (R), left (L), or remain unchanged (U)?

   a.   _____   Increase in the price of hamburger meat
   b.   _____   Increase in the price of hamburgers

c.   _____ Increase in the price of chicken nuggets
d.   _____ Introduction of new cost-saving technology
            in the hamburger industry

Concept: Market equilibrium price and quantity; shortages and surpluses

7. The table below contains the price, quantity supplied, and quantity demanded data from column a of questions 1 and 4.

Price per Bushel	Quantity Demanded		Quantity Supplied	
	(000s of bushels per year)			
	(a)	(b)	(c)	(d)
$4.00	850	_____	1600	_____
3.75	900	_____	1400	_____
3.50	950	_____	1200	_____
3.25	1000	_____	1000	_____
3.00	1050	_____	800	_____
2.75	1100	_____	600	_____
2.50	1150	_____	400	_____

a. From the table above, determine the market equilibrium price and quantity in bushels.

b. On the diagram below, plot both the demand and supply curves. Identify the equilibrium price and quantity.

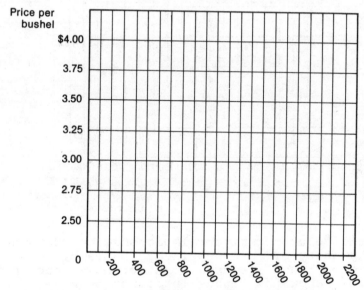

Quantity of corn demanded and supplied
(000s of bushels per week)

c. At a price of $3.75, a _____ exists in the amount of _____ because quantity demanded is _____ than quantity supplied.

d. At a price of $2.75, a _____ exists in the amount of _____ because quantity demanded is _____ than quantity supplied.

e. What is meant by the statement that competitive markets are self-equilibrating?

Concept: Changes in supply and demand and market equilibrium

8.   Referring to the supply and demand schedules in question 7 above:

   a.   Suppose that an increase in income causes the demand for corn to
        increase by 250,000 bushels at each price. Show the change in
        question 7, column b. Plot the new demand curve on the diagram in
        question 7.

   b.   The market equilibrium price has _____ from $_____ to
        $_____ . Market equilibrium output has _____ from _____
        bushels to _____ bushels.

   c.   Suppose that because of excellent weather, corn production increases
        at every price by 500,000 bushels. Show the change by completing
        column d from question 7. Plot the new supply curve on the diagram
        in question 7.

   d.   Comparing the original equilibrium--demand curve a and supply curve
        c--to the new equilibrium with supply curve d, market equilibrium
        price has _____ from $_____ to $_____ . Market
        quantity has _____ from _____ bushels to _____
        bushels.

   e.   Comparing the original equilibrium--demand curve a and supply curve
        c--to a new equilibrium with demand curve b and supply curve d,
        market equilibrium price has _____ from $_____ to $_____
        and market quantity has _____ from _____ to _____
        bushels.

9.   Indicate below if the market price and quantity of concert tickets
     increases (+), decreases (-), or is indeterminate (0):

                                              Price   Quantity

   a.   Stock market losses reduce wealth   _____   _____
   b.   Income increases   _____   _____
   c.   Season ticket prices are
        expected to rise   _____   _____
   d.   Musicians union wins large
        pay increase   _____   _____
   e.   Price of movie tickets falls   _____   _____
   f.   Population migrating to an
        area increases   _____   _____

10. <u>Advanced Question.</u> Let the following equations represent demand and
     supply curves for some good:

              Demand curve: $Qd = a - bP$
              Supply curve: $Qs = c + dP$

                       where   a, b, c, and d are positive
                                 constants
                                 Qd = quantity demanded
                                 Qs = quantity supplied
                                 P = price

   a.   Solve the above equations for the market equilibrium price.
   b.   Solve for the equilibrium quantity.
   c.   Interpret the equations for price and quantity. What causes price or
        quantity to rise or fall?

SELF-TEST FOR MASTERY

Select the best answer.

1.   In a free and unregulated competitive economy:

     a.   Wants are communicated to producers by the purchase orders of
          wholesalers.
     b.   Wants of buyers are communicated to sellers through the determination
          of prices in markets.
     c.   Sellers use market survey instruments to determine what and how much
          to produce.
     d.   Markets play an insignificant role.

2.   The quantities of goods that buyers are willing and able to purchase at a
     specific price over a period of time, other influences held unchanged, is
     a definition for:

     a.   Quantity demanded.
     b.   Supply.
     c.   Total sales.
     d.   Demand.

3.   The demand _____ is a table of price and quantity demanded data in
     which the ceteris paribus assumption is employed. The _____ is a
     plot of that data.

     a.   Table/scatter diagram
     b.   Schedule/marginal cost curve
     c.   Curve/schedule
     d.   Schedule/demand curve

4.   The law of demand states that, other things being the same:

     a.   Price and income are positively related.
     b.   Income and sales are positively related.
     c.   Price and quantity demanded are positively related.
     d.   Price and quantity demanded are inversely related.

5.   Which of the following will not cause a change in demand?

     a.   Change in income
     b.   Change in the price of the good in question
     c.   Change in the prices of related goods, such as complements or
          substitutes
     d.   Expectation of higher prices

6.   If two goods are substitutes and the price of one good increases, the
     demand for the other good will:

     a.   Not change.
     b.   Increase.
     c.   Not be related.
     d.   Decrease.

7.   If two goods are complementary goods and the price of one good increases,
     the demand for the other will:

     a.   Not change.
     b.   Increase.

c.   Not be related.
d.   Decrease.

8.   If a good is a normal good, an increase in income will:

a.   Increase supply.
b.   Decrease demand.
c.   Increase demand.
d.   Decrease supply.

9.   The quantities of a good that sellers are willing and able to produce and make available to the market at a specific price over a given period, other things being constant, is a definition of:

a.   Demand.
b.   Equilibrium.
c.   Demand curve.
d.   Supply.

10. The law of supply states that, other influences being unchanged:

a.   Price and quantity demanded are inversely related.
b.   Price and quantity supplied are inversely related.
c.   Income and quantity supplied are unrelated.
d.   Price and quantity supplied are positively related.

11. A change in quantity supplied can be caused by a change in

a.   Price.
b.   Income.
c.   Technology.
d.   Price of inputs.

12. A shift in a supply curve is known as a:

a.   Supply shift.
b.   Change in quantity supplied.
c.   Rotation.
d.   Change in supply.

13. Which of the following will not cause a leftward shift in the supply curve?

a.   Decrease in input prices
b.   Increase in the prices of other goods that could be produced with the same resources and technology
c.   Expectation of lower product prices
d.   Decrease in the number of sellers

14. Market equilibrium occurs when:

a.   The forces of supply and demand oppose each other.
b.   The forces of price and quantity oppose each other.
c.   A market price just equates quantity demanded and quantity supplied.
d.   A market quantity just equates quantity supplied and quantity demanded.

15. A price above the market equilibrium price results in:

a.   A shortage.
b.   Inflation.

c. Excess demand.
d. A surplus.

16. A price below the market equilibrium price results in:

a. A shortage.
b. Inflation.
c. Insufficient demand.
d. A surplus.

17. An increase in the demand for a good will _____ price and _____ quantity.

a. Decrease/decrease
b. Increase/decrease
c. Increase/increase
d. Decrease/increase

18. A decrease in supply of a good will _____ price and _____ quantity.

a. Decrease/decrease
b. Increase/decrease
c. Increase/increase
d. Decrease/increase

19. An increase in both demand and supply will _____ price and _____ quantity.

a. Decrease/ decrease
b. Have an indeterminate effect on/increase
c. Increase/increase
d. Increase/have an indeterminate effect on

20. If the price of movie tickets increases significantly, then the price of VCRs will probably _____ and the market quantity of VCRs will _____.

a. Increase/decrease
b. Increase/increase
c. Decrease/decrease
d. Decrease/increase

THINK IT THROUGH

1. A market economy is a type of economy that relies on the market to .... (Complete the statement as thoroughly as you can.)

2. Use supply and demand analysis to assess the impact of the drought that occurred in the farm belt in the Spring and Summer of 1988.
   a. Discuss the impact of the drought on the market for corn.
   b. Discuss the probable impact on feedlots that use corn as feed.

3. If a market is currently in equilibrium and an increase in demand occurs, what happens to the market price? Explain.

4. If the price of golf course greens fees increases nationally, using supply and demand analysis, discuss the impact on the market for golf balls.

5.   Suppose that you operate a dry cleaning firm in a small city and you and the other dry cleaners are earning handsome profits. Because of the profit potential, a national dry cleaning firm enters the area and opens several new dry cleaners. Assess the impact on the market for dry cleaning in this city.

POP QUIZ   Read the news brief at the end of this chapter and answer the question below.

Identify the forces affecting the supply and demand for gasoline and explain the probable impact on market price and quantity.

CHAPTER ANSWERS

In Brief: Chapter Summary

1. Markets 2. Market price 3. Supply and demand analysis 4. Demand schedule 5. Demand curve 6. Demand 7. Change in quantity demanded 8. Change in demand 9. Supply schedule 10. Supply curve 11. Supply 12. Change in quantity supplied 13. Change in supply 14. Equilibrium 15. Price 16. Surplus 17. Shortage 18. Cutting prices 19. Surplus 20. Increasing 21. Equal to 22. Can

Vocabulary Review

1. Change in relative price 2. Demand curve 3. Supply schedule 4. Supply 5. Quantity supplied 6. Demand schedule 7. Market 8. Supply and demand analysis 9. Market equilibrium 10. Shortage 11. Equilibrium 12. Surplus 13. Change in supply 14. Change in quantity demanded 15. Change in demand 16. Complements 17. Substitutes 18. Supply curve 19. Law of demand 20. Change in quantity supplied 21. Quantity demanded 22. Demand schedule 23. Demand

Skills Review

1.   a.

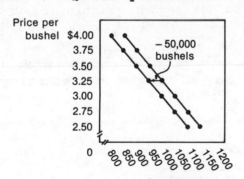

Price per bushel

Quantity of corn demanded (000s bushels per week)

b.   Negative or inverse
c.   If other vegetables are considered substitutes for corn, the demand for corn falls and the demand curve shifts leftward as the prices of other vegetables are falling.

d.

(b)
800
850
900
950
1000
1050
1100

e. The demand curve shifts leftward as shown in the diagram above in part a.

2. a. Income b. Wealth c. Prices of substitutes and complements d. Price expectations e. Tastes f. Number of buyers

3. a. U b. L c. L d. R e. L f. R

4. a.

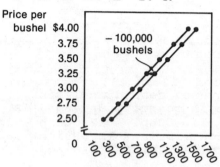

Quantity of corn supplied
(000s bushels per week)

b. Positive, higher prices increase the willingness and ability of suppliers to increase production.

c.

(b)
1500
1300
1100
900
700
500
300

d. The supply curve shifts leftward as shown in the diagram above in part a.

5. a. Prices of other goods b. Prices of inputs c. Technology d. Price expectations e. Number of sellers

6. a. L b. U c. L d. R

7. a. $3.25, 1,000,000

b.

Price per bushel $4.00
3.75
3.50
3.25
3.00
2.75
2.50

+ 500,000 bushels
+ 250,000 bushels

Quantity of corn demanded and supplied (000s of bushels

64

c. Surplus, 500,000 bushels, less
d. Shortage, 500,000 bushels, greater
e. Competitive markets are self-equilibrating because market forces will eliminate shortages and surpluses. Shortages are eliminated as market prices rise and surpluses are eliminated as suppliers lower prices to sell excess inventory.

8. a. (b)   b. Increased, $3.25, $3.50, increased,
        1100   1,000,000, 1,200,000
        1150
        1200
        1250
        1300
        1350
        1400

   c. (d)   d. Decreased, $3.25, $2.75, increased,
       2100   1,000,000, 1,100,000
       1900
       1700   e. Decreased, $3.25, $3, increased,
       1500   1,000,000, 1,300,000
       1300
       1100
        900

9.   Price   Quantity
   a.   -   -
   b.   +   +
   c.   +   +
   d.   +   -
   e.   -   -
   f.   +   +

10. Market equilibrium requires that Qd = Qs. Setting the supply and demand curves equal to each other:

    $$a - bP = c + dP$$

    and solving for P, the market equilibrium price, gives:

    a. $P = (a - c)/(d + b)$

    Substituting this expression for P into either the demand or supply equation and solving for Q, the market equilibrium quantity, yields:

    b. $Q = (ad + bc)/(d + b)$

    c. Q is positive and P must be positive. P is positive if the intercept of the demand curve a exceeds the intercept of the supply curve c. This always is expected to be the case. Changes in the nonprice determinants of supply and demand influence the supply and demand equations by changing the value of the intercept terms, a or c. For instance, an increase in income would increase a assuming the good is a normal good. If it is an inferior good, the increase in income will reduce a. As can be seen from the equations above, an increase in a will increase P and Q. A decrease in a will decrease P and Q. An increase in c caused by a nonprice determinant of supply causes P to decrease and Q to increase.

1. b 2. d 3. d 4. d 5. b 6. b 7. d 8. c 9. d 10. d 11. a 12. d 13. a 14. c 15. d 16. a 17. c 18. b 19. b 20. b

Think it Through

1.   A market economy is a type of economy that relies on the market to allocate resources and distribute output. The impersonal interaction of the forces of supply and demand communicate the wishes of consumers to sellers via the market price. Changes in demand alter the price, and it is the change in price that causes a supplier to respond by altering production. As producers alter levels of production, they alter their levels of employment of resources. Thus markets determine what is to be produced and in what quantities. Resources flow to markets experiencing increases in quantity and away from markets experiencing decreases in production. Output is distributed based upon a buyer's ability to pay. Other things being constant, rising market prices reduce the ability to pay, whereas decreases in market prices increase the ability to pay.

2.   a. As is shown in the diagram below, the drought reduces the supply of corn increasing the price per bushel of corn and reducing the market quantity of corn.

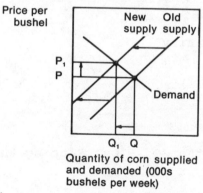

Quantity of corn supplied
and demanded (000s
bushels per week)

   b.   If corn is an input to feedlot operations and the price of corn is increasing, the supply of feedlot services will decrease, causing the price of those services to increase and the quantity of feedlot services to fall.

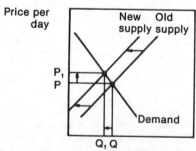

Quantity of feedlot days
supplies and demanded

3.   If demand increases, then at the current market price there is a shortage because quantity demanded exceeds quantity supplied. In order to ration the limited number of goods or services among many buyers, the price of the good or service is increased. Increases in price reduce quantity demanded but increase quantity supplied. This in turn reduces the shortage. As long as a shortage exists, the rationing function of prices implies that prices will continue to rise. Prices will no longer increase when the shortage is eliminated. The shortage no longer exists at the new market equilibrium.

4. Greens fees and golf balls are complementary goods. If the price of greens fees increases, the demand for golf balls will decrease. As can be seen in the figure below, a decrease in the demand for golf balls reduces the market price and quantity.

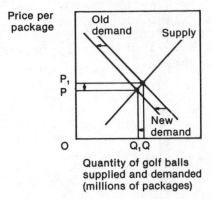

Quantity of golf balls
supplied and demanded
(millions of packages)

5. If several new dry cleaners open for business, the local market supply of dry cleaning services will increase. This causes a decrease in the price of dry cleaning services, but an increase in total market quantity.

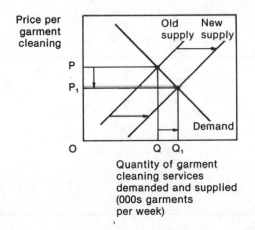

Quantity of garment
cleaning services
demanded and supplied
(000s garments
per week)

Pop Quiz

Gasoline prices have remained "firm" in spite of a $4 decline in the price of crude oil. In the long run, the price of crude oil is an important determinant of gasoline prices, but in the short run other forces affecting the supply of and demand for gasoline may be changing and thus offsetting the effect of lower crude prices on gasoline prices. On the demand side of the gasoline market, demand is expected to increase 2% in 1988 in part because many states raised speed limits, resulting in increased fuel consumption. Further, a decline in the international value of the dollar made foreign vacations more expensive relative to domestic vacations. The American Automobile Association projected that 10 million more automobile vacations would be taken in 1988 than in 1987.

On the supply side of the gasoline market, the summer drought reduced shipments of gasoline on the Mississippi River by 50,000 barrels per day. Gasoline barges required several more days between river terminals than normal. Coastal refineries had to purchase and bring in fresh water because river levels were not high enough to prevent the intrusion of salt water. Several refineries experienced breakdowns. Refineries were able to produce only 294 million gallons daily at capacity and quantity demanded was 319 million gallons per day. The number of refineries has fallen by about one-third from 213 in the early 1980s. Finally, the yield of gasoline per barrel of crude has fallen because of the government's ban on the use of lead additives.

In short, demand is strong and expected to grow, but supply is constrained--
there are bottlenecks in delivery and refineries are operating at capacity.
These forces would normally result in an increase in market price and in time
market quantity, but the decline in crude prices and the 11% increase in the
stocks of crude oil have been an offsetting factor. Also, the industry is
becoming less competitive; 80% of all gasoline used in the U.S. is produced by
just 15 refineries. Major oil companies have been eliminating the independent
retail segment of the market and have increasingly marketed and sold at retail
the gasoline output of their refineries.

Array of Forces Bolstering
The Pump Price of Gasoline

By ALLANNA SULLIVAN

Staff Reporter of THE WALL STREET JOURNAL

For years, the cost of a road trip to, say, Yellowstone National Park has been largely determined by the councils of OPEC. But not this summer.

Long-term changes in the gasoline business—as well as some special, short-term factors—have drastically altered the dynamics of pricing in the more than $150 billion-a-year gasoline market. "Things aren't crystal clear anymore," says Thomas Burns, manager of economics at Chevron Corp. "The underlying reasons for price moves are more obscure."

The effect, however, is clear enough: Retail gasoline prices have remained firm, despite depressed prices for crude oil. In the long run, of course, the price of crude will continue to control whether gasoline prices rise or fall. But this summer, at least, "the gasoline market is marching to its own drummer," says Trilby Lundberg, whose Lundberg Letter tracks retail gasoline prices across the country.

Gasoline prices currently average around $1 a gallon nationwide, up about one cent from a year ago, even though the spot-market price of crude has dropped more than $4 a barrel in the same period, to $15.45 as of Friday. What's more, U.S. gasoline inventories have fallen sharply in recent weeks, to almost 10% below last year's levels, while stocks of crude oil are nearly 11% higher than they were a year ago. (Last week's explosion of a huge North Sea oil platform could help to shrink those inventories somewhat by eliminating for a time 300,000 barrels a day of production from the glutted crude market.)

The Role of Big Oil

One reason for the resilience of gasoline prices, some independent marketers say, is that the major oil companies' grip on the market is growing tighter in many areas. The majors can exclude costly middlemen by refining and selling their own products, in addition to producing the crude from which they're made. With their lower costs and deeper pockets, the major companies have been gobbling up larger chunks of regional markets at a time when independent station owners and marketers are abandoning their businesses because of slim profit margins.

Steven Riggins, whose family runs 16 gas stations in New Jersey, says half of the independent gasoline wholesalers in his market have dropped out in just the past year. As a result, he notes, he's stuck with buying more often from major companies, and pricing is less competitive. "There's definitely not the pick anymore," he says.

Demand, which averaged 7.2 million barrels a day in 1987 and is expected to jump a hefty 2% this year, is also bolstering gasoline prices. Even as the price creeps up, gasoline remains a bargain in the minds of most U.S. motorists. Only five years ago, regular unleaded in such areas as New York City cost $1.24 a gallon, compared with a top price there of $1.07 a gallon today. And with many states abolishing the 55-mile-an-hour speed limit, autos are soaking up more fuel.

Moreover, the declining value of the U.S. dollar is promoting more domestic vacations while attracting tourists from overseas. The American Automobile Association expects Americans to take 10 million more driving vacations this year than the 243 million taken last year. Through May, the Automobile Club of New York had fielded nearly 120 million requests for highway-travel information, up 7% from a year ago. "Our branches have never been so crowded," says a club spokesman.

The supply side, too, is keeping gasoline prices strong. On a regional basis, a number of special factors are tipping the balance against the consumer. For one thing, the delivery each day of at least 50,000 barrels of gasoline along the Mississippi River has been slowed because of drought conditions in that area. The tugboat Amoco Missouri River, for instance, is spending 15 days rather than the usual five to push its gasoline barges between two terminals.

Another drought-related problem: Low river levels are permitting saltwater to reach farther north in Louisiana. This has forced some coastal refineries to use barges, at great expense, to bring in the fresh water needed for their operations.

Meanwhile, a spate of breakdowns and maintenance stoppages has caused at least five major refineries to cut back on gasoline production in recent weeks. The explosion in May of Shell Oil Co.'s huge Norco, La., refinery alone took 130,000 barrels of gasoline a day off the market. "The Shell explosion sure hasn't helped," says Ted Eck, chief economist for Amoco Corp.

Indeed, even while operating nearly flat out last month, U.S. refineries were able to supply only about 294 million gallons of gasoline daily—against demand of 319 million gallons a day. The shortfall was filled from inventories and through imports from Venezuela, Brazil and Canada.

Fewer Refineries

A broader factor in the production squeeze is that the number of refineries in the U.S. has dwindled by almost a third, to 213, since the abolition earlier this decade of oil price controls, which virtually assured refiners of a profit. Of the survivors, no more than 15 provide 80% of the gasoline used by U.S. motorists, says Vic Rasheed, executive director of Service Station Dealers of America, a Washington-based trade group.

As refining capacity has shrunk, so, too, has the yield of gasoline from a barrel of crude, thanks to a government ban on using lead additives to boost octane. This problem is likely to become only more acute as motorists clamor for greater quantities of high-octane premium gasoline to fuel increasingly popular high-performance automobiles.

"The industry is producing (gasoline) at close to sustainable capacity already," says Rodger W. Murtaugh, vice president of operations, planning and transportation for Amoco. He calls current gasoline supplies "tight but manageable."

Mr. Burns, the Chevron economist, says similarly that, after years of glut, gasoline supplies are in "fairly good balance." But this, he adds, means "any accumulation of small things can tip that balance."

5

Using Supply and Demand Analysis

CHAPTER CHALLENGES

After studying your text, attending class, and completing this chapter, you should be able to:

1. Demonstrate how market equilibrium prices deal with the problem of scarcity by rationing goods and services and explain why prices would be zero for nonscarce goods.
2. Explain how supply and demand conditions affect the price and sales potential for new products.
3. Show how wages and interest are determined in competitive markets.
4. Use supply and demand analysis to show how government control of prices in competitive markets can result in shortages or surpluses.
5. Discuss nonprice rationing systems and show how these alternatives work when the rationing function of prices in markets is impaired.

IN BRIEF: CHAPTER SUMMARY

Fill in the blanks to summarize chapter content.

Supply and demand analysis is a useful tool for analyzing personal, business, and social problems and issues. It shows the importance of prices in the allocation of resources. Prices help us deal with the problem of scarcity in both the allocation of resources and the distribution of output. Do prices have a role when scarcity does not exist? Goods in abundant supply such as air are called (1)_____ (essential commodities, nonscarce goods) because there is no positive price for which quantity demanded exceeds quantity supplied. If a positive price is not possible, markets do not develop. Markets develop only when positive prices are possible.

But even at positive prices, a market may not develop if the minimum price required by sellers exceeds the maximum price that buyers are willing and able to pay for the first unit of output. A market for new products can only develop when demand and supply have reached a point where the (2)_____(maximum, minimum) price buyers are willing and able to pay for the first unit of output exceeds the (3)_____(maximum, minimum) price sellers are willing to take for that unit.

In addition to the markets for goods and services, supply and demand analysis can be used to assess changes in competitive labor and credit markets. The price per unit of labor is called the (4)_____(labor cost, wage). When the supply of labor equals the demand, there is a market wage and quantity of labor employed. Everyone who wants to work at that wage is employed. If the demand for the product produced by that labor increases, the demand for labor by employers will likewise increase. This causes the wage to (5)_____(rise, fall) and the quantity of labor employed to (6)_____(decrease, increase). In a recession, as the demand for goods and services falls, the demand for labor declines, causing both wages and employment to also (7)_____(rise, fall).

Changes in the demand and supply of loanable funds determine interest rate movements. In an economic expansion, individuals, businesses, and government as a group borrow more. Interest rates (8)_____(rise, fall) as the demand for loanable funds increases. If the supply of loanable funds increases, say as a result of an increase in savings by both businesses and individuals, interest rates will (9)_____(rise, fall) and (10)_____(more, less) credit will be extended by lenders.

Prices are not always allowed to perform the rationing function. Society will often sanction government price controls as an attempt to aid certain interest groups, such as farmers, unskilled workers, and low-income renters and borrowers. (11)_____ (Price ceilings, Price floors) are government-mandated prices that are set below market equilibrium prices. A price below the market price causes (12)_____(surpluses, shortages). Rent controls, while helping those fortunate enough to pay controlled rents, cause (13)_____(surpluses, shortages) of low-income housing and reduce the incentive of landlords to maintain properties. Usury laws that prevent interest rates from rising to their market levels, while benefiting those people able to obtain the regulated credit, will cause a (14)_____ (surplus, shortage) of loanable funds. The least credit worthy (and also the lowest income) members of society will have difficulty finding credit. Price ceilings will cause (15)_____ (surpluses, shortages) only when the regulated price is (16)_____(below, above) the market price. If market interest rates were to fall, for example, below the usury ceiling, there would be no (17)_____(shortage, surplus) of loanable funds.

When shortages develop there must be a way to allocate the limited goods and services among the buyers. A market system relies on prices to do this. But with price ceilings, prices are not allowed to perform that function. Waiting in line, eligibility criteria, and ration stamps are three methods of nonprice rationing. All three are less efficient than prices in responding to shortages. There will still be those people willing and able to pay prices above the controlled price. In response to this potential market, illegal or (18)_____ (new markets, black markets) develop.

(19)_____(Price ceilings, Price floors) are controlled prices that are set above the market price. Prices above market equilibrium prices cause (20)_____(surpluses, shortages). Whereas prices fall to eliminate the surplus, other means have to be used to deal with surpluses, such as with agricultural price-support programs. Farmers either have to be rewarded to reduce plantings or the surpluses have to be purchased, stored, and distributed by government. Resources that could have been used elsewhere in the economy are being used to eliminate or deal with surpluses that would have been efficiently eliminated by a functioning price system. Although farmers as a special interest group benefit, consumers lose in that they pay (21)_____(lower, higher) prices, and the allocation of resources in the economy is (22)_____(less, more) efficient.

Minimum wage laws set minimum wages at a level above the market wage in most labor markets. The intent of such legislation is to increase the income of the poorest members of society, those individuals who also happen to have the lowest skill levels. But as was the case with agricultural price supports, (23)_____(surpluses, shortages) develop. The unemployment rate among the unskilled is (24)_____(lower, higher). The minimum wage benefits those lucky enough to find employment at that wage, but causes (25)_____(more, less) unemployment in that segment of society that can least afford to be unemployed.

Price controls distort the economy. They benefit some at the expense of others and prohibit a competitive economy from efficiently rationing resources. If the motives underlying price controls are socially desirable, society would gain if methods other than price controls could be employed to make certain interest groups better off without impairing the functioning of a competitive economy.

VOCABULARY REVIEW

Write the key term from the list below next to its definition.

Key Terms

Nonscarce good   Price ceiling
Wages   Nonprice rationing
Credit   Black market
Interest   Price floor

Definitions

1. _____: a good for which the quantity demanded does not exceed the quantity supplied at a zero price.

2. _____: establishes a maximum price that can legally be charged for a good or service.

3. _____: the price paid for labor services.

4. _____: the price for the use of funds, expressed as a percentage per dollar of funds borrowed.

5. _____: a minimum price established by law.

6. _____: a market in which sellers sell goods to buyers for more than the legal prices.

7. _____: the use of loanable funds supplied by lenders to borrowers, who agree to pay back the funds borrowed, according to an agreed-upon schedule.

8. _____: a device that distributes available goods and services on a basis other than willingness to pay.

SKILLS REVIEW

Concept: **The determination of wages and interest rates in competitive markets**

1. You are a manager of a business and you are trying to decide if you should borrow funds for plant expansion today at the current interest rate of 12%. The morning newspaper reports that the Federal Reserve System has announced that within the next month it will begin to expand the funds that banks have on hand to extend credit.

a.   Show the impact on the supply of loanable funds curve in the diagram below.

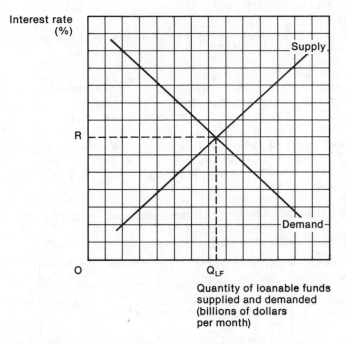

Interest rate (%)

R

O   Q_LF

Supply

Demand

Quantity of loanable funds
supplied and demanded
(billions of dollars
per month)

b.   How will your analysis of future interest rates influence your decision to borrow today?

2.   You are a college sophomore trying to decide if you should major in mechanical engineering. Employability and income prospects are important considerations in your choice. As shown in the diagram below, the market for engineers is currently producing high entry market wages.

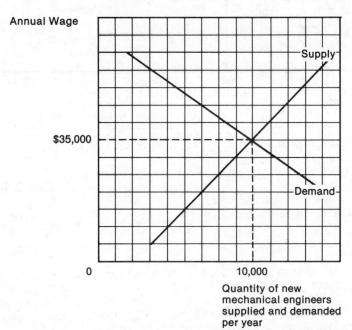

Annual Wage

$35,000

0   10,000

Supply

Demand

Quantity of new
mechanical engineers
supplied and demanded
per year

a.   If you and thousands of other college students are induced by the high entry wages to become majors in engineering, in time the supply

73

of engineers will _____. Show the future supply curve on the diagram above.

b. Entry wages in the future would _____, and the total employment of engineers would _____.

c. How might these expected future wages and employment levels influence your decision today to major in engineering?

3. Advanced Question. As a portfolio manager you must react to anticipated changes in interest rates with respect to your company's holding of financial assets such as stocks, cash, and bonds. Based on the current interest rate of 10%, our research shows that for each one percentage point change in the interest rate, the quantity of loanable funds supplied changes by $2 billion and the quantity of loanable funds demanded changes by $3 billion. If you anticipate that the demand for loanable funds will increase by $5 billion, what would you predict regarding the future rate of interest?

Concept: Government price controls--shortages and surpluses

4. The diagram below represents the market for good X.

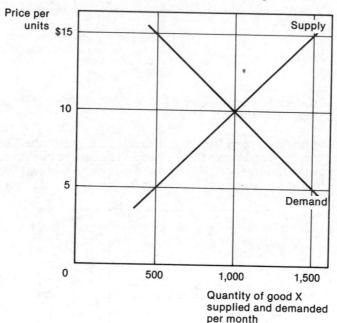

a. The market price is $_____, and the market quantity equals _____ units of X.

b. If a price ceiling is established at $5, a _____ would exist in the amount of _____ units. Show on the diagram above the impact of this price ceiling.

c. If a price floor is set at $15, a _____ would exist in the amount of _____ units. Show this on the graph above.

5. Given the market for unskilled labor in the diagram below:

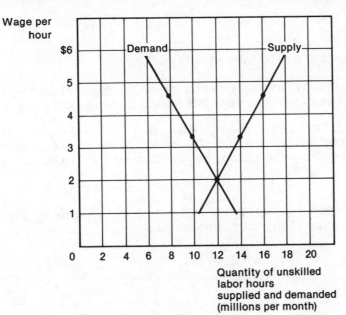

Wage per hour

Quantity of unskilled
labor hours
supplied and demanded
(millions per month)

a. The market wage and level of employment equals $_____ and _____ hours, respectively.

b. A minimum wage is now established at $3.35 per hour.
    (1) Show on the graph above.
    (2) Wages _____ from $_____ to $_____ and employment _____ from _____ hours to _____ hours.

c. What would happen if the minimum wage increased from $3.35 to $4.70 per hour?
    (1) Show on the above graph.
    (2) Wages _____ from $_____ to $_____ and employment _____ from _____ hours to _____ hours.

Concept: Nonprice rationing systems

6. List three forms of nonprice rationing:

    a. _____
    b. _____
    c. _____

SELF-TEST FOR MASTERY

Select the best answer.

1. Markets for new products would not develop if:

    a. The price required by producers to produce the first unit of output exceeded the price that buyers are willing and able to pay for that first unit.
    b. Profits exceeded that which could be earned on financial assets.
    c. The price required by producers to produce the first unit of output was less than the price buyers are willing and able to pay for the first unit.
    d. None of the above

2. Goods for which there is no positive price in which the quantity demanded exceeds the quantity supplied, are known as:

    a. Scarce goods.
    b. Normal goods.
    c. Inferior goods.
    d. Nonscarce goods.

3. An important function of prices in competitive markets is:

    a. The rationing function.
    b. To ensure that producers make profits.
    c. To eliminate any unemployment.
    d. To communicate to buyers the wishes of sellers.

4. In a competitive labor market, wages are determined:

    a. By buyers.
    b. By unions.
    c. By sellers.
    d. By the forces of supply and demand.

5. An increase in the demand for labor by businesses _____ wages and _____ employment.

    a. Increases/decreases
    b. Decreases/decreases
    c. Increases/increases
    d. Decreases/increases

6. If because of a recession the demand for loanable funds decreases, what would happen to market interest rates and the quantity of credit extended?

    a. Interest rates would increase and the quantity of credit would decrease.
    b. Interest rates would decrease and the quantity of credit would not change.
    c. Interest rates would not change but the quantity of credit would fall.
    d. Both interest rates and the quantity of credit would decline.

7. Usury laws that prevent interest rates from rising to market levels are called:

    a. Monetary regulations.

    b.   Price ceilings.
    c.   Price floors.
    d.   Rationing methods.

8.   Rents controls:

    a.   Are price ceilings.
    b.   Cause shortages of low-income housing.
    c.   Result in the deterioration of low-income housing through the lack of maintenance.
    d.   All of the above.

9.   The minimum wage law is an example of:

    a.   An employment enhancement strategy.
    b.   A price ceiling.
    c.   A price floor.
    d.   A well-designed policy intended to reduce teenage unemployment.

10.   Price ceilings cause:

    a.   No change in market quantities.
    b.   Shortages.
    c.   Quantity supplied to increase.
    d.   Surpluses.

11.   Price floors cause:

    a.   No change in market quantities.
    b.   Shortages.
    c.   Quantity demanded to increase.
    d.   Surpluses.

12.   Agricultural price supports:

    a.   Benefit farmers.
    b.   Harm consumers.
    c.   Require the use of scarce resources to deal with surpluses.
    d.   All of the above

13.   If in some labor markets the market wage for unskilled labor exceeds the minimum wage:

    a.   Unemployment would result.
    b.   Wages would rise.
    c.   The minimum wage law would not have an adverse impact on unemployment.
    d.   Wages would fall.

14.   Which of the following cannot be considered true regarding price controls?

    a.   Some people within special interest groups gain.
    b.   Some people within the targeted special interest groups may actually lose.
    c.   Resources are more efficiently used in the economy.
    d.   Resources are less efficiently used in the economy.

15.   Which of the following is not a nonprice form of rationing?

    a.   Grouped staging
    b.   Waiting in line

        c.   Ration stamps
        d.   Eligibility criteria

16.   Price ceilings create an environment conducive to the development of:

        a.   New products.
        b.   Black markets.
        c.   Higher employment.
        d.   A saving ethic.

THINK IT THROUGH

1.   Discuss the importance of the price system in a market-based economy.

2.   Discuss how interest rates are determined in a competitive market for loanable funds. Identify the gainers and losers from usury laws. Under what conditions would the usury laws be ineffective? If it is socially desirable to make credit available at below-market interest rates, what are other ways to benefit the targeted interest group without resulting in as much economic inefficiency as usury laws.

3.   In 1988 Democrats in Congress began a push to increase the minimum wage from its present level of $3.35 per hour to around $5 per hour. Identify the likely gainers and losers. If it is socially desirable to increase the incomes of the unskilled beyond the levels that would prevail in a competitive labor market, what are other ways of doing this so that unskilled workers can be better off without causing as much inefficiency as would be the case with price controls?

4.   In the early 1970s, President Nixon installed a series of wage and price controls. Prices were temporarily frozen on all goods and services. The supply of and demand for gasoline put upward pressure on gasoline prices, but these prices were temporarily controlled. In effect, the price freeze acted as a price ceiling. What do you think occurred in the gasoline market? Explain.

CHAPTER ANSWERS

In Brief: Chapter Summary

1. Nonscarce goods 2. Maximum 3. Minimum 4. Wage 5. Rise 6. Increase 7. Fall 8. Rise 9. Fall 10. More 11. Price ceilings 12. Shortages 13. Shortages 14. Shortage 15. Shortages 16. Below 17. Shortage 18. Black markets 19. Price floors 20. Surpluses 21. Higher 22. Less 23. Surpluses 24. Higher 25. More

Vocabulary Review

1. Nonscarce good 2. Price ceiling 3. Wages 4. Interest 5. Price floor 6. Black market 7. Credit 8. Nonprice rationing

Skills Review

1. a.

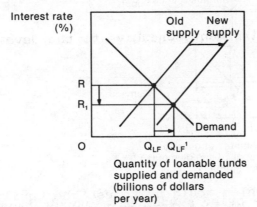

Interest rate
(%)

Quantity of loanable funds
supplied and demanded
(billions of dollars
per year)

b. If you expect interest rates to fall, then other things being equal, you could lower borrowing costs by delaying borrowing until interest rates have fallen.

2. a. Increase

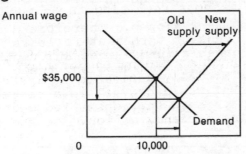

Annual wage

Quantity of mechanical engineers
supplied and demanded
per year

b. Decease, increase
c. You might be deterred from becoming an engineering major in anticipation of lower market wages that might prevail at the time you graduate and enter the labor force. This, of course, assumes that nothing else is expected to influence wages in the future and that you are placing a very high priority on entry level wages relative to other benefits received from an occupation or course of study.

3. This question can be solved graphically or algebraically with just the information given. Assume that the demand and supply curves for loanable funds are linear. This means that the slopes of both curves are constant. Assume also that no other influences are shifting the supply or demand curves other than the increase in demand of $5 billion. We are told that the current interest rate is 10%. This is the rate at which the supply and demand curves intersect. Increasing or decreasing the interest rate by one percentage point increases or decreases the quantity of loanable funds supplied by $2 billion and decreases or increases the quantity of loanable funds demanded by $3 billion. As can be seen in the figure below, this produces supply and demand curves that intersect at a market interest rate of 10%. Shifting the demand curve rightward by $5 billion increases the market interest rate to 11%.

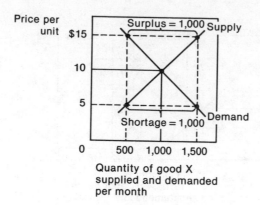

Price per unit

Quantity of good X
supplied and demanded
per month

Another way to solve the problem would be to use the equilibrium price equation derived in question 10 from Chapter 5. Except in this case let's call the price the interest rate.

Let R = (a - c)/(d + b), where R = the interest rate

A change in R = 1/(d + b) x the change in (a - c)

Recall that we are assuming constant slopes. Therefore d and b remain unchanged. The a term is the constant term that reflects noninterest rate influences on the demand for loanable funds--that shifts the demand curve. Since we are making the <u>ceteris paribus</u> assumption, the c term is held constant.

A change in R = 1/(2 + 3) x $5 billion
= 1%

Interest rates are expected to rise from 10% to 11%

4. a. $10, 1000
    b. Shortage, 1000

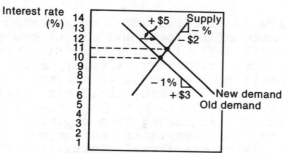

Interest rate (%)

Quantity of loanable funds
supplied and demanded
(billions of dollars
per month)

    c. Surplus, 1000

5. a. $2, 12 million
    b. (1)

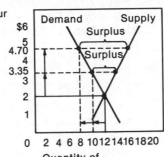

Wage per hour

        (2) Increase, $2, $3.35, decreases, 12 million, 10 million
    c. (1) Answer on the above diagram
        (2) Increase, $3.35, $4.70, decreases, 10 million, 8 million

6. a. Waiting in line
    b. Ration stamps
    c. Eligibility criteria

Self-Test for Mastery

1. a 2. d 3. a 4. d 5. c 6. d 7. b 8. d 9. c 10. b 11. d 12. d 13.
c 14. c 15. a 16. b

Think it Through

1.   Your answer needs to emphasize the rationing function of prices. Price
changes will in time eliminate shortages or surpluses. The price system
allocates resources efficiently. Prices represent the vehicle by which the
wishes of buyers are communicated to sellers. In short, prices coordinate the
purchase plans of buyers with the production plans of sellers.

2.   In a competitive market for loanable funds, the forces of supply and
demand determine the market rate of interest and the market quantity of credit.
Usury laws benefit those lucky enough to obtain loans at the controlled rate
(those people with higher incomes and credit ratings), but impose costs on
those who must go without credit (those people with lower incomes and poorer
credit ratings). One alternative to regulated interest rates might be
subsidies to low-income borrowers or those with poor credit ratings to be used
to defer the cost of borrowing at the market rate of interest. Lenders could
be encouraged to make loans to these people if lenders were protected from loan
defaults by some form of government guarantee. This alternative would still
require the use of scarce resources that would not have been required in a
market involving no intervention. But at least the price system can perform
its rationing function.

3.   An increase in the minimum wage will increase the incomes of those able to
find employment at that wage. But the level of unemployment will increase
among those least able to afford the loss of a job--the poor and unskilled.
Incomes and employability can be increased a number of ways without having to
resort to price controls. Job training programs that increase the productivity
of the unskilled will increase their prospects for employment and better wages.
Income transfers (such as Aid to Families with Dependent Children) can be used
to supplement the incomes of the poor and unskilled. Again, these alternatives
require the use of scarce resources but at least do not prevent the price
system from functioning.

81

4.   Severe gasoline shortages developed at the frozen price. Because prices could not perform their rationing function, people waited endlessly in line at service stations all across the nation. The problem continued to be serious until the price controls were removed.

6

The Price System: How It Functions and When It Fails

CHAPTER CHALLENGES

After studying your text, attending class, and completing this chapter, you should be able to:

1. Examine the framework of a pure market economy and show how the circular flow of income and expenditure in a capitalistic economy keeps it functioning.
2. Provide an overview of the price system as a mechanism for coordinating decisions and allocating resources to influence what is to be produced, how it is produced, and how output is distributed.
3. Point out the defects of a pure market system by showing how the price system doesn't attain all possible gains from resource use and how it sometimes results in low living standards for large numbers of people.
4. Briefly outline the functioning of the modern mixed economy.

IN BRIEF: CHAPTER SUMMARY

Fill in the blanks to summarize chapter content.

(1)_____ (Capitalism, Socialism) is an economic system characterized by private ownership, freedom of choice and enterprise, and a limited economic role for government. A capitalistic economy relies on the (2)_____ (benevolence of sellers, price system) to answer the "what, how, and to whom" questions basic to all economies. (3)_____ (Profit, Money) is the guiding force in capitalistic systems. It is what induces sellers to acquire resources to produce goods that are profitable to produce and to withdraw resources from other uses that are less profitable or involve no profit. (4)_____ (Economic chivalry, Economic rivalry) is also an essential characteristic in which there are large numbers of both buyers and sellers in markets and in which economic power is dispersed among many sellers and buyers such that no one seller or buyer dominates market outcomes.

For a market system to operate efficiently, it must not only produce output efficiently, but buyers and sellers must also be allowed to engage in mutually gainful trades or transactions. An economy attains the state of (5)_____ (allocative efficiency, production efficiency) when it is producing the maximum output for a given quantity of resources and buyers and sellers have engaged in mutually beneficial trades to the point where no further mutual gains can be achieved.

Transactions in a (6)_____ (money, barter) economy do not involve the exchange of money for goods, but the exchange of goods for goods. It is an inefficient form of exchange because of the high transaction costs involved in finding "producers-consumers" with which to trade. Barter requires a (7)_____ (single coincidence of wants, double coincidence of wants). Money greatly facilitates the exchange process because it allows individuals to specialize in the production of a single good, to convert any surplus into money by selling it in the market, and to spend the money on goods and services produced by other sellers. With money, a double coincidence of wants (8)_____(is, is not) required.

A (9)_____(supply and demand diagram, circular flow diagram) is a useful way of identifying the major sectors in a pure market economy and the relationships among those sectors. Businesses purchase resources from households in order to produce the output of goods and services consumed by households. Households derive their income from the sale of resources to the business sector. It is in this market for resources that supply and demand conditions determine the market prices that businesses must pay for resources and therefore the market wages, rents, and interest plus profits received by households. A household's income is the result of the quantities of resources sold in the resource market and the market prices at which those resources sell.

Households use their income, in part, to purchase the output of business. Household expenditures become the firm's sale revenue. The revenue from sales is used by businesses to purchase the resources necessary to produce output. In the markets for goods and services, supply and demand determine prices, which in turn influence the quantities of goods and services demanded and supplied.

In a pure market economy, the price system answers the three basic questions: What is produced? How are goods produced? To whom are goods distributed? Goods are produced if they are profitable to produce. Resources are used first to produce the most (10)_____(profitable, desirable) goods and services. Profitability depends, in part, upon the prices prevailing in both product and resource markets. Because of economic rivalry, successful producers are those that are able to earn enough income over time to continue in business. Sellers who introduce new technology can realize lower costs and, as a result, higher profits. But increased production resulting from higher profits increases market supply and reduces prices. This requires other sellers to adopt the new technology just to maintain profits. The (11)_____(newest, least costly) methods of production are adopted and quickly disseminated among other sellers. The market distributes goods based upon a buyer's willingness and ability to pay. Ability to pay is determined by household income and the prices of goods and services purchased.

Markets often fail to achieve allocative efficiency. Private firms will not produce some goods that benefit society because prices cannot be used to exclude those unwilling to pay. These goods are known as (12)_____(private goods, public goods). Markets may overproduce or underproduce if market prices do not reflect all benefits and costs associated with the production or consumption of output. (13)_____(Negative, Positive) externalities occur when costs accrue to parties other than sellers and buyers. Sellers in this case make decisions based upon marginal costs that do not reflect these external or "third-party" costs. Their costs are lower than if all costs were considered and that induces them to produce (14)_____(less, more) than they would otherwise. In contrast, the production or consumption of goods may confer benefits on third parties, implying that market demand curves do not reflect all benefits associated with goods, but just those benefits received by the buyer of the good. (15)_____(Negative, Positive) externalities result in too (16)_____(much, little) output in that persons other than direct consumers benefit from the good. Sellers respond only to the effective demands registered by buyers, not third parties.

Externalities occur because property rights do not exist or because the property rights are not enforced. Property rights are not enforced when the

transaction costs involved in enforcing these rights are very
(17)_____(high, low). Some of the environment, such as air and navigable
waterways, involve common ownership and are often polluted because no one
individual has a property right or the capacity to enforce the right.

Other problems of a market system involve the absence of competition in markets
and the ability of sellers to control market outcomes to the disbenefit of
society. A market system can produce a skewed distribution of income in which
a small percentage of families receive a much larger percentage of income and
own an even larger percentage of the nation's wealth. A market system does not
guarantee the absence of unemployment or poverty. Because of market
shortcomings, modern economies rely on (18)_____(significant, limited)
government intervention in the economy to improve upon the allocation of
resources or to correct other market problems. These modern market economies
are known as (19)_____(mixed economies, pure market economies) because
decisions regarding resource use are made by both the private and public
sectors of the economy.

VOCABULARY REVIEW

Write the key term from the list below next to its definition.

Key Terms

Capitalism	Market failure
Mixed economy	Public goods
Price system	Externalities
Allocative efficiency	Property rights
Barter	Transaction costs
Money	

Definitions

1. _____: costs incurred in enforcing property rights to
traded goods, locating trading partners, and actually carrying out the
transaction.

2. _____: goods consumed equally by everyone whether they
pay or not.

3. _____: what sellers usually accept as payment for goods
and services.

4. _____: attained when all possible mutual gains from
exchange can be enjoyed.

5. _____: a mechanism by which resource use in an economy
is guided by prices.

6. _____: privileges to use or own goods, services, and
economic resources.

7. _____: characterized by private ownership of economic
resources and freedom of enterprise in which owners of factories and other
capital hire workers to produce goods and services.

8. _____: the process of exchanging goods and services.

9. _____: occurs when the price system fails to allocate resources so as to achieve allocative efficiency.

10. _____: costs or benefits of market transactions that are not reflected in the prices buyers and sellers use to make their decisions.

11. _____: an economy in which governments as well as business firms provide goods and services.

SKILLS REVIEW

Concept: **Framework of a pure market economy; circular flow of income and expenditure**

1. List six characteristics of a pure market economy:

   a. _____
   b. _____
   c. _____
   d. _____
   e. _____
   f. _____

2. In the diagram below, match the flow or box with one of the following:

   a. _____
   b. _____
   c. _____
   d. _____
   e. _____
   f. _____

   1. Market for goods and services
   2. Resource market
   3. Rents, interest, wages, and profits
   4. Economic resources
   5. Goods and services
   6. Expenditures on goods and services

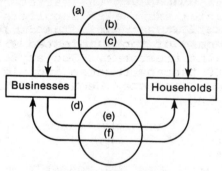

Concept: **Defects of a pure market economy**

3. List four failings of a market economy:

   a. _____
   b. _____
   c. _____
   d. _____

86

4. The diagram below represents the market for electricity. Electric power
    companies are burning bituminous coal and emitting sulfur into the
    atmosphere, creating acid rain that destroys forests and kills lakes.

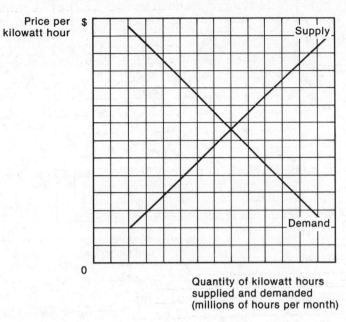

Price per $
kilowatt hour

Supply

Demand

0

Quantity of kilowatt hours
supplied and demanded
(millions of hours per month)

a. This is an example of a good involving _____ externalities.
b. On the diagram, show what would happen if these electric power
    companies were required to install scrubbers to remove sulfur from
    their emissions?
c. Market price of electricity _____ and market quantity
    _____.
d. Why is government required to correct the market failure?

5. Suppose the following diagram represents the market for AIDS therapy.
    Private pharmaceutical companies and health suppliers are in a race to
    discover and market a successful treatment. The demand for AIDS therapy
    reflects only the private demand of those infected with the virus and
    willing and able to pay for the treatment. Society as a whole, however,
    benefits from successful AIDS therapy because individuals who would have
    otherwise been infected are not infected because of the treatment that
    persons with AIDS are receiving.

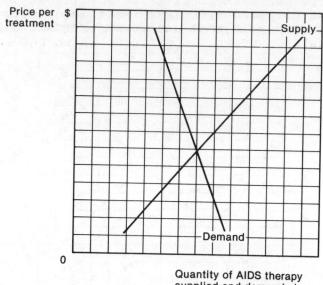

Price per $ treatment

Supply

Demand

0

Quantity of AIDS therapy
supplied and demanded
(000s treatments per month)

a. This is an example of a good involving _____ externalities.
b. Presently, there are too _____ resources allocated to AIDS therapy.
c. If government subsidizes AIDS research and the development of successful treatments, show on the diagram the likely impact on the market for AIDS therapy.
d. Market price of AIDS treatment _____ and market quantity _____.
e. Why must government be involved?

6. Advanced Question. The Sleaze E Chemical Company is presently dumping untreated effluent into a river. Downstream residents and other users of the river suffer from pollution. You are a policy maker in charge of determining the socially desirable level of pollution for the river and the appropriate effluent tax or charge per gallon of untreated effluent to impose on Sleaze E. You want to impose a tax high enough to induce Sleaze E to treat its discharge up to the point at which the proper level of pollution is reached.

Sleaze E Treated Discharge (000s gallons)	Units of Pollution Reduction	Marginal Benefits	Marginal Costs
0	0	$0	$0
10	1	10	2
20	2	8	4
30	3	6	6
40	4	4	8
50	5	2	10

a. Using the marginal benefits and marginal costs columns, determine the units of pollution reduction that maximize the net gain to society. Assume that the marginal benefit and cost data include external costs and benefits. How many gallons of discharge will Sleaze E have to treat in order to reach that level of pollution reduction?

b.   The diagram below represents the relationship between Sleaze E's
       marginal cost of treating discharge and the quantity of discharge
       treated. What tax per unit of untreated effluent would be sufficient
       to induce Sleaze E to treat its effluent up to the level desired by
       society?

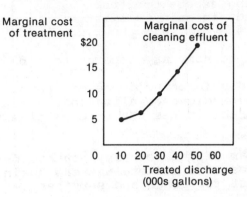

Select the best answer.

1.   Which of the following is not true of a pure market system?

       a.   Private ownership
       b.   Freedom of enterprise and choice
       c.   Significant economic role of government
       d.   Presence of economic rivalry

2.   A pure market economy relies on which of the following to answer the three
       basic questions: (1) What is produced? (2)   How are goods produced? (3)
       To whom are goods distributed?

       a.   Barter
       b.   Money
       c.   Property rights
       d.   Price system

3.   The catalyst or driving force in a market system that induces sellers to
       acquire resources to produce products is:

       a.   Money.
       b.   Profit.
       c.   Price.
       d.   Benevolence.

4.   Economic rivalry means:

       a.   That there are large numbers of consumers, but not sellers in
              markets.
       b.   That the survival of the fittest criterion of business behavior is
              operative in the economy.
       c.   There are large numbers of buyers and sellers in markets such that no
              one buyer or seller dominates market outcomes.
       d.   That competitive firms produce profitable goods.

5. When an economy is operating at a point on its production possibilities curve and buyers and sellers have engaged in trade to the point where no further mutual gains from trade are possible:

    a. Production efficiency is said to exist.
    b. All firms are earning excess profits.
    c. Allocative efficiency is said to exist.
    d. Distributive efficiency is said to exist.

6. The advantage of a money economy as compared to a barter economy is :

    a. The avoidance of a double coincidence of wants.
    b. That money allows economic specialization and the division of labor.
    c. That money greatly facilitates the process of exchange.
    d. All of the above

7. In a circular flow diagram of the economy, households represent the _____ side of the resource market, whereas business represents the _____ of the market for goods and services.

    a. Demand/demand
    b. Supply/supply
    c. Demand/supply
    d. Supply/demand

8. In a circular flow diagram of the economy, households provide _____ and receive _____, which when _____ become the _____ of businesses.

    a. Goods/money/saved/capital
    b. Money/bonds/employed/capital
    c. Economic resources/money income/expended/sales revenue
    d. Money income/employment/used/property

9. Economic rivalry in a pure market economy ensures that:

    a. Only the healthiest firms use the most advanced technology.
    b. New cost-saving technology is rapidly disseminated among sellers in the economy.
    c. Firms will adopt the least-cost combination of resources.
    d. B and c
    e. A and c

10. Goods are distributed in a pure market economy:

    a. By government.
    b. By both the private and public sectors.
    c. On the basis of the buyer's willingness and ability to pay for goods and services.
    d. To those with the highest wages.

11. Private businesses will not allocate resources to the production of goods when prices cannot be used to exclude those unwilling to pay. These goods are known as:

    a. Inferior goods.
    b. Public goods.
    c. Loss goods.
    d. External goods.

12. Goods that when consumed or produced impose costs on third parties involve:

    a. Public external effects.
    b. Positive externalities.
    c. Marginal costs.
    d. Negative externalities.

13. Goods that when consumed or produced confer benefits on third parties involve:

    a. Public external effects.
    b. Positive externalities.
    c. Marginal benefits.
    d. Negative externalities.

14. Goods involving positive externalities result in :

    a. An efficient allocation of resources.
    b. Productive efficiency, but not allocative efficiency.
    c. An overallocation of resources to the production of the good.
    d. An underallocation of resources to the production of the good.

15. Externalities exist because:

    a. Businesses are often operated by uncaring individuals.
    b. Businesses do not investigate production problems as thoroughly as they should.
    c. Property rights are completely assigned and enforced.
    d. Property rights either do not exist, are not enforced, or are too costly to enforce.

16. High transaction costs associated with the assignment and enforcement of property rights increase the likelihood that:

    a. Externalities will not exist.
    b. Government will not intervene in the economy.
    c. Externalities will exist.
    d. Allocative efficiency will be achieved.

17. Actual market economies give rise to all but one of the following:

    a. A skewed distribution of income
    b. Poverty among plenty
    c. Full employment
    d. Less than competitive markets

18. In a market economy subject to market failures, society's well-being can be improved:

    a. By no government intervention.
    b. By government intervention that corrects resource misallocation and modifies other market outcomes consistent with the desires of society.
    c. By the price system.
    d. If decisions regarding public goods production are left to the private sector.

19. Modern market economies that rely on both the private and public sectors of the economy to answer the three basic questions are known as:

a. Modern market economies.
b. Pure market systems.
c. Pure capitalistic economies.
d. Mixed economies.

THINK IT THROUGH

1. Distinguish between concepts of productive efficiency and allocative efficiency.

2. During inflationary periods of the 1970s, a number of barter services were established as a means of eliminating inflation. These barter arrangements made use of computers to register the goods and services that the users were willing to supply and the goods that would be acceptable in exchange. Would such a barter system be as efficient as one with money? Explain.

3. A basic function of government in a pure market economy is to facilitate the functioning of the economy, but not to modify market outcomes. Discuss.

4. For a pure market economy, explain why producers employ the least costly techniques of production. If the price of labor rises relative to the price of capital and other inputs, how would this affect a competitive seller's combination of resources employed in production?

5. Education in the United States is provided by both the private and public sectors. Why?

POP QUIZ   Read the news brief at the end of this chapter and answer the question below.

In addition to the sources of market failure discussed in the text, markets may also fail to allocate resources efficiently if they do not operate competitively. Briefly describe the credit-card industry and indicate how resource allocation might be affected.

CHAPTER ANSWERS

In Brief: Chapter Summary

1. Capitalism 2. Price system 3. Profit 4. Economic rivalry 5. Allocative efficiency 6. Barter 7. Double coincidence of wants 8. Is not 9. Circular flow diagram 10. Profitable 11. Least costly 12. Public goods 13. Negative 14. More 15. Positive 16. Little 17. High 18. Significant 19. Mixed economies

Vocabulary Review

1. Transaction costs 2. Public goods 3. Money 4. Allocative efficiency 5. Price system 6. Property rights 7. Capitalism 8. Barter 9. Market failure 10. Externalities 11. Mixed economy

Skills Review

1. a. Private ownership
    b. Freedom of choice and enterprise
    c. Limited economic role for government
    d. Reliance on the price system to allocate resources
    e. Profit motive
    f. Economic rivalry

2. a. 2 b. 3 c. 4 d. 1 e. 5 f. 6

3. a. Externalities
    b. Lack of competition in markets
    c. Skewed distribution of income
    d. Doesn't eliminate poverty or unemployment

4. a. Negative
    b. If power companies are required to bear the cost of cleaning their emissions, the market supply curve would shift leftward.

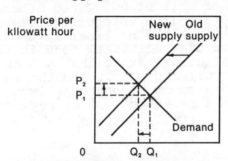

Quantity of kilowatt hours
supplied and demanded
(millions of hours per month)

    c. Increases, decreases
    d. Individual property rights do not exist to the atmosphere and to most lakes and a good portion of timber lands. Where property rights do exist in the ownership of forests and lakes, it is far too costly for any one property owner to identify the source of pollution and to seek remedy in court. Therefore government must intervene and enforce the collective property rights of society to commonly owned resources. Government can also reduce the transaction costs of enforcing property rights for individual property owners. In both cases, government improves resource allocation.

5. a. Positive
    b. Few
    c. Government subsidies increase the net gain to those conducting AIDS research and developing therapies. In time there will be a rightward shift in the supply curve.

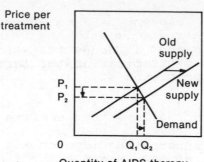

Price per
treatment

Old
supply

New
supply

P_1

P_2

Demand

0          $Q_1 Q_2$

Quantity of AIDS therapy
supplied and demanded
(000s treatments per month)

d. Decreases, increases

e. A market system relies on pricing to allocate resources. Market prices do not reflect the external benefits accruing to third parties. Markets will underproduce goods involving positive externalities. Governments can produce net gains for society by engaging in activities that reallocate more resources to the production of goods with positive externalities.

6. a. Marginal benefits and costs become equal at three units of pollution reduction. This is the level of pollution that maximizes society's net gain. Sleaze E will have to treat 30,000 gallons of discharge for this level of pollution reduction to be realized.

b. $10. A tax of $10 per unit of untreated discharge will result in a net gain to Sleaze E for each unit of treated discharge up to 30,000 gallons. This is because the marginal cost of treating a gallon of effluent is less than the additional benefit associated with not having to pay the pollution tax on that gallon. This holds true up to the level of 30,000 gallons at which the marginal cost of treatment is $10. Treatment beyond this level would not take place because Sleaze E would be better off by paying the tax than treating the discharge.

Self-Test for Mastery

1. c 2. d 3. b 4. c 5. c 6. d 7. b 8. c 9. d 10. c 11. b 12. d 13. b 14. d 15. d 16. c 17. c 18. b 19. d

Think It Through

1. Production efficiency occurs when an economy is operating on its production possibilities curve. Here, resources are efficiently and fully employed. But allocative efficiency is not achieved if any trades can occur between buyers and sellers such that some people can be made better off without making anyone worse off. Allocative efficiency is reached only when trades and exchanges have taken place to the point at which the gains to some parties can only come at the expense of others.

2. Barter systems, whether or not they are operated by computers, must develop "prices" or exchange ratios for the goods involved. This requires scarce resources. A double coincidence of wants is required, which reduces the efficiency of exchange. A middleman must be paid to provide a service that is naturally provided as part of the functioning of a market economy using money.

3. In a pure market system, there are no failures. There are no externalities, markets provide employment for everyone willing and able to work at prevailing wages, all markets involve economic rivalry, and incomes are based strictly on the resources that households supply to the market and the prices at which they sell. In short, it is assumed that allocative efficiency

is achieved by the market without government interference. Government, nevertheless, performs a vital economic role by assigning property rights and enforcing those rights via a system of laws, courts, and police protection. Government also provides money and the basic infrastructure of roads, water supply, sewerage, etc., necessary for the efficient functioning of a market system.

4. Economic rivalry implies that sellers must operate at least cost. If they did not, in time they would incur insufficient profits to remain in business. Firms that stay in business in a pure market system are those that are able to use the least costly combination of inputs and technology in order to at least generate a minimally sufficient level of profit. If the price of labor rises relative to the cost of other inputs, a least cost producer will substitute the relatively less costly resources for labor. By making capital more productive relative to labor, technology reduces the cost of capital relative to labor in the production of output. This is what happened in American agriculture. Technology made farm labor more expensive relative to capital, inducing farmers to mechanize.

5. Education is a good involving positive externalities. A market system produces too little education from society's point of view. Government can increase the net gain to society by providing more education than that provided by a market system alone. But this does not necessarily mean the we have to have the current public-private system in order to achieve this outcome. Education could be entirely publicly provided or it could be provided entirely by a private sector encouraged to produce more with subsidies. Alternatively, students could be given education vouchers that supplement their own funds for education. These funds could be spent entirely in the private sector or even in the current public-private system.

Pop Quiz

Jeff Bailey poses an important question regarding the social consequences of the current structure of the credit-card industry: "A plastic OPEC?" Although 3000 financial institutions are issuing Visa and MasterCard, the ten largest credit-card issuers now have a 50% share of the market, up from about one-third in 1980. While other rates of interest have fallen markedly in the 1980s, credit-card rates have remained in the 17.5% to 20% range. These dominant credit-card issuers are oligopolists and have avoided a rate war by refusing to lower rates. Instead, they compete by spending huge sums in advertising on television and through direct mailings, whereas most of the other more price competitive issuers have inadequate resources to compete through advertising. Critics argue that there is not "prominent disclosure" of interest rates and fees and that issuers should be required to prominently display this information. Other critics contend that if the industry does not engage in price competition, rate caps should be employed, limiting the interest income earned by the large issuers.

Dominant credit-card companies are able to prevent interest rates from reflecting changes in the supply of and demand for consumer credit. If rates do not change to equate supply and demand, then there is a misallocation of resources in that there is either a shortage or surplus of consumer credit. If rates are prevented from falling given a decline in demand, less credit is demanded than would be the case if interest rates fell to restore equilibrium in the market. If consumers are being persuaded through mailings or other advertising to make choices with incomplete or misleading information, then consumer choices will result in a combination of goods and services consumed that is inferior to the combination chosen when consumers have access to full and complete information. Also, Jeff Bailey notes that for the dominant card issuers, the credit-card business is "hugely" profitable--three times as profitable as banking in general in terms of pretax profits as a percent of outstanding loans. These excess profits are received at the expense of possibly ill-informed consumers. This constitutes a redistribution of income from credit-card holders to issuers.

Major Credit-Card Issuers Tighten Grip On Market Despite High Interest Charges

YOUR
MONEY
MATTERS

By Jeff Bailey
Staff Reporter of The Wall Street Journal

A plastic OPEC?

Some banking industry critics contend that something close to that is emerging in the credit-card business. They are worried that a small number of card issuers are increasingly dominating the business and keeping card interest rates high.

"The business is really an oligopoly," says Rep. Charles E. Schumer, a New York Democrat who backs legislation that would force bank-card issuers to disclose their interest rates and fees rates more prominently. "There isn't true (price) competition," he says.

What bothers Mr. Schumer and other critics is that, since 1980, the 10 largest Visa and MasterCard issuers have expanded their combined share of the hugely profitable business to about half of the market from one third. And despite all the talk about credit-card wars, they have managed to do so without a rate battle.

Indeed, instead of falling sharply along with other interest rates, as many people expected, credit-card rates have edged down only slightly during the 1980s. A look at the top 10 card issuers shows current rates bunched in a range of 17.5% to 20%.

Rates Set Independently

The two bank card associations, Visa International and MasterCard International, along with the banks, see nothing wrong with that. They say interest rates are set independently and certainly aren't ever discussed among issuers. "We would never talk to anybody about pricing," says Ira Rimmerman, who heads Citicorp's card business.

That apparently includes consumers, too. Most promotions aimed at getting consumers to take new cards are distinguished by features other than the basic price of using the card, such as the size of the credit limit, the color of the card, free travel insurance and extra frequent flier miles. The issuers who do promote their cards based on a low interest rate represent only a tiny segment of the market.

With a lack of competition on pricing, the dominant issuers have little incentive to lower their rates. In fact, "the industry's resolve to *not* lower rates has stiffened," says a banker who runs one of the 10 biggest card operations.

That resolve was in question a year and a half ago when American Express Co. introduced its Optima bank card at 13.5%. Rate wars were predicted. But Optima has since won little of the market and earlier this month raised its rate to 14.25%.

In the meantime, borrowing by plastic is actually getting more expensive because

> **I**SSUERS that do promote their credit cards based on a low interest rate represent only a tiny segment of the market.

provisions of the 1986 tax law are rapidly phasing out deductions for credit-card interest payments. They'll be gone completely by 1991. Borrowing nevertheless has continued to grow.

Consumers are at least partly to blame for the fact that out of some 3,000 financial institutions issuing Visa and MasterCards, a handful dominate the business. For one thing, few people shop for cards. Instead, they are more likely to respond to direct-mail solicitations, the vast majority of which come from the major credit-card companies.

Generally, as few as 1% of consumers respond to a mailing. But some big issuers are able to back up mailings with heavy advertising and thus increase response rates. Citicorp, which aims to add three million new accounts this year, says its television advertising campaign—"Not just MasterCard. Citibank MasterCard"—has helped response rates to its mailings, though it won't say by how much.

Those consumers who seek out banks that charge lower rates find that they often require a better credit history and won't offer the big credit limits that larger issuers will. Despite its 10.92% rate and a periodic listing in this newspaper and other publications, Arkansas Federal Savings in Little Rock has attracted less than $3 million in credit-card loans. But Arkansas Federal is among those with more stringent credit requirements and lower credit limits.

Card issuers have found, too, that many consumers disregard interest rates because they never intend to borrow money by plastic, but then do. "Most people believe they will pay the balance every month," says Philip J. Purcell, who oversees Sears, Roebuck & Co.'s Discover bank-card business. Only about half do, according to Visa.

Pretax Profits

It's clear why the large credit-card issuers want to increase their share of the business. Combined Visa and MasterCard loans total nearly $100 billion. And the profits on that business are huge. Citicorp's pretax profit on its $16 billion in credit-card loans appears to run at about $800 million a year, a figure that Citicorp's Mr. Rimmerman doesn't dispute. BankAmerica Corp., with about $6 billion in loans, makes more than $300 million before taxes. And First Chicago Corp., with about $4.5 billion in loans, makes more than $200 million before taxes.

For the larger issuers, the credit-card business brings in revenue generally totaling 21% of their loans outstanding. This includes interest payments and annual fees from cardholders and merchants. After subtracting the cost of funds, loan losses and operating costs—including processing, labor and marketing—the pretax profit is roughly 5% of the loans outstanding. That figure is roughly three times the level of a healthy bank's overall profit margin.

But some public officials would like to see the government trim card issuers' earnings. Rep. Schumer says that if the prominent disclosure of interest rates and fees on credit cards doesn't lead to more price competition, he would favor a national cap on credit-card rates.

Jerry Cosentino, Illinois state treasurer, isn't waiting. He wants a rate cap now and last year pulled state funds out of First Chicago to protest its 19.8% rate on credit cards. "They're gouging the consumer every day. There is so much greed in those top 10 issuers," he says. "It's like a conspiracy."

7

Elasticity of Supply and Demand

CHAPTER CHALLENGES

After studying your text, attending class, completing this chapter, you should be able to:

1. Explain the purpose and concept of price elasticity of demand.
2. Show how price elasticity of demand can be calculated for points on a given demand curve and discuss some uses of elasticity.
3. Explain how to use other elasticity measures, including the income elasticity of demand, the cross-elasticity of demand, and the price elasticity of supply.
4. Show how the price elasticities of demand and supply are relevant for explaining the impact of taxes on market prices of goods and services.

IN BRIEF: CHAPTER SUMMARY

Fill in the blanks to summarize chapter content.

The laws of supply and demand indicate the direction in which quantity supplied or demanded changes in response to a price change but they do not reveal the sensitivity of sellers or buyers to given price changes. The concept of elasticity is employed to gauge the sensitivity of buyers and sellers to price changes. Specifically, the (1)_____(income, price) elasticity of demand is a number measuring the sensitivity of buyers to a 1% change in price. If the percentage change in quantity demanded is (2)_____(greater, smaller) than the percentage change in price, demand is said to be elastic, and the price elasticity of demand coefficient is (3)_____(greater, smaller) than 1 (ignoring the minus sign). If the percentage change in quantity demanded is (4)_____(greater, smaller) than the percentage change in price, demand is said to be inelastic, and the price elasticity of demand coefficient is (5)_____ (more, less) than 1 (ignoring the minus sign)but greater than 0. A coefficient equal to (6)_____(1, 0) means that demand is unit elastic. Unit elasticity means that a given percentage change in price will result in (7)_____(a greater, the same) percentage change in quantity demanded.

The price elasticity of demand is determined by taking the percentage change in (8)_____(price, quantity demanded) divided by the percentage change in (9)_____ (price, quantity demanded). The elasticity coefficient or number is influenced by (a) the availability of substitutes, (b) time, and (c) the percentage of income spent on a good. Demand becomes (10)_____(more, less) elastic with increases in the availability of substitute goods, time, and increases in the proportion of income spent on the good. Decreases in the availability of substitutes, time, or the percentage of income expended on a good cause demand to become (11)_____(more, less) elastic.

The price elasticity of demand is not the slope of the demand curve. For a linear demand curve with a constant slope, the price elasticity of demand changes from being (12)_____ (inelastic, elastic) in the upper portion of the demand curve to being (13)_____(inelastic, elastic) in the lower segment of the curve. Exceptions to this would be the cases of perfectly elastic and perfectly inelastic demand curves. A vertical demand curve is perfectly inelastic and has a price elasticity coefficient of (14)_____(1, 0). A horizontal demand curve is perfectly elastic and has a price elasticity coefficient of (15)_____(0, infinity).

A useful application of the price elasticity of demand is an analysis of the behavior of total revenue or expenditures given percentage price changes. If demand is elastic over the range of a price decrease, total revenues and expenditures will (16)_____(fall, rise). This is because the increase in quantity demanded more than offsets the decline in price. If demand is inelastic over the range of a price increase, total revenue and expenditures also (17)_____(fall, rise). In this case, the price increase more than dominates the decline in quantity demanded. Therefore price and total revenue or expenditures are positively related when demand is inelastic and are negatively related when demand is elastic. When the price elasticity of demand is unit elastic, a change in price (18)_____(increases, has no impact on) revenue or expenditures.

Other elasticity concepts include the income elasticity of demand, the cross-elasticity of demand, and the price elasticity of supply. The income elasticity of demand measures the sensitivity of consumer purchases to changes in income. If the income elasticity coefficient is (19)_____ (greater, smaller) than 0, the good in question is a normal good. If the coefficient is (20)_____(greater, smaller) than 0, the good is an inferior good. The cross-elasticity of demand is a way to identify goods as being substitutes, complements, or unrelated. If the cross-elasticity is (21)_____ (negative, positive), the two goods in question are substitutes. The percentage quantity demanded of one good increases when the price of the other good increases by a given percentage. Two goods are complements when the cross-elasticity coefficient is (22)_____(negative, positive). In this case, the percentage quantity demanded of one good decreases when the price of the other good increases by a given percentage. Two goods are unrelated when the cross-elasticity is (23)_____(1, 0).

The price elasticity of supply measures the sensitivity of sellers to percentage price changes. If the percentage change in quantity supplied is greater than the percentage change in price, supply is (24)_____ (elastic, inelastic), with an elasticity coefficient greater than 1. If the percentage change in quantity supplied is less than the percentage change in price, supply is (25)_____(elastic, inelastic), with an elasticity coefficient greater than 0 but less than 1. A coefficient of 0 represents unit supply elasticity, where quantity supplied does not change given a change in price. Supply is (26)_____(more, less) elastic when (a) the additional costs of producing a unit of output rise slowly with increases in output and (b) sufficient time is allowed for the firm or industry to respond to price changes. As with demand, supply can also be perfectly inelastic or perfectly elastic. A vertical supply curve, one that is perfectly (27)_____ (elastic, inelastic), has a supply elasticity coefficient of 0. A horizontal supply curve is perfectly (28)_____(elastic, inelastic) with a coefficient of infinity.

Price elasticities of supply and demand can be used in determining the portion of a tax levied on producers that is shifted to buyers. A tax per unit of output levied on sellers will shift the supply curve (29)_____ (downward, upward) by the amount of that tax per unit. Prices rise, but if they rise less than the tax, some of the tax is borne by sellers and the remainder is borne by consumers. A firm would be successful in passing or shifting all of the tax to consumers when the demand curve is perfectly (30)_____ (inelastic,

elastic) or when the supply curve is perfectly (31)_____(inelastic, elastic). In the opposite case, where the demand curve is (32)_____(horizontal, vertical) and the supply curve is (33)_____(horizontal, vertical), the entire tax would be borne by sellers. With conventionally sloped demand and supply curves, both sellers and buyers bear a portion of the tax.

VOCABULARY REVIEW

Write the key term from the list below next to its definition.

Key Terms

Price elasticity of
  demand
Elastic demand
Inelastic demand
Total revenue
Unit elastic demand
Total expenditure
Income elasticity of
  demand

Normal goods
Inelastic supply
Inferior goods
Price elasticity of
  supply
Elastic supply
Unit elastic supply
Tax shifting
Cross-elasticity of
  supply

Definitions

1. _____: goods that have positive income elasticity of demand.

2. _____: prevails if the price elasticity of demand for a good is a number that exceeds 1, ignoring the minus sign.

3. _____: occurs when a tax levied on sellers of a good causes the market price of the good to increase.

4. _____: a number representing the percentage change in quantity demanded of a good resulting from each 1% change in the price of a good.

5. _____: a number used to measure the sensitivity of consumer purchases of one good to each 1% change in the prices of related goods.

6. _____: prevails when the price elasticity of supply is equal to or greater than 0 but less than 1.

7. _____: the dollars sellers of a product take in; the amount sold over a period multiplied by the price (PQ).

8. _____: prevails if the price elasticity of demand for a good exactly equals 1 when the minus sign is ignored.

9. _____: goods that have negative income elasticity of demand.

10. _____: a number used to measure the sensitivity of

changes in quantity supplied to each 1% change in the price of a good, other things being equal.

11. _____: prevails if the price elasticity of demand for a good is equal to or greater than 0, but less then 1, ignoring the minus sign.

12. _____: prevails when the price elasticity of supply is greater than 1.

13. _____: over any given period, the number of units of a product purchased multiplied by the price of the product (PQ); equals the total revenue of sellers.

14. _____: a number that measures the sensitivity of consumer purchases to each 1% change in income.

15. _____: prevails when elasticity of supply just equals 1.

SKILLS REVIEW

Concept: **Price elasticity of demand; measurement, uses, determinants**

1. Referring to the diagram below:

   a. Calculate the price elasticity of demand over the demand curve segment a-b. _____ Demand is _____.

   b. Calculate the price elasticity of demand over segment e-f. _____ Demand is _____.

   c. Calculate the price elasticity of demand over segment c-d. _____ Demand is _____.

   d. Total revenue (P X Q) at point   a = _____
       b = _____
       c = _____
       d = _____
       e = _____
       f = _____

   e. A decline in price from $6 to $5 _____ total revenue by $_____.

   f. A decline in price from $2 to $1 _____ total revenue by $_____.

   g. A decline in price from $4 to $3 _____ total revenue by $_____.

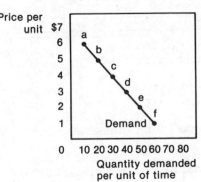

101

2. Will the following make the elasticity of demand more elastic or less elastic?

    a. _____ Decrease in the percentage of income spent on a good
    b. _____ Import tariffs reduce the availability of substitute goods
    c. _____ More time to respond to price changes
    d. _____ Increase in the availability of substitutes

3. Given your knowledge of the determinants of the price elasticity of demand, which of the following goods are likely to have elastic demands and which are likely to be inelastic?

    a. _____ Diamonds
    b. _____ Hamburgers
    c. _____ Toothpaste
    d. _____ Automobiles
    e. _____ Gasoline
    f. _____ Cigarettes
    g. _____ Movies

Concept: Other concepts of elasticity; measurement, uses, determinants

4. Suppose you observe that as incomes increase by 10%, the quantity of some good purchased:

    a. Increases by 20%. Determine the income elasticity of demand. The good in question is a/an_____ good.
    b. Decreases by 5%. Determine the income elasticity of demand. The good is a _____ good.

5. Determine the cross-elasticity of demand if a 5% decrease in the price of good X:

    a. Increases the quantity of good Y purchased by 15% ____. Good Y is a _____ to good X.
    b. Decreases the quantity of good Y purchased by 5% ____. Good Y is _____ to good X.
    c. Does not change the quantity of good Y purchased ____. Good Y is _____ to good X.

6. Referring to the diagram below:

    a. Calculate the elasticity of supply over the supply curve segment a-b. ____ Supply is _____.
    b. Calculate the elasticity of supply over segment e-f. ____ Supply is _____.
    c. List two determinants of the elasticity of supply:
       (1)_____
       (2)_____

Price per unit

Quantity supplied per unit of time

Concept: Price elasticity of demand and supply; impact of taxes on prices

7.   Referring to the diagram below:

a.   Show the impact on the supply curve for cigarettes of a tax of $1 per pack.
b.   Market price _____ from $_____ to $_____.
c.   Consumers pay _____ cents of the tax and sellers pay the other _____ cents.
d.   Assume that cigarette smoking is such an addiction that the demand for cigarettes is perfectly inelastic.
      (1)   Show a perfectly inelastic demand curve on the diagram.
      (2)   How much of the tax is paid by consumers? _____ cents By sellers? _____ cents

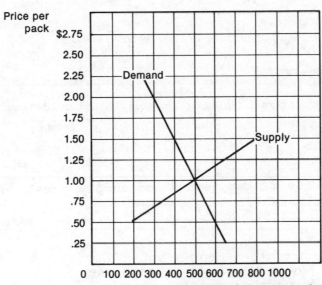

8. For which of the following diagrams is a per unit tax completely borne by:
    a. Consumers?_____
    b. Sellers?_____

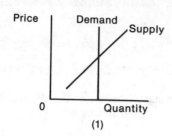

(1)

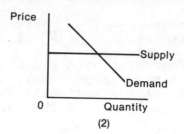

(2)

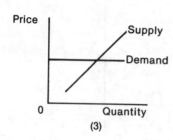

(3)

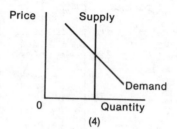

(4)

9. <u>Advanced Question</u>. The market demand and supply equations from Chapter 4, question 10, are as follows:

$$Qd = a - bP$$
$$Qs = c + dP$$

where a, b, c, and d are positive constants
Qd = quantity demanded
Qs = quantity supplied
P = price

Suppose that in the absence of per unit taxes on output, Qs is a positive function of P. If a tax, T, is levied on sellers, Qs becomes a function of the after-tax price rather than the before-tax price, P.

a. Modify the supply equation to incorporate a per unit tax, T.
b. Derive an expression for the market equilibrium price.
c. How can that expression be used to determine the portion of a tax, T, that is shifted to buyers?

SELF-TEST FOR MASTERY

Select the best answer.

1. The price elasticity of demand is measured by:

    a. Dividing the percentage change in quantity demanded into the percentage change in income.
    b. Dividing the percentage change in quantity demanded into the percentage change in supply.

    c.   Dividing the percentage change in price into the percentage change in quantity demanded.
    d.   Dividing price into quantity demanded.

2.   If the price elasticity of demand is greater than 1, it is said to be:

    a.   Unit elastic.
    b.   Elastic.
    c.   Inelastic.
    d.   A normal good.

3.   If the price elasticity of demand is greater than 0, but less than 1, it is said to be:

    a.   Unit elastic.
    b.   Elastic.
    c.   Inelastic.
    d.   A normal good.

4.   A _____ elastic demand curve is one where the price elasticity coefficient is infinity.

    a.   Unit
    b.   Less
    c.   Completely
    d.   Perfectly

5.   A demand curve for insulin is likely to be:

    a.   Perfectly inelastic.
    b.   Perfectly elastic.
    c.   Somewhat elastic.
    d.   Moderately inelastic.

6.   Moving from the upper range of a linear demand curve southeast to the lower portions is associated with a price elasticity of demand that becomes increasingly:

    a.   Elastic.
    b.   Inelastic.
    c.   Large.
    d.   Difficult to estimate.

7.   Which of the following is a determinant of the price elasticity of demand?

    a.   Time
    b.   The percentage of income spent on the good
    c.   The availability of substitutes
    d.   All of the above

8.   Other things being equal, an increase in the availability of substitutes:

    a.   Has no impact on the price elasticity of demand.
    b.   Decreases the price elasticity of demand.
    c.   Increases the price elasticity of demand.
    d.   None of the above

9.   If demand is elastic and the price falls, total revenue will:

    a.   Not change.
    b.   Increase.

c. Decrease.
d. Increase if the supply elasticity is not 0.

10. If demand is inelastic and the price falls, total revenue will:

a. Not change.
b. Increase.
c. Decrease.
d. Increase if the supply elasticity is not 0.

11. A good having a positive income elasticity of demand is called a:

a. Positive good.
b. Public good.
c. Inferior good.
d. Normal good.

12. A good having a negative income elasticity of demand is called a:

a. Positive good.
b. Public good.
c. Inferior good.
d. Normal good.

13. Two goods that are substitutes in consumption have a _____ cross-elasticity of demand.

a. Positive
b. Elastic
c. Inelastic
d. Negative

14. Two goods that are complements in consumption have a _____ cross-elasticity of demand.

a. Positive
b. Elastic
c. Inelastic
d. Negative

15. Which of the following is not a determinant of the price elasticity of supply?

a. Availability of substitutes
b. Time
c. The marginal cost associated with producing additional units of output
d. Percentage of income spent on a good
e. A and d

16. A perfectly elastic supply curve is:

a. Positively sloped.
b. Vertical.
c. Negatively sloped.
d. Horizontal.

17. If the supply of some good is unit elastic and the price of the good increases by 10%:

a. Quantity supplied increases by more than 10%.

b.   Quantity demanded decreases by at least 10%.
c.   Quantity supplied increases by 10%.
d.   Quantity supplied does not change.

18. If a per unit tax is levied on sellers and the demand for the good is perfectly elastic, sellers:

a.   Will pass all of the tax to consumers in the form of higher prices.
b.   Will not be able to shift the tax.
c.   Will share the burden of the tax equally with buyers.
d.   None of the above

19. If a per unit tax is levied on sellers and the demand for the good is perfectly inelastic, sellers:

a.   Will pass all of the tax to consumers in the form of higher prices.
b.   Will not be able to shift the tax.
c.   Will share the burden of the tax equally with buyers.
d.   Will pay most of the tax.

20. If a per unit tax is levied on sellers and the supply and demand curves are conventionally sloped, sellers:

a.   Will pass all of the tax to consumers in the form of higher prices.
b.   Will not be able to shift the tax.
c.   Will share the burden of the tax equally with buyers.
d.   Will share the burden of the tax with buyers.

THINK IT THROUGH

1.   You have been asked by a physician to determine if his fees should be increased. He wants to generate additional revenues. Based upon what you know about the determinants of the price elasticity of demand, determine first if the demand for physicians services is elastic or inelastic and then determine what fee change will increase the physician's revenues.

2.   The demand for unskilled labor is generally regarded as elastic. Why? An increase in the minimum wage will increase wages for those employed, but will reduce the total wages paid to unskilled labor as a whole.   Why?

3.   How could knowledge of the price, cross-price, and income elasticities of demand for various goods be useful in helping a discount store manager predict the probable consequences of price changes?

4.   Sumptuary taxes are taxes intended to discourage the consumption of goods considered harmful to individuals. A tax per quart of whiskey is such a tax. Based upon what you know about determinants of the price elasticity of demand, is a per unit tax on whiskey likely to curb consumption?

CHAPTER ANSWERS

In Brief: Chapter Summary

1. Price 2. Greater 3. Greater 4. Smaller 5. Less 6. 1 7. The same 8. Quantity demanded 9. Price 10. More 11. Less 12. Elastic 13. Inelastic

14. 0 15. Infinity 16. Rise 17. Rise 18. Has no impact on 19. Greater 20. Smaller 21. Positive 22. Negative 23. 0 24. Elastic 25. Inelastic 26. More 27. Inelastic 28. Elastic 29. Upward 30. Inelastic 31. Elastic 32. Horizontal 33. Vertical

Vocabulary Review

1. Normal goods 2. Elastic demand 3. Tax shifting 4. Price elasticity of demand 5. Cross-elasticity of demand 6. Inelastic supply 7. Total revenue 8. Unit elastic demand 9. Inferior goods 10. Price elasticity of supply 11. Inelastic demand 12. Elastic supply 13. Total expenditure 14. Income elasticity of demand 15. Unit elastic supply

Skills Review

1. a. 3.67, elastic
    b. 0.27, inelastic
    c. 1, unit elastic
    d. (a) $60, (b) $100, (c) $120, (d) $120, (e) $100, (f) $60
    e. Increase, $40
    f. Decrease, $40
    g. Changes, $0

2. a. More
    b. Less
    c. More
    d. More

3. a. Elastic
    b. Elastic
    c. Inelastic
    d. Inelastic
    e. Inelastic
    f. Inelastic
    g. Elastic

4. a. +2, normal
    b. -1/2, inferior

5. a. -3, complement
    b. +1, substitute
    c. 0, unrelated

6. a. 1, unit elastic
    b. 1, unit elastic
    c. (1) Additional cost of producing a unit of output as more output is produced
        (2) Time

7. a.

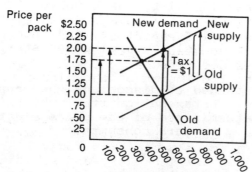

Quantity of cigarette packs
supplied and demanded
(millions of packs
per year)

    b. Increase, $1, $1.75
    c. 75, 25
    d. (1) Shown on diagram above
        (2) 100, 0

108

8. a. Figures (1) and (2)
   b. Figures (3) and (4)

9. a. Let Qs = c + d (P - T)
   b. Equilibrium requires setting Qd = Qs. Therefore:

$$a - bP = a + d (P - T)$$

   Solving for P gives:

$$P = (a - c + dT)/(b + d)$$

   c. Let the change in P = [d/(b + d)] x change in T

   If d/(b + d) is greater than 0 but less than 1, both sellers and
   buyers share the tax burden. If d/(b + d) equals 0, the tax is borne
   by sellers. If d/(b + d) equals 1, the tax is borne by buyers. When
   d/(b + d) is 0, d = 0 or b equals infinity. d = 0 when supply is
   perfectly inelastic. b = infinity when demand is perfectly elastic.
   d/(b + d) is 1 when b = 0 or when d = infinity. b = 0 when demand is
   perfectly inelastic and d = infinity when supply is perfectly
   elastic. Conventionally sloped supply and demand curves yield a
   value for d/(b + d) greater than 0 but less than 1.

Self-Test for Mastery

1. c 2. b 3. c 4. d 5. a 6. b 7. d 8. c 9. b 10. c 11. d 12. c 13.
a 14. d 15. e 16. d 17. c 18. b 19. a 20. d

Think it Through

1. People perceive physician services as having no close substitutes.
Because care usually cannot be delayed, the demand for physician services is
regarded as inelastic. If the physician wants to increase revenues from his
practice, he should increase his fees.

2. Unskilled labor is considered to have an elastic demand, in part because
many types of labor can be substituted for unskilled labor, but unskilled
workers are not substitutes for those requiring special skills, education, or
training. Also, there is typically a ready pool of unskilled labor that can be
employed with minimal training cost to the firm.

   If the demand for unskilled labor is elastic and the minimum wage
increases, total wages (minimum wage x quantity of labor hours employed) paid
to unskilled labor as a group will decrease, even though those employed at the
minimum wage are better off. This occurs because the unemployment caused by
the minimum wage more than offsets the impact of the higher wage on the total
wages paid to labor.

3. Knowledge of price elasticities of demand for various goods would allow
the manager to predict percentage changes in quantities demanded for given
percentage price changes. Cross-price elasticities would allow predictions
regarding the quantities demanded of complementary and substitute goods.
Income elasticities of demand would allow predictions for those goods that are
normal or inferior. This would be useful, for instance, in areas experiencing
a significant influx of higher income households. All of this assumes that the
national or regional data used to estimate these coefficients are applicable to
a local economy. In other words, the relationships that hold for the economy
as a whole are assumed to pertain to the local economy as well.

4.   For whiskey consumers, there are probably few close substitutes for whiskey. The demand for whiskey is probably inelastic. A sumptuary tax would primarily increase the price of whiskey, having only a modest negative impact on the quantity of whiskey demanded.

8

Gross National Product and the Performance of the National Economy

CHAPTER CHALLENGES

After studying this chapter, attending class, and completing this chapter, you should be able to:

1. Explain what GNP is and how it is measured and discuss the shortcomings of GNP as a measure of national well-being.
2. Understand the distinction between final products and intermediate products. Explain how gross national product can be measured as the sum of value added at each stage of production and how value added must equal the earnings accruing to owners of resources used in production.
3. Understand the distinction between nominal GNP and real GNP and explain how real GNP can be used to measure aggregate production over time.
4. Show how gross national product can be viewed as either a flow of expenditures or a flow of income.
5. Use a circular flow analysis to understand the interrelationships in the economy among households, business firms, financial transactions, governments, and international trade and explain how leakages and injections of spending affect the economy.
6. Understand how supply and demand analysis is used in macroeconomics and show how changes in aggregate demand or aggregate supply can cause real GNP and prices to change.

IN BRIEF: CHAPTER SUMMARY

Fill in the blanks to summarize chapter content.

The National Income and Product Accounts are designed to measure economic activity--flows of income and expenditures over a period of time. The broadest measure of economic activity is (1)_____(gross national product, aggregate output). GNP is the market value of an economy's (2)_____(total, final) goods and services produced over a period of 1 year. It is designed to measure economic activity that gives rise to income, output, and employment. Some transactions during the year do not affect production and employment and are thus excluded from GNP. These include changes in the value of existing assets, (3)_____ (nonfinancial, financial) transactions, sale of used goods, and most goods not sold in markets.

GNP can be thought of as the total value added in a nation over a given year. The market value of all products and services (4)_____(less, plus) the market value of all intermediate goods equals the value added in producing and making final goods and services available to the market. Value added (5)_____(is greater than, also equals) the payments to suppliers of labor, capital, and raw materials, including profit to entrepreneurs. Because GNP is defined in terms of its market value, inflation can cause the value of GNP to change. In order to remove this inflationary bias so as to uncover the movements in GNP that affect output and employment, it is necessary to deflate

111

GNP--to remove the effect of inflation. This is accomplished by dividing a general price index into (6)_____ (nominal, real) GNP. Doing so yields (7)_____ (real, nominal) GNP, a measure of the value of a nation's aggregate output of final products using market prices defined by the price index base year.

GNP should not be considered a perfect measure of a nation's well-being. It excludes nonmarket goods and services, such as the services of spouses in maintaining a home, that contribute to society's welfare. It also excludes the value of leisure, does not consider the impact of environmental damage caused by the production or consumption of output, (8)_____ (but does, and does not) reflect the market value of goods and services produced in the underground economy.

Gross national product can be measured by determining the total aggregate expenditures on final output during the year or by determining the income generated by the economy in producing that final output. GNP can be estimated by summing personal consumption expenditures of households, gross private domestic investment, government purchases of goods and services, and net (9)_____(exports, imports). Personal consumption expenditures are household expenditures on durable goods, nondurable goods, and services. Gross private domestic investment represents spending on producer durables, residential and nonresidential construction, and (10)_____ (the, changes in the) value of inventories. Government expenditures include the expenditures of all levels of government on goods and services (including labor services) less transfer payments. Net exports are total (11)_____ (exports, imports) less (12)_____(exports, imports).

Gross national product can also be determined by summing the incomes received by resource suppliers during the year. The five types of income are compensation of employees, proprietors' income, corporate profits, net interest, and rental income. Compensation of employees includes wages and salaries and employer-provided contributions to Social Security and pension plans. (13)_____(Enterprise income, Proprietors' income) is the income of unincorporated enterprises. Corporate profits are the incomes of corporations and equal the sum of dividends and retained earnings, and corporate profits taxes. Net interest includes the interest paid by business (14)_____ (and, but not) the interest paid by government. Rental income is received by those supplying land, mineral rights, and structures for the use of others. It (15)_____ (excludes, also includes) the imputed rent earned by homeowners. Adding these components of total income to indirect business taxes and depreciation gives GNP.

As can be shown in a circular flow diagram, total aggregate expenditures on final output generate the income necessary to sustain those expenditures. But if leakages from the circular flow exceed injections into the flow of spending, the level of economic activity will (16)_____(decline, increase). Leakages include net taxes, saving, and imports. These reduce the amount of funds available to purchase domestic output. Injections include gross private domestic investment, government spending on goods and services, and exports. These expenditures increase total spending on domestic output. If leakages are less than injections, economic activity will (17)_____(decline, increase). If leakages equal injections, the level of economic activity will just be maintained, neither increasing nor decreasing.

Gross national product and the level of prices can be modeled using an aggregate supply and demand model. The aggregate demand curve shows the relationship between the general price level and total expenditures on final output. The price level is (18)_____(positively, negatively) related to aggregate expenditures on final output. The aggregate supply curve shows a (19)_____(positive, negative) relationship between the price level and the total production of final output. Where the aggregate supply and demand curves intersect, the macroeconomy is in a state of balance or equilibrium. There is only one combination of GNP and the price level consistent with this state. A change in aggregate demand or a change in aggregate supply will alter the equilibrium level of GNP and prices.

VOCABULARY REVIEW

Write the key term from the list below next to its definition.

Key Terms

Gross national product
Net exports
National Income and
  Product Accounts
Aggregates
Net taxes
Intermediate products
Aggregate expenditure
Total value added in
  a nation
Nominal GNP
Real GNP
Aggregate real income
Personal consumption
  expenditures

Gross private domestic
  investment
Depreciation (capital
  consumption allowances)
Net private domestic
  investment
Government purchases of
  goods and services
Transfer payments
Leakages
Indirect business taxes
Corporate profits taxes
Disposable income
Injections

Definitions

1. _____: the market value of an economy's final goods and services produced over a period of 1 year.

2. _____: broad totals of economic variables such as production or unemployment.

3. _____: the market value of a nation's aggregate production of final output based on current prices for the goods and services produced during the year.

4. _____: the nominal (money) income of a nation, adjusted for inflation.

5. _____: investment purchases by business firms: expenditure on new machinery and equipment (producer durables), the value of new residential and nonresidential construction, and the change in business inventories during the year.

6. _____: expenditure on final products of business firms and all input costs, including labor costs, incurred by all levels of government in the United States.

7. _____: taxes levied on business firms that increase their costs and are therefore reflected in the market value of goods and services sold.

8. _____: the difference between taxes and transfer payments.

9. _____: a portion of income that is not used to purchase domestically produced goods during the year.

10. _____: the official system of accounting to measure the flows of income and expenditures in the United States.

11. _____: products produced by business firms for resale by other firms or for use as materials or services that will be included in the value of resold goods.

12. _____: a measure of the value of a nation's aggregate output of final products obtained by using market prices prevailing for products during a certain base or reference year.

13. _____: any excess of expenditure on exports over imports.

14. _____: an estimate of the value of capital goods that wear out or become obsolete over the year.

15. _____: payments for which no good or service is currently received in return and that therefore do not represent expenditures for the purchase of final products.

16. _____: those amounts corporations pay as taxes to governments out of their annual receipts from the sale of goods and services.

17. _____: the amount of income available for households to spend after receipt of government transfer payments and payment of taxes.

18. _____: a purchase made by business firms, governments, or foreign buyers that increases the flow of income in a nation.

19. _____: the difference between the market value of <u>all</u> products of business firms and the market value of all intermediate products.

20. _____: the sum of consumption, investment expenditures, government purchases, and net exports during the year.

21. _____: household and individual purchases of both durable and nondurable goods and services.

22. _____: gross private domestic investment less depreciation.

SKILLS REVIEW

Concept: GNP and its shortcomings

1. List four catagories of items excluded from GNP.

    a. _____
    b. _____
    c. _____
    d. _____

2. Indicate whether the following cause GNP to be understated or overstated as a measure of well-being.

    a. _____ GNP excludes most nonmarket goods.
    b. _____ GNP excludes the value of leisure.
    c. _____ The environmental damage that results from production is not accounted for in GNP.
    d. _____ GNP excludes the value of goods and services produced by the underground economy.

Concept: Nominal and real GNP

3. Consider the production and price data below for a nation producing only automobiles. (Assume that all automobiles are identical.)

Year	Price per Auto	Output (units)	Nominal GNP	Price Index	Real GNP
1	$10,000	1,000	_____	_____	_____
2	10,500	1,200	_____	_____	_____
3	11,000	1,400	_____	_____	_____
4	11,500	1,600	_____	_____	_____
5	12,000	1,800	_____	_____	_____

    a. Complete the nominal GNP column.
    b. Complete the price index column. Assume that year 3 is the base year. Price index = (current year price/base year price) x 100.
    c. Prices have increased _____ % from year 3 to year 5.
    d. Complete the real GNP column. (Hint: Divide the price index by 100 prior to dividing into nominal GNP.)

Concept: GNP and the flow of expenditures and income

4. The following are national income and product accounts for a nation for a given year.

National Income and Product Accounts

Government purchases of goods and services	$ 580
Indirect business taxes	230
Personal consumption expenditures	1,520
Depreciation	310
Proprietors' income	175
Employer contributions to public and private pension plans	325
Net interest	98
Gross private domestic investment	410
Rental income	45
Exports	460
Imports	260
Corporate profits	225
Wages and salaries	1,302

    a. Using the expenditure side of GNP, determine GNP. _____
    b. Using the income side of GNP, determine GNP. _____
    c. Net private domestic investment = _____
    d. Net national product = _____
    e. Net exports = _____
    f. Capital consumption allowances = _____

5. a. List the components of personal consumption expenditures.
        (1) _____
        (2) _____
        (3) _____
    b. List the components of gross private domestic investment.
        (1) _____
        (2) _____
        (3) _____
    c. List the components of corporate profits.
        (1) _____
        (2) _____
        (3) _____

Concept: Circular flow, leakages, and injections

6. Regarding a circular flow diagram:

    a. List the leakages from the flow of income.
        (1) _____
        (2) _____
        (3) _____
    b. List the injections to the flow of final expenditures on domestic output.
        (1) _____
        (2) _____
        (3) _____
    c. Economic activity _____ when leakages exceed injections.
        Economic activity _____ when leakages are less than injections.
        Economic activity _____ when leakages equal injections.
    d. Saving is composed of:
        (1) _____
        (2) _____
        (3) _____

Concept: **Aggregate supply and demand**

7.   An aggregate demand-aggregate supply model for an economy is shown in the diagram below.

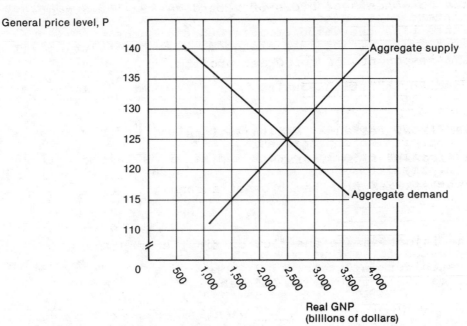

General price level, P

Real GNP
(billions of dollars)

a.   Find the equilibrium level of real GNP and the price level. GNP = _____ , P = _____

b.   If government reduces the level of government purchases, show the impact on the figure above. GNP _____ , and P _____

c.   An increase in aggregate demand _____ GNP and _____ P.

d.   An increase in aggregate supply _____ GNP and _____ P.

e.   An increase in both aggregate demand and aggregate supply _____ GNP and _____ P.

SELF-TEST FOR MASTERY

Select the best answer.

1.   Which of the following defines GNP?

a.   Total output produced by an economy
b.   Total final output produced by an economy
c.   The market value of the total final output produced by an economy during a given year
d.   The market value of the total output produced by an economy during a given year

2.   Which of the following are excluded from GNP?

a.   Changes in the value of existing assets
b.   Financial transactions
c.   Sale of used goods
d.   All of the above

3. The value added for a nation equals:

   a. All goods and services less the intermediate goods used in production.
   b. The market value of all products and services less the market value of all intermediate goods.
   c. Input costs plus the value of intermediate goods.
   d. The market value of intermediate goods less the value of all goods and services.

4. The value added for a nation equals:

   a. GNP.
   b. The payments to suppliers of labor, capital, and raw materials, including profit to entrepreneurs.
   c. The market value of all products and services less the market value of all intermediate goods.
   d. All of the above.

5. Nominal GNP is:

   a. A preliminary estimate of GNP.
   b. GNP unadjusted for inflation.
   c. GNP adjusted for inflation.
   d. GNP less capital consumption allowances.

6. Real GNP is:

   a. The final estimate of GNP for a period.
   b. GNP unadjusted for inflation.
   c. GNP adjusted for inflation.
   d. Total income minus indirect business taxes.

7. GNP overstates economic well-being if:

   a. Nonmarket goods are included in GNP.
   b. Leisure time is not included in GNP.
   c. Production in the underground economy is included in GNP.
   d. The environmental damage caused by economic activity is not considered in GNP.

8. GNP can be estimated by summing :

   a. Personal consumption expenditures, net private domestic investment, and federal government spending.
   b. Personal consumption expenditures, gross private domestic investment, government spending on goods and services, and net exports.
   c. All services and goods purchased by households, businesses, and government.
   d. Household spending, investment, financial transactions, and government transfers.

9. What two items must be added to net interest, corporate profits, proprietor's income, rental income, and employee compensation in order to derive GNP?

   a. Depreciation and capital consumption allowances
   b. Capital consumption allowances and indirect business taxes
   c. Dividends and retained earnings
   d. Household consumption and business investment

10. Gross private domestic investment equals the sum of:

   a. Changes in the value of inventories, new residential and nonresidential construction, and producer durables.
   b. The value of inventories, residential construction, and machines.
   c. Business structures and machines.
   d. Plant and equipment.

11. Which of the following categories absorbs the largest percentage of household expenditures?

   a. Nondurable goods
   b. Services
   c. Durable goods
   d. Taxes

12. The most volatile components of GNP are:

   a. Defense spending and net exports.
   b. Personal consumption expenditures.
   c. Services and government spending.
   d. Investment and net exports.

13. Rental income is composed of:

   a. Income from rental properties.
   b. Lease payments and apartment rents.
   c. Income received by suppliers of land, mineral rights and structures.
   d. Imputed rent attributed to owner-occupied housing.
   e. C and d.

14. Leakages from the flow of income include:

   a. Saving.
   b. Imports.
   c. Taxes.
   d. All of the above.

15. Which of the following is not an injection to the flow of spending?

   a. Investment
   b. Government spending
   c. Imports
   d. Exports

16. If leakages exceed injections, economic activity will:

   a. Expand.
   b. Remain unchanged.
   c. Decline.
   d. Experience a slight decline, then a robust expansion.

17. If injections exceed leakages, economic activity will:

   a. Expand.
   b. Remain unchanged.
   c. Decline.
   d. Expand, then decline upon reaching the point of diminishing returns.

18. If injections equal leakages, economic activity will:

    a. Expand.
    b. Remain unchanged.
    c. Decline.
    d. None of the above.

19. In an aggregate supply and demand model of the economy, an increase in aggregate demand will _____ GNP and _____ the price level.

    a. Decrease, decrease
    b. Increase, decrease
    c. Increase, increase
    d. Decrease, increase

20. In an aggregate supply and demand model of the economy, an increase in aggregate supply will _____ GNP and _____ the price level.

    a. Decrease, decrease
    b. Increase, decrease
    c. Increase, increase
    d. Decrease, increase

THINK IT THROUGH

1. Discuss two methods of estimating gross national product.

2. If capital consumption allowances exceed gross private domestic investment, what will happen to the nation's capital stock?

3. Discuss how the effect of inflation can be removed from GNP. Of what use is this?

4. Recently, the U.S. trade balance has improved. Exports are rising at a faster rate than imports. How is this likely to affect the U.S. economy?

5. Using the value added concept, explain why total expenditures on the nation's output of final goods and services are conceptually equal to the total income earned by suppliers of economic resources.

POP QUIZ   Read the news brief at the end of this chapter and answer the following question.

Explain why measured real GNP might today overstate actual GNP. Should an increase in real GNP be interpreted as an improvement in quality of life?

CHAPTER ANSWERS

In Brief: Chapter Summary

1. Gross national product 2. Final 3. Financial 4. Less 5. Also equals 6. Nominal 7. Real 8. And does not 9. Exports 10. Changes in the 11. Exports 12. Imports 13. Proprietors' income 14. But not 15. Also includes 16. Decline 17. Increase 18. Negatively 19. Positive

Vocabulary Review

1. Gross national product 2. Aggregates 3. Nominal GNP 4. Aggregate real income 5. Gross private domestic investment 6. Government purchases of goods and services 7. Indirect business taxes 8. Net taxes 9. Leakages 10. National income and product accounts 11. Intermediate products 12. Real GNP 13. Net exports 14. Depreciation 15. Transfer payments 16. Corporate profits taxes 17. Disposable income 18. Injections 19. Total value added in a nation 20. Aggregate expenditure 21. Personal consumption expenditures 22. Net private domestic investment

Skills Review

1. a. Changes in the value of existing assets
    b. Sale of used goods
    c. Financial transactions
    d. Most goods not sold in markets

2. a. Understated
    b. Understated
    c. Overstated
    d. Understated

3.
Nominal GNP	Price Index	Real GNP
$10,000,000	90.9	$11,001,100
12,600,000	95.5	13,193,717
15,400,000	100.0	15,400,000
18,400,000	104.5	17,607,656
21,600,000	109.1	19,798,350

    c. 9.1%

4. a. $2,710
    b. $2,710
    c. $100
    d. $2,400
    e. $200
    f. $310

5. a. (1) Durable goods
        (2) Nondurable goods
        (3) Services
    b. (1) New residential and nonresidential construction
        (2) Producer durables
        (3) Changes in the value of inventories
    c. (1) Corporate profits taxes
        (2) Retained earnings
        (3) Dividends

6. a. (1) Saving
        (2) Net taxes
        (3) Imports
    b. (1) Gross private domestic investment
        (2) Government purchases of goods and services
        (3) Exports
    c. Declines, increases, remains unchanged
    d. (1) Personal saving
        (2) Business saving
        (3) Foreign saving

7. a. $2,500, 125
    b. Falls, falls

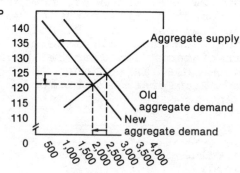

General price level, P

Aggregate supply

Old aggregate demand

New aggregate demand

Real GNP
(billions of dollars)

    c. Increases, increases
    d. Increases, decreases
    e. Increase, may either increase, decrease or leave unchanged

Self-Test for Mastery

1. c 2. d 3. b 4. d 5. b 6. c 7. d 8. b 9. b 10. a 11. b 12. d 13. e 14. d 15. c 16. c 17. a 18. b 19. c 20. b

Think it Through

1.   GNP can be estimated by summing the aggregate expenditures on the nation's final output or by summing the income generated by the economy in producing that output. The expenditure approach requires the summation of personal consumption expenditures, government purchases of goods and services, gross private domestic investment, and net exports. The income approach involves the addition of the five types of income (proprietors' income, corporate profits, compensation of employees, rental income, and net interest) to indirect business taxes and capital consumption allowances.

2.   Although gross private domestic investment is positive, net private domestic investment is negative. Total investment is insufficient to replace the capital that has worn out during the year's production of GNP. The total capacity of the economy to produce output has declined. Future economic growth will likely be impaired.

3.   Real GNP can be derived by dividing a general price index into nominal GNP. Changes in real GNP are the result of changes in output and not prices because real GNP is valued at a given set of prices as determined by the base year. Economists are interested in real GNP because changes in real GNP reflect real changes in economic activity that produce output and employment rather than the image of changes in economic activity caused merely by inflation.

4.   If exports are rising faster than imports, net exports are rising.   The total level of aggregate expenditures on domestic output is therefore also rising.   In the context of the aggregate supply and demand model, aggregate demand is rising, causing an increase in real GNP and the price level.

5.   Total expenditures on a nation's final output equal the market value of the final output produced.   But the market value of all final output less the market value of all intermediate inputs must equal the value added at the last stage of production.   This value added is made possible by the combined services of labor, raw materials, capital, and entrepreneurs.   The value added just equals the payments to suppliers of labor, capital, and raw materials, including profits to owners.   The sum of the value added at each stage of production equals GNP, but it also equals the total aggregate income generated in producing that value added.   Thus total expenditures on a nation's final output are conceptually equal to the total income generated by the economy in producing that final output.

Pop Quiz

Since 1960, fundamental changes have occurred in the composition of the labor force.   These changes have influenced real GNP without necessarily improving the quality of life.   From 1960 to 1980, women as a percentage of the labor force grew from 33% to 43%.   Furthermore, women are on average working more hours on the job per year than previously.   This means that the time available for non-paid work outside the job has fallen.   Household goods and services that were once produced by women are now increasingly being purchased in markets.   This reduces the extent to which GNP understates actual output, because now a greater percentage of production involves market transactions which are accounted for in measured real GNP.   Laura Stern argues that the household goods and services now purchased in markets are in many cases inferior to home-produced items--child care, for instance.   Measured Real GNP rises as a result of this shift from nonmarket to market production, causing real GNP to possibly overstate actual GNP.   Quality of life does not necessarily increase when measured real GNP increases.

I Work This Hard So I Can Eat Tuna Surprise?

By Laura Stern

Staring forlornly at the "meal" I've prepared for my family, at the end of a 10-hour day employed as an economist, I see convincing evidence here that the gap between measured gross national product and social welfare has widened radically. The omission of nonmarket activities (like a home-cooked meal) is a distortion of GNP that is readily admitted by economists, but the different composition of goods and services constituting GNP today has made the problem somewhat different. Although our rising real GNP (up 6.8% in 1984, less since) may give an impression of "material well-being," the taste of tuna and Tostitos that we chomp down for dinner tells the true story.

The advance of women into paid jobs is one of the fundamental changes of this generation. Women's share of the labor force grew to 43% from 33% between 1960 and 1980. Also, the average hours women work in a paid job have increased more than 50%, to 873 a year from 572, according to the Census Bureau. Since the number of hours in a day has remained remarkably stable at 24, it should come as no surprise that average nonmarket hours worked by women have declined to 1,497 in 1979 from 1,854 in 1959, according to a recent study by Victor Fuchs.

What kinds of nonmarket activities have been abandoned, hurriedly done or substituted for as a result of women exchanging non-paid for paid work? The list is long: housework, child care, chauffeuring of children to lessons or friends' houses, volunteerism, pickling and preserving, ironing, decorating, crafts, sports, sleeping, reading the paper, and so on.

Now, the astute reader will necessarily point out that many of the nonmarket activities previously performed by women have been replaced by market activities that will raise GNP and do represent an increase in the production of goods and services, or, as GNP represents, "a measure of national economic performance." Let's be serious—does a meal at Red Lobster truly compare with a meal of oysters Rockefeller served on rock salt, lovingly prepared at home, rock by rock? Is the perfunctory greeting from a housekeeper as a youngster bounds in the door from school nearly as meaningful as the harsh scream from Mom to "hang up your coat before you grab for the cookies"? Can the despair of finding out that you have no more clean underwear (albeit you own 13 luxurious pairs) ever be appropriately quantified?

What is being suggested is that with the changing composition of the labor force, and specifically the change in activities that women perform today, there are many missed activities that have made the nation worse off but have not lowered real GNP as it is currently measured. Our method of GNP accounting, then, rather than understating GNP as in the past, now probably overstates GNP due to the omission of activities not now being performed. Although poking holes in GNP accounting is nothing new, the changed role of women has radically affected the impact of this problem.

In Mr. Fuchs's study, entitled "His and Hers: Gender Differences in Work and Income, 1959-1979," he concludes that if you combine market and nonmarket hours, women worked more hours in 1979 than in 1959 and even more hours relative to men in 1979 than in 1959. Most distressingly, he found that the women-to-men ratio of total income rose very slightly or *not at all*, depending on the set of assumptions used. It was an immense relief to discover that my feeling this year of being "more tired and no richer" was not a figment of my imagination.

It is not being suggested for a minute that women abandon their roles in the labor force and defer career ambitions for the warmth of a baby bottom on a lap from 9 to 5. Rather, it is advisable to use caution in interpreting GNP statistics, and specifically to avoid automatically linking rises in GNP to improvements in quality of life. Future estimates of real GNP peg a trend growth of about 3% a year over the rest of the decade. This may be cause for celebration in some circles, but I'd settle for being able to stay conscious after 10 p.m. or having some time to make my infamous homemade graham cracker cake with mocha frosting. Mmm, remember that one?

Ms. Stern, a former university instructor, is a happy but tired public utility economist, wife and mother of three.

9

Business Cycles and Unemployment

CHAPTER CHALLENGES

After studying this chapter, attending class, and completing this chapter, you should be able to:

1. Discuss the phases of the business cycle and give examples of recent periods of recession and expansion of the U.S. economy.
2. Understand the concept of the unemployment rate and discuss different possible causes of fluctuations in the unemployment rate.
3. Define the concept of full employment and show how it is related to the natural rate of unemployment. Also, show how the actual unemployment rate is the sum of the natural unemployment rate and the cyclical unemployment rate.
4. Understand the concept of potential real GNP and the difficulties involved in estimating it.
5. Discuss the social costs of unemployment and programs designed to cushion those costs.

IN BRIEF: CHAPTER SUMMARY

Fill in the blanks to summarize chapter content.

The business cycle describes the ups and downs in real GNP over time. Although no two business cycles are identical, they all have four distinct phases: expansion, peak, contraction, and trough. An economy is in a recession or contraction when real GNP has declined for (1)_____(three, two) consecutive 3-month periods. Although real GNP fluctuates up and down, its long-run average annual growth trend is just over (2)_____(3%, 5%). When the economy is in a recession, such in the Great Depression of the 1930s or more recently the 1981-82 recession, unemployment (3)_____(rises, falls). As the economy expands out of a trough, the unemployment rate (4)_____(rises, falls).

The unemployment rate is the percentage of the labor force that is unemployed. The labor force includes all persons over the age of 16 with jobs and those actively seeking employment. A person is considered unemployed if the person is over age 16 and is available for work (5)_____(but not, and) actively seeking employment. The unemployment rate may understate or overstate the true extent of unemployment. The unemployment rate (6)_____ (does not, does) include discouraged workers. Also, part-time employment is considered as full-time employment, not as partial employment or unemployment. People may respond to unemployment surveys that they are looking for work when in fact their expectations of a job will likely not materialize because those expectations are unrealistic. The rate of unemployment is higher among (7)_____ (married, single) workers than among (8)_____ (married, single) workers. It is also higher among (9)_____(whites, blacks) than (10)_____(whites, blacks). Teenagers, particularly nonwhite teens, face some of the highest unemployment rates.

The three types of unemployment are frictional unemployment, structural unemployment, and cyclical unemployment. (11)_____ (Structural, Frictional) unemployment is due to the length of time it takes to find employment upon entering the labor force or between jobs. (12)_____ (Structural, Frictional) unemployment results from changes in the composition of output produced by the economy or by technological changes that cause some industries to expand and others to decline. Cyclical unemployment is unemployment caused by economic decline or recession. Most cyclical unemployment is the result of layoffs. Full employment is defined as a level of economic activity where the actual unemployment rate (13)_____ (is less than, equals) the sum of structural and frictional unemployment and exists even when the economy is operating at the peak of the business cycle--at a high rate of capacity utilization. When the sum of frictional and (14)_____ (structural, cyclical) unemployment is expressed as a percentage of the total labor force, the ratio is known as the natural rate of unemployment.

(15)_____(Actual, Potential) GNP is the level of output that results if the economy operates for an entire year at the natural rate of unemployment. The difference between potential and actual GNP is called the (16)_____(natural rate of unemployment, GNP gap). If actual GNP falls short of potential GNP, the sacrificed output constitutes a major cost of cyclical unemployment. For instance, for each 1% increase in the unemployment rate, real GNP falls by (17)_____(3.5%, 2.5%). This is known as Okun's Law. Using Okun's Law, the GNP gap for 1982 is estimated at approximately $300 billion. Other social costs of unemployment include the monetary and nonmonetary costs associated with suicide, crime, mental illness, physical illness, stress, and other problems attributed to unemployment.

Unemployment insurance was established in 1935 as part of the Social Security Act in order to soften the blow of unemployment. Generally, only those people who lose their jobs due to layoff, economic contraction, or (18)_____ (firings, plant closings) get unemployment benefits. Evidence shows that unemployment benefits, while softening the trauma of unemployment, (19)_____ (increase, decrease) frictional unemployment.

VOCABULARY REVIEW

Write the key term from the list below next to its definition.

Key Terms

Business cycle	Job search
Contraction	Job finding
Recession	Frictional
Layoff	unemployment
Expansion	Structural
GNP gap	unemployment
Recovery	Cyclical
Job separation	unemployment
Labor force	Natural rate of
Okun's Law	unemployment
Unemployment rate	Full employment
Unemployed person	Potential real GNP
Discouraged worker	

Definitions

1. _____: the term used to describe the fluctuations in aggregate production as measured by the ups and downs of real GNP.

2. _____: an upturn of economic activity between a trough and a peak during which real GNP increases.

3. _____: the sum of the number of persons over age 16 with jobs and workers who are actively seeking a job but currently do not have one.

4. _____: the temporary suspension of employment without pay for a period of 7 consecutive days or more.

5. _____: occurs when a worker leaves a job for any reason: quitting, being fired, or being laid off.

6. _____: the amount of unemployment resulting from declines in real GNP during periods of contraction or recession or in any period when the economy fails to operate at its potential.

7. _____: the level that would prevail if the economy achieved the natural rate of unemployment over a period.

8. _____: the difference between potential and actual GNP.

9. _____: states that each 1% increase in the unemployment rate is associated with a 2.5% reduction in real GNP.

10. _____: a downturn from peak economic activity in the business cycle during which real GNP declines from its previous value.

11. _____: the term used to describe an expansion in economic activity after a trough if the expansion follows a period of contraction severe enough to be classified as a recession.

12. _____: measures the ratio of the number of people classified as unemployed to the total labor force.

13. _____: a worker who leaves the labor force (stops actively seeking work) after unsuccessfully searching for a job for a certain period.

14. _____: the process of looking for suitable work either by those just entering the labor force or by those having just experienced a job separation.

15. _____: the percentage of the labor force that can normally be expected to be unemployed for reasons other than cyclical fluctuations in real GNP.

16. _____: exists when the decline in real GNP measured at an annual rate occurs for two consecutive 3-month reporting periods.

17. _____: a person over age 16 who is available for work and has actively sought employment during the previous 4 weeks.

18. _____: occurs when an unemployed worker accepts an offer of a new job.

19. _____: occurs when the actual rate of unemployment is no more the natural rate of unemployment.

20. _____: represents the usual amount of unemployment resulting from people who have left jobs that did not work out and are searching for new employment, or people who are either entering or reentering the labor force to search for a job.

21. _____: unemployment resulting from shifts in the pattern of demand for goods and services or changes in technology in the economy that affect the profitability of hiring workers in specific industries.

SKILLS REVIEW

Concept: **Phases of the business cycle; record of recent fluctuations in the U.S. economy**

1. Identify the phases of the business cycle in the diagram below.

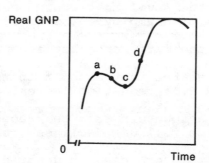

     a. _____
     b. _____
     c. _____
     d. _____

2. a. During the 1930s, the unemployment rate _____ to _____ and real GNP _____ by _____ of its 1929 value.

     b. As a result of World War II, the unemployment rate _____ and real GNP _____, but recessions did occur _____. The 1950s can be characterized as a period of _____, although _____ occurred in _____ and _____.

     c. The 1960s was a period of economic expansion lasting from _____ to _____, which was due in part to _____.

     d. The decade of the 1970s experienced periods of rising _____ and _____. The last half of the decade can be characterized as _____.

     e. There have been _____ recessions in the 1980s, with the most severe recession since the Great Depression occurring from _____ to _____.

Concept: Unemployment rate

3.   Find the size of the labor force, the number of unemployed persons, and
     the unemployment rate from the data below.

       1.   Total population   200 million
       2.   Persons over age 16 working   95
       3.   Institutional population
           (prisons, hospitals, etc.)   12
       4.   Discouraged workers   2
       5.   Persons over age 16 actively
           seeking work and available for
           employment   5
       6.   Part-time workers   1

   a.   Total labor force = _____
   b.   Unemployed persons = _____
   c.   Unemployment rate = _____

4.   List three reasons why the unemployment rate may not reflect the true
     extent of unemployment.

   a.   _____
   b.   _____
   c.   _____

5.   Identify each of the following as either frictional, structural, or
     cyclical unemployment.

   a.   _____   You quit your job and spend time searching for new
                          employment.
   b.   _____   You are temporarily unemployed due to layoff.
   c.   _____   Advances in office automation reduce the need for
                         secretaries.
   d.   _____   Movie theaters reduce employment because more people
                         are watching home videos.
   e.   _____   You graduate from high school and begin your search
                         for a job.
   f.   _____   A decline in demand for the nation's output causes
                         both GNP and employment to decline.

Concept: Potential GNP, actual GNP, and GNP gap

6.   Determine potential GNP and the GNP gap from the data below.

       1.   Natural rate of unemployment   6%
       2.   Actual rate of unemployment   5%
       3.   Annual labor hours (4% unemployment)   200 billion
       4.   Annual labor hours (5% unemployment)   250 billion
       5.   Annual labor hours (6% unemployment)   300 billion
       6.   Output per labor hour $15
       7.   Actual GNP $ 4 trillion

   a.   Potential GNP = _____
   b.   GNP gap = _____
   c.   If there are 100 million households, find the GNP gap per household.
       _____

d.   On the diagram below, shade in the area representing the GNP gap.

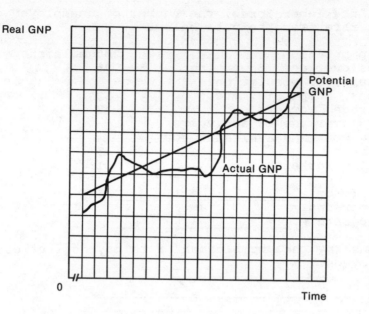

Concept: Social costs of unemployment

7.   In addition to the GNP gap, other social costs of unemployment include the costs associated with:

a. _____
b. _____
c. _____
d. _____

SELF-TEST FOR MASTERY

Select the best answer.

1.   Which of the following best defines the business cycle?

a.   Recessions and expansions
b.   Ups and downs in business activity
c.   Ups and downs in real GNP
d.   None of the above

2.   The phase of a business cycle just following a trough is called a/an:

a.   Recession.
b.   Decline.
c.   Expansion.
d.   Peak.

3. The economy is defined as being in a recession if:

   a. Economic activity declines.
   b. Real GNP declines.
   c. Real GNP declines for four consecutive 3-month periods.
   d. Real GNP declines for two consecutive 3-month periods.

4. Since the turn of the century, real GNP has expanded at an average annual rate of:

   a. 2%.
   b. 3%.
   c. 4%.
   d. 5%.

5. Unemployment rises in _____ and declines in _____.

   a. Expansions, recessions
   b. Recessions, expansions
   c. Expansions, expansions
   d. Recessions, recessions

6. The total labor force consists of:

   a. All persons working plus those not working.
   b. All persons over age 16 working.
   c. Discouraged workers, part-time and full-time workers, and the armed forces.
   d. All persons over age 16 either working or actively seeking work and available for employment.

7. The unemployment rate is defined as:

   a. The percentage of the population that is unemployed.
   b. The percentage of the labor force that is unemployed.
   c. All unemployed workers, including discouraged workers, divided by the total labor force.
   d. All unemployed workers, including discouraged workers, divided by the total population.

8. Which of the following is not a reason why the unemployment rate may not reflect the true extent of unemployment?

   a. Discouraged workers are excluded.
   b. Part-time work is considered as full-time work.
   c. People may respond to employment surveys that they are looking for work when in fact the likelihood of their finding employment that meets their expectations is remote.
   d. None of the above.

9. Which of the following groups experiences the highest unemployment rates?

   a. Teenagers, whites, single persons
   b. Middle-aged persons, blacks, single persons
   c. Teenagers, blacks, married persons
   d. Teenagers, blacks, single persons

10. Unemployment due to the length of time it takes to find employment upon entering the labor force or voluntarily between jobs is called:

    a. Cyclical unemployment.
    b. Frictional unemployment.
    c. Structural unemployment.
    d. Natural unemployment.

11. Unemployment that results from changes in the composition of output produced by the economy or from technological changes is called:

    a. Cyclical unemployment.
    b. Frictional unemployment.
    c. Structural unemployment.
    d. Natural unemployment.

12. Unemployment caused by economic decline or recession is called:

    a. Cyclical unemployment.
    b. Frictional unemployment.
    c. Structural unemployment.
    d. Natural unemployment.

13. Most cyclical unemployment is the result of:

    a. Layoffs.
    b. Voluntary job separations.
    c. Job findings.
    d. Firings.

14. The unemployment rate that exists even when the economy is at the peak of a business cycle is:

    a. The sum of the frictional and structural unemployment rates.
    b. The actual unemployment rate.
    c. The cyclical unemployment rate.
    d. The natural rate of unemployment.
    e. A and d.

15. Today most economists consider the natural rate of unemployment to be:

    a. 4%.
    b. 8%.
    c. 6%.
    d. 2%.

16. _____ is the level of output that would result if the economy operated for an entire year at the natural rate of unemployment.

    a. Real GNP
    b. Natural rate of GNP
    c. Capacity GNP
    d. Potential GNP

17. The difference between potential GNP and actual GNP is the:

    a. GNP gap.
    b. Major economic cost of unemployment.
    c. Forgone output resulting from the actual rate of unemployment exceeding the natural rate of unemployment.
    d. All of the above.

18. Costs associated with unemployment include:

   a.   The GNP gap.
   b.   Costs associated with suicide and mental illness.
   c.   Costs associated with stress, physical illness, and crime.
   d.   All of the above.

19. Unemployment insurance:

   a.   Covers all workers.
   b.   Is federally administered.
   c.   Primarily covers those workers who lose their jobs due to layoff, economic contraction, or plant closings.
   d.   Was established in 1970.

20. Evidence shows that unemployment benefits:

   a.   Decrease structural unemployment.
   b.   Increase structural unemployment.
   c.   Decrease frictional unemployment.
   d.   Increase frictional unemployment.

THINK IT THROUGH

1.   Define the unemployment rate and discuss why it may not accurately reflect the true extent of unemployment.

2.   Discuss the factors that influence the unemployment rate.

3.   Of what use is the concept of the natural rate of unemployment?

4.   What are the social costs associated with unemployment?

5.   Discuss one way in which society softens the blow of unemployment.

POP QUIZ   Read the news brief at the end of this chapter and answer the questions below.

1.   According to the news brief, what is the natural rate of unemployment?

2.   What forces have been responsible for the rise in the natural rate of unemployment in the 1960s and 1970s?

3.   Are there any reasons to believe it is falling today?

CHAPTER ANSWERS

In Brief: Chapter Summary

1. Two 2. 3% 3. Rises 4. Falls 5. And 6. Does not 7. Single 8. Married
9. Blacks 10. Whites 11. Frictional 12. Structural 13. Equals 14.

Structural   15. Potential   16. GNP gap   17. 2.5%   18. Plant closings   19.
Increase

Vocabulary Review

1. Business cycle 2. Expansion 3. Labor force 4. Layoff 5. Job separation
6. Cyclical unemployment 7. Potential real GNP 8. GNP gap 9. Okun's law 10.
Contraction 11. Recovery 12. Unemployment rate 13. Discouraged worker 14.
Job search 15. Natural rate of unemployment 16. Recession 17. Unemployed
person 18. Job finding 19. Full employment 20. Frictional unemployment 21.
Structural unemployment

Skills Review

1.   a. Peak b. Recession c. Trough d. Expansion

2.   a.   Increased, 25%, fell, one third
     b.   Fell, increased, at the end of the war and in 1949; growth and
          stability, recessions, 1954, 1958
     c.   1961, 1970; military expansion and the Vietnam War
     d.   Inflation, unemployment; growth and rampant inflation
     e.   Two, 1981, 1982

3.   a.   100 million
     b.   5 million
     c.   5%

4.   a.   Discouraged workers are excluded.
     b.   Part-time work is counted as full-time work.
     c.   Survey responses may be misleading.

5.   a. Frictional b. Cyclical c. Structural d. Structural e. Frictional
     f. Cyclical

6.   a. $4.5 trillion b. $.5 trillion c. $5,000

     d.

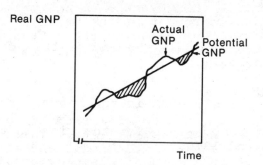

7.   a.   Crime b. Suicide c. Mental illness d. Physical illness

Self-Test for Mastery

1. c 2. c 3. d 4. b 5. a 6. d 7. b 8. d 9. d 10. b 11. c 12. a 13.
a 14. e 15. c 16. d 17. d 18. d 19. c 20. d

Think it Through

1.   The unemployment rate is the percentage of the total labor force that is
unemployed. The labor force consists of all persons over age 16 either working
or actively seeking employment but not currently employed. Unemployed persons
are those individuals over age 16 available for work and actively searching for
employment. The unemployment rate may not reflect the true extent of
unemployment because discouraged workers are unemployed but not counted as part
of the labor force. Also, part-time work is counted as full-time employment.
Further, employment surveys include responses from individuals that may be
misleading.

2.   The factors that influence the unemployment rate are the factors that
influence frictional, structural, and cyclical unemployment. The rates of
voluntary job separation and job finding affect frictional unemployment. The
length of time that it takes to find a job varies with the business cycle. The
decision to enter or reenter the labor force may also be associated with the
level of economic prosperity. Technological progress often displaces certain
workers who have skills specific to the obsolete technologies. Changes in
society's preferences regarding the composition of GNP will cause some
industries to expand and some to decline, even at a state of full employment in
the economy as a whole. Broad forces causing economic contraction or expansion
will decrease or increase the cyclical component of the unemployment rate.

3.   The natural rate of unemployment is a useful benchmark for determining the
potential output of the economy. Policies that are intended to spur economic
activity and reduce unemployment must have a benchmark indicating possible
courses of action in the short run.

4.   The social costs of unemployment include the output that is forgone when
an economy operates at a level of unemployment above the natural rate of
unemployment. This is known as the GNP gap. Other social costs include the
costs associated with crime, suicide, mental and physical illness, and stress.

5.   Unemployment insurance was established as part of the Social Security Act
of 1935 in order to alleviate to some extent the problems associated with
unemployment. Unemployment benefits replace some of the lost purchasing power
resulting from unemployment, although there is not universal coverage of
unemployed workers. Critics contend that the benefits are too high and
available for too many weeks, thus reducing the urgency with which workers
search for employment. Evidence seems to indicate that unemployment benefits
increase frictional unemployment.

Pop Quiz

1.   According to the news item, the natural rate of unemployment is defined as
the nonaccelerating-inflation unemployment rate. This rate of unemployment is
assumed to be equally divided between frictional and structural unemployment.
Most economists believe that this rate of unemployment is approximately 6%.

2.   The natural rate of unemployment rose from the 4 to 5% range because of
the marked entry of women and baby boomers (teenagers) into the labor force in
the 1960s and 1970s. In the 1970s, the labor force grew 24 million, double the
increase in the 1960s and almost 3 and one-half times the increase in the
1950s. In 1978, 24.5% of the labor force was composed of 16- to 24-year-olds.
These new entrants brought fewer skills and less experience to labor markets
causing the rate of frictional unemployment to increase at given rates of
inflation. As a result, the nonaccelerating-inflation rate of unemployment
rose.

3. Today, the natural rate of unemployment is likely falling and should continue to fall for a time. By 1990, it is expected that the natural rate of unemployment will again be down to the 4% range. Women have been integrated into the labor force and baby boomers are no longer teenagers, but in the most productive 25- to 44-year-old group. Labor force participants 16 to 24 years of age have become a smaller percentage of the labor force, falling to 19.2% last year. It is also suggested that the natural rate of unemployment is falling because firms, increasingly cost conscious, are unlikely to increase wages as rapidly as labor markets tighten, resulting in lower nonaccelerating-inflation rates of unemployment.

The Outlook

Has Unemployment Finally Hit Its Low?

NEW YORK

Has the U.S. unemployment rate, which hit a 14-year low of 5.3% in June, dropped about as far as it's going?

That it got that low surprises many economists. As long as 3½ years ago, with the economic expansion apparently aging and the jobless rate at 7.4% of the labor force, they suspected that unemployment had already hit bottom. And beginning in 1968, the lows in unemployment from one business cycle to the next had trended alarmingly higher, from 3.4% to 4.6% in 1973, to 5.6% in 1979, to 7.2% in 1981.

As the figures soured, the non-accelerating-inflation rate of unemployment—the rate that can't be reduced without speeding up inflation—was generally believed to have risen to about 6%. That 6% was evenly divided, most economists held, between frictional unemployment—workers voluntarily between jobs—and structural unemployment—workers with inadequate skills.

This concept of a natural rate of unemployment is admittedly vague; you can't pin it down with statistics. Audrey Freedman, a labor economist at the Conference Board, comments that it can't be known "until we get wage inflation due to tight labor-supply conditions"—a bit like saying you can't see that truck coming until it hits you.

But it's important. If unemployment has already fallen to its natural rate, it can't safely be reduced further. So, hunches about that natural rate strongly influence notions of appropriate fiscal and monetary policy.

Even though economists can't pinpoint the natural rate, most believe it rose in the 1970s and now has fallen.

"Before the baby-boomers and women entered the labor force in substantial numbers," says Roger H. Fulton, an economist at A. Gary Shilling & Co., "a general unemployment rate of 4%-5% was viewed as full employment. Because the two groups lacked experience and training, which limited the types of jobs they could handle, economists concluded that the economy could be faced with greater structural unemployment."

But today, Mr. Fulton notes, "women have become an integral part of the nation's work force and most baby-boomers have moved into the 25-44 year age group, generally considered to be the prime productivity age ranges. . . . And because of declining birth rates, teen-agers now comprise an abnormally small percentage of workers."

Edward Yardeni of Prudential-Bache Securities believes that these "demographic forces should push the unemployment rate down to 4% by 1990"—and perhaps sooner. He notes that during the 1970s, when "the baby-boomers overwhelmed the job market," the labor force grew 24 million, up from 12.3 million in the 1960s and only seven million in the 1950s. But last year, he says, 16-to-24-year-olds fell to 19.2% of the labor force from the 1978 peak of 24.5%.

"The 'birth dearth' which followed the baby boom is already helping push the unemployment rate back down toward levels not seen since the mid-1970s," he adds.

However, Mrs. Freedman contends that the non-inflationary rate of unemployment has dropped not because of demographic trends, which peaked in the mid-1970s, but because "employers' wage-setting practices have changed. They no longer engage in a great deal of wage imitation. Now, employers are not looking at each other but at their own companies' competitive situations and their own unit labor costs."

Still worried about foreign competition and still able to take advantage of labor unions' weakness, employers probably won't start bidding wars to get workers. "Corporate managers are unlikely to suddenly offer big wage hikes after they spent five years cutting costs," Mr. Yardeni says.

The point at which low unemployment becomes inflationary also is affected by what is driving it down. If it is low because of genuine prosperity, it isn't as inflationary as demand force-fed by government, whose borrowing tends to flood the economy with too much money.

Also important is how people react.

If consumers see inflation rising, they may step up their spending to try to beat price increases. The faster money is flowing through the economy, the more inflationary bang for a given rise in the number of bucks.

And if workers demand more pay, they also can boost inflation. So far, a Smith Barney research report sees "no clear proof that wage inflation is accelerating." Gregory Gieber, an economist at the securities firm, cites the year-to-year gains in a key private-sector employment-cost index. "After holding relatively flat around 3.2% from mid-1986 through the first quarter of 1988," he writes, "wage inflation jumped to 3.7% in the second quarter. . . . However, the rate is still low relative to the late 1970s-early 1980s and less than might be expected, based on historical relationships between economic or employment growth and wage rates."

The fact that New England's unemployment averaged only 3.4% last year may indicate that the jobless rate could fall considerably below 5% elsewhere, too.

But the closer to plant capacity the economy is operating, the faster low unemployment pushes up costs and prices. And operating rates are rising; in July, they reached 83.5%, the highest since March 1980. Meanwhile, productivity gains, which can offset rising costs, are lagging, held down by slow growth in the service sector. Productivity fell in the second period, and Merrill Lynch sees it up less than 1% in the second half.

The risk of inflation is clearly rising, and, once again, many analysts doubt unemployment can fall much further. Mr. Gieber calculates that unemployment, adjusted for the demographic changes, was 5.5% in July, matching its level in 1979, "when the economy appeared to be starting to overheat."

—HENRY F MYERS

10

Inflation and Its Consequences

CHAPTER CHALLENGES

After studying your text, attending class, and completing this chapter, you should be able to:

1. Understand how price indexes are used to measure the price level.
2. Define the concepts of inflation and deflation and show how they are measured.
3. Distinguish nominal income from real income and nominal wages from real wages.
4. Explain the consequences of inflation for incomes and decisions.
5. Explain how inflation affects interest rates and explain the difference between real and nominal interest rates.

IN BRIEF: CHAPTER SUMMARY

Fill in the blanks to summarize chapter content.

A price index is used to measure the price level. The (1)_____ [producer price index, consumer price index (CPI)] is used to measure the impact of changes in prices on households. It is determined by dividing the (2)_____ (current, base-year) value of a market basket of products and services by the value of the same market basket in the (3)_____ (current, base) year. The quotient is then multiplied by 100. In the (4)_____ (current, base) year, the price index is always 100. The CPI is actually a weighted average of a number of component price indexes. The weights are determined from household expenditure surveys conducted every (5)_____ (year, 10 years). Other price indexes include the producer price index and the implicit GNP deflator. The (6)_____ (producer price index, implicit GNP deflator) measures the price level of producer goods such as materials, chemicals, intermediate products, and capital equipment. The (7)_____ (producer price index, implicit GNP deflator) is used in calculating real GNP.

Inflation is the percentage increase from period to period in a price index. If the price index is decreasing, the percentage change in the index is called (8)_____ (disinflation, deflation). From 1913 until 1950, the CPI exhibited periods of both inflation and deflation. (9)_____ (Deflation, Inflation) usually occurred immediately following wars and depressions. Since 1950, the CPI has shown a consistent (10)_____ (decrease, increase), although the rate of inflation has been variable. From 1960 to the 5-year period ending in 1980, the 5-year average rate of inflation increased from 1.3% to 8.9%. Between 1980 and 1985 inflation decreased to an average of 5.9%, and between 1985 and 1987 inflation decreased further to a 2-year average of (11)_____ (3.1%, 5.5%).

Price indexes can be used to remove the effect of inflation from nominal variables such as nominal income, nominal wages, and nominal GNP. Inflation

(12)_____ (increases, erodes) the purchasing power of a dollar. Since nominal variables are defined in terms of current dollars, changes in the purchasing power of nominal variables (13)_____ (are necessarily, are not necessarily) fully reflected by dollar changes in the variable. For instance, if a household's nominal income doubled over a 10-year period but the level of prices confronting the household also doubled, the household's purchasing power would (14)_____ (remain unchanged, double). Nominal values can be converted to real values by dividing the nominal variable by the relevant price index itself (15)_____ (multiplied, divided) by 100. By removing the effect of inflation, we can determine how much of an increase in a nominal variable is due to inflation and how much is due to real increases in purchasing power. During periods of rapid inflation, nominal wage inflation (16)_____ (lags behind, exceeds) price inflation, causing real wages to (17)_____ (rise, fall). In effect, income is redistributed from workers to employers. Over the long run, however, wage inflation has exceeded price inflation, resulting in an/a (18)_____ (increase, decrease) in real wages.

In addition to reducing purchasing power, inflation can redistribute income and wealth. Borrowers (19)_____ (lose, benefit) during a period of inflation because the future dollars that they pay in principal and interest are worth (20)_____ (more, less) in purchasing power than the dollars at the time they were borrowed. The government borrows vast sums of money to finance its annual budget deficit. During periods of inflation, the purchasing power of the federal debt actually decreases. Over time, inflation may transfer purchasing power (21)_____ (to, away from) government (or taxpayers that are not creditors of government) and (22)_____ (to, away from) those holding government debt. Because households headed by young individuals and those with middle incomes tend to have large debt as a percentage of income relative to other age and income groups, inflation benefits young and middle-income households relative to other households. In general, if inflation is unanticipated, debtors benefit at the expense of creditors.

(23)_____ (Anticipated, Unanticipated) inflation affects present choices. If expectations of inflation are in error, choices are likely to result in a (24)_____ (more, less) efficient allocation of the economy's resources. If anticipated inflation is greater than the nominal interest rate, the real rate of interest is negative. If anticipated inflation increases more than the nominal rate of interest, the real rate of interest (25)_____ (falls, rises). Planned investment spending depends in part on the real rate of interest. Changes in anticipated inflation that cause changes in real rates of interest will affect planned investment. If those expectations are in error, businesses will likely over- or underinvest.

Similarly, expected inflation might cause households to consume (26)_____ (later rather than now at current prices, now rather than wait for prices to rise). Given a level of income, an increase in consumption of goods and services means that saving will decline. If anticipated inflation reduces saving, economic growth is (27)_____ (promoted, impaired). Also during periods of anticipated inflation, individuals tend to purchase goods that rise in value as fast as or faster than the general price level. If funds are being used to purchase real estate, gold, art, and other similar goods, those funds are not available as saving for use by businesses for capital investment. Inflation also redistributes wealth to households having these inflation-hedging assets away from those having assets that do not inflate in value as rapidly.

VOCABULARY REVIEW

Write the key term from the list below next to its definition.

Key Terms

Price level   Purchasing power of a dollar
Price index   Nominal income
Inflation   Real income
Deflation   Nominal wages
Consumer price   Real wages
   index (CPI)   Nominal interest rate
Pure inflation   Real interest rate
Producer price   Implicit GNP deflator
   index

1. _____: an index number whose value varies with the ratio of nominal GNP to real GNP.

2. _____: measures movements in a broad aggregate of products purchased by producers rather than consumers.

3. _____: a measure of how much a dollar can buy.

4. _____: occurs when the prices of all goods rise by the same percentage over the year.

5. _____: the actual number of dollars received over a year.

6. _____: commonly used to measure the impact of changes in prices on households. The index is based on a standard market basket of goods and services purchased by a typical urban family.

7. _____: hourly payments to workers in current dollars.

8. _____: the rate of downward movement in the price level for an aggregate of goods and services.

9. _____: nominal wages deflated to adjust for changes in the purchasing power of the dollar since a certain base year.

10. _____: the rate of upward movement in the price level for an aggregate of goods and services.

11. _____: the annual percentage amount of money that is earned on a sum that is loaned or deposited in a bank.

12. _____: a number used to measure the price level. The value of the index is set at 100 in the base year.

13. _____: the actual annual percentage change in the purchasing power of interest income earned on a sum of money that is loaned out.

14. _____: an indicator of how high or low prices are in a given year compared to prices in a certain base year.

15. _____: the purchasing power of nominal income.

SKILLS REVIEW

Concept: Price indexes and inflation

1. a. Given the annual values of a given market basket of goods and
        services, compute the price index assuming the base year is year 3.

Year	Current Value of Market Basket	Price Index (base year = 3)
1	$18,000	_____
2	20,000	_____
3	24,000	_____
4	27,000	_____
5	29,500	_____
6	33,000	_____

    b. Determine the rate of inflation from the price index values above:

        (1) From year 3 to year 4 _____ %
        (2) From year 4 to year 5 _____ %
        (3) From year 5 to year 6 _____ %

2. If housing has a weight of 42.6% in the CPI and housing prices increase
    20% over the year, assuming all other prices rise at 5%, what is the rate
    of inflation for the year as measured by the rate of change in the
    CPI?_____ %

Concept: Nominal and real income

3. a. Suppose you cleaned your closet and found income tax records for
        several consecutive years. Assuming your nominal income was shown in
        the table below and given the consumer price index, determine your
        real income for each year in the table.

Year	Nominal Income	CPI (base year = year 1)	Real Income
1	$29,000	100	$_____
2	31,000	110	_____
3	34,100	125	_____
4	35,000	131	_____
5	37,200	144	_____
6	39,500	160	_____

    b. Are you better off in year 6 as compared to year 1?

4. The data below consist of a household's nominal hourly wage and the CPI
    for given consecutive years.

Year	Nominal Hourly Wage	CPI	Real Hourly Wage
1	$6.25	110	_____
2	7.50	115	_____
3	8.50	125	_____
4	10.00	133	_____
5	12.00	145	_____

    a. Complete the table.

b. Assume nominal wage growth is the result of two factors--inflation and increases in labor productivity. Determine what portion of the year-to-year change in the nominal hourly wage is due to inflation and what portion is due to increases in labor productivity.

Year 1 to 2: _____% due to inflation, _____% due to labor productivity.

Year 2 to 3: _____% due to inflation, _____% due to labor productivity.

Year 3 to 4: _____% due to inflation, _____% due to labor productivity.

Year 4 to 5: _____% due to inflation, _____% due to labor productivity.

Concept: **Consequences of inflation**

5. Identify how inflation affects purchasing power, the distribution of income and wealth, and economic choices.

a. Purchasing power:

b. Distribution of income and wealth:

c. Economic choices:

SELF-TEST FOR MASTERY

Select the best answer.

1. Which of the following is an indicator of how high or low prices are in a given year compared to prices in a certain base year?

a. Inflation
b. Deflation
c. Price level
d. Price index

2. Which of the following is defined as a rate of downward movement in the price level for an aggregate of goods and services?

a. Inflation
b. Deflation
c. Price level
d. Price index

3. Which of the following price indexes measures the impact of changes in prices on households?

   a. Inflation index
   b. CPI
   c. Producer price index
   d. Implicit GNP deflator
   e. Explicit GNP inflator

4. A price index has a value of _____ in the base year.

   a. 100
   b. 10
   c. 50
   d. 1000
   e. 0

5. A price index for a market basket of goods can be found by:

   a. Multiplying the value of the market basket by the rate of inflation.
   b. Dividing the value of the market basket by the rate of inflation.
   c. Dividing the current-year value of the market basket by the base-year value of the basket and multiplying the result by 100.
   d. Dividing the base-year cost of the basket by the current-year cost of the basket.

6. If the CPI in year 1 equals 100 and the CPI in year 2 equals 113, it can be concluded that:

   a. Year 2 is the base year.
   b. The rate of inflation from year 1 to year 2 is 113%.
   c. The rate of inflation from year 1 to year 2 is 13%.
   d. More information is needed to determine the rate of inflation.

7. Which of the following is not true regarding the consumer price index?

   a. The CPI is a weighted average.
   b. Most households actually experience rates of inflation somewhat different from that measured by percentage changes in the CPI.
   c. The CPI covers all goods consumed by households.
   d. Since 1950 the CPI has risen, although prior to that time there were times when consumer prices fell.

8. Beginning in 1960, the 5-year average rate of inflation in the United States:

   a. Has continually increased.
   b. Has continually decreased.
   c. Increased until 1975-1980 and then decreased to the present.
   d. Increased until 1980-1985 and then decreased to the present.

9. If the rate of inflation for a year is 10% but the rate of nominal income growth is 5%, real income:

   a. Will rise.
   b. Will fall.
   c. Will remain the same.
   d. Cannot be determined.

10. Over the long run _____ has exceeded _____, resulting in _____ real hourly wages in the United States.

   a. Inflation, the rate of wage growth, rising
   b. The rate of wage growth, inflation, falling
   c. The rate of wage growth, inflation, rising
   d. Inflation, the rate of wage growth, rising
   e. Income, wages, falling

11. During periods of rapid inflation, _____ lags _____, causing real wages to _____.

   a. Inflation, wage growth, rise
   b. Wage growth, inflation, rise
   c. Inflation, wage growth, fall
   d. Wage growth, inflation, fall

12. Debtors benefit during periods of unanticipated inflation because:

   a. The money they pay lenders is worth more than the money originally borrowed.
   b. Inflation outpaces wage growth.
   c. Interest rates fall.
   d. The purchasing power of the dollars borrowed is greater than the purchasing power of the dollars repaid to lenders.

13. Which of the following groups lose as a result of unexpected inflation?

   a. Lenders
   b. Savers
   c. Taxpayers holding government debt
   d. Retirees on fixed pensions
   e. All of the above

14. Which of the following defines the anticipated real rate of interest?

   a. The nominal interest rate less the expected rate of inflation
   b. Inflation less the nominal rate of interest
   c. The nominal rate of interest plus the ex post rate of interest
   d. The real rate of interest adjusted for inflation

15. Anticipated inflation:

   a. Affects the choices we make as individuals.
   b. Constitutes a perfect forecast of actual inflation.
   c. May result in too much saving.
   d. May cause errors in consumption, but planned investment levels will always be correct because profit-maximizing producers use marginal analysis.
   e. None of the above.

16. Anticipated inflation:

   a. Results in less funds available for productive investment.
   b. Causes individuals to buy inflation "hedges" such as real estate, art and gold.
   c. May cause individuals to consume now rather than wait until prices rise.
   d. If erratic causes problems for planning and designing long-term contracts.
   e. All of the above.

17. Extremely high inflation such as that experienced by Germany in 1922 is called:

    a. Deflation.
    b. Inflation.
    c. Stagflation.
    d. Disinflation.
    e. Hyperinflation.

THINK IT THROUGH

1.   It is likely that you experience a rate of inflation different from that derived from the rate of change in the consumer price index. Explain.

2.   Explain the difference between nominal and real GNP. Can you think of any reasons why it is necessary to distinguish between nominal and real GNP? Discuss.

3.   Explain what is meant by the following statement: " Inflation is a distorter of choices and a capricious redistributor of income."

CHAPTER ANSWERS

In Brief: Chapter Summary

1. Consumer price index (CPI) 2. Current 3. Base 4. Base 5. 10 years 6. Producer price index 7. Implicit GNP deflator 8. Deflation 9. Deflation 10. Increase 11. 3.1% 12. Erodes 13. Are not necessarily 14. Remain unchanged 15. Divided 16. Lags behind 17. Fall 18. Increase 19. Benefit 20. Less 21. To the 22. Away from 23. Anticipated 24. Less 25. Falls 26. Now rather than wait for prices to rise 27. Impaired

Vocabulary Review

1. Implicit GNP deflator 2. Producer price index 3. Purchasing power of the dollar 4. Pure inflation 5. Nominal income 6. Consumer price index (CPI) 7. Nominal wages 8. Deflation 9. Real wages 10. Inflation 11. Nominal interest rate 12. Price index 13. Real interest rate 14. Price level 15. Real income

Skills Review

1.   a.   Price Index (base year = year 3)
             75
             83.3
            100
            112.5
            122.9
            137.5

     b.   (1) 12.5%   (2) 9.2%   (3) 11.9%

2.   Compute a weighted-average inflation rate as follows:

$$.426(20\%) + .574(5\%) = 11.39\%$$

3. a. Real Income

        $29,000.00
         28,181.82
         27,280.00
         26,717.56
         25,833.33
         24,687.50

    b. You are worse off in year 6 as compared to year 1 because your real income has declined.

4. a. Real Hourly Wage
            $5.68
             6.52
             6.80
             7.52
             8.28

    b. In order to determine the year-to-year percentage change in nominal hourly wages due to increases in labor productivity, find the year-to-year change in real hourly wages and divide this by the year-to-year change in nominal hourly wages. Subtract the result from 1 to determine the year-to-year percentage change in nominal hourly wages due to inflation.

	Due to Inflation	Due to Increases in Productivity
Year 1 to 2	32.8%	67.2%
2 to 3	72.0	28.0
3 to 4	52.0	48.0
4 to 5	62.0	38.0

5. a. Inflation reduces the purchasing power of a dollar and reduces the purchasing power of all nominal variables, such as nominal wages, nominal income, and nominal GNP.

    b. Unexpected inflation harms creditors such as financial institutions, savers, and holders of government debt, but benefits borrowers, including the federal government. It also benefits those households with a high debt burden such as middle-income households and households headed by young individuals. Inflation redistributes wealth from households having assets that do not increase in value as rapidly as the price level to households having assets that rise in value at a rate faster than the general price level.

    c. Anticipated inflation affects economic choices in the present. Expectations of inflation may cause an increase in consumption in an effort to beat the expected price increase. Or it may induce people to purchase inflation-hedging assets. Both forms of spending reduce current saving, impairing future economic growth. Errors are likely to be made in decision making because long-term plans and contracts will be based in part on an expected rate of inflation that may or may not materialize. Because of the uncertainty regarding future price levels, planned investment may be lower.

Self-Test for Mastery

1. c 2. b 3. b 4. a 5. c 6. c 7. c 8. c 9. b 10. c 11. d 12. d 13. e 14. a 15. a 16. e 17. e

Think it Through

1.   The consumer price index is a weighted average of several price indexes
for certain classes of goods or services such as housing or food and beverages.
The weight for each class of goods represents the percentage of a typical urban
family's budget that is spent on that class of goods. For instance, the weight
for housing is .426, meaning that the typical urban family spends 42.6% of its
budget on housing. These weights are based upon a 1982 to 1984 survey. These
surveys are updated once a decade.

If you differ in any way in your spending as compared to the "typical" urban
family, you will face a different rate of inflation than that given by
percentage changes in the CPI. The further in time we are away from the date
of the survey, the less accurate are the weights. New products such as VCRs
and personal computers and the changing spending patterns in response to these
new goods would not be reflected in the weights of the CPI until the next
survey.

2.   Nominal GNP is the current-dollar value of GNP. Increases in prices or
output will cause GNP to rise. While economists and others are certainly
interested in inflation, it is of value to know how much real output the
economy produces from year to year. It is increases in real output not
inflation that ultimately result in increased employment and living standards.
To remove the effect of rising prices from nominal GNP in order to reveal the
changes in real output, nominal GNP can be divided by a price index (the
implicit GNP deflator) itself divided by 100. The result is real GNP, which is
a much better indicator of economic growth over time than is nominal GNP.

3.   See question 5 in the Skills Review section for the answer. Inflation is
"capricious" in its redistribution of income in that there are gainers and
losers and it is difficult to assess the net outcome. Further, these changes
in income distribution result not from deliberated public policy, but from
unanticipated changes in price levels.

11

The Forces of Aggregate Supply and Demand: Investigating the Causes of Cyclical Unemployment and Inflation

CHAPTER CHALLENGES

After studying your text, attending class, and completing this chapter, you should be able to:

1. Distinguish an aggregate demand curve from a market demand curve and explain why an aggregate demand curve is downward sloping.
2. Distinguish an aggregate supply curve from a market supply curve and explain the shape of an aggregate supply curve prevailing in the short run.
3. Use aggregate supply and demand analysis to show how we determine the equilibrium level of real GNP and the price level over a given year.
4. Use aggregate supply and demand analysis to show how changes in aggregate demand and aggregate supply affect the equilibrium levels of real GNP and the price level for a given year.
5. Use aggregate supply and demand analysis to explain the possible causes of recessions, excessive unemployment, and inflation.
6. Understand the classical model of macroeconomic equilibrium and explain why the self-correction mechanism implied by the model does not work quickly and reliably in modern economies to ensure full employment.

IN BRIEF: CHAPTER SUMMARY

Fill in the blanks to summarize chapter content.

Macroeconomics is concerned with explaining the forces affecting aggregate production and the general level of prices rather than with specific market quantities and prices. Aggregate supply and demand analysis is used to explain the factors that cause aggregate production and the price level to change. The aggregate demand curve shows the relationship between (1)_____ (the general price level, aggregate income) and the aggregate domestic production demanded. The aggregate quantity demanded is (2)_____ (positively, inversely) related to the general price level--the aggregate demand curve is (3)_____ (downward sloping, upward sloping). A change in the price level will change the aggregate quantity demanded, but influences other than the change in the price level that affect aggregate quantity demanded will (4)_____ (result in a movement along an aggregate demand curve, shift the aggregate demand curve).

The aggregate demand curve shows an inverse relationship between the price level and aggregate quantity demanded. As the price level rises, real wealth falls, causing saving to (5)_____ (increase, decrease) and consumption to (6)_____ (increase, decrease). Higher prices increase the demand for credit, thus increasing real interest rates which (7)_____ (increases, reduces) planned investment. Finally, a higher price level reduces exports and increases imports. Thus a higher price level (8)_____ (increases, reduces) aggregate purchases.

The aggregate supply curve shows an/a (9)_____(inverse, positive)
relationship between aggregate output produced (real GNP) and the price level
as potential real GNP is approached. As the price level rises, individual
producers experience rising prices for the products that they produce. If
input prices are not rising, opportunities for additional profits arise,
causing some producers to increase production. Because producers confront
(10)_____ (falling, rising) marginal costs with increases in output, they
must have higher product prices to cover the (11)_____ (falling, rising)
marginal and unit costs of production. At output levels associated with
considerable cyclical unemployment, increases in production do not increase
unit production costs. As potential real GNP is approached, unit production
costs begin to (12)_____ (rise, fall). If output expands beyond potential
real GNP, unit production costs rise even faster for given increases in output.

Macroeconomic equilibrium occurs when the quantity of real GNP demanded equals
the quantity of real GNP supplied--where the aggregate demand and supply curves
intersect.   In equilibrium, there are no tendencies for the price level or
aggregate output level to change (13)_____(and there will be no,
even though there may be) shortages or surpluses in individual product or
resource markets. If aggregate demand rises relative to aggregate supply,
unintended inventories fall, inducing firms to eventually (14)_____
(increase, decrease) production. If aggregate demand falls relative to
aggregate supply, unintended inventories (15)_____ (rise, fall)
causing firms to eventually (16)_____ (increase, cut) production and
employment.

Factors that shift the aggregate demand curve include: (a) changes in
investment demand by business, (b) changes in consumers' willingness to consume
and save, (c) changes in exports sold or imports demanded, and (d)
(17)_____ (changes in the price level, changes in government
purchases of final products and input services). If changes in these factors
reduce aggregate demand, the aggregate demand curve shifts to the left, causing
real GNP to fall relative to potential real GNP. An/a (18)_____
(inflationary, recessionary) gap arises equal to the difference between the
potential and actual levels of real GNP. If changes in these factors cause
aggregate demand to increase and the aggregate demand curve to shift rightward,
both real output and the price level will increase. Continual increases in
aggregate demand cause (19)_____ (demand-pull, cost-push) inflation. The
increase in the price level and the level of real GNP depend on the point on
the aggregate supply curve at which the economy is operating. If actual real
GNP exceeds potential real GNP, an/a (20)_____ (inflationary,
recessionary) gap exists by the amount of the difference between the potential
and actual levels of real GNP.

Changes in aggregate supply will alter the equilibrium level of real GNP and
the price level. If aggregate supply decreases relative to aggregate demand,
the price level will (21)_____ (fall, rise) while the level of employment and
output will fall. If aggregate supply increases relative to aggregate demand,
output (22)_____ (decreases, increases) and the price level falls. Rising
input prices shift the aggregate supply curve (23)_____ (leftward,
rightward), causing the price level to increase and employment and real GNP to
(24)_____ (rise, fall). Continual decreases in aggregate supply cause
(25)_____ (demand-pull, cost-push) inflation.

The (26)_____ (Keynesian, classical) model of macroeconomic equilibrium
assumes that any departure of real GNP from its full-employment level will
cause wages and prices to adjust in such a way as to quickly restore full
employment. If the economy is initially at potential real GNP and aggregate
demand increases, the price level will rise, inducing firms to increase
production. But in time, input prices (27)_____ (fall, rise), shifting the

149

aggregate supply curve leftward, and real output falls back to its potential level. In the long run, real GNP is fixed at (28)_____ (an inflationary level, its potential level) regardless of the price level. The classical long-run aggregate supply curve is therefore (29)_____ (vertical, upward sloping) at the potential level of real GNP.

(30)_____ (Keynesian, Classical) macroeconomic analysis criticizes the (31)_____ (Keynesian, classical) model's assumption of flexible wages and prices. If wages and prices are rigid in the downward direction, a decline in aggregate demand will not result in sufficient wage and price level changes to restore full employment. As a result, Keynes argued that (32)_____ (government policies, the economy's self-adjustment mechanism) could be used to increase aggregate demand to move the economy toward its potential level of real GNP.

VOCABULARY REVIEW

Write the key term from the list below next to its definition.

Key Terms

Aggregate demand curve
Aggregate quantity demanded
Aggregate supply curve
Aggregate quantity supplied
Macroeconomic equilibrium
Recessionary GNP gap
Demand-pull inflation
Change in aggregate demand
Keynesian model of macro-
    economic equilibrium

Inflationary GNP gap
Change in aggregate
    supply
Cost-push inflation
Classical model of
    macroeconomic equi-
    librium
Long-run aggregate supply
    curve (LRAS)

Definitions

1. _____: inflation caused by increases in aggregate demand.

2. _____: a shift in the economy's aggregate demand curve, causing the economy to move to a new macroeconomic equilibrium.

3. _____: the difference between equilibrium real GNP and potential real GNP when the economy is overheated.

4. _____: the difference between the equilibrium level of real GNP and potential real GNP when the economy is operating at less than full employment.

5. _____: a shift in the economy's aggregate supply curve as the relationship is altered between the price level and real GNP supplied.

6. _____: occurs when the quantity of real GNP demanded equals the quantity of real GNP supplied.

7. _____: inflation caused by continual decreases in aggregate supply.

8. _____: the quantity of real GNP supplied by producers that is associated with a given price level.

9. _____: implied that excessive unemployment of workers and unused productive capacity would set up forces that would eventually result in increases in real GNP and eliminate the unemployment of workers.

10. _____: shows the aggregate output of final products, as measured by real GNP, that will be produced at each possible price over a given period.

11. _____: shows the relationship between the aggregate quantity supplied and the price level that would be observed if nominal wages and other money prices were flexible enough to allow the classical self-correction mechanism to work.

12. _____: the amount of real GNP that buyers are willing and able to purchase at each possible price level.

13. _____: assumes that because of rigid nominal wages the economy's self-correction mechanism cannot be expected to restore full employment when aggregate demand declines.

14. _____: shows how the amount of aggregate domestic production demanded, measured by real GNP, will vary with the price level.

SKILLS REVIEW

Concept: Slope of the aggregate demand curve; shifts in the aggregate demand curve

1. Assume that the economy is currently operating at a level of real GNP of $2200 billion with a price level equal to 120. Plot this coordinate on the figure below.

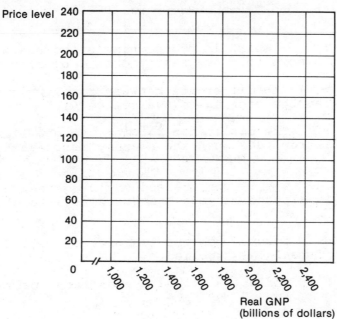

a. An increase in the price level to 180 will cause real wealth to
    _____, causing saving to _____ and consumption to
    _____ by $200 billion.
b. This price level increase will also cause real interest rates to
    _____, resulting in a/an _____ in planned investment of
    $100 billion.
c. The increase in the price level _____ imports by $80 billion and
    _____ exports by $20 billion, causing net exports (exports minus
    imports) to _____ by $100 billion.
d. The total change in aggregate quantity demanded due to the increase
    in the price level to 180 is $_____. Plot this new price level-
    aggregate quantity demanded coordinate on the figure above. The
    aggregate demand curve has a/an _____ slope.

2. List four factors that shift the aggregate demand curve and indicate
    whether an increase in the factor shifts the aggregate demand to the right
    or left.

    a. _____
    b. _____
    c. _____
    d. _____

Concept: Aggregate supply

3. Match the statement with the proper segment of the aggregate supply curve
    shown in the figure below.

    a. _____: Output can increase without much upward pressure on
                     unit costs of production.
    b. _____: Unit production costs rise very rapidly.
    c. _____: Higher prices are required by producers to cover the
                     rising unit costs of production as potential real GNP
                     is approached.
    d. _____: There is idle capacity and much cyclical unemployment.
    e. _____: The economy is overheated.

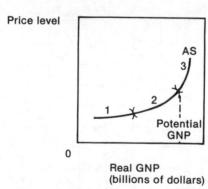

152

Concept: **Changes in aggregate demand and macroeconomic equilibrium**

4.   a.   Show on the figure below the effect of an increase in aggregate
         demand and label the new AD curve AD1.   Identify on the figure the
         change in real GNP and the price level.   Real GNP _____
         potential real GNP, resulting in a/an _____ gap.

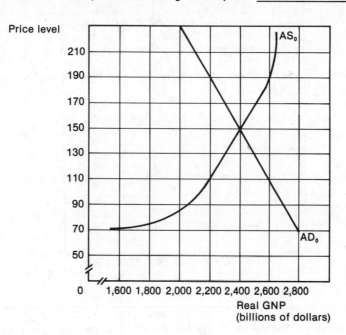

   b.   Given ADo as the initial aggregate demand curve, show on the figure
         above the effect of a decrease in aggregate demand and label the new
         AD curve AD2.   Identify the changes in real GNP and the price level.
         Real GNP _____ potential GNP, resulting in a/an
         _____ gap.

Concept: **Changes in aggregate supply and macroeconomic equilibrium**

5.   The economy shown in the figure below is currently operating at its potential level of real GNP.

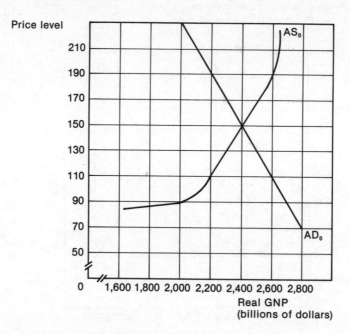

a.   If the nation experiences a significant increase in oil prices, the aggregate supply curve will shift _____ by $200 billion dollars at every price level. Show this in the figure above and label the new aggregate supply curve AS1.

b.   Real GNP _____ potential GNP by $_____, causing a/an_____ gap. The price level _____ to _____.

c.   Assume that the economy is currently at potential real GNP. Show the effect of a decline in input prices and label the new aggregate supply curve AS2. Real GNP _____, and the price level _____.

Concept: Classical long-run aggregate supply curve

6. The economy shown in the figure below is currently operating at its potential level of real GNP.

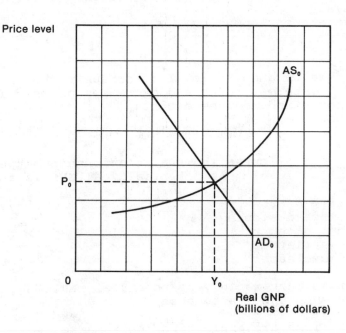

a. Show the effect of an increase in aggregate demand. Label the new aggregate demand curve AD1.
b. According to classical macroeconomics, in the short run real GNP will_____ and the price level will _____. In the long run wages and prices will _____, ensuring that real GNP _____ potential real GNP. Graphically, in the long run the short-run aggregate supply curve will shift _____.
c. Show on the figure above the classical long-run aggregate supply curve and label it LRAS.
d. Keynes argued that in a recessionary GNP gap, wages and prices _____ and automatic forces in the economy _____ (will, will not) quickly restore full employment. Keynes argued that full employment could be restored by _____ aggregate demand with _____ in government spending.

SELF-TEST FOR MASTERY

Select the best answer.

1. The aggregate demand curve shows:

a. A positive relationship between prices and quantities.
b. An inverse relationship between the price level and the aggregate quantity demanded.
c. An independent relationship between the price level and the aggregate quantity demanded.
d. An inverse relationship between the product price and the quantity of a good demanded.

2.	Which of the following will not shift the aggregate demand curve?

	a.	Changes in exports
	b.	Changes in planned investment by businesses
	c.	The price level
	d.	Changes in government spending

3.	A higher price level:

	a.	Reduces real wealth and the level of consumption.
	b.	Increases real interest rates and decreases planned investment.
	c.	Increases imports and reduces exports.
	d.	All of the above.
	e.	A and b.

4.	The aggregate _____ curve shows a relationship between real GNP produced and the price level. As potential real GNP is approached this curve _____.

	a.	Demand, is downward sloping
	b.	Supply, becomes steeper
	c.	Supply, becomes flatter
	d.	Demand, becomes steeper

5.	The price level rises more rapidly as potential real GNP is approached along an aggregate supply curve because:

	a.	Profit-taking firms are exploiting their market size and power.
	b.	Of the profit incentive.
	c.	The costs of additional units of aggregate output begin to rise more rapidly, causing firms to seek higher prices to cover these rising costs.
	d.	None of the above.

6.	Macroeconomic equilibrium occurs when:

	a.	Aggregate demand equals price.
	b.	Price equals the value of the marginal product.
	c.	Market demand equals market supply.
	d.	Aggregate quantity demanded equals aggregate quantity supplied.

7.	Starting initially at potential real GNP, an increase in aggregate demand shifts the aggregate demand curve _____, causing real GNP to _____ and the price level to _____.

	a.	Rightward, rise, rise
	b.	Rightward, rise, fall
	c.	Leftward, fall, fall
	d.	Rightward, fall, fall
	e.	Leftward, fall, rise

8.	If actual real GNP exceeds potential real GNP:

	a.	The economy is overheated.
	b.	Prices rise more rapidly.
	c.	An inflationary gap exists.
	d.	Real GNP increases less for given increases in aggregate demand.
	e.	All of the above.

9. Starting initially at potential real GNP, a decrease in aggregate demand
    shifts the aggregate demand curve _____, causing real GNP to _____
    and the price level to _____.

    a. Rightward, rise, rise
    b. Rightward, rise, fall
    c. Leftward, fall, fall
    d. Rightward, fall, fall
    e. Leftward, fall, rise

10. If actual real GNP is below potential real GNP:

    a. The economy is overheated.
    b. Prices rise more rapidly.
    c. An inflationary gap exists.
    d. A recessionary gap exists.

11. If domestic consumers reduce their demand for imports, aggregate demand
    will _____, causing real GNP to _____.

    a. Fall, rise
    b. Fall, fall
    c. Rise, fall
    d. Rise, rise

12. Demand-pull inflation:

    a. Is caused by rising prices.
    b. Is caused by rising input prices.
    c. Is due to the decline over time in aggregate demand.
    d. Is caused by continual increases in aggregate demand beyond the
        potential real GNP level.

13. An increase in input prices shifts the aggregate _____ curve _____,
    causing real GNP to _____ and the price level to _____.

    a. Demand, upward, fall, rise
    b. Demand, leftward, rise, rise
    c. Demand, rightward, rise, fall
    d. Supply, leftward, fall, rise
    e. Supply, rightward, rise, fall

14. Which of the following cause cost-push inflation?

    a. A one-time increase in aggregate demand
    b. Continual increases in aggregate demand
    c. A one-time decrease in aggregate supply
    d. Continual decreases in aggregate supply

15. Which of the following assumptions is crucial to the classical
    macroeconomic model's assertion that the economy has built-in forces that
    automatically eliminate unemployment and quickly move the economy to its
    potential level of real GNP?

    a. Profit motive
    b. Rigid wages and prices
    c. Flexible wages and prices
    d. Natural rate of unemployment

16. The classicists argued that an increase in aggregate demand would
_____ in the short run, but in the long run real GNP would
_____.

    a.   Decrease real GNP, increase
    b.   Increase real GNP, return to its potential level
    c.   Increase real GNP, rise further, causing inflation
    d.   Decrease aggregate supply, rise

17. The classical long-run aggregate supply curve:

    a.   Is vertical at a level of output below potential real GNP.
    b.   Is upward sloping.
    c.   Is upward sloping at the level of potential real GNP.
    d.   Is vertical at the level of potential real GNP.

18. John Maynard Keynes argued that:

    a.   Downward nominal-wage rigidity prevented the classical self-correction mechanism from working to eliminate recessionary GNP gaps.
    b.   The automatic forces of the market would restore the economy to full employment very quickly.
    c.   The classical macroeconomists' argument that government spending should be used in recessions would not eliminate a recessionary GNP gap.
    d.   Fluctuations in aggregate demand were the primary cause of recessions.
    e.   A and d.

THINK IT THROUGH

1. Distinguish between demand-pull and cost-push inflation.

2. Discuss the macroeconomic effects of a significant increase in the price of oil.

3. Why did Keynes believe that government policies designed to change aggregate demand should be used in recessions?

CHAPTER ANSWERS

In Brief: Chapter Summary

1. The general price level 2. Inversely 3. Downward sloping 4. Shift the aggregate demand curve 5. Increase 6. Decrease 7. Reduce 8. Reduces 9. Positive 10. Rising 11. Rising 12. Rise 13. Even though there may be 14. Increase 15. Rise 16. Cut 17. Changes in government purchases of final products and input services 18. Recessionary 19. Demand-pull 20. Inflationary 21. Rise 22. Increases 23. Leftward 24. Fall 25. Cost-push 26. Classical 27. Rise 28. Its potential level 29. Vertical 30. Keynesian 31. Classical 32. Government policies

Vocabulary Review

1. Demand-pull inflation 2. Change in aggregate demand 3. Inflationary GNP gap 4. Recessionary GNP gap 5. Change in aggregate supply 6. Macroeconomic equilibrium 7. Cost-push inflation 8. Aggregate quantity supplied 9. Classical model of macroeconomic equilibrium 10. Aggregate supply curve 11. Long-run aggregate supply curve (LRAS) 12. Aggregate demand 13. Keynesian model of macroeconomic equilibrium 14. Aggregate quantity demanded

Skills Review

1.

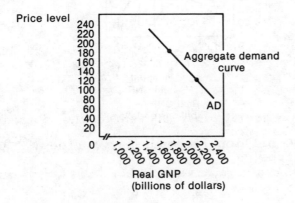

   a.   Decrease, increase, decrease b. Rise, decrease
   c.   Increases, decreases, decrease
   d. $400 billion; negative

2.   a.   Government expenditures on goods and input services; right
    b.   Planned investment spending by business; right
    c.   The willingness to consume; right
    d.   Net exports (exports less imports); right

3.   a.   1 b. 3 c. 2 d. 1 e. 3

4.   a.   Exceeds, inflationary

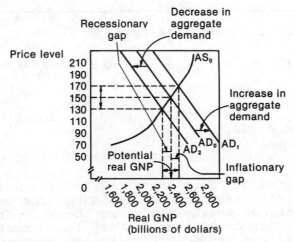

   b.   Falls below, recessionary

5. a.   Leftward

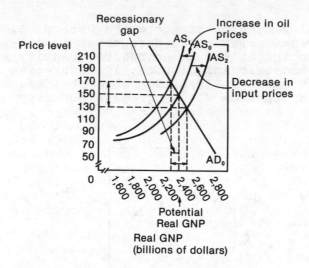

b. Falls below, $100 billion, recessionary; rises, 170
c. Increases, decreases

6. a.

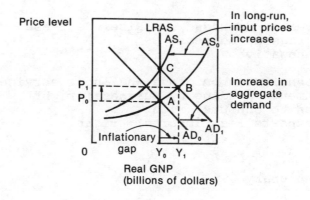

b. Increase, rise; rise, equals; leftward
c. On figure above
d. Are rigid downward, will not; increasing, increases

Self-Test for Mastery

1. b 2. c 3. d 4. b 5. c 6. d 7. a 8. e 9. c 10. d 11. d 12. d 13. d 14. d 15. c 16. b 17. d 18. e

Think it Through

1. Demand-pull inflation results from continual increases in aggregate demand when the economy is close to or beyond potential GNP. The price level rises more rapidly when the economy is overheated along the very steep portion of the aggregate supply curve beyond potential real GNP. In contrast to demand-pull inflation where high inflation is associated with low unemployment, cost-push inflation results in the simultaneous occurrence of inflation and rates of unemployment above the natural rate of unemployment. Cost-push inflation results from continual decreases in aggregate supply caused by increases in input prices.

2.   An increase in oil prices shifts the aggregate supply curve leftward. The aggregate supply curve shifts leftward (or upward) because businesses require higher prices to cover rising oil prices in order to be induced to continue producing at their current levels of output. If prices do not rise sufficiently to fully cover the increase in oil prices, firms will cut back production. As the aggregate supply curve shifts leftward, real GNP falls, unemployment rises, and the price level increases.

3.   Keynes believed that in recessions wages and prices would not fall quickly enough to restore real GNP to its potential level without significant social costs of prolonged unemployment. Wages and prices are rigid in the downward direction in part because of institutional factors such as multi-year labor contracts. Keynes believed that recessions were due to inadequate levels of aggregate demand. Because the economy's self-adjustment mechanism would not eliminate a recessionary GNP gap in the short run, Keynes argued that government policies could be used to increase aggregate demand to a level that would restore higher levels of employment.

12

The Components of Aggregate Demand: Consumption, Investment, Government Purchases, and Net Exports

CHAPTER CHALLENGES

After studying your text, attending class, and completing this chapter, you should be able to:

1. List the determinants of annual consumer purchases in an economy.
2. Use a consumption function graph and the concepts of marginal propensity to consume and marginal propensity to save to show how consumption and saving in a given year vary with disposable income.
3. List the major determinants of business investment purchases and explain why such purchases are extremely unstable from year to year.
4. Discuss how government influences aggregate demand and understand why government purchases in a given year are independent of disposable income.
5. Discuss how exports and imports for a year are likely to vary with disposable income, and draw a nation's net export function graph.
6. Draw an aggregate purchases line and explain how it shows the way purchases of final products that comprise GNP will vary with disposable income in a given year.

IN BRIEF: CHAPTER SUMMARY

Fill in the blanks to summarize chapter content.

Personal consumption purchases are the major component of aggregate demand, accounting for (1)_____ (one half, two thirds) of GNP. Consumption is primarily determined by the (2)_____ (level of disposable income, real interest rate). Households on average use in excess of 90% of their disposable income for consumption purchases. Disposable income that is not consumed is saved. That percentage of consumption due to disposable income is referred to as (3)_____ (induced, autonomous) consumption. The percentage of consumption due to influences on other than disposable income is referred to as (4)_____ (induced, autonomous) consumption. Changes in autonomous consumption result from changes in aggregate household wealth, aggregate household debt, and household expectations about future income and wealth.

The consumption function is a line or curve showing an/a (5)_____ (independent, positive) relationship between consumption and disposable income. The saving function is also a line or curve showing an/a (6)_____ (independent, positive) relationship between disposable income and saving. Given that disposable income must be either consumed or saved, saving can be derived by subtracting consumption from disposable income and the saving function can be derived by subtracting the consumption function from the 45-degree line. The slope of the consumption function is called the (7)_____ (marginal propensity to consume, rate of change in consumption). For a linear curve (straight line), it is found by a change in consumption (8)_____ (divided, multiplied) by a change in disposable income. The marginal propensity to save is the slope of the saving function and is defined as a change in (9)_____ (disposable income, saving) divided by a change in (10)_____ (disposable income, saving). Because disposable income must be consumed or saved, the marginal propensities to consume and save must sum to (11)_____ (zero, one).

Autonomous changes in consumption shift the consumption function, but they also shift the saving function because the saving line is derived from the consumption line. An increase in wealth (12)_____ (increases, decreases) consumption and (13)_____ (increases, decreases) saving at a given level of disposable income. The consumption function shifts (14)_____ (downward, upward) by the same amount that the saving function shifts (15)_____ (downward, upward). An increase in household debt reduces consumption (increases saving) at a given level of disposable income and vice versa. Expectations can also shift the saving and consumption functions. Expectations of a decline in future income will likely cause some households to save more and consume less out of their current income.

Investment spending is a (16)_____ (volatile, stable) component of GNP. It includes expenditures on machines, structures, equipment, and inventories. (17)_____ (Unplanned, Planned) investment purchases are those investment purchases that businesses make on the basis of profit expectations. If businesses overproduce output relative to sales, the unsold output is added to inventories. This is an increase in inventory investment even though it is unplanned. Planned investment demand is determined by the real interest rate, the real marginal return to investment, and other factors that shift the investment demand curve. A profit-maximizing business will invest up to the point at which the expected return for each additional dollar invested (the real marginal return to investment) is (18)_____ (just equal to, greater than) the opportunity cost of using a dollar to make the investment (or the real interest rate). The (19)_____ (aggregate purchases, investment demand) curve shows an inverse relationship between the real interest rate and the level of investment. A decline in the real interest rate relative to the real marginal return to investment will cause businesses to (20)_____ (decrease, increase) investment purchases.

Several factors can change the level of investment at a given real interest rate. These include: (a) expectations about aggregate demand, (b) expectations about the profitability of investments, (c) (21)_____ (disposable income, capacity utilization), (d) technological change, and (e) the tax treatment of investment and income. When plotted against disposable income, the investment function is a horizontal line at the annual level of investment. Any of the influences listed above, including the real interest rate, will shift the investment function either up or down. For example, an increase in the real rate of interest will (22)_____ (reduce, increase) investment purchases at a given level of disposable income and will shift the investment function (23)_____ (upward by the increase, downward by the reduction) in investment spending.

Government spending, like investment, is assumed to be (24)_____ (independent of, dependent on) the current year's level of disposable income. Government purchases of goods and input services constitute about (25)_____ (40%, 20%) of real GNP. The government purchases function is horizontal and shifts either up or down depending upon the change in government spending. An increase in government spending shifts the curve upward and vice versa. Government can also influence aggregate demand by changing taxes and transfer payments. An increase in taxes or a reduction in transfers (26)_____ (increases, reduces) disposable income and consumption and vice versa.

The last component of aggregate demand is net exports. Net exports are defined as the difference between exports and imports. If the difference is positive, international trade results in an/a (27)_____ (increase, decrease) in domestic aggregate demand. If the difference is negative, trade (28)_____ (reduces, increases) aggregate demand. Net exports are determined by the level of disposable income and the prices of imported goods relative to domestic prices. A/An (29)_____ (decrease, increase) in disposable income increases imports and reduces net exports. If the international value of the dollar (30)_____ (increases, decreases) relative to foreign currencies, U.S. exports become less price competitive in foreign markets, reducing net exports. The net export function shows a/an (31)_____ (positive, inverse) relationship between net exports and disposable income.

VOCABULARY REVIEW

Write the key term from the list below next to its definition.

Key Terms

Wealth
Aggregate household wealth
Aggregate household debt
Consumption function
Autonomous consumption
Induced consumption
Real marginal return to
   investment

Marginal propensity to
   consume
Marginal propensity to
   save
Planned investment
   purchases
Aggregate purchases

Definitions

1. _____: purchases of new or replacement residential and nonresidential structures, producer durable equipment, and additions to inventories that business firms intentionally make during the year.

2. _____: an estimate of the percentage of each dollar invested that will be returned to a firm as additional revenue per year (adjusted for the effects of changes in the price level).

3. _____: the fraction of each additional dollar of annual disposable income that is saved.

4. _____: the market value of final goods and services that will be purchased at any given level of income.

5. _____: the fraction of each additional dollar of annual disposable income that is allocated to consumer purchases.

6. _____: the portion of annual consumer purchases in a given year that responds to changes in current disposable income.

7. _____: the purchasing power of the sums of money outstanding that households have borrowed and are currently obligated to repay.

8. _____: the portion of annual consumer purchases that is independent of current disposable income.

9. _____: the purchasing power of all assets owned by households.

10. _____: a relationship between aggregate consumer purchases and disposable income in a certain year given all other determinants of consumption.

11. _____: the sum of the current values of all assets a person owns.

SKILLS REVIEW

Concept: Consumption, saving, and the consumption and saving functions

1. Below are annual data for an economy.

Disposable Income ($ billions)	Consumption ($ billions)	Saving ($ billions)
$ 0	$ 200	$_____
250	350	_____
500	500	_____
750	650	_____
1,000	800	_____
1,250	950	_____
1,500	1,100	_____

   a. Complete the table.
   b. There exists a/an _____ relationship between disposable income and consumption and a/an _____ relationship between disposable income and saving.
   c. Marginal propensity to consume equals _____; marginal propensity to save equals _____. The sum of the marginal propensities to consume and save equal _____.
   d. Plot the consumption line in a in the figure below and plot the saving line in b. At what level of disposable income is saving zero? $_____

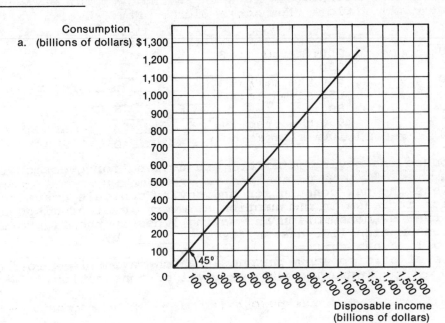

Consumption
a. (billions of dollars) $1,300
1,200
1,100
1,000
900
800
700
600
500
400
300
200
100
45°
0   100 200 300 400 500 600 700 800 900 1,000 1,100 1,200 1,300 1,400 1,500 1,600
Disposable income
(billions of dollars)

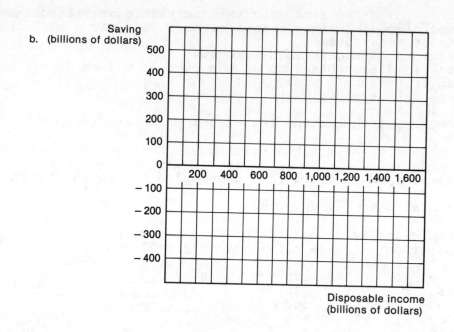

Saving
b. (billions of dollars)

Disposable income
(billions of dollars)

2. List three factors that will shift the consumption and saving lines.

a. _____
b. _____
c. _____

3. The stock market has produced impressive gains in household wealth over the last several months. Because of this, consumption increased by $200 billion at every level of disposable income. Answer the questions below based upon the data reproduced from question 1.

Disposable Income	Consumption Old	Consumption New (1)	Saving Old (2)	Saving New (3)
$ 0	$ 200	$_____	$_____	$_____
250	350	_____	_____	_____
500	500	_____	_____	_____
750	650	_____	_____	_____
1,000	800	_____	_____	_____
1,250	950	_____	_____	_____
1,500	1,100	_____	_____	_____

a. Reproduce the saving data that you derived for question 1 in column 2 above.
b. Complete the new consumption and saving schedule assuming a $200 billion increase in consumption at every level of disposable income.
c. Plot the new consumption and saving lines in the figure above.
d. The consumption line has shifted _____ by $_____, and the saving line has shifted _____ by $_____.
e. The level of disposable income at which saving is zero is $_____ assuming the new level of consumption.

166

4. Indicate for each of the following whether the consumption line and saving line will shift and in which direction.

    a. Expectations of higher future income
    b. Increase in disposable income
    c. Decline in household wealth
    d. Increase in household debt

Concept: **Investment demand and the investment purchases line**

5. The figure below represents the relationship between the real marginal return on investment and the aggregate level of investment purchases for an economy.

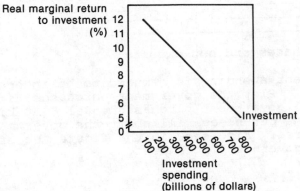

    a. Profit-maximizing firms will engage in investment spending up to the point at which the _____ is just equal to the
        _____.

    b. At a real interest rate of 10%, the level of investment purchases equals $_____. If the rate of interest falls to 8%, the level of investment _____ to $_____.

    c. On the figure below, plot the economy's investment purchases line for a 10% real rate of interest.

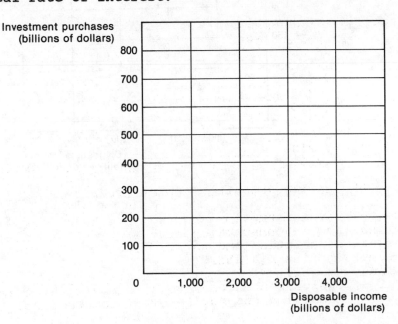

167

d. On the figure above, plot the investment purchases line for an 8% rate of interest.

e. An increase in the real interest rate will shift the investment line _____, and a decrease in the real interest rate will shift the investment line _____.

6. List five factors other than the real interest rate that will shift the investment purchases line and discuss for two of the five factors how the investment purchases line is affected.

a. _____
b. _____
c. _____
d. _____
e. _____

Concept: **Government purchases and net exports**

7. The level of government spending is assumed to be independent of the level of disposable income. Plot the government purchases line in the figure below assuming annual government purchases equal $150 billion. An increase in government purchases will shift the government purchases line _____ and vice versa. Also show in the figure the effect of a $50 billion increase in government purchases.

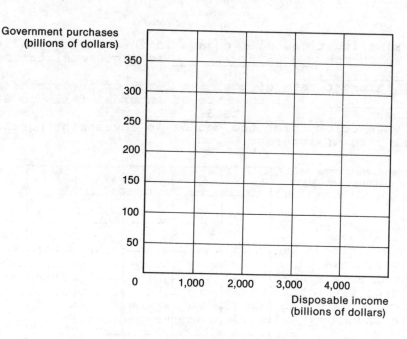

8. The data below show the relationship among disposable income, exports, and imports for an economy.

Disposable Income ($ billions)	Imports	Exports ($ billions)	Net Exports
$ 0	$ 0	$ 150	$_____
400	50	150	_____
800	100	150	_____
1,200	150	150	_____
1,600	200	150	_____
2,000	250	150	_____
2,400	300	150	_____

a. Complete the table.
b. Plot the net exports line in the figure below.

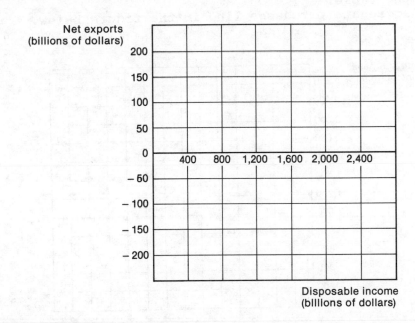

c. Net exports are _____ related to disposable income.
d. If the international value of the dollar falls relative to the foreign currencies of U.S. trading partners, assume that U.S. export goods become more price competitive abroad, resulting in an increase in exports of $50 billion at every level of disposable income. Show in the figure the effect on the net exports line. The level of disposable income at which net exports equal zero _____ to $_____.

Concept: Aggregate purchases line

9.   Derive the aggregate purchases schedule and aggregate purchases line from the table below. (All data are in billions of dollars.)

Disposable Income	C	Ip	G	NE	Aggregate Purchases
$ 0	$200	$100	$150	$100	$_____
400	500	100	150	75	_____
800	800	100	150	50	_____
1,200	1,100	100	150	25	_____
1,600	1,400	100	150	0	_____
2,000	1,700	100	150	-25	_____
2,400	2,000	100	150	-50	_____

a.   Complete the table.
b.   Plot the aggregate purchases line in the figure below.

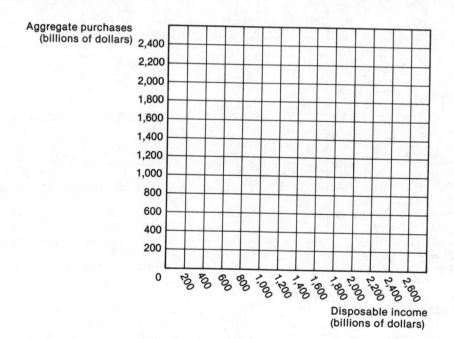

SELF-TEST FOR MASTERY

Select the best answer.

1.   Consumption represents what proportion of gross national product?

    a.   One fourth
    b.   One half
    c.   Two fifths
    d.   Two thirds
    e.   Three fourths

2. From 1960 to 1987, Americans have used what percentage on average of their disposable income for household consumption?

   a. 60%
   b. 70%
   c. 80%
   d. Over 90%

3. Induced consumption is caused by which of the following?

   a. Aggregate household wealth
   b. Aggregate household debt
   c. Expectations of future income and wealth
   d. Disposable income
   e. Interest rate

4. Autonomous consumption is influenced by all but one of the following.

   a. Aggregate household wealth
   b. Aggregate household debt
   c. Expectations of future income and wealth
   d. Disposable income

5. The slope of the consumption function:

   a. Is positive.
   b. Is called the marginal propensity to consume.
   c. Is found by dividing a given change in disposable income into a change in consumption.
   d. Is one minus the marginal propensity to save.
   e. All of the above.

6. An increase in wealth will _____ consumption at every level of disposable income and will shift the saving function _____.

   a. Decrease, upward
   b. Decrease, downward
   c. Increase, upward
   d. Increase, downward

7. The level of disposable income where the consumption function intersects the 45-degree line:

   a. Is the point of maximum returns to investment.
   b. Is the point of maximum saving.
   c. Is the point at which saving is zero.
   d. None of the above.

8. Expectations of future higher income and wealth will cause the consumption function to shift _____ and the saving function to shift _____.

   a. Upward, upward
   b. Downward, downward
   c. Upward, downward
   d. Downward, upward

9. Which of the following components of aggregate demand is the most unstable?

    a. Consumption
    b. Investment
    c. Government purchases
    d. Net exports

10. Which of the following is true of planned investment expenditures?

    a. Planned investment is inversely related to the real interest rate.
    b. Planned investment is positively related to the real interest rate.
    c. Planned investment includes inventory investment resulting from unexpectedly low sales.
    d. Profit-maximizing firms plan to invest on the basis of a comparison between the nominal rate of interest and the absolute cost of the investment project.
    e. None of the above.

11. If the real rate of interest increases relative to the real marginal return to investment:

    a. Planned investment will decrease.
    b. There is an upward movement along a fixed investment demand curve.
    c. The investment line or function relating investment purchases to disposable income will shift downward.
    d. All of the above.

12. If the rate of capacity utilization falls markedly, investment spending will _____ and the investment purchases function will shift _____ .

    a. Decrease, downward
    b. Increase, upward
    c. Decrease, upward
    d. Increase, downward

13. Which of the following will not shift the investment demand curve?

    a. Expectations about aggregate demand
    b. Changes in capacity utilization
    c. Changes in the real interest rate
    d. Technological change
    e. Changes in the tax treatment of investment purchases

14. In 1987, government purchases accounted for what percentage of GNP?

    a. 10%
    b. 20%
    c. 30%
    d. 40%
    e. 26%

15. The government purchases function is :

    a. Horizontal.
    b. Upward sloping.
    c. Downward sloping.
    d. Vertical.

16. Given the level of exports, as disposable income rises, imports
    _____ and net exports _____.

    a. Rise, rise
    b. Fall, rise
    c. Fall, fall
    d. Rise, fall

17. If the international value of the dollar increases relative to foreign
    currencies, U.S. exports will _____, causing   both net exports
    and aggregate purchases to _____.

    a. Rise, rise
    b. Fall, rise
    c. Fall, fall
    d. Rise, fall

18. An increase in exports will shift the net exports curve _____ and
    shift the aggregate purchases line _____.

    a. Upward, downward
    b. Downward, upward
    c. Upward, upward
    d. Downward, downward

19. Which of the following defines aggregate purchases?

    a. GNP + C - S + NE
    b. C + G - NE - S + Ip
    c. C + G + Ip - S
    d. C + NE + G + Ip

20. The market value of final goods and services that will be purchased at any
    given level of income is known as:

    a. Aggregate purchases.
    b. Aggregate household wealth.
    c. Aggregate household debt.
    d. Aggregate household disposable income.

THINK IT THROUGH

1. Discuss the likely consequences of a crash in the stock market that
results in large losses in the value of household real wealth.

2. Can you think of any reasons why it is not uncommon for businesses to
invest more as interest rates rise?

3. How can government influence the level of aggregate purchases other than
by changing the level of government spending on goods and input services?

4. Explain how the nation's aggregate purchases function is affected when the
international value of the dollar falls relative to the value of foreign
currencies.

POP QUIZ   Read the news brief at the end of this and answer the questions
                  below.

1.   Why is a high debt burden considered a threat to the economy?

2.   Mickey D. Levy of First Fidelity Bancorp is forecasting a 2.3% increase in
consumption purchases for 1988, less than half the average annual increase for
the first 4 years of the economic expansion that began at the end of 1982.
What factors are expected to slow the rate of growth in consumer spending?

CHAPTER ANSWERS

In Brief: Chapter Summary

1. Two thirds 2. Level of disposable income 3. Induced 4. Autonomous 5.
Positive 6. Positive 7. Marginal propensity to consume 8. Divided 9. Saving
10. Disposable income 11. One 12. Increases 13. Decreases 14. Upward 15.
Downward 16. Volatile 17. Planned 18. Just equal to 19. Investment demand
20. Increase 21. Capacity utilization 22. Reduce 23. Downward by the
reduction 24. Independent of 25. 20% 26. Reduces 27. Increase 28. Reduces
29. Increase 30. Increases 31. Inverse

Vocabulary Review

1. Planned investment purchases 2. Real marginal return to investment 3.
Marginal propensity to save 4. Aggregate purchases 5. Marginal propensity to
consume 6. Induced consumption 7. Aggregate household debt 8. Autonomous
consumption 9. Aggregate household wealth 10. Consumption function 11.
Wealth

Skills Review

1.   a.   Saving

            $-200
             -100
                0
              100
              200
              300
              400

      b.   Positive, positive c. .6, .4; 1 d. $500 billion

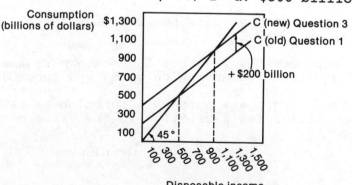

Disposable income
(billions of dollars)

174

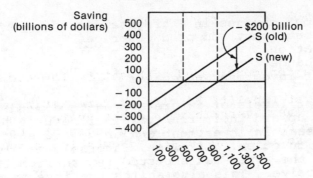

Saving (billions of dollars)

Disposable income (billions of dollars)

2. a. Changes in aggregate household wealth
    b. Changes in aggregate household debt
    c. Expectations of future income and wealth

3. a. Shown above in answer 1. a

    b.
New Consumption	New Saving
$ 400	$-400
550	-300
700	-200
850	-100
1,000	0
1,150	100
1,300	200

    c. Shown in figure above
    d. Upward, $200 billion, downward, $200 billion
    e. $1,000 billion

4. a. The consumption function will shift upward and the saving function downward.
    b. Neither the consumption nor saving functions will shift.
    c. The consumption function will shift downward and the saving function will shift upward.
    d. The consumption function will shift downward and the saving function will shift upward.

5. a. Real rate of interest, real marginal return to investment
    b. $300 billion, rises, $500 billion
    c. Shown on figure below
    d. Shown on figure below

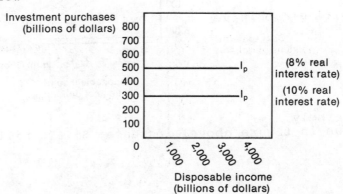

Investment purchases (billions of dollars)

Disposable income (billions of dollars)

    e. Downward, upward

175

6. a. Expectations about changes in aggregate demand
    b. Expectations about input and product prices
    c. Capacity utilization
    d. Technological change
    e. Tax treatment of investment purchases

    Expectations of higher levels of future aggregate demand will likely cause businesses to revise upward their real marginal returns to investment, resulting in an increase in investment and an upward shift in the investment purchases function. Likewise, favorable tax treatment of investment increases the after-tax expected return from the investment making it more attractive. This also shifts the investment function upward.

7. Upward

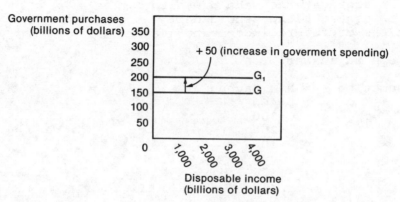

8. a. Net Exports
    $150
     100
      50
       0
     -50
    -100
    -150

    b.

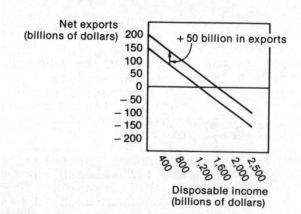

    c. Inversely
    d. Shown in figure above, increase, $1,600 billion

9. a.   Aggregate Purchases
                $ 550
                  825
                1,100
                1,375
                1,550
                1,925
                2,200

    b.

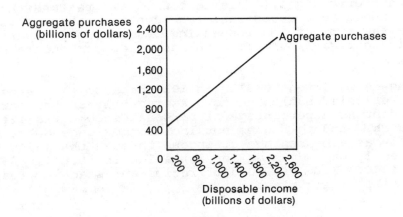

Self-Test for Mastery

1. d 2. d 3. d 4. d 5. e 6. d 7. c 8. c 9. b 10. a 11. d 12. a 13. c 14. b 15. a 16. d 17. c 18. c 19. d 20. a

Think It Through

1. If households experience large losses in household wealth, they will reduce consumption expenditures and increase saving. The consumption function will shift downward, and the saving function will shift upward. The October 1987 crash reduced real consumer spending for a short period, but other forces that cause consumption to increase eventually offset the impact of the decline in wealth.

2. The real rate of interest is just one of several influences affecting investment. In an expansion, interest rates at some point usually rise, but other factors affecting investment in the opposite direction are also changing. In an expansion, capacity utilization is rising and expectations of future growth in aggregate demand may be optimistic. Further, there may be expectations of rising product prices and profitability of expanded capacity. In other words, the real marginal return to investment is being revised upward faster than the increase in real interest rates.

3. In addition to changing the level of government purchases, the government can influence the level of aggregate demand by influencing the level of disposable income and therefore consumption. An increase in income taxes reduces disposable income and causes a reduction in household consumption and aggregate purchases and vice versa. An increase in transfer payments to households supplements household disposable income, resulting in an increase in consumption and aggregate purchases. A decrease in transfers reduces aggregate purchases.

4. When the international value of the dollar falls relative to the value of foreign currencies, the prices of U.S. exports become relatively lower to foreigners as compared to their foreign-produced output. Foreigners purchase more U.S. goods and less of their own output. As U.S. exports rise, net

exports and aggregate purchases increase. The net export function shifts upward and, since the net export function is a component of the aggregate purchases function, the aggregate purchases function likewise shifts upward.

Pop Quiz

1.   A high and rising debt burden is considered a threat to the economy because at some point consumers can no longer sustain increases in spending by borrowing. Some experts feel we have reached this point. Consumer debt to income ratios are at historic highs. This is one of the reasons that economists have been expecting a recession. Consumption makes up 65% of GNP. When consumers reduce the rate of their spending, the economy experiences a significant decline in aggregate purchases unless other components of aggregate demand are increasing.

2.   Consumer spending is expected to slow in 1988 because of rising debt burdens and stagnant real disposable income. As recently as the early 1980s, consumer installment debt as a percentage of personal income was 12%. Today it is 16%--an all-time high. And this does not include mortgage debt, which has increased significantly as a percentage of income through the 1970s and into the 1980s. Average weekly pay adjusted for inflation is actually $5 lower today than it was in 1980. With rising debt ratios and stagnant real incomes, consumption spending will likely slow.

Economists Fret Over Consumer Outlays

Delicate Balance Is Required to Avoid a Slump

By LINDLEY H. CLARK JR.
And ALFRED L. MALABRE JR.
Staff Reporters of THE WALL STREET JOURNAL

Will economists ever run out of things to worry about?

Through much of the economy's long expansion and especially after the stock market crash, many forecasters feared that consumers, burdened by debt, skimpy pay gains and low savings, would slash their spending and thus spark a recession. So far, that hasn't happened.

Now, many forecasters fear that consumers may step up their spending and

Consumer Spending

In billions of 1982 dollars, plotted quarterly, seasonally adjusted annual rate

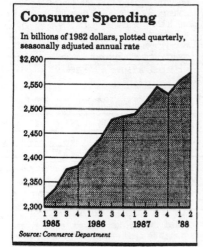

Source: Commerce Department

thus spark—you guessed it—a recession. So far, that hasn't happened, either.

In fact, most economists don't even expect it to happen. But they also can't quite rule it out. And therefore they can't help worrying that if consumers should spend too freely now, while capital outlays and exports are surging, they could overtax the economy, accelerate inflation, force the Federal Reserve to tighten credit and, ultimately, cause a new slump.

Odd 'Bad News'

So, most economists hope that consumers keep spending—because such outlays perennially account for about two-thirds of all business activity—but that they won't spend too lavishly. Such hopes can produce odd-seeming analyses. In a recent report, Edward S. Hyman, the chief economist of C.J. Lawrence, Morgan Grenfell Inc., called a brisk increase in retail sales in June "bad news."

But despite that increase and the strong 1% gain in June consumer spending, the evidence suggests, on balance, that consumers are indeed relatively restrained.

"It's a delicate transition, getting from a consumer-led expansion to one powered by capital outlays and exports, and to do so without interruption in overall economic growth," says Donald Straszheim, the chief economist of Merrill Lynch & Co. But "the transition seems to be working. Capital spending is booming, as are exports, while consumer spending is neither racing ahead nor coming to a complete halt."

Washington's statistics mills are grinding out data, adjusted for inflation and seasonal factors, that appear to confirm that the economy is undergoing a sea change. Business fixed investment in the 1988 first half rose at a swift annual rate of 10.8%, and exports soared at a 16.8% rate. Meanwhile, consumer outlays climbed at an annual rate of only 3.4%; in last year's final quarter, which encompassed the market crash, they slipped a bit.

Trends Likely to Continue

Most economists expect these trends to continue. Mickey D. Levy, the chief economist of First Fidelity Bancorp, forecasts double-digit gains in business investment and exports this year but only a 2.3% increase in consumer outlays—less than half the average annual rise in the first four years of the current expansion.

"We're going to see very modest consumption growth," Mr. Levy predicts, calling this a "better" prospect than most forecasters had earlier anticipated. So, barring an unexpected change in government policy, consumer prices will keep rising at an annual rate below 5% at least through the next six months, he says. This, in turn, suggests continuing economic expansion through next year, he adds.

Factors that point to only slight gains in consumer spending in the months ahead are generally the same ones that earlier had prompted concern about a spending collapse.

Topping the list is consumer debt. It has surged during the economic expansion, which is nearing the six-year mark. Consumer installment debt, now above 16% of personal income, is at a record. Early in the 1980s, it was about 12%. Home-mortgage debt shows a similar progression.

Meanwhile, pay gains continue to be modest, generally failing to keep abreast of price increases. Weekly paychecks are

still edging up, on the average, but not if inflation is taken into account. Adjusted for rising prices, average weekly pay is nearly $5 less now than it was as long ago as 1980, and average hourly pay also has dwindled. A broader earnings gauge—all personal income, adjusted for inflation, taxes and population growth—has barely budged in two years.

Low Savings Rate

Moreover, the share of income saved hovers below 5%. The second-quarter savings rate, at 3.8%, topped last year's 3.2% average but remained far below the 7%-plus levels of the early 1980s.

For the second half, Charles B. Reeder, an economic consultant in Wilmington, Del., forecasts "sluggish" consumer spending, largely because of "a heavy debt burden and wage rates rising more slowly than prices." Like most forecasters, however, he doesn't expect "an actual decline in consumer spending." And F. Thomas Juster, an economist at the University of Michigan, says recent polls by its Survey Research Center find "consumers still to be confident."

Other factors less obvious than the mounting consumer debt are expected to help buoy consumers. Despite the higher debt, a Federal Reserve Board study finds that consumers' "debt-service payments have risen at a much slower rate." Among the reasons: longer loan-contract maturities and lower interest rates than those early in the decade.

Ratio of Installment Debt to Income

(In percent)

July 1986   Jan. 1987   July   Jan. 1988

Sources: Federal Reserve Board; Department of Commerce

In a recent three-year period, consumer installment debt outstanding surged 64% to $551.8 billion from $337 billion, but monthly payments on that debt climbed only 38% to $10.6 billion from $7.7 billion. Significantly, delinquency rates on installment and home-mortgage loans, though relatively high, have been lower in recent months than early last year.

Demographic factors also may explain why the outlook for consumer finances may be brighter than overall debt numbers indicate. "Part of the increase in debt is related to the age profile of the population and should be considered natural and not threatening," a Dean Witter Reynolds study says.

So far in this decade, the fastest-growing population group has been the 25-to-44-year-olds—typically, the age group that, relative to income, uses the most credit. As these people age, their borrowing should ebb and their incomes should rise appreciably. Furthermore, relatively few

Index of Consumer Sentiment

First quarter 1966 = 100

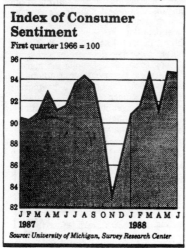

Source: University of Michigan, Survey Research Center

people will be entering the 25-44 age bracket in the years just ahead.

Also apparently showing a brighter side is the savings picture. Although the share of income saved has long been extraordinarily low, this doesn't take into account

the surge in the value of housing and, despite the crash, of securities holdings. The Federal Reserve study finds that more than "80% of the families that have consumer installment debt also have financial

Home Mortgage Loans

Percent delinquent 30 days or more

Source: Mortgage Bankers Association

Installment Loans

Percent delinquent 30 days or more

Source: American Bankers Association

assets or home equity sufficient to permit liquidating their debts in emergencies."

Similarly, Mr. Hyman suggests that the big rise in home-mortgage debt be viewed against the big rise in the value of consumer-owned housing and land. Last year, he estimates, mortgage debt amounted to 45.6% of the value of the underlying homes and land. This was up from 37.3% at the start of the decade but slightly less than the comparable reading as long ago as the early 1960s. "Maybe the consumer isn't so leveraged," Mr. Hyman comments.

Helping sustain consumer spending is the surprising strength in employment, which partly offsets the modest size of pay

gains. Lacy Hunt, the chief economist of CM&M Group, a New York securities concern, predicts that "with such strength evident in the employment numbers—nearly four million new jobs in the past year—consumer spending certainly isn't going to collapse." He adds, "Most of the new jobs have been in the better-paid categories, including manufacturing and construction."

Nature of Job Growth

And the Labor Department estimates that "since 1982, part-time employment has accounted for only about 8% of overall job growth" and that the temporary-help industry comprises less than 1% of all payroll jobs.

Persistent strength on the job front is widely seen as a major reason for the

Population Trend Since 1980

AGE	% OF POP. IN 1980	% OF POP. IN 1987	% OF POP. IN 1995
25-34	16.8%	17.8%	15.7%
35-44	11.3	14.1	16.3
45-54	10.1	9.6	12.0
55-64	9.6	9.0	8.2

stock market crash's mild impact on consumer spending. A Federal Reserve economist says that, for all the attention accorded the market, "stock equities are among the most concentrated of all asset holdings." A Fed study shows that the top 10% of wealth-holders own over 90% of all stock. Affluent people usually aren't under heavy pressure to cut their spending.

Far more important than the stock market to consumer spending, the Fed economist says, is the housing market. He shares the consensus that consumers will keep on spending, though at a modest pace, but he cautions that "we could see an actual decline in outlays if housing turns sour and home prices drop across a broad front. Then you would see the purse strings tighten fast." No broad price drop is evident, he adds, though home prices have recently softened in some areas.

13

Aggregate Demand and Keynesian Analysis of Macroeconomic Equilibrium

After studying your text, attending class, and completing this chapter, you should be able to:

1. Explain the conditions required for macroeconomic equilibrium and why equilibrium sometimes occurs at a level of real GNP below the level that can provide full employment.
2. Discuss the possible causes of recessions using the Keynesian aggregate purchases aggregate production approach.
3. Discuss how the multiplier works and how it can be calculated.
4. Discuss how changes in net exports can affect aggregate demand and macroeconomic equilibrium.
5. Discuss how changes in the price level can affect aggregate demand and equilibrium real GNP.
6. Show how an inflationary GNP gap can result from an increase in aggregate demand and how an overheated economy implies that an inflationary process will decrease equilibrium real GNP.

IN BRIEF: CHAPTER SUMMARY

Fill in the blanks to summarize chapter content.

In Keynesian analysis of the macroeconomy, (1)_____ (aggregate demand, inflation) is the key cause of fluctuations in real GNP. Macroeconomic equilibrium occurs when aggregate production (2)_____ (exceeds, equals) aggregate purchases. For an economy without government purchases, taxes or net exports, another condition for equilibrium is that planned investment equal (3)_____ (consumption, saving) and unintended inventory investment (4)_____ (exceed, equal) zero. If aggregate purchases exceed aggregate production, planned investment will exceed saving and unintended inventory investment will be (5)_____ (positive, negative). This puts (6)_____ (upward, downward) pressure on real GNP. Just the opposite is true of levels of income where aggregate purchases are less than aggregate production. In equilibrium, there is no tendency for real GNP to rise or fall. Graphically, macroeconomic equilibrium occurs where the aggregate purchases line intersects the (7)_____ (45-degree, consumption) line and where the saving function intersects the planned investment line.

In Keynesian analysis, shifts in the aggregate purchases line cause expansions and recessions. For example, a/an (8)_____ (decline, increase) in planned investment will reduce aggregate purchases relative to aggregate production, resulting in an unintended (9)_____ (decline, increase) in inventory investment. Businesses will (10)_____ (increase, cut) production due to the increase in unsold output. As production and income fall, real GNP, saving, and unintended inventory investment will fall. When saving falls to equal the new and lower level of planned investment, unintended inventory investment is zero and aggregate purchases are once again equal to aggregate production but

at a lower level of real GNP--a recessionary level. As real GNP falls,
employment also falls. Anything that causes a downward shift in the aggregate
purchases line will cause equilibrium real GNP to (11)_____ (rise, fall).
Conversely, anything that causes the aggregate purchases function to shift
upward will cause equilibrium real GNP to (12)_____ (increase, decrease).
In the short run, the economy can attain a recessionary level of equilibrium
real GNP and employment. Because of (13)_____ (downward wage and
price rigidity, flexible wages and prices), Keynes believed that recessionary
levels of employment would persist for long periods unless government
intervened by stimulating aggregate demand. In effect, Keynes viewed the
aggregate (14)_____ (demand, supply) curve as horizontal below the level
of potential real GNP.

A change in (15)_____ (induced, autonomous) purchases (a shift in the
aggregate purchases curve) produce larger changes in equilibrium real GNP.
This is known as the multiplier effect. The (16)_____ (marginal
propensity to consume, multiplier) is a number that when multiplied by either a
positive or negative change in autonomous purchases gives the resulting change
in equilibrium real GNP. The multiplier process occurs because income spent
becomes the income of input suppliers to the industries in which the income was
originally spent. Input suppliers in turn spend a portion of the new income
and save a portion. When they spend, input suppliers elsewhere in the economy
receive income, a portion of which they eventually spend. For the case of an
economy without government or foreign sectors, this process of spending and
respending continues until the change in saving (17)_____ (just equals, is
greater than) the initial change in planned investment. The multiplier can be
found by taking the reciprocal of (18)_____ [(1 - MPC), (1 - MPS)] or the
reciprocal of the (19)_____ (MPS, MPC).

Adding the government and international sectors to the Keynesian model requires
reflecting all four components of aggregate purchases in the aggregate
purchases curve: C, Ip, G, and NE. The conditions for macroeconomic
equilibrium also change. Aggregate production must still equal aggregate
purchases, now defined as including G and NE, (20)_____ (and S =
Ip continues to be, but S = Ip is no longer) valid as a condition for
equilibrium. The sum of the uses of income for purposes other than purchasing
domestic output (saving, taxes less transfers, and imports) must just be offset
by the sum of planned investment, government purchases, and exports. That is,
Ip + G + E = S + T + M or, alternatively, Ip + G + NE = S + T. The multiplier
must also be modified because like saving, imports and taxes are positive
functions of real income. The new multiplier can be defined as
(21)_____ [the reciprocal of (1 - MRR), MRR times MPC] where the
marginal respending rate (MRR) is influenced by the marginal propensity to
consume (MPC), the marginal propensity to import (MPI), and the tax rate.
Fluctuations in real GNP can be caused by autonomous changes in any of the
components of aggregate purchases, including G and NE.

Thus far, Keynesian analysis has assumed that the price level is constant. In
order to understand the inflationary implications of fluctuations in autonomous
purchases, it is necessary to introduce a price variable to the Keynesian
model. As an initial step, the aggregate demand curve must be derived. The
aggregate demand curve shows a relationship between the (22)_____
(real disposable income, price level) and aggregate purchases. An increase in
the price level will (23)_____ (increase, reduce) aggregate purchases
because real wealth decreases, causing consumption to (24)_____ (rise,
fall); real interest rates, rise causing planned investment to (25)_____
(rise, fall); and the prices of U.S. goods relative to foreign goods rise,
causing exports to (26)_____ (rise, fall) and imports to (27)_____
(rise, fall). The aggregate demand curve is downward sloping. When the
aggregate purchases curve shifts upward, causing an inflationary gap where real
GNP exceeds potential GNP, the price level rises. This will eventually cause

the aggregate purchases line to shift (28)_____ (to a level
higher than; back down to) its original position where real GNP equals
potential GNP. Thus the price variable acts as a long-run corrective
mechanism, eventually returning real GNP to its potential level.

VOCABULARY REVIEW

Write the key term from the list below next to its definition.

Key Terms

Multiplier   Marginal respending rate (MRR)
Autonomous purchases   Marginal propensity to
                                 import (MPI)

Definitions

1. _____: the fraction of each extra dollar of income used
   to purchase imported products.

2. _____: the extra purchases that result from each extra
   dollar of income.

3. _____: a number that can be used to multiply a change in
   purchases that results in a shift of the aggregate purchases line to
   obtain the change in equilibrium real GNP that results from those
   purchases.

4. _____: purchases such as investment or autonomous
   consumption that cause the economy's aggregate purchases line to shift.

SKILLS REVIEW

Concept: Macroeconomic equilibrium

1. Assume that an economy does not engage in international trade and there
   are no taxes, transfers, or government purchases. Answer the following
   questions based upon the data in the table below. (All data are in
   billions of dollars.)

Aggregate Production	Planned Investment	Consumption	Aggregate Purchases	Unintended Inventory Investment
$ 500	$300	$ 600	$_____	$_____
1,000	300	1,000	_____	_____
1,500	300	1,400	_____	_____
2,000	300	1,800	_____	_____
2,500	300	2,200	_____	_____
3,000	300	2,600	_____	_____
3,500	300	3,000	_____	_____

   a. Complete the table.
   b. The conditions for macroeconomic equilibrium are that _____
      equal _____ and _____ equal zero. In equilibrium,
      planned investment must equal _____.

183

c. Equilibrium GNP = $_____. In equilibrium, aggregate purchases
    = $_____, aggregate production = $_____, unintended
    inventory investment = $_____, saving = $_____, and
    planned investment = $_____.
d. Plot the aggregate purchases curve in the figure below and identify
    the equilibrium level of real GNP.

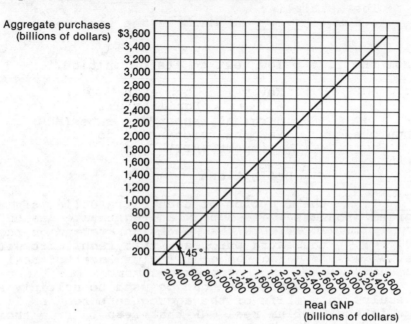

Aggregate purchases
(billions of dollars)

Real GNP
(billions of dollars)

e. At a level of aggregate production of $1,500 billion, aggregate
    purchases _____ aggregate production by $_____, resulting
    in an unintended inventory investment of $_____. This causes
    the level of real GNP to _____.
f. At a level of aggregate production of $3,500 billion, aggregate
    purchases _____ aggregate production by $_____, resulting
    in an unintended inventory investment of $_____. This causes
    real GNP to _____.

Concept: **Changes in autonomous purchases, macroeconomic equilibrium, and the
          multiplier**

2. For the economy shown in the table above in question 1, analyze the effect
    of an increase in planned investment of $100 billion. (All data are in
    billions of dollars.)

Aggregate Production	Planned Investment		Consumption	Aggregate Purchases		Unintended Inventory Investment	
	Old	New		Old	New	Old	New
$ 500	$300	$400	$ 600	$___	$___	$___	$___
1,000	300	400	1,000	___	___	___	___
1,500	300	400	1,400	___	___	___	___
2,000	300	400	1,800	___	___	___	___
2,500	300	400	2,200	___	___	___	___
3,000	300	400	2,600	___	___	___	___
3,500	300	400	3,000	___	___	___	___

a. Complete the table.

b. For the new level of planned investment, equilibrium real GNP =
    $_____.
c. On the figure above, draw the new aggregate purchases curve and
    identify the new equilibrium real GNP.
d. Equilibrium real GNP has _____ from $_____ to $_____.
    Equilibrium autonomous purchases have _____ from $_____ to
    $_____. The multiplier = _____.
e. MPC = _____, MPS = _____. What is the reciprocal of the MPS or
    (1 - MPC)?

3. Complete the table.

Change in Autonomous Purchases	MPC	MPS	Multiplier	Change in Equilibrium Real GNP
$50 billion	.8			$_____
-30 billion	.75	____	____	_____
700 billion	____	.4	____	_____
-80 billion	____	____	2	_____

4. In the figure below is an aggregate supply and aggregate demand model.
    The aggregate supply curve reflects the Keynesian assumption regarding
    wage and price rigidity. Assuming the MPS is .25, show what will happen
    to the aggregate demand curve and the equilibrium level of real GNP given
    a decline in household wealth that reduces autonomous purchases by $75
    billion.

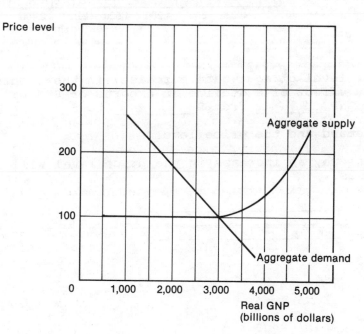

5. Show on the figure below the effect of an increase in government purchases
    of $100 billion. Identify the new equilibrium real GNP. The multiplier =
    _____. If after the increase in government spending the level of
    equilibrium real GNP is short of potential GNP by $200 billion and
    government desires to increase its spending to move the economy to its
    potential level, how much more of an increase in government purchases is
    required? $_____

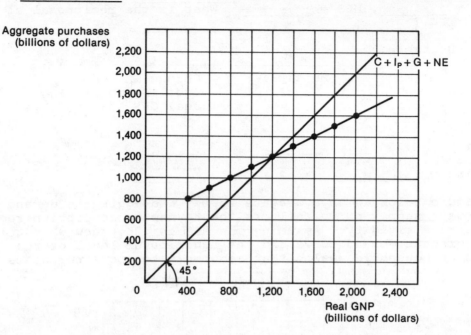

6. Given the initial level of aggregate purchases in the figure above, show
    on the figure the effect of a decline in exports of $50 billion.
    Equilibrium real GNP _____ from $_____ to $_____.

Concept: **Aggregate demand and the price level**

7. List three reasons why an increase in the price level will reduce
    aggregate purchases.

    a. _____
    b. _____
    c. _____

8.   In the figure below, a represents three aggregate purchases curves, each
      associated with a different price level. Curve 1 is associated with price
      level P1, curve 2 with P2, and curve 3 with P3. In b, find the price
      level-real GNP coordinates consistent with macroeconomic equilibrium.
      (Plot the aggregate demand curve.)

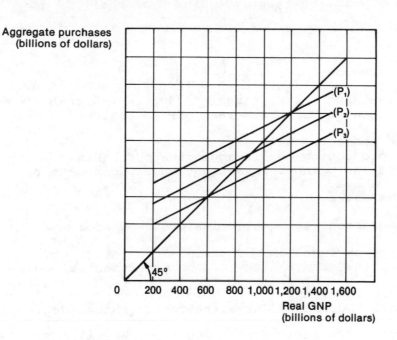

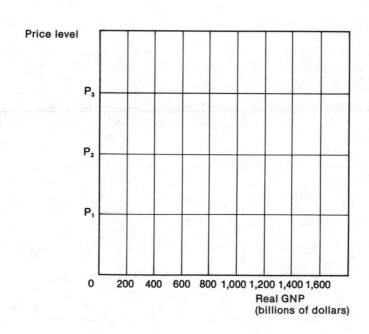

Select the best answer.

1. In Keynesian analysis, the key determinant of real GNP is:

    a. Profits.
    b. Investment.
    c. Inflation.
    d. Aggregate demand.

2. For an economy without international trade, taxes, transfers and government spending, equilibrium real GNP is achieved when

    a. Planned investment equals saving.
    b. Aggregate production equals aggregate purchases.
    c. Consumption and planned investment equal aggregate production.
    d. All of the above.
    e. None of the above.

3. Graphically, macroeconomic equilibrium occurs where:

    a. The consumption function and saving line intersect.
    b. The planned investment line and the government spending line intersect.
    c. Spending equals saving.
    d. The aggregate purchases curve intersects the 45-degree line.

4. At a level of real GNP greater than equilibrium real GNP, aggregate production _____ aggregate purchases and unintended inventory investment _____.

    a. Equals, equals zero
    b. Exceeds, is positive
    c. Is less than, is negative
    d. Equals, is negative
    e. Exceeds, equals zero

5. At a level of real GNP less than equilibrium real GNP, aggregate production _____ aggregate purchases and unintended inventory investment _____.

    a. Equals, equals zero
    b. Exceeds, is positive
    c. Is less than, is negative
    d. Equals, is negative
    e. Exceeds, equals zero

6. A decline in planned investment:

    a. Causes aggregate purchases to increase and aggregate production to decrease.
    b. Reduces aggregate purchases relative to aggregate production causing unintended inventories to rise and putting pressure on real GNP to rise.
    c. Increases aggregate purchases relative to aggregate production causing unintended inventories to rise and putting pressure on real GNP to fall.
    d. Reduces aggregate purchases relative to aggregate production causing

unintended inventories to rise and putting pressure on real GNP to fall.

7. If households experience a substantial increase in aggregate household wealth:

    a.   Unintended inventory investment falls initially, but eventually equilibrium real GNP will rise.
    b.   Unintended inventory investment rises initially, but eventually equilibrium real GNP will fall.
    c.   Unintended inventory investment falls initially, but eventually equilibrium real GNP will fall.
    d.   Initially equilibrium real GNP will rise, but eventually unintended inventory investment will fall.

8. If the economy is operating at a level of equilibrium real GNP below its potential real GNP:

    a.   The economy is experiencing inflation.
    b.   Government can move the economy toward its potential level by reducing government purchases.
    c.   The economy is at full employment, but is at least not experiencing inflation.
    d.   Government can move the economy toward its potential level by increasing government purchases.

9. A change in autonomous purchases produces a larger change in real GNP. This concept is represented by the:

    a.   MPC.
    b.   MRR.
    c.   Multiplier.
    d.   1/MPI.
    e   C and d.

10. Which of the following expressions represents the multiplier?

    a.   1/MPI
    b.   1/MPC
    c.   1/MPS
    d.   1/(1 - MPC)
    e.   C and d

11. If the current level of equilibrium real GNP is $2,000 billion and the MPS equals .25, an increase in planned investment of $50 billion will change real equilibrium GNP to:

    a. $1,800 billion.
    b. $2,300 billion.
    c. $3,200 billion.
    d. $2,200 billion.
    e. $2,100 billion.

12. If the MPC is .8 and a decline in consumer wealth reduces aggregate purchases by $100 billion, equilibrium real GNP will change by:

    a.   -$200 billion.
    b. $200 billion.
    c. $400 billion.
    d.   -$500 billion.

13. Which of the following equilibrium conditions applies to an economy with foreign trade, government spending, taxes, and transfers?

    a. Aggregate production = aggregate purchases
    b. C + Ip + G + NE = real GNP
    c. Ip + G + E = S + T + M
    d. All of the above
    e. B and c

14. The multiplier for an economy with taxes and imports as a function of income:

    a. Is larger than the multiplier for an economy without foreign trade, taxes, transfers, and government spending.
    b. Is expressed as the reciprocal of the MRR.
    c. Is expressed as the reciprocal of (1 - MRR).
    d. Is smaller than the multiplier for an economy without foreign trade, taxes, transfers, and government purchases.
    e. C and d

15. A/An _____ in exports can cause a/an _____ gap.

    a. Decrease, recessionary
    b. Decrease, inflationary
    c. Increase, recessionary
    d. Increase, will leave real GNP unchanged

16. Which of the following is not a reason why aggregate purchases and the price level are inversely related?

    a. Higher prices cause higher wages, inducing firms to cut employment and production.
    b. Higher prices reduce real wealth, decreasing consumption and aggregate purchases.
    c. Higher prices reduce real interest rates, reducing planned investment and aggregate purchases.
    d. Higher prices reduces exports and increase imports, reducing aggregate purchases.

17. A point on the aggregate demand curve represents a price level- real GNP coordinate at which:

    a. Aggregate purchases equal aggregate government spending.
    b. Aggregate demand equals aggregate purchases.
    c. Aggregate purchases equal aggregate production.
    d. S + C = Ip + real GNP.

18. An inflationary gap exists where equilibrium real GNP _____ potential or full-employment GNP. In the long run, an inflationary gap will cause the aggregate purchases curve to shift _____.

    a. Equals, upward
    b. Equals, downward
    c. Is less than, downward
    d. Is greater than, downward
    e. Is greater than, upward

THINK IT THROUGH

1.   Suppose that the international value of the dollar on foreign exchange markets increases, causing the prices of U.S. goods abroad to become less competitive. If exports fall, what is the likely impact on the economy?

2.   If business becomes more optimistic regarding future sales such that the expected marginal rate of return to investment rises relative to the real interest rate, discuss the likely macroeconomic effects.

3.   Explain intuitively the multiplier process.

CHAPTER ANSWERS

In Brief: Chapter Summary

1. Aggregate demand 2. Equals 3. Saving 4. Equal 5. Negative 6. Upward 7. 45-degree 8. Decline 9. Increase 10. Cut 11. Fall 12. Increase 13. Downward wage and price rigidity 14. Supply 15. Autonomous 16. Multiplier 17. Just equals 18. (1 - MPC) 19. MPS 20. But S = Ip is no longer 21. The reciprocal of (1 - MRR) 22. Price level 23. Reduce 24. Fall 25. Fall 26. Fall 27. Rise 28. Back down to

Vocabulary Review

1.   Marginal propensity to import 2. Marginal respending rate (MRR) 3. Multiplier 4. Autonomous purchases

Skills Review

1. a.

Aggregate Purchases	Unintended Inventory Investment
$ 900	$-400
1,300	-300
1,700	-200
2,100	-100
2,500	0
2,900	100
3,300	200

   b.   Aggregate purchases, aggregate production, unintended inventory investment; saving

   c. $2,500; $2,500, $2,500, $0, $300, $300

d.

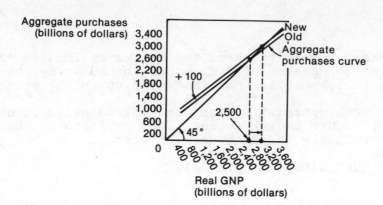

Aggregate purchases
(billions of dollars)

Real GNP
(billions of dollars)

e. Exceed, $200, -$200; rise
f. Are less than, $200, $200; fall

2. a. Aggregate Purchases   Unintended Inventory
                                               Investment

Old	New		Old	New
$ 900	$1,000		$-400	$-500
1,300	1,400		-300	-400
1,700	1,800		-200	-300
2,100	2,200		-100	-200
2,500	2,600		0	-100
2,900	3,000		100	0
3,300	3,400		200	100

b. $3000
c. On figure above
d. Increased, $2,500, $3,000; increases, $2,500, $3,000; 5
e. .8, .2; the multiplier

3.

Change in Autonomous Purchases	MPC	MPS	Multiplier	Change in Equilibrium Real GNP
$50 billion	.8	.2	5	$250 billion
-30 billion	.75	.25	4	-120 billion
700 billion	.6	.4	2.5	1,750 billion
-80	.5	.5	2	-160 billion

4.

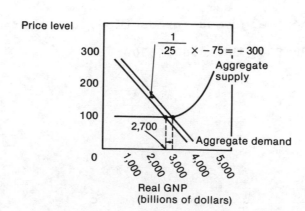

Price level

Real GNP
(billions of dollars)

192

5.

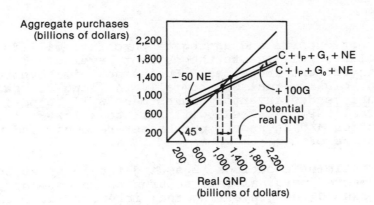

2, $100 billion

6. Shown on figure above; decreases, $1,200, $1,100

7. a. An increase in the price level will reduce real wealth, reducing consumption and aggregate purchases.
   b. An increase in the price level will increase real interest rates, reducing planned investment and causing aggregate purchases to fall.
   c. An increase in the prices of U.S. goods relative to foreign goods increases imports and decreases exports, causing aggregate purchases to decline.

8.

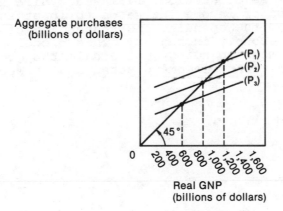

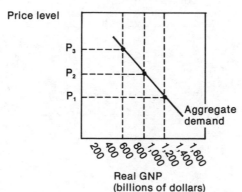

Self-Test for Mastery

1. d 2. d 3. d 4. b 5. d 6. d 7. a 8. d 9. c 10. e 11. d 12. d 13. d 14. e 15. a 16. a 17. c 18. d

Think it Through

1.   If exports fall, net exports and aggregate purchases will decline. As aggregate spending declines relative to the current level of real GNP, unintended inventory investment increases. Businesses will eventually reduce the rate of production, causing real GNP to fall. As long as real GNP exceeds aggregate purchases, unintended inventory investment will be positive putting downward pressure on real GNP. Real GNP will fall to a lower equilibrium level where aggregate production and aggregate purchases are equal and unintended inventory investment is zero.

2.   If because of an optimistic outlook regarding future sales businesses revise upward their expected marginal real returns to investments, the expected marginal returns will exceed the prevailing real interest rate, causing profit-maximizing firms to increase planned investment. This will cause an autonomous increase in aggregate purchases, which in turn will produce a multiple increase in real GNP assuming that the economy initially was in equilibrium at less than full employment. If the economy was initially at full employment, the increase in planned investment will cause an inflationary gap.

3.   An increase in autonomous expenditures causes an equal increase in output and income. Businesses produce output to meet increases in spending, and households receive income for supplying inputs to the industry experiencing the autonomous spending. Input suppliers save a portion of the new disposable income and spend a portion. But when they spend, they create a demand for goods and services, which causes the producers of those items to increase production. In order to increase production, firms must hire additional inputs, providing another round of income increases to input suppliers. The multiplier process results from the spending and respending of income. At each round, output produced by the economy increases. This process continues until the initial increase in autonomous spending just equals the growth of saving. At this point, there is no additional income created and consequently no growth in spending or production.

A Complete Keynesian Model

IN BRIEF: APPENDIX SUMMARY

Fill in the blanks to summarize appendix content.

The complete Keynesian model considers aggregate purchases to be the sum of C + Ip + G + NE. Consumption, C, is a function of disposable income. In determining disposable income, DI, a net tax function is employed where net taxes collected equal the marginal tax rate times the level of (1)_____ (consumption, income). The (2)_____ (average, marginal) tax rate is the fraction of each extra dollar of income earned in a nation that is collected as taxes. Planned investment, Ip, and government purchases, G, are treated as autonomous variables. The net exports function, NE, is an/a (3)_____ (inverse, positive) function of income. Specifically, NE = exports - imports where imports are a (4)_____ (negative, positive) function of income. Thus as national income rises, imports rise relative to exports, causing net exports to (5)_____ (rise, fall).

A condition for economic equilibrium is that aggregate purchases equal aggregate production.

$$\text{Aggregate purchases} = C + Ip + G + (E - M)$$
$$\text{Aggregate production} = Y = C + S + T$$

Setting aggregate production equal to aggregate purchases and simplifying yields:

$$(E - M) + (G - T) = S - Ip$$

The sum of the foreign trade balance and the government budget balance must equal the difference between saving and planned investment. This can be alternatively stated as:

$$\text{Balance of trade deficit} = S - (Ip + \text{budget deficit})$$

If a nation has a balance of trade deficit, domestic saving (6)_____ (falls short of, exceeds) the sum of planned investment purchases and the budget deficit.

In order to algebraically solve for the equilibrium level of real GNP and the multiplier, the individual functions for the components of aggregate purchases must be summed to obtain the aggregate purchases function. This is then set equal to the level of aggregate production, Y, and solved for Y--the equilibrium level of real GNP. The collection of coefficients preceding autonomous C, Ip, G, and E are the multipliers pertaining to each component.

$$Y = C + Ip + G + NE$$
$$Y = A + MPC[(1 - t)]Y + Ip + G + [E - MPI(Y)]$$
$$Y = [1/(1 - MRR)]A + [1/(1 - MRR)]Ip + [1/(1 - MRR)]G + [1/(1 - MRR)]E$$
$$\text{where } MRR = [MPC(1 - t) - MPI]$$

A change in planned investment, for instance, would change real GNP by
[1/(1 - MRR)] times the change in (7)_____ (planned investment, real
GNP).

VOCABULARY REVIEW

Write the key term from the list below next to its definition.

Key Terms

Marginal tax rate   Balance of trade deficit

Definitions

1. _____: prevails when expenditures on imported products
over the year exceed receipts by domestic firms from sales of exports.

2. _____: the fraction of each extra dollar of income
earned in a nation that is collected as taxes.

SKILLS REVIEW

Answer questions 1, 2, and 3 given the values below.

    A = $300 billion, Ip = $400 billion, G = $500,
    E = $200, MPC = .9, t = .3, MPI = .15

1. MRR = _____
    Multiplier = _____
    Equilibrium real GNP = $_____

2. If the marginal tax rate, t, is reduced to .2, what is the impact on real
    GNP? Real GNP _____ from $_____ to $_____.

3. If the international value of the dollar falls relative to the values of
    foreign currencies, exports rise. If exports rise by $50 billion, by how
    much will equilibrium income change? (Assume t = .2.) $_____

SELF-TEST FOR MASTERY

Select the best answer.

1. The fraction of each extra dollar of income earned in a nation that is
    collected as taxes is called:

    a.   Net taxes.
    b.   Average tax rate.
    c.   Marginal tax rate.
    d.   Marginal income.

2. In the complete Keynesian model, which of the following represents the consumption function?

   a. $C = A - (MPC)Y$
   b. $C = A + (MPC - t)Y$
   c. $C = MPC - A(1 - t)Y$
   d. $C = A - MPC[(1 - t)]Y$

3. In the complete Keynesian model, the multiplier is expressed as:

   a. $1/MPC$
   b. $1/(1 - MPS)$
   c. $1/(MRR - 1)$
   d. $1/(1 + MRR)$
   e. $1/\{1 - [MPC(1 - t) - MPI]\}$

4. The equilibrium condition can be expressed to yield an implication regarding a nation running a balance of trade deficit. Which of the following is a statement of that implication?

   a. Real GNP is always larger given balance of trade deficits.
   b. A balance of trade deficit implies that planned investment and the budget deficit exceed saving.
   c. A balance of trade deficit implies that domestic saving falls short of the sum of planned investment purchases and the budget deficit.
   d. None of the above.

CHAPTER APPENDIX ANSWERS

In Brief: Appendix Summary

1. Income 2. Marginal 3. Inverse 4. Positive 5. Fall 6. Falls short of
7. Planned investment

Vocabulary Review

1. Balance of trade deficit 2. Marginal tax rate

Skills Review

1. .48, 1.923, $2,692.3 billion

2. Increases, $2,692.3 billion, $3,255.8 billion

3. +$116.28 billion

Self-Test for Mastery

1. c 2. d 3. e 4. c

14

Aggregate Supply: Its Influence on Macroeconomic Equilibrium and Economic Growth

CHAPTER CHALLENGES

After studying your text, attending class, and completing this chapter, you should be able to:

1. Understand why an increase in aggregate demand can cause the price level to increase even when the economy is operating at a level below full employment.
2. Explain how a wage-price spiral and stagflation can result when an economy overheats.
3. Use aggregate demand and supply analysis to show how an unfavorable supply-side shock can cause a recession and put upward pressure on the price level, thus causing a period of stagflation.
4. Show how an increase in aggregate supply has favorable effects on macroeconomic equilibrium by putting upward pressure on real GNP while at the same time putting downward pressure on the price level.
5. Discuss long-term influences on aggregate supply and explain the economy's long-run aggregate supply curve.
6. Discuss the sources and importance of economic growth as well as its benefits and costs.

IN BRIEF: CHAPTER SUMMARY

Fill in the blanks to summarize chapter content.

If a nation's aggregate supply curve is upward sloping, increases in aggregate demand increase both real GNP and the price level. The rate of increase in the price level is likely to (1)_____ (increase, remain the same) as the economy approaches potential real GNP. If increases in aggregate demand cause an inflationary GNP gap, rising prices eventually will induce labor and other input suppliers to demand higher wages and resource prices to compensate for the loss in purchasing power due to the price level increase. This shifts the aggregate supply curve (2)_____ (rightward, leftward), thus returning the economy to (3)_____ (its potential, a recessionary) level of real GNP. But this results in still higher prices. A wage-price spiral will occur if further increases in aggregate demand take place.

(4)_____ (Expansion, Stagflation) results when the aggregate supply curve shifts to the left. Unemployment is rising while the price level is rising. If workers begin to anticipate continued increases in inflation, they ask for even higher wages, shifting the aggregate supply curve (5)_____ (rightward, leftward) by an even larger amount. Prices can be rising even when unemployment falls below the natural rate of unemployment. Stagflation can also result from (6)_____ (adverse, favorable) supply-side shocks such as sharp increases in the cost of resources that shift the aggregate supply curve leftward. But (7)_____ (adverse, favorable) supply-side shocks such as the decline in oil prices in 1986 have just the opposite effect, shifting the aggregate supply curve rightward and putting downward pressure on the price level and increasing real GNP.

In the long run, as wages and other input prices adjust to the prevailing rate of inflation and assuming that there are no other forces influencing the level of real GNP, the economy will eventually return to its potential level of real GNP at the natural rate of unemployment. The (8)_____ (long-run aggregate supply, short-run aggregate demand) curve is vertical at the potential level of real GNP. In the long run, this curve will shift to the right due to (9)_____ (decreases, increases) in the quantity of resources available for use by the economy, (10)_____ (decreases, increases) in resource productivity, improvements in technology, and improvements in the efficiency with which inputs are used.

(11)_____ (Labor productivity, The quantity of labor supplied) is the key source of real GNP growth. It is influenced by the level of work experience, education, training, (12)_____ (the amount of profit, the amount of capital per worker), the age composition of the labor force, technological improvements, and improvements in managerial techniques. The growth of capital per worker is dependent on the rate of planned investment and the (13)_____ (stock market, rate of saving). According to the text, (14)_____ (two thirds, one half) of real GNP growth from 1929 to 1982 can be attributed to increases in labor productivity, with the remainder due to increases in the quantity of labor. The increases in (15)_____ (the quantity of labor supplied, labor productivity) are primarily due to improved technology and managerial techniques, increases in the quantity of capital, and improved education and training.

Over time, even though aggregate demand is subject to cyclical variation, it exhibits a long-term upward trend. But in the long run, aggregate supply increases as well. The increase in a nation's aggregate supply satisfies its rising aggregate demand, but also (16)_____ (increases, moderates) the rate at which prices rise.

VOCABULARY REVIEW

Write the key term from the list below next to its definition.

Key Terms

Wage-price spiral   Long-run aggregate supply curve
Stagflation   Productivity
Supply-side shock

Definitions

1. _____ : a measure of output per unit of input.

2. _____ : a sudden and unexpected shift of the aggregate supply curve.

3. _____ : exists when higher product prices result in higher wages, which in turn increase prices still further through a decrease in aggregate supply.

4. _____ : term coined to describe an economy in which real GNP stagnates at a given level or actually declines from one period to the next while inflation ensues at relatively high rates.

5. _____: shows the relationship between the aggregate quantity supplied and the price level that would be observed if nominal wages and other money prices were flexible enough to allow the classical self-correction mechanism to work.

SKILLS REVIEW

Concept: **Changes in aggregate demand and the price level**

1. The figure below shows an aggregate demand and supply model.

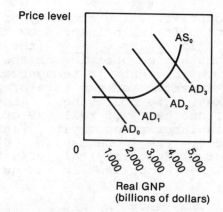

a. If potential real GNP equals $4000 billion, is the economy experiencing a recessionary or inflationary gap at ADo? _____ Equilibrium real GNP = $_____

b. If an increase in aggregate demand shifts the AD curve from ADo to AD1, the price level will _____ and the level of real GNP will _____.

c. If demand increases from AD1 to AD2, the price level _____ and the level of real GNP _____.

d. If aggregate demand increases from AD2 to AD3, the price level will _____ and the level of real GNP will _____.

Concept: Wage-price spiral and the long-run aggregate supply curve

2. Suppose the economy shown in the figure below is currently in equilibrium at its potential level of real GNP.

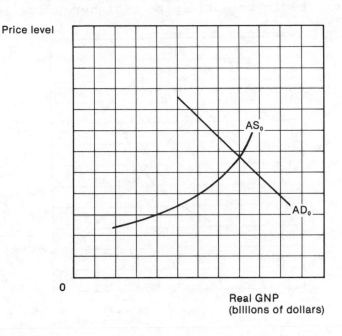

a. On the figure above, show a new aggregate demand curve reflecting an increase in demand and label it AD1. The price level _____ while real GNP _____. Identify the new price level and level of real GNP on the figure above.

b. Eventually, workers and other input suppliers will react to the loss of purchasing power resulting from the increase in the price level by _____. Show the impact on the aggregate supply curve assuming that input suppliers have completely adjusted to the new price level and label the curve AS1. The price level _____ while the level of real GNP _____. Identify graphically the new equilibrium price and real GNP levels.

c. Suppose that aggregate demand increases again, shifting the AD curve from AD1 to AD2. Show graphically and identify the new price level and level of real GNP. Workers will again eventually respond by _____, which causes the AS curve to shift _____. Show the new AS curve and label it AS2.

d. The process described above produces a _____-_____ spiral.

e. In the long run, when input suppliers have completely adjusted to the price level, the equilibrium level of real GNP equals _____. Find the long-run aggregate supply curve in the figure above and label it AS3. The long-run aggregate supply curve is (upward sloping, vertical).

Concept: Stagflation, price expectations, and supply-side shocks

3. The figure below shows an economy at its potential level of real GNP.
    Assume that this economy has been experiencing a wage-price spiral such
    that input suppliers begin to anticipate a higher price level.

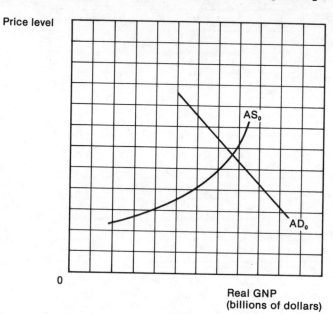

Price level

AS₀

AD₀

0

Real GNP
(billions of dollars)

a. Show on the figure above, what happens to the aggregate supply curve
    when workers begin to anticipate higher prices. Label the new AS
    curve AS1. Real GNP _____, and the price level _____.
b. Given the aggregate demand curve and the new AS curve, AS1, assume
    that an oil price shock occurs. Show the effect on the AS curve.
    Label the new AS curve AS2. The oil price shock is known as a
    _____. Equilibrium real GNP _____ while the price level
    _____.
c. Rising price-level expectations and adverse supply-side shocks
    produce the dual incidence of _____ and _____, which is
    otherwise known as _____.

Concept: Economic growth and the aggregate supply and demand model

4. List four influences that shift the aggregate supply curve rightward.

    a. _____
    b. _____
    c. _____
    d. _____

202

5.   In the United States, aggregate demand and aggregate supply have both
     exhibited a long-term increase. Because of downward wage-price rigidity
     or the sluggishness with which prices and wages fall, the price level over
     the long run has increased. In a in the figure below, show this process
     of economic growth. In b in the figure, show this process of economic
     growth.

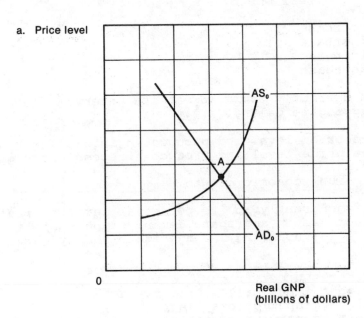

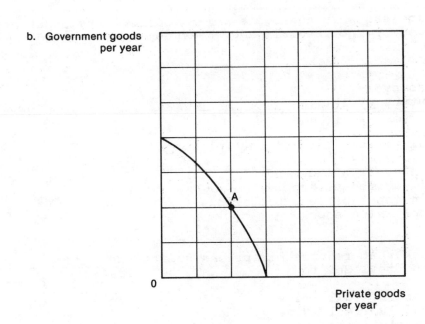

SELF-TEST FOR MASTERY

Select the best answer.

1.   For an economy operating on the upward sloping portion of the aggregate
     supply curve, an increase in aggregate demand will _____ the price
     level and _____ real GNP.

     a.   Increase, decrease
     b.   Increase, increase
     c.   Decrease, increase
     d.   Decrease, decrease

2.   If an economy is currently operating at its potential level of real GNP,
     an increase in aggregate demand will:

     a.   Increase the price level and produce an inflationary gap.
     b.   Decrease the price level and produce a recessionary gap.
     c.   Cause stagflation.
     d.   Produce long-run economic growth.

3.   When an economy is currently at its potential level of real GNP and
     experiences an increase in aggregate demand, input suppliers will
     eventually _____, causing the aggregate supply curve to shift
     _____.

     a.   Withdraw from resource markets, leftward
     b.   Press for higher input prices, rightward
     c.   Press for higher input prices, leftward
     d.   Increase the productivity of their resources, rightward

4.   The process of increases in aggregate demand followed by input price
     pressures followed by increases in aggregate demand is called:

     a.   A recession.
     b.   Stagflation.
     c.   The business cycle.
     d.   The real output cycle.
     e.   A wage-price spiral.

5.   Stagflation results from which of the following?

     a.   Increases in aggregate demand
     b.   Increases in aggregate supply
     c.   Increases in input price expectations
     d.   Adverse supply-side shocks
     e.   C and d

6.   An oil price shock that reduces oil prices shifts the _____ curve
     rightward, causing real GNP to _____ and the price level to_____.

     a.   Aggregate demand, fall, rise
     b.   Aggregate supply, fall, rise
     c.   Aggregate supply, rise, rise
     d.   Aggregate supply, rise, fall
     e.   Aggregate demand, rise, fall

7.   An adverse supply-side shock shifts the aggregate supply curve _____ causing real GNP to _____ and the price level to _____.

     a.   Leftward, fall, rise
     b.   Rightward, fall, rise
     c.   Leftward, rise, fall
     d.   Rightward, rise, fall
     e.   Leftward, fall, fall

8.   Which of the following increases potential real GNP over the long run?

     a.   An increase in demand
     b.   Inflation
     c.   Government spending
     d.   Consumption
     e.   None of the above

9.   Which of the following shift the long-run aggregate supply curve rightward?

     a.   Increases in the quantity of resources available to a nation
     b.   Increases in the productivity of productive resources
     c.   Improvements in technology
     d.   Improvements in the efficiency with which resources are used
     e.   All of the above

10. The long-run aggregate supply curve is:

     a.   Upward sloping.
     b.   Horizontal.
     c.   Downward sloping.
     d.   Vertical.

11. Which of the following is a key to the process of economic growth?

     a.   Improvements in labor productivity
     b.   Increases in the stock of resources
     c.   Increases in the money supply
     d.   Reducing the federal budget deficit

12. In order of importance, what factors are responsible for the growth in labor productivity in the United States from 1929 to 1982?

     a.   Improvements in education, increases in the amount of capital per worker, increases in investment spending
     b.   Increases in the capital stock, saving, cuts in income tax rates
     c.   Improvements in technology and management, increases in the amount of capital per worker, improvements in education and training
     d.   Saving and investment, technological improvements, increases in the quantity of labor and other resources

13. An increase in saving reduces _____ in the short run but if it is invested in physical and human capital over the long run, the level of potential real GNP will _____.

     a.   Aggregate supply, decrease
     b.   Aggregate supply, increase
     c.   Aggregate demand, decrease
     d.   Consumption, increase

14. In a growing economy, both _____ and _____ increase, but because prices do not fall as quickly or easily as they rise, the general price level over the long run _____.

    a. Aggregate demand, aggregate supply, falls
    b. Aggregate supply, unemployment, falls
    c. Inflation, unemployment, rises
    d. Aggregate demand, aggregate supply, rises

15. Supply-side shifts in the aggregate supply curve resulting from economic growth serve to:

    a. Increase inflation.
    b. Reduce the price level over time.
    c. Moderate inflation resulting from shifts in the aggregate demand curve.
    d. Increase real GNP beyond the level possible by shifts in the aggregate demand curve alone.
    e. C and d.

THINK IT THROUGH

1. Assume that an adverse-side supply shock occurs. Discuss the effects of the supply-side shock. Suppose that workers increase their expectations of inflation at the same time that the supply-side shock is occurring. Discuss the likely effects.

2. Why is the long-run aggregate supply curve independent of shifts in the aggregate demand curve?

3. Assume that the United States imports copper, which is used widely in business and industry. Discuss the effects on the U.S. economy of a major reduction in the world price of copper.

POP QUIZ   Read the news brief at the end of this chapter and answer the following questions.

1. In June of 1988 the economy appeared to be operating on what point of its aggregate supply curve?
2. Approximately what level of capacity utilization is consistent with the economy's potential level of real GNP?
3. If the economy continues to experience increases in aggregate demand, what are the likely consequences?

CHAPTER ANSWERS

In Brief: Chapter Summary

1. Increase 2. Leftward 3. Its potential 4. Stagflation 5. Leftward 6. Adverse 7. Favorable 8. Long-run aggregate supply 9. Increases 10. Increases 11. Labor productivity 12. The amount of capital per worker 13. Rate of saving 14. Two thirds 15. Labor productivity 16. Moderates

Vocabulary Review

1. Productivity 2. Supply-side shock 3. Wage-price spiral 4. Stagflation 5. Long-run aggregate supply curve

Skills Review

1. a.   Recessionary gap; $1,000 billion
   b.   Not change, increase
   c.   Increases, increases
   d.   Increase more rapidly, increase

2. a.

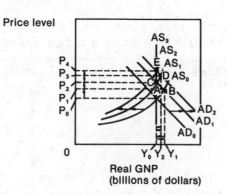

Price level

Real GNP
(billions of dollars)

Increases, increases
   b.   Pressing for higher wages and other input prices; increases, falls back to its potential level of real GNP
   c.   Pressing for higher wages; leftward
   d.   Wage, price
   e.   The potential level of real GNP; vertical

3. a.

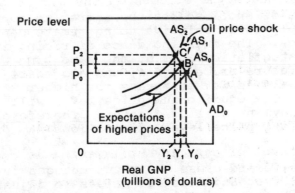

Price level

Real GNP
(billions of dollars)

Decreases, increases
   b.   Supply-side shock; falls, increases
   c.   Rising unemployment and rising inflation; stagflation

4. a.   Increases in the quantity of resources available to a nation
   b.   Increases in resource productivity
   c.   Improved technology and managerial techniques
   d.   Improvements in the efficiency with which resources are used

207

5.

Price level

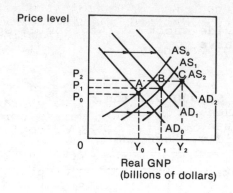

Real GNP
(billions of dollars)

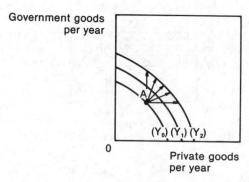

Self-Test for Mastery

1. b 2. a 3. c 4. e 5. e 6. d 7. a 8. e 9. e 10. d 11. a 12. c 13. d 14. d 15. e

Think it Through

1.   An adverse supply-side shock shifts the aggregate supply curve to the left. As aggregate supply falls relative to aggregate demand, real GNP falls and the price level rises. The dual incidence of rising inflation and rising unemployment is called stagflation. If at the same time workers have expectations of higher future price levels, the aggregate supply curve will shift even further leftward as workers press for higher wages to offset the expected higher prices. The equilibrium price level will increase even more, and the extent of unemployment will be greater. Therefore adverse supply-side shocks combined with rising price level expectations may produce a serious stagflation.

2.   Shifts in aggregate demand cause short-run changes in real GNP, but if given enough time for product and resource prices to adjust completely, the economy will return to its potential level of real GNP. For instance, if an increase in aggregate demand causes inflation, workers and other resource suppliers will in time push for higher wages and resource prices. Businesses either will require higher product prices to cover the increases in resource prices or they will reduce output at given prices. Either way, the aggregate supply curve shifts leftward and real GNP returns to its potential level in the long run. The long-run aggregate supply curve is vertical at the potential level of real GNP. Only supply-side influences such as the quantity and productivity of resources can shift the long-run aggregate supply curve rightward.

3.   A major reduction in the world price of copper is an example of a favorable supply-side shock. Businesses increase output because the

profitability of producing goods has increased at given price levels. The aggregate supply curve shifts rightward, putting downward pressure on the price level and increasing real GNP. In this case, a falling price level and unemployment rate occur simultaneously.

Pop Quiz

1.   As of June 1988, the economy appeared to be operating at its potential level of real GNP. The economy's aggregate demand curve intersected its aggregate supply curve at the potential level of real GNP.

2.   The level of economic activity beyond which inflation is likely to accelerate is a level of capacity utilization of about 82% to 83%.

3.   If the economy continues to experience growth in aggregate demand, capacity utilization could reach 84% by the end of 1988. This level has indicated the beginning of considerable inflationary pressures in past expansions. Investment in capacity is occurring at a brisk pace, but the aggregate supply curve will not shift to the right fast enough to moderate inflationary pressures.

The Outlook

As Output Climbs So Do Capacity Fears

NEW YORK

The two developments, we suspect, aren't entirely unrelated. The remarkable American economy is cruising through its 70th straight month of expansion, a record for peacetime. And the cruise-control mechanism on our family's 1986 Ford Taurus station wagon remains inoperable, cruising nowhere while we await a part ordered many, many weeks ago.

There's no sure way to ascertain just how typical such experiences may be for car owners, or for that matter for owners of all sorts of other items. But evidence keeps mounting of strain on the economy's physical ability to meet demand. And the pattern sends a troubling message about the economy's possible behavior in coming months.

It suggests an environment where business activity, as it continues to gain momentum, will come under increasing difficulty, marked not only by parts shortages but dislocations ranging from costly production bottlenecks to accelerating price increases.

Early indications of such an environment can already be detected, among other places, in the fine print of this month's report of the National Association of Purchasing Management, which regularly polls more than 250 buyers at major corporations. It finds that 20 industrial products are in short supply, up from 18 in July. The scarce products include such diverse items as aluminum, paperboard, methanol and titanium dioxide.

Not surprisingly, the survey also shows that far more companies are experiencing lengthening delivery delays than prompter service, an imbalance that has prevailed now for nearly two years. The survey also lists 35 products whose prices are rising, up from 29 in July. Only one item, fuel oil, shows a drop in price.

The survey isn't so finely focused as to pinpoint the status of cruise-control parts at Ford Motor Co. However, as recently reported in this paper, Ford's car and truck assembly plants are running at capacity, with some 20% of the vehicles sold last quarter produced on overtime shifts, and the firm is weighing building new plants.

Not all manufacturers, to be sure, are keeping as busy as Ford. But there seems little question that capacity usage in general is on the rise. Indeed, it appears to be approaching levels that in the past have usually signaled the onset of strained business operations. In June, the latest month available, U.S. industry as a whole—factories, mines and utilities—used 83.1% of its capacity, after adjustment for seasonal factors. This was up from 82.9% in May and marked the highest monthly rate of operations in more than eight years.

With such a level of operations, "it seems prudent to assume that the economy has started to overheat somewhat," declares Edward S. Hyman Jr., chief economist of C. J. Lawrence, Morgan Grenfell Inc. "From here," he adds, even modest economic growth "will increase these overheating pressures."

Of course, a rapid increase in capacity would presumably serve to prevent any such pressure buildup. But as Richard B. Hoey, chief economist of Drexel Burnham Lambert Inc., remarks, increases in capacity "unfortunately are likely to be too little and too late to head off a progressive tightening of capacity utilization." He foresees, as a result, an acceleration of inflation typical of the "final stages" of a business-cycle upswing.

Parenthetically, it should be noted that economists at Goldman, Sachs & Co. estimate that plant-and-equipment outlays, adjusted for inflation, will climb a robust 8% or 9% this year, which suggests to some analysts an easing of capacity constraints. Lawrence A. Kudlow, chief economist of Bear, Stearns & Co., says that, with capital outlays "hitting new record highs, capacity worries look increasingly unrealistic."

But Mr. Hoey cautions that "a capacity boom isn't guaranteed by the investment boom." Indeed, he notes that most new spending is "for replacement purposes and has only limited benefit for capacity levels." He adds that "many of the larger plant expansions currently under way are unlikely to be fully operational until late 1989 or 1990, too late to ameliorate price pressures in the next 18 months."

A similar assessment comes from Donald H. Straszheim, chief economist of Merrill Lynch & Co., who feels that "despite a pickup in capital spending, capacity growth will continue to lag behind gains in production." By late this year, he estimates, "capacity utilization could exceed 84%," a level, he recalls, that in earlier expansions marked the onset of substantial inflationary pressure.

The record hardly encourages the hope that the current spending surge will translate rapidly and effectively into expanded production facilities. In a recent 12 months, while capital spending rose sharply, capacity edged up less than 3%. The strongest spending increases, moreover, continue to come in outlays for new equipment, which often involves replacement rather than expansion. Spending for structures, brick-and-mortar projects that are more apt to boost capacity, remains relatively weak.

Most economists, it should be added, regard capacity statistics, which the Federal Reserve Board assembles, as woefully imprecise, and Fed officials offer no ready remedy. So no one can be very certain just how much—or how little—elbowroom really does exist in the economy right now. But we do know that our cruise-control unit still needs a part.

—ALFRED L. MALABRE JR.

210

15

The Functions of Money

CHAPTER CHALLENGES

After studying your text, attending class, and completing this chapter, you should be able to:

1. List the four major functions of money.
2. Discuss the major components of the stock of money.
3. Explain the concept of near money and the official measures of the U.S. money stock and liquid assets held by the public.
4. Discuss the determinants of the demand for money.
5. Explain how, given the demand for money, changes in the stock of money influence interest rates and spending decisions.
6. Explain how, given the stock of money, changes in the demand for money can affect interest rates.

IN BRIEF: CHAPTER SUMMARY

Fill in the blanks to summarize chapter content.

In order to understand the operation of the macroeconomy, it is necessary to understand the role of money. But first it is necessary to define money, identify its functions, consider operational measures of money, and explain how changes in the demand for and supply of money affect interest rates and spending in the economy.

Money is defined according to its functions. Money serves as a medium of (1)_____(exchange, value), a standard of value, a standard of deferred payment, and a store of (2)_____ (exchange, value). Anything performing these functions is money. Money does not have to have intrinsic value such as (3)_____(fiat, commodity) money in order to perform these functions. Fiat money and checkable deposits are considered money not because they have intrinsic value, but because they are accepted as a medium of exchange and fulfill the other functions of money. Bonds and credit cards are (4)_____(not, also) money. Money is an asset--a store of value. Even though credit cards can be used as a medium to facilitate exchange, a liability or debt is incurred when credit cards are used.

Three of the official definitions of money are M1, M2, and M3. M1 is the sum of (5)_____(checkable, savings) deposits, currency, and traveler's checks held by the public on a given day. M2 is the sum of M1 and near monies. Near monies are assets that can easily be converted to money because they can be liquidated easily, quickly, and at little cost. M3 is the sum of M2 and (6)_____(small-, large-) denomination certificates of deposit.

Individuals and businesses hold money for two reasons: to carry out transactions in the economy and because money is an asset. Modern economies require a medium of exchange to facilitate transactions. As an economy experiences growth in nominal GNP, the number and volume of transactions increase, causing the transaction demand for money to (7)_____(increase, decrease). The degree to which receipts and payments are synchronized also affects the need for transaction money balances. In addition, expectations of future interest rates will affect the desire to hold transaction money balances because interest rates influence the (8)_____(liquidity, opportunity cost) of holding money.

Money, like other assets, has certain characteristics that make it more or less attractive to hold relative to other financial assets. Money is held as an asset not because of its income, return, or yield, but because it is (9)_____(totally riskless, liquid). Because individuals and businesses have a (10)_____ (hedging, precautionary) and speculative motive for holding money, liquidity is required to satisfy these motives. Expectations of future interest rates and bond prices affect the desire to hold money relative to other assets. Even expectations of future rates of inflation affect the desirability of holding money as an asset.

The total demand for money is the sum of the transaction and asset demands for money. The quantity of money demanded varies (11)_____(inversely, directly) with the interest rate. Higher interest rates (12)_____(decrease, increase) the opportunity cost of holding money and therefore reduce the quantity of money demanded and vice versa. The factors mentioned above that influence either the transaction or asset demand for money will affect the total demand for money. The money demand curve is (13)_____(upward sloping, downward sloping), but will shift to the right or left depending upon changes in the noninterest rate determinants of money demand, which include (a) the degree to which receipts and payments are synchronized, (b) expectations of future interest rates, stock and bond prices, and rates of inflation, and (c) the level of nominal GNP.

The interest rate is determined by the supply of and demand for loanable funds. A change in the stock of money or demand for money influences the market rate of interest. A change in the interest rate in turn influences the level of spending in the economy and GNP. For instance, given the demand for money, an increase in the supply of money will create a (14)_____(surplus, shortage) of money at the current rate of interest. Since (15)_____(more, less) money is on hand than is desired for transactions or as assets, saving and the buying of bonds are likely to (16)_____(decrease, increase). This (17)_____(decreases, increases) the supply of loanable funds resulting in an/a (18)_____ (increase, decrease) in the interest rate. Interest rates must (19)_____(fall, rise) in order to increase the quantity of money demanded to equal the higher level of the money stock. Likewise, a decline in the money stock (20)_____ (increases, decreases) the interest rate.

Given the stock of money, a change in the demand for money will create either a shortage or a surplus of money at the current market rate of interest, causing the loanable funds market to be influenced such that interest rates change in the direction necessary to once again equate the supply of and demand for money. Changes in the interest rate affect interest-sensitive expenditures and thus the level of aggregate demand and GNP.

VOCABULARY REVIEW

Write the key term from the list below next to its definition.

Key Terms

Money
Commodity money
Fiat money
Checkable deposits
Commercial banks
Saving and loan associations
Mutual savings banks
Credit unions
Bonds

M1
Near monies
M2
Time deposits
M3
Transaction demand for money
Demand for money
Money demand curve
Change in money demanded

Definitions

1. _____: money that is accepted as a medium of exchange because of government decree rather than because of its intrinsic value as a commodity.

2. _____: depository institutions whose depositors are called "members" and belong to a particular organization such as a business firm or government; they make loans only to their members for the purpose of financing homes or personal goods and services.

3. _____: assets that are easily converted to money because they can be liquidated at low cost and little risk of loss.

4. _____: the sum of M2 and large-denomination certificates of deposit.

5. _____: the sum of money people wish to hold per day as a convenience in paying their bills.

6. _____: shows a relationship between the level of interest rates in the economy and the stock of money demanded at a given point in time.

7. _____: a change in the relationship between the level of interest rates and the stock of money demanded in the economy caused by a change in economic conditions.

8. _____: an item that serves the functions of money but also has value in uses other than as the medium of exchange.

9. _____: depository institutions operating in some states that are similar to savings and loan associations in that they primarily attract savings deposits and in the past have specialized in making mortgage loans; they are also owned by their depositors.

10. _____: the stock of money measured by the sum of currency, traveler's checks, and checkable deposits held by the public on a particular day of the year in the United States.

11. _____: interest-bearing accounts at commercial banks and thrift institutions for which the bank can legally request a 30-day notice before paying out the funds.

12. _____: the relationship between the sums of money people willingly hold and the level of interest rates in the economy given all other influences on the desirability of holding money instead of other assets.

13. _____: anything that is generally accepted as payment for goods or services; also serves as a standard of value, a standard of deferred payment, and a store of value.

14. _____: depository institutions that acquire funds chiefly through attracting savings deposits and have in the past specialized in making mortgage loans.

15. _____: securities issued by corporations and governments representing the promise to make periodic payments of interest and repay a debt of borrowed funds at a certain time.

16. _____: the sum of M1 and certain near monies; a measure of liquid assets held by the public.

17. _____: firms that acquire funds by accepting checkable deposits and savings deposits of households and business firms and use these funds to make loans for a wide variety of purposes.

18. _____: represents money deposited in bank accounts that can be used to write checks that are accepted to pay debts, or that can easily be converted to currency.

SKILLS REVIEW

Concept: **Functions of money**

1. List four functions of money.

    a. _____
    b. _____
    c. _____
    d. _____

Concept: **Definitions of money; measures of money**

2. Using the items given below, define M1, M2, and M3.

    Currency held by the public
    Money market mutual funds
    Money market deposit accounts
    Traveler's checks held by the public
    Checkable deposits held by the public
    Large-denomination certificates of deposit
    Savings accounts, small-denomination certificates of deposit, and
        certain other near monies

    a. M1 = _____

    b. M2 = _____
            _____

    c. M3 = _____
            _____
            _____

d. Near monies = _____
_____

e. Silver dollars are examples of _____ money.

f. Federal Reserve Notes are examples of _____ money.

g. Why are credit cards not considered money?

Concept: Determinants of the demand for money; money demand curve

3. a. List and discuss three factors that influence the transaction demand for money.

    (1) _____
    (2) _____
    (3) _____

   b. List and discuss three factors that influence the asset demand for money.

    (1) _____
    (2) _____
    (3) _____

4. The data below show the relationship between the quantity of money demanded and the nominal interest rate holding all other influences unchanged.

Quantity of Money Demanded per Day ($ billions)			Interest Rate (%)
(a)	(b)	(c)	(d)
$ 740			12%
760			11
780			10
800			9
820			8
840			7

a.   Plot the money demand curve on the diagram below.

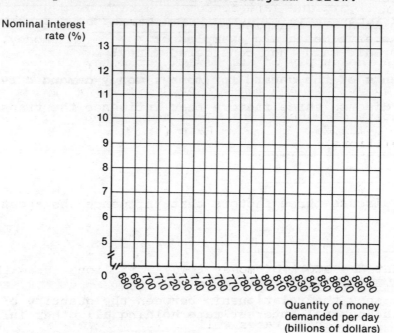

Nominal interest rate (%)

Quantity of money demanded per day (billions of dollars)

b.   Why is the money demand curve downward sloping?
c.   List the factors that shift the money demand curve.
     (1)   _____
     (2)   _____
     (3)   _____
d.   Assume that the data above are for a level of nominal GNP of $4 trillion. Assume nominal GNP increases by $40 billion at each interest rate.
     (1)   Complete column b in the table above.
     (2)   Plot the new money demand curve on the figure above. The money demand curve has shifted _____.
e.   Assume again that the current money demand data are reflected in column a. Assume that expectations of higher future inflation reduce the desirability of holding money as an asset, causing the demand for money to decrease by $60 billion at each interest rate.
     (1)   Complete column c in the table above.
     (2)   Plot the new money demand curve on the figure above. The money demand curve has shifted _____.

5.   For each of the following, indicate whether the money demand curve will shift to the right or left.

     a.   Technology and new banking regulations allow employers to electronically deposit paychecks in employees' checkable deposit accounts, and the accounts are automatically drafted to pay the employees' fixed monthly payments such as mortgage payments._____
     b.   Merchants allow customers to use "debit" cards whereby the merchant can electronically transfer funds for a purchase from the customer's checkable deposit account to the merchant's account._____
     c.   Credit cards are used more frequently._____
     d.   Employers and consumers coordinate their payments and receipts such that paychecks are received and payments are due the first of each month._____
     e.   Nominal GNP increases._____

216

f. The price level increases._____
g. New highly liquid and safe financial assets become available earning
    a rate of interest in excess of that earned by checkable
    deposits._____

Concept: Changes in the supply of and demand for money

6. The data from question 4 above are reproduced below.

Quantity of Money Demanded ($ billions)			Interest Rate (%)
(a)	(b)	(c)	
$740			12%
760			11
780			10
800			9
820			8
840			7

a. Assume that the stock of money is $780 billion. Draw the money stock
    curve on the diagram above. The equilibrium rate of interest is
    _____%.
b. If the demand for money changes from that shown in column a to that
    in column b, interest rates will _____ to _____%.
c. If the demand for money changes from that shown in column a to that
    in column c, interest rates will _____ to _____%.
d. On the diagrams below:
    (1) Show the effect of an increase in the stock of money.
         Interest rates _____.
    (2) Show the effect of a decrease in the stock of money.
         Interest rates _____.
    (3) Show the effect of an increase in both the demand for and
         supply of money by the same amount. Interest rates
         _____.

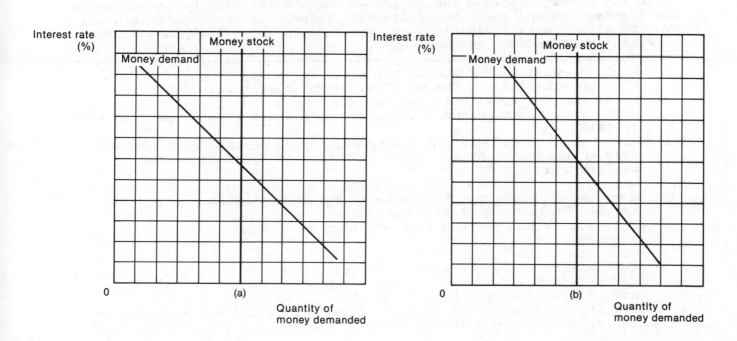

217

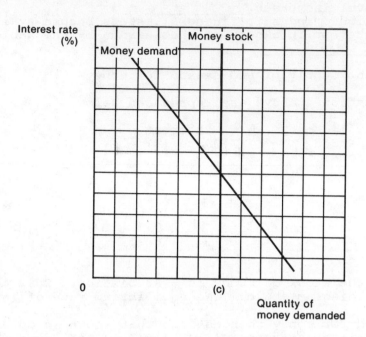

Interest rate (%)

Money demand

Money stock

0

(c)

Quantity of money demanded

7. <u>Advanced Question</u> Let the supply of and demand for money be given by the equations below.

MT = a - bR
MA = c - dR
MS = M1

where MT = transaction demand
MA = asset demand
MS = money stock
M1 = currency, checkable deposits, and traveler's checks held by the public
R = interest rate

Constants a and c reflect the impact of noninterest rate determinants on the transaction and asset money demands, respectively. Constants b and d are the slope terms indicating the magnitude of the effect that a change in R has on MT and MA, respectively.

a. Find an equation for the total demand for money, MD.
b. Find an equation for the equilibrium interest rate. (Hint: The condition for equilibrium is that MD = MS.)
c. Using your equation for R, discuss the factors that cause R to rise or fall.
d. Given the values below, plot MA, MT, and MD on the figure below. Draw in the money stock curve. Identify on the diagram the equilibrium rate of interest.

a = $800 billion   b = $10 billion   c = $400 billion
d = $40 billion   M1 = $850 billion

218

Interest rate
(%)

18
16
14
12
10
8
6
4
2
0

100 200 300 400 500 600 700 800 900 1,000 1,100 1,200 1,300

Quantity of
money demaned
(billions of dollars)

SELF-TEST FOR MASTERY

Select the best answer.

1. Money allows dissimilar goods and services to be valued according to a single common denominator--a nation's basic monetary unit, such as the dollar. Which of the following represent this function?

   a. Medium of exchange
   b. Store of value
   c. Standard of value
   d. Standard of deferred payment

2. Money is an asset. Which of the following represents this function?

   a. Medium of exchange
   b. Store of value
   c. Standard of value
   d. Standard of deferred payment

3. _____ money has value in exchange and intrinsic value in nonmoney uses.

   a. Fiat
   b. Commodity
   c. Valuable
   d. All

4. Money that, by government decree must be accepted in exchange and for the payment of debt is known as:

   a. Fiat money.
   b. Commodity money.

    c.   Demand deposits.
    d.   Gold.

5.   One function of money that credit cards are unable to fulfill is:

    a.   The medium of exchange function.
    b.   The store of value function.
    c.   The standard of value function.
    d.   The standard of deferred payment function.

6.   The sum of currency, traveler's checks, and checkable deposits held by the public is known as:

    a.   M1.
    b.   M2.
    c.   M3.
    d.   L.

7.   The sum of currency, traveler's checks, checkable deposits, and certain near monies held by the public is known as:

    a.   M1.
    b.   M2.
    c.   M3.
    d.   L.

8.   _____ are assets that can easily be converted to money because they can be liquidated easily, quickly, and at little cost.

    a.   Large-denomination certificates of deposit
    b.   Near monies
    c.   Pension funds
    d.   Real estate

9.   Individuals and businesses hold money because:

    a.   Money is necessary to carry out transactions, and it is also an asset.
    b.   It is profitable to do so.
    c.   It must be used to make exchanges.
    d.   Nothing else can be used in a commercial transaction.

10.   Which of the following financial characteristics makes money attractive as an asset?

    a.   Liquidity
    b.   Return or yield
    c.   Risk
    d.   Availability

11.   A/An _____ in nominal GNP shifts the money demand curve _____.

    a.   Decrease, rightward
    b.   Increase, leftward
    c.   Decrease, leftward
    d.   Increase, rightward
    e.   C and d.

12. Which of the following will shift the money demand curve leftward?

   a. Payments and receipts become more synchronized.
   b. The price level declines.
   c. The level of nominal GNP decreases.
   d. All of the above.

13. The quantity of money demanded varies _____ with the nominal interest rate. Higher interest rates _____ the opportunity cost of holding money and therefore reduce the quantity of money demanded.

   a. Directly, reduce
   b. Inversely, increase
   c. Directly, increase
   d. Inversely, reduce

14. An increase in the stock of money creates a _____ of money at the current rate of interest. This in turn _____ the supply of loanable funds, which, given the demand for loanable funds, causes the market rate of interest to _____.

   a. Shortage, reduces, rise
   b. Shortage, reduces, fall
   c. Surplus, reduces, rise
   d. Surplus, increases, fall

15. A decrease in the stock of money causes interest rates to:

   a. Fall.
   b. Rise.
   c. Not change.
   d. None of the above.

16. If the demand for money and the stock of money increased by the same amount at each interest rate, interest rates would:

   a. Fall.
   b. Rise.
   c. Not change.
   d. None of the above.

17. If the demand for money decreases, interest rates will _____ and nominal GNP will _____.

   a. Fall, fall
   b. Rise, fall
   c. Fall, rise
   d. Rise, rise

THINK IT THROUGH

1. Can you think of any problems associated with the use of commodity money?

2. Why can't government bureaucrats simply make up their minds and select a single definition of money? Can you think of any reasons why are there several official definitions and why these definitions change over time?

3.   Why do individuals and businesses hold money? What factors influence the desirability of holding money?

4.   Suppose you are a producer of household appliances. Further assume that most appliance purchases are made on credit. You also have observed in the past that sales increase when nominal GNP increases. What would you predict for sales if you knew that the nation's central banking authorities were deliberately reducing the stock of money?

CHAPTER ANSWERS

In Brief: Chapter Summary

1. Exchange 2. Value 3. Commodity 4. Not 5. Checkable 6. Large- 7. Increase 8. Opportunity cost 9. Liquid 10. Precautionary 11. Inversely 12. Increase 13. Downward sloping 14. Surplus 15. More 16. Increase 17. Increases 18. Decrease 19. Fall 20. Increases

Vocabulary Review

1. Fiat money 2. Credit unions 3. Near monies 4. M3 5. Transaction demand for money 6. Money demand curve 7. Change in money demanded 8. Commodity money 9. Mutual savings banks 10. M1 11. Time deposits 12. Demand for money 13. Money 14. Savings and loan associations 15. Bonds 16. M2 17. Commercial banks 18. Checkable deposits

Skills Review

1.   a.   Medium of exchange
      b.   Store of value
      c.   Standard of value
      d.   Standard of deferred payment

2.   a.   M1 = currency + traveler's checks + checkable deposits held by the public.
      b.   M2 = M1 + money market mutual funds + money market deposit accounts + savings accounts, small-denomination certificates of deposit, and certain other near monies.
      c.   M3 = M2 + large-denomination certificates of deposit.
      d.   Near monies = money market mutual funds + money market deposit accounts + savings accounts, small-denomination certificates of deposit, and certain other near monies.
      e.   Commodity
      f.   Fiat
      g.   Money is an asset, whereas a liability or debt is incurred when credit cards are used. Credit cards do not satisfy the store of value function of money.

3.   a.   (1) Nominal GNP (2) Synchronization of receipts and payments
            (3) Interest rates
      b.   (1) Interest rates (2) Expectations of inflation
            (3) Expectations of interest rates and bond prices

4. a.

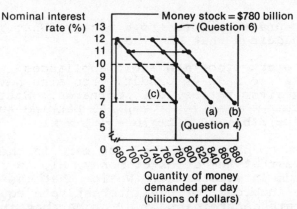

Nominal interest rate (%)

Money stock = $780 billion (Question 6)

(c)

(a) (b)
(Question 4)

Quantity of money demanded per day (billions of dollars)

b. The money demand curve is downward sloping because the nominal interest rate and the quantity of money demanded are inversely related. As interest rates rise, the opportunity cost of holding money increases, which reduces the desirability of holding noninterest-bearing or low interest-yielding assets such as money.

c. (1) Synchronization of receipts and payments (2) Changes in real GNP (3) Changes in the price level (4) Expectations of inflation, interest rates, and bond prices

d. (1) (2) Rightward   e. (1) (2) Leftward
    $780 $680
    800   700
    820   720
    840   740
    860   760
    880   780

5. a. Left b. Left c. Left d. Left e. Right f. Right g. Left

6. a. 10% b. Increase, 12% c. Decrease, 7%
d. (1) Decrease (2) Increase (3) Remain unchanged

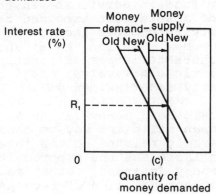

Interest rate (%)

Money supply
New Old

R_2

R_1

0   (b)

Quantity of money demanded

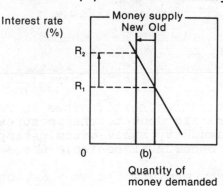

Interest rate (%)

Money supply
Old New

Money demand

R_1

R_2

0   (a)

Quantity of money demanded

Interest rate (%)

Money demand
Old New

Money supply
Old New

R_1

0   (c)

Quantity of money demanded

223

7. a. MD = MT + MA = (a + c) - (b + d)R
    b. Equilibrium requires that MD = MS

        M1 = (a + c) - (b + d)R

        Solving for R gives

        R = (a + c)/(b + d) - [1/(b + d)] x M1

    c. The negative sign preceding the last term in the interest rate
        equation shows that the stock of money, M1, is inversely related to
        the equilibrium interest rate. Notice that the shift terms, a and c,
        appear in the intercept of the interest rate equation. Any
        noninterest rate determinant of MT or MA that increases (a + c) will
        increase the interest rate. A change in one of these determinants
        that reduces (a + c) will reduce the interest rate. Likewise,
        changes in the slope of the transaction and asset money demand curves
        will change the interest rate.
    d. MT = 800 - 10R   MA = 400 - 40R   MD = 1200 - 50R
        R = 24 - (1/50)R

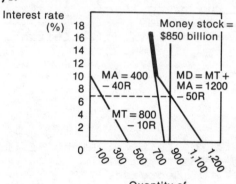

Self-Test for Mastery

1. c 2. b 3. b 4. a 5. b 6. a 7. b 8. b 9. a 10. a 11. e 12. d 13.
b 14. d 15. b 16. c 17. c

Think it Through

1. Besides being difficult or hazardous to transport, such as was the case
with gold and silver coins, commodity money often disappears from circulation
when the market value of the commodity rises above the exchange value of money.

2. As new financial instruments are created such as NOW accounts and money
market mutual funds, individuals in their own self-interest alter the
composition of assets that are used to meet liquidity, risk, and income needs.
Utility-maximizing choices lead us to use certain items to fulfill the
functions of money. As long as financial innovations continue to occur and as
long as the characteristics of assets change relative to one another, the money
stock will continue to evolve. As a result, the central banking authorities
must continually redefine money.

3. Individuals hold money (a) as an asset because it is liquid and (b)
because it is an efficient way to consummate transactions. The demand for
money is inversely related to the interest rate because an increase in the
interest rate increases the opportunity cost of holding money and reduces the
quantity of money demanded. Other factors that influence the demand for money
include the synchronization of receipts and payments, the level of real GNP,

the price level, and expectations of inflation, interest rates, and bond prices.

4.   If the money stock decreases, it is likely that, other things being equal, interest rates will rise, making credit more costly to your customers. Total spending and GNP will decrease due to the higher rates of interest. Two factors therefore indicate that household appliance sales will fall: higher interest rates making credit more expensive, and a decline in nominal GNP.

16

The Banking System

CHAPTER CHALLENGES

After studying your text, attending class, and completing this chapter, you should be able to:

1. Discuss the origins of banking and explain the concept of fractional reserve banking.
2. Examine bank balance sheets and show how the balance sheets are affected when the bank makes loans.
3. Show how multiple expansion of the money stock can result from an inflow of excess reserves into banks and calculate the reserve multiplier.
4. Discuss bank portfolio management practices.

IN BRIEF: CHAPTER SUMMARY

Fill in the blanks to summarize chapter content.

In order to understand the role of money and financial institutions in the economy, it is necessary first to understand how the activities of financial institutions influence the nation's stock of money. The goldsmiths of England and the moneychangers of Italy engaged in "banking" by accepting gold for safekeeping and issuing gold receipts. In time, the receipts began to trade as a medium of exchange or money. But these early bankers discovered that (1)_____(all of the, only a fraction of the) gold had to be held in reserve at any one time to honor redemption of the gold receipts. They could therefore make loans (2)_____(equal to, in excess of) the gold they had on hand. They did this by issuing additional gold receipts--they in essence created money. The fractional reserve banking that developed meant that the stock of money (3)_____ (must equal, could be larger than) the gold reserves upon which it was based.

In depository institutions today, only a fraction of the funds acquired through deposits have to be kept back as reserves. A bank's (4)_____ (total, required) reserves consist of cash and deposits held at a regional Federal Reserve Bank. But banks and other depository institutions that issue checkable deposits are required to keep reserves equal to between 3% and 12% of various deposit liabilities. A bank will balance profit, liquidity, and risk considerations in deciding the amount of (5)_____ (total, excess) reserves it desires to use to acquire income-producing assets such as loans and government securities. Excess reserves are the difference between total reserves and required reserves. While a depository institution does not have to use all of its excess reserves, it (6)_____(can, cannot) make loans or purchase securities in amounts greater than the amount it has as excess reserves. When a bank uses excess reserves to make a loan, new checkable deposits are created--money is created. Even if the borrower spends the proceeds of the loan by writing a check, the funds eventually end up in the check recipient's checkable deposit account elsewhere in the banking system.

An individual bank can increase checkable deposits or the money supply to the extent of its excess reserves by (7)_____(making loans or purchasing securities, advertising bank services), but the banking system as a whole can increase the stock of money by (8)_____(less than, a multiple of) its excess reserves. For instance, when a bank makes a loan, not only does it create new checkable deposits somewhere in the banking system, but it also passes excess reserves to other banks through the (9)_____ (financial, check clearing) system. Banks receiving deposits and reserves likewise make loans, increasing deposits and passing excess reserves to still other banks, which in turn do the same.

Each bank, however, has to keep some percentage of the new deposits back as required reserves, thus reducing the quantity of excess reserves available for loans and the quantity of reserves passed on to other banks. The percentage of deposit liabilities that must be held back is called the (10)_____ (required reserve ratio, discount rate). This process of deposit growth continues until there are no additional excess reserves in the system. At this point banks are (11)_____ (deficient, "loaned up"), meaning they have no excess reserves and can no longer make loans and create money. The stock of checkable deposits (money) can potentially expand by the reciprocal of the required reserve ratio times the quantity of excess reserves. The reciprocal of the required reserve ratio is known as the (12)_____(reserve multiplier, expansion coefficient). The process works just the opposite when banks find that their total reserves are less than required reserves. To acquire reserves or reduce required reserves in order to eliminate this deficiency, banks engage in activities that (13)_____(increase, reduce) the volume of checkable deposits.

As of January 1988, U.S. banks had reserves equal to 7.5% of total assets. Their (14)_____ (primary, secondary) reserves or government securities and other liquid securities were 18.4% of total assets. Loans accounted for (15)_____ (67%, 34%) of total assets. The largest share of funds (50%) acquired to purchase assets was obtained from saving deposits and certificates of deposits. Checkable deposits accounted for (16)_____ (40%, 20%) of total liabilities and capital. Net worth equaled 6% of total assets.

As of the beginning of the 1980s, with the enactment of the Depository Institutions Deregulation and Monetary Control Act of 1980, depository institutions such as credit unions, mutual savings banks, and savings and loan associations began to compete with banks by offering traditional banking services such as checking accounts. Whereas prior to 1980 only banks could create money, today all depository institutions with checkable deposits are involved in the process of money creation.

VOCABULARY REVIEW

Write the key term from the list below next to its definition.

Key Terms

Depository institutions	Excess reserves
Bank	Default
Financial intermediaries	Check clearing
Fractional reserve banking	Reserve multiplier
Fractional reserve ratio	Prime rate
Reserves	Collateral
Required reserve ratio	Government securities
Required reserves	Secondary reserves

Definitions

1. _____: firms that specialize in borrowing funds from savers and lending those funds to investors and others.

2. _____: a process by which a banking system creates checkable deposits by making loans in some multiple of the reserves it actually has on hand to pay withdrawals.

3. _____: balances (of a modern U.S. bank) kept on deposit with the Federal Reserve Bank in its district or a currency in its vault.

4. _____: nonrepayment of the principal and interest on a loan.

5. _____: the process of transferring Federal Reserve deposits among banks as checks are paid.

6. _____: the maximum amount of new money stock that can be created from each dollar increase in excess reserves available to the banking system.

7. _____: government securities held by banks.

8. _____: a commercial bank or thrift institution that offers checkable deposits.

9. _____: the ratio of actual reserves to total receipts for deposits.

10. _____: the difference between total reserves and required reserves of a bank held against deposits.

11. _____: interest-bearing debts of the federal government in the form of Treasury bills, Treasury notes, and Treasury bonds.

12. _____: those that make loans and offer checkable deposit and time deposit accounts for use by households and business firms.

13. _____: the dollar value of currency and deposits in Federal Reserve Banks that a bank must hold to meet current regulations.

14. _____: an asset a borrower pledges to a bank in case of default.

15. _____: the minimum percentage of deposits that a bank must hold in reserves to comply with regulatory requirements.

16. _____: the interest rate a bank charges its most credit worthy customers for short-term loans of less than 1 year.

SKILLS REVIEW

Concept: Examine a bank's balance sheet; impact of making a loan on the balance sheet

1. Identify the following as either an asset (A) or a liability (L) of a commercial bank.

   a. ____ Certificates of deposit
   b. ____ Cash
   c. ____ Total reserves
   d. ____ Bank building and property
   e. ____ Checkable deposits
   f. ____ Time and saving deposits
   g. ____ Reserve deposits at Federal Reserve
   h. ____ Loans
   i. ____ Government securities
   j. ____ Borrowings

2. a. Discuss the logic of the basic accounting identity.
   b. Why must balance sheets balance at a given point in time?

3. Given a balance sheet for a commercial bank, answer parts a-d assuming a required reserve ratio on checkable deposits of 10%.

Assets		Liabilities and Net Worth	
Cash	$ 200	Checkable deposits	$ 2,000
Reserve deposits	550	Savings and time	
Loans	6,700	deposits	5,000
Securities	1,840	Borrowings	2,400
Bank building		Net worth	600
and property	710		
Total Assets	$10,000	Total Liabilities and Net Worth	$10,000

   a. Total reserves = _____.
   b. Required reserves = _____.
   c. Excess reserves equal = _____.
   d. This bank can make loans of $_____.

4. Reserve deposits, loans, and checkable deposits are reproduced from the balance sheet above in the balance sheet below.

Assets		Liabilities and Net Worth	
Reserve deposits	$ 550	Checkable deposits	$2,000
Loans	6,700		

   a. Indicate on the balance sheet above the impact of a loan of $550 to one of the bank's customer-depositors. Designate your entries with an (a). (Hint: For every entry there must be an offsetting entry.) Total assets have _____ to $_____, and total liabilities have _____ to $_____.
   b. Assume now that the customer spends the proceeds of the loan by writing a check to a merchant for $550. Assume that the merchant deposits the check in a bank in the same Federal Reserve district and the check is routed to the Fed and back to the originating bank via the check clearing process. Indicate the impact of this on the balance sheet above and designate your entries with a (b). This

bank's checkable deposits have _____ to $_____, but total reserves have _____ to $_____. Excess reserves equal $_____. Total loans equal $_____.

   c.   Can this bank make loans in excess of its excess reserves? Why?

   d.   As a result of this loan, the stock of money has _____ by $_____.

Concept: Multiple expansion of the money stock

5.   The following assumptions pertain to the banking system:

   i.   Commercial Bank A has $100 in excess reserves.
   ii. Required reserve ratio = 20%
   iii. Other banks are presently "loaned up."
   iv. All banks use all of their excess reserves to make loans.
   v.   Bank A makes loans to its customers that, after the check clearing process, end up as deposits in Bank B. Similarly, Bank B makes loans to its customers that end up as deposits in Bank C, and so on.

   a.   Make the final entries on each bank's balance sheet assuming initially that Bank A makes a loan to the extent of its excess reserves. Trace the impact from Bank A through Bank D on the balance sheets below. (The final entries are after banks have loaned excess reserves, customers have spent the proceeds of the loans, and the checks have cleared.)

Bank A

Assets	Liabilities and Net Worth
Reserve deposits	Checkable deposits
Loans	

Bank B

Assets	Liabilities and Net Worth
Reserve deposits	Checkable deposits
Loans	

Bank C

Assets	Liabilities and Net Worth
Reserve deposits	Checkable deposits
Loans	

Bank D

Assets	Liabilities and Net Worth
Reserve deposits	Checkable deposits
Loans	

230

b.   Complete the following table.

Bank	Change in Required Reserves	Change in Money Stock
A	_____	_____
B	_____	_____
C	_____	_____
D	_____	_____

c.   The expansion of the money supply continues until the
_____ just equals the initial excess reserves of
$100.   At this point, excess reserves in the banking system equal
$_____.   When this occurs, the money stock has increased by
$_____.

6.   Find the change in the money stock for the banking system by filling in
the blanks below.

	Required Reserve Ratio	Change in Excess Reserves	Change in Checkable Deposits
a.	.1	+$1 billion	_____
b.	.2	0	_____
c.	.25	-$500 million	_____
d.	.4	+$10 billion	_____
e.	.5	-$5 billion	_____

SELF-TEST FOR MASTERY

Select the best answer.

1.   Early bankers, the goldsmiths of England and the moneychangers of Italy,
accepted deposits of gold for safekeeping and in return issued gold
receipts.   These early bankers were similar to modern bankers in that:

a.   They created a medium of exchange.
b.   They had a fractional reserve (gold) system.
c.   They accepted deposits and made loans.
d.   Gold receipts (medium of exchange) could be issued in greater volume
than the gold (reserves) upon which they were based.
e.   All of the above.

2.   The fractional reserve system means that:

a.   Only a fraction of bank assets at any one time may be used to create
money.
b.   A bank receives only a fraction of the reserves that it needs at any
given time.
c.   Only a fraction of a bank's liabilities must be held back as reserves
to meet withdrawals at any one time.
d.   None of the above.

3. A bank's total reserves consist of:

    a. Liquid assets such as private commercial paper and Treasury bills.
    b. Cash and Treasury bills.
    c. Cash only.
    d. Cash and reserve deposits held at a regional Federal Reserve Bank.

4. A bank's required reserves are determined by:

    a. Multiplying the required reserve ratio by certain deposit liabilities.
    b. Dividing total assets by net worth.
    c. Dividing the required reserve ratio into demand deposits.
    d. The U.S. Treasury.
    e. A and d.

5. The difference between total and required reserves is known as:

    a. The required reserve ratio.
    b. Fractional reserves.
    c. Extra reserves.
    d. Excess reserves.

6. Excess reserves are important to a banker because:

    a. If they are not met, the banking regulators will shut the bank down.
    b. They represent the funds available to acquire income-producing assets such as loans and securities.
    c. They are typically deposited in special high-yielding investment accounts.
    d. They are the profits that are divided among the bank's owners.

7. An individual bank can create deposits to the extent of its:

    a. Excess reserves.
    b. Required reserves.
    c. Total reserves.
    d. Deposits.
    e. Net worth.

8. A bank is "loaned up" when:

    a. Deposits are no longer coming in.
    b. Excess reserves are negative.
    c. Excess reserves are zero.
    d. Total reserves are zero.

9. The banking system can increase the stock of money by an amount _____ an increase in excess reserves.

    a. Less than
    b. The same as
    c. Greater than
    d. Less than or equal to

10. The reserve multiplier is:

   a. The ratio of required reserves to total reserves.
   b. The required reserve ratio multiplied by certain deposit liabilities.
   c. The number by which the total stock of reserves changes given a change in excess reserves.
   d. The number by which the total stock of money changes given a change in excess reserves.

11. The reciprocal of the required reserve ratio is the:

   a. Depository institutions capital ratio.
   b. Reserve multiplier.
   c. Bank's required reserves.
   d. Measure of excess reserves that the banker desires to use to make loans.

12. Assume that a bank in the banking system has $1,000 in total reserves and $5,000 in checkable deposits, and the required reserve ratio on checkable deposits is 10%. This bank's excess reserves equal:

   a. Zero; it is loaned up.
   b. $250.
   c. $500.
   d. $750.

13. Assume that a bank in the banking system has $2 million in reserves and checkable deposits of $9 million, and the required reserve ratio on checkable deposits is 20%. The maximum amount of loans this bank can make is:

   a. $1 million.
   b. $500,000.
   c. $700,000.
   d. $200,000.

14. Assume that a bank in the banking system has $1 billion in reserves and checkable deposits of $6 billion, and the required reserve ratio on checkable deposits is 10%. The maximum amount by which the banking system can expand the money supply is:

   a. $4 billion.
   b. $6 billion.
   c. $8 billion.
   d. $10 billion.

15. Total reserves of the banking system of $400 billion could potentially support $_____ of checkable deposits assuming a required reserve ratio of 25%.

   a. $400 billion
   b. $700 billion
   c. $1200 billion
   d. $1600 billion

16. If a banking system is loaned up and the Federal Reserve engages in activities that withdraw reserves from the system:

   a. The money supply will expand.
   b. The money supply will decrease.

c. The FDIC will intervene to replace the reserves.
d. Checkable deposits will increase.

17. As of January 1988, U.S. banks on average held _____ % of their total assets as loans and _____ % of their total liabilities and capital as checkable deposits.

    a. 67, 20
    b. 40, 30
    c. 34, 58
    d. 20, 67
    e. 50, 18.4

18. As of January 1988, U.S. banks' reserves as a percentage of total bank assets equaled:

    a. 15%.
    b. 12%.
    c. 6%.
    d. 7.5%.

19. Whereas prior to 1980 only banks could create money, today because of _____ all depository institutions with checkable deposits are involved in the process of money creation.

    a. The Federal Reserve Act
    b. The FDIC
    c. The Fiscal Responsibility Act of 1980
    d. The Depository Institutions Deregulation and Monetary Control Act of 1980

20. Secondary reserves consist of:

    a. Cash.
    b. Cash and government securities.
    c. Cash, reserve deposits, and government securities.
    d. Government securities and other liquid securities.

THINK IT THROUGH

1. Discuss the philosophy behind fractional reserve banking. What is the implication of fractional reserve banking for the multiple expansion of the money stock in terms of the role of depository institutions?

2. Suppose you are a banker and you have difficulty predicting deposits and withdrawals. At times you unexpectedly experience large withdrawals from checkable deposits. How might this influence your decision to use excess reserves? If there are many other bankers like you in the banking system, how might the deposit expansion process be affected?

3. Why can't a bank make loans in amounts greater than the bank's excess reserves? What would happen if more loans were extended than could be supported by excess reserves?

4. Discuss the reserve multiplier and the multiple expansion of the money stock.

5.   What is the significance of the Depository Institutions Deregulation and Monetary Control Act of 1980 for the money expansion process?

CHAPTER ANSWERS

In Brief: Chapter Summary

1. Only a fraction of the 2. In excess of 3. Could be larger than 4. Total
5. Excess 6. Cannot 7. Making loans or purchasing securities 8. A multiple of 9. Check clearing 10. Required reserve ratio 11. "Loaned up" 12. Reserve multiplier 13. Reduce 14. Secondary 15. 67% 16. 20%

Vocabulary Review

1. Financial intermediaries 2. Fractional reserve banking 3. Reserves 4. Default 5. Check clearing 6. Reserve multiplier 7. Secondary reserves 8. Bank 9. Fractional reserve ratio 10. Excess reserves 11. Government securities 12. Depository institutions 13. Required reserves 14. Collateral 15. Required reserve ratio 16. Prime rate

Skills Review

1.   a. L b. A c. A d. A e. L f. L g. A h. A i. A j. L

2.   a.   Assets must be exactly equal to the sum of liabilities and net worth. Assets are acquired with funds that you either own or borrow. For a depository institution, assets represent the uses of funds and deposits, and borrowings and net worth represent the sources of funds.
      b.   For the accounting identity to hold, any change in assets or liabilities and net worth must have an offsetting change in the asset or liability and net worth accounts on the balance sheet. Therefore, regardless of the entries made to a balance sheet, the offsetting entries ensure that the two sides of the balance sheet always balance.

3.   a. $750 b. $200 c. $550 d. $550

4.   a.

Assets		Liabilities and Net Worth	
Reserve deposits $	550	Checkable deposits	$2,000
(b)	-550	(a)	550
Loans	6,700	(b)	-550
(a)	550		

      Increased, $7,250; increased, $2,550
      b.   Decreased, $2000; fallen, $200, $0; $7,250
      c.   No. If this bank makes loans in excess of its excess reserves, $550, then after borrowers spend the proceeds of the loans and the checks clear, the bank will not have enough total reserves to meet its legal reserve requirement.
      d.   Increased, $550

5.   a.

	Bank A	
Assets		Liabilities and Net Worth
Reserve deposits	-$100	Checkable deposits
Loans	100	

Bank B

Assets		Liabilities and Net Worth
Reserve deposits	$20	Checkable deposits $100
Loans	80	

Bank C

Assets		Liabilities and Net Worth
Reserve deposits	$16	Checkable deposits $80
Loans	64	

Bank D

Assets		Liabilities and Net Worth
Reserve deposits	$12.8	Checkable deposits $64
Loans	51.2	

b.

A	---	---
B	$20	$100
C	16	80
D	12.8	64

c.   Increase in required reserves; $0; $500

6.   a. $10 billion b. $0 c. -$2 billion d. $25 billion e. -$10 billion

Self-Test for Mastery

1. e 2. c 3. d 4. a 5. d 6. b 7. a 8. c 9. c 10. d 11. b 12. c 13. d 14. a 15. d 16. b 17. a 18. d 19. d 20. d

Think It Through

1.   On any given day, deposit withdrawals are only a fraction of total deposits. Therefore, to meet withdrawals banks need to keep only a fraction of total assets in the form of liquid assets such as cash and reserve deposits. The upshot of this is that banks can create deposits by making loans with excess reserves and the banking system can create a money stock that is a multiple of the reserve base upon which it rests.

2.   Given the uncertainty regarding the fluctuations in checkable deposit balances, it would be wise to maintain a cushion of excess reserves as a contingency against deposit outflows that might otherwise put the bank in a deficient reserve position. Of course, in doing this you sacrifice potential income, but you also reduce the risk confronting the bank. For the banking system as a whole, this implies that some portion of excess reserves is held back, thus reducing the stock of money that can be supported by a given stock of bank reserves. The reserve multiplier will also be smaller.

3.   If more loans were extended than could be funded with excess reserves, a bank would not be meeting its legal reserve requirement. This is because once the proceeds of the loans are spent and the checks clear, the bank loses total reserves equal to the loans--which are greater than excess reserves. The bank would then either have to increase total reserves by borrowing or selling other assets, or it would have to reduce checkable deposits in order to reduce required reserves.

4.   The expansion process occurs because of the fractional reserve
system. A portion of a bank's excess reserves is passed on to other banks in
the banking system as a result of loans and cleared checks. The only thing
that prevents this expansion from occurring indefinitely is that some of the
excess reserves must be held back as required reserves by those banks
experiencing deposit inflows. Eventually all of the initial excess reserves
will be absorbed in the banking system as required reserves, leaving none as
excess reserves for further expansion of deposits. The process is an infinite
geometric progression that can be solved yielding the reserve multiplier,
1/required reserve ratio, as part of the solution.

5.   The act allows credit unions, savings and loan associations, and mutual
savings banks to compete with banks for checkable deposits and consumer and
business loans. The significance of the act for the money expansion process is
that banks are no longer the only institutions that can create money by making
loans. Now all depository institutions having checkable deposits can create
money by making loans. The act also brings all depository institutions
offering checkable deposits under uniform reserve ratios administered by the
Federal Reserve System.

17

The Federal Reserve System and Its Influence on Money and Credit

After studying your text, attending class, and completing this chapter, you should be able to:

1. Discuss the organization and structure of the Federal Reserve System.
2. Examine the balance sheet of the Federal Reserve Banks and discuss the techniques used by the Fed to influence the money supply.
3. Show how the Fed's open market operations affect bank reserves, securities prices, interest rates, and the money supply.
4. Analyze the nation's money supply curve and show how desires by banks to hold excess reserves affect the quantity of money supplied.

IN BRIEF: CHAPTER SUMMARY

Fill in the blanks to summarize chapter content.

The Federal Reserve System was established in 1913. It consists of a Board of Governors, (1)_____(twelve, seven) regional Federal Reserve Banks and their branch banks, the Federal Open Market Committee, and the Federal Advisory Council. The Chairman of the Board of Governors is appointed by the President to a 4-year term, whereas the other (2)_____(three, six) board members are appointed to 14-year terms. The Federal Reserve Banks are owned by the member banks in their respective districts. The Federal (3)_____ (Advisory, Open Market) Committee is the principal policy-making body within the Federal Reserve System. It issues directives to the account manager at the trading desk of the New York Federal Reserve Bank to achieve some level of money growth during a given time period. The account manager does this by buying and selling U.S. government securities. The Fed is to some extent independent of the legislative and administrative levels of the federal government in that it does not rely upon Congressional funding, but instead earns its own operating revenues.

The major asset of the Federal Reserve System is its holdings of (4)_____ (U.S. government securities, Federal Reserve Notes). Other assets include loans to banks (discounts and advances), certificates issued by the U.S. Treasury, cash items in process of collection, coin, foreign currencies, debt obligations of federal agencies, and bank property and equipment. The largest liability of the system is (5)_____(U.S. government securities, Federal Reserve Notes). Other liabilities include deposits by banks, foreign nations, and the U.S. Treasury.

The supply of money equals the monetary base times the reserve multiplier. The (6)_____(monetary base, reserve sum) is the sum of currency in the hands of the public and total bank reserves. Total checkable deposits equal total reserves times the reserve multiplier. The Fed can influence both the monetary base (volume of reserves) and the reserve multiplier. The money expansion process is also influenced by the decisions of bankers regarding the quantity of excess reserves that are held and not used to make loans. The Fed can influence the money supply in three ways: changing the required reserve ratio, changing the (7)_____ (interest, discount) rate, and either buying or selling U.S. government securities.

An/A (8)_____(increase, decrease) in the reserve ratio does not affect total reserves, but it does reduce excess reserves and therefore contracts the money stock. An/A (9)_____ (increase, decrease) in the reserve ratio increases excess reserves and the money stock. An/A (10)_____ (increase, decrease) in the discount rate relative to the yields on short-term government securities reduces both total and excess reserves in the banking system and contracts the money supply. An/A (11)_____(increase, decrease) in the discount rate increases total and excess reserves and increases the money stock. Open market (12)_____(purchases, sales) of securities to banks reduce reserves, the monetary base, and the money supply. (13)_____(Purchases from, Sales to) the public will have the same effect if the public pays for the securities by check rather than by cash. Open market (14)_____ (purchases from, sales to) banks or the public will increase reserves, the monetary base, and the money stock. The most important of the three tools of monetary control is (15)_____ (open market operations, the discount rate, the required reserve ratio). Changes in the discount rate are important but often lag behind rather than cause changes in interest rates. The required reserve ratio, while very powerful, is not used as a money management tool.

Open market transactions affect the economy immediately in that the Fed buys and sells such a large volume of securities that securities prices and their yields (interest rates) are affected. A Fed purchase of securities (16)_____ (increases, reduces) the outstanding supply of securities held by the public and causes securities prices to (17)_____ (rise, fall) and interest rates to (18)_____ (rise, fall). A Fed sale of securities (19)_____ (increases, decreases) the supply of securities held by the public, which (20)_____ (increases, reduces) securities prices and (21)_____ (increases, decreases) interest rates. But open market transactions also affect bank excess reserves and the total stock of money. As the supply of money changes relative to the demand for money, interest rates will change. A purchase of securities (22)_____ (decreases, increases) excess reserves and (23)_____ (decreases, increases) the supply of money relative to the demand for money causing the interest rate to (24)_____ (fall, rise). A sale of securities (25)_____ (increases, reduces) excess reserves and the supply of money relative to the demand for money and causes the interest rate to (26)_____ (decrease, increase).

The supply of money is positively related to the interest rate because of the relationship between the interest rate and bankers' propensities to hold some excess reserves rather than use them for loans. Interest rates rise as the economy approaches a higher level of economic activity, but this is the time when loan demand is strong and the opportunity cost of holding noninterest-bearing assets is high. Therefore bankers (27)_____ (reduce, increase) their holdings of excess reserves. Just the opposite is generally true of recessions. The demand for loans is less, interest rates are lower, and the opportunity cost of holding reserves is lower. Bankers prefer to hold (28)_____ (less, more) excess reserves in recessions. So when interest rates are high, excess reserves held are (29)_____(smaller, larger) and the stock of money is correspondingly (30)_____(smaller, larger). Conversely, at lower rates of interest, excess reserves held are (31)_____ (smaller, larger) and the stock of money is (32)_____ (larger, smaller). This produces a/an (33)_____(vertical, upward sloping) money supply curve.

239

VOCABULARY REVIEW

Write the key term from the list below next to its definition.

Key Terms

Board of Governors of the
   Federal Reserve System
Regional Federal Reserve Banks
Monetary base
Federal Open Market Committee

Discount rate
Open market operations
Discount loans
Money supply

Definitions

1. _____: an arm of the Federal Reserve System; affects the amount of excess reserves available to banks by instructing the Federal Reserve Bank of New York to buy or sell government securities on the open market.

2. _____: the sum of currency in circulation and total bank reserves outstanding at any given time.

3. _____: the Federal Reserve System's purchases and sales of government securities, conducted by the Federal Open Market Committee.

4. _____: bank borrowings from the Federal Reserve System; also called <u>advances</u>.

5. _____: a relationship between the quantity of money supplied in the form of currency and checkable deposits and the level of interest rates prevailing at a given point in time.

6. _____: perform central banking functions for banks within each of 12 Federal Reserve districts.

7. _____: the interest rate Federal Reserve Banks charge member banks for loans.

8. _____: supervises the operation of the nation's banking system and acts as an authority to regulate the money supply.

SKILLS REVIEW

Concept: **Balance sheet of the Federal Reserve; techniques to control the money stock**

1. Identify each of the following as either an asset (A) or a liability (L) of the Federal Reserve.

    a. _____ U.S. government securities
    b. _____ Loans to banks (discounts and advances)
    c. _____ Deposits of the U.S. Treasury
    d. _____ Federal Reserve Notes
    e. _____ Deposits by foreign nations
    f. _____ Deposits by banks
    g. _____ Coin
    h. _____ Foreign currency

2. Determine what happens to checkable deposits in the banking system if the Fed lowers the required reserve ratio from 20% to 19%, total reserves equal $200 billion, and banks are presently loaned up. (Hint: Total checkable deposits = reserve multiplier X total reserves.)

a. Reserve multiplier (reserve ratio = 20%) = _____
b. Checkable deposits (reserve ratio = 20%) = _____
c. Reserve multiplier (reserve ratio = 19%) = _____
d. Checkable deposits (reserve ratio = 19%) = _____

3. a. Complete the table.

Reserve Ratio	Reserve Multiplier	Total Reserves	Checkable Deposits
.1	_____	$100 billion	$_____
.2	_____	100	_____
.25	_____	100	_____

b. An increase in the required reserve ratio _____ checkable deposits. A decrease in the reserve ratio _____ checkable deposits.

4. Below are balance sheets for the Federal Reserve and a commercial bank, Bank A. Assume that this and all other commercial banks are presently loaned up, no excess reserves are held, and the reserve ratio is 20%.

Federal Reserve

Assets	Liabilities and Net Worth
Loans to banks	Deposits of banks

Bank A

Assets	Liabilities and Net Worth
Reserve deposits	Borrowings

a. Assume that Bank A borrows $10 million from the Fed. Make the appropriate entries in the balance sheets above.
b. Bank A now has $_____ in excess reserves and can extend loans equal to $_____.
c. The banking system can increase checkable deposits by a maximum of $_____.
d. If the Fed increases the discount rate relative to short-term interest rates (Treasury Bill rates), the volume of discounts _____, causing bank total and excess reserves to _____, which causes a/an _____ in checkable deposits.
e. If the Fed decreases the discount rate relative to other short-term rates of interest, the volume of discounts _____, causing bank total and excess reserves to _____, which causes a/an _____ in checkable deposits.

5. Below are balance sheets for the Federal Reserve and Commercial Bank A. Assume that this and all other banks are loaned up, the current reserve ratio is 20%, and no excess reserves are held.

                        Federal Reserve

        Assets   Liabilities and Net Worth

        Securities   Deposits of banks

                        Bank A

        Assets   Liabilities and Net Worth

        Reserve deposits
        Securities

    a. The Fed purchases $25 million of securities from Bank A. Make the appropriate entries on the balance sheets above.
    b. Bank A's total reserves _____ by $_____.
        Bank A's required reserves _____ by $_____.
        Bank A's excess reserves _____ by $_____.
    c. Bank A can _____ loans by $_____ and the banking system can _____ checkable deposits by $_____.
    d. If the Fed purchases securities from the public rather than a bank, would the impact on checkable deposits be any different from that which you showed in part c?
    e. Fed purchases of U.S. government securities _____ bank excess reserves and the monetary base and _____ the money stock.

6. Suppose the Fed sells $20 billion in U.S. government securities to banks. Assume the reserve ratio is 10% and banks are loaned up.

    a. Make the appropriate entries on the balance sheets below.

                        Federal Reserve

        Assets   Liabilities and Net Worth

        Securities   Deposits of banks

                        All Banks

        Assets   Liabilities and Net Worth

        Reserve deposits
        Securities

    b. Bank total reserves _____ by $_____.
    c. Checkable deposits in the banking system_____ by $_____.
    d. If the securities are sold to the public, total checkable deposits _____ by $_____ if the public pays for the securities with checks, but _____ if payments are made with cash.
    e. Assuming no cash transactions, Fed sales of securities _____ bank reserves and the monetary base and_____ the money stock.

Concept: Money supply curve; equilibrium interest rate

7. When interest rates rise, the quantity of excess reserves held and not used _____, causing the supply of money to _____. When interest rates fall, the quantity of excess reserves held and not used _____ causing the supply of money to _____. The relationship between the interest rate and the quantity of money supplied is a _____ relationship, resulting in a _____ sloped money supply curve.

8. a.   On the diagram below, show the effect of an increase in the stock of money.

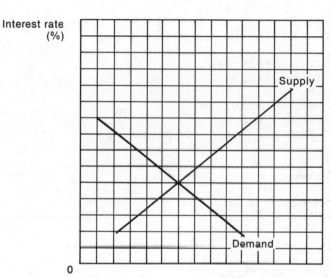

An increase in the stock of money, given the demand for money, _____ the equilibrium interest rate.

b.   Show on the figure above the impact of a reduction in the supply of money. A decrease in the stock of money, given the demand for money, _____ the equilibrium interest rate.

c.   Indicate whether each of the following increases (+), decreases (-), or remains unchanged (0).

	Fed Policy	Change in Monetary Base	Change in Excess Reserves	Change in Checkable Deposits
1.	Increase reserve ratio			
2.	Securities sales	____	____	____
3.	Securities purchases	____	____	____
4.	Decrease reserve ratio			
		____	____	____
5.	Increase discount rate			
		____	____	____
6.	Decrease discount rate			
		____	____	____

SELF-TEST FOR MASTERY

Multiple Choice   Select the best answer.

1.   The Board of Governors of the Federal Reserve System consists of how many members?

     a.   4
     b.   5
     c.   6
     d.   7
     e.   8

2.   The principal policy-making body of the Federal Reserve System with regard to the regulation of the nation's money stock is:

     a.   The Federal Advisory Committee.
     b.   The trading desk in New York.
     c.   The U.S. Treasury.
     d.   The Federal Open Market Committee.

3.   The major asset of the Federal Reserve System is:

     a.   Bank deposits.
     b.   Government securities.
     c.   Treasury deposits.
     d.   Federal Reserve notes.
     e.   Discounts and advances.

4.   The major liability of the Federal Reserve System is:

     a.   Bank deposits.
     b.   Government securities.
     c.   Treasury deposits.
     d.   Federal Reserve notes.
     e.   Discounts and advances.

5.   Which of the following is not a function of the Federal Reserve System?

     a.   Regulation of the money supply
     b.   Administering federal matching funds used in the banking industry
     c.   Clearing checks
     d.   Providing banks with currency and coin
     e.   Making loans to banks

6.   The sum of currency in circulation and total bank reserves equals:

     a.   The total required reserves.
     b.   The money stock.
     c.   The total assets of the banking system.
     d.   The monetary base.
     e.   The money multiplier.

7.   The Federal Reserve System controls the money supply primarily by controlling:

     a.   The monetary base.
     b.   Checkable deposits.
     c.   The interest rate.
     d.   Paper currency and coin.

8. An increase in the required reserve ratio _____ excess reserves and _____ the money stock.

   a. Increases, decreases
   b. Decreases, increases
   c. Decreases, decreases
   d. Increases, increases

9. A decrease in the discount rate _____ both total and excess reserves and _____ the money stock.

   a. Increases, decreases
   b. Decreases, increases
   c. Decreases, decreases
   d. Increases, increases

10. Sales of government securities to banks _____ total and excess reserves and _____ the money stock.

    a. Increase, decrease
    b. Decrease, increase
    c. Decrease, decrease
    d. Increase, increase

11. Federal Reserve purchases of securities _____ the money stock, and sales of securities _____ the money stock.

    a. Increase, decrease
    b. Increase, also increase
    c. Decrease, increase
    d. Decrease, also decrease

12. The most important tool for monetary control is:

    a. Changing the reserve ratio.
    b. The interest rate.
    c. The discount rate.
    d. Open market operations.

13. The least used tool of monetary control is:

    a. The reserve ratio policy.
    b. The interest rate.
    c. The discount rate.
    d. Open market operations.
    e. The statutory ability to impose price controls.

14. An open market purchase of securities by the Fed will _____ the supply of securities and cause the price of securities to _____ and interest rates to _____.

    a. Increase, increase, increase
    b. Decrease, increase, decrease
    c. Increase, increase, decrease
    d. Decrease, decrease, increase

15. Which of the following best explains the slope of the money supply curve?

   a. Interest rates and loans are directly related.
   b. Interest rates and total bank reserves are inversely related.
   c. Interest rates and the monetary base are positively related.
   d. Interest rates vary inversely with excess reserves.

16. An increase in the supply of money, given the demand for money, will:

   a. At the prevailing interest rate cause a surplus of money, which in turn reduces the rate of interest.
   b. At the prevailing interest rate cause no change in the stock of money or the interest rate.
   c. At the prevailing interest rate cause a shortage of money, which in turn increases the rate of interest.
   d. At the prevailing interest rate cause a surplus of money, which in turn decreases the rate of interest.

17. A decrease in the supply of money, given the demand for money, will _____ interest rates and _____ interest-sensitive expenditures in the economy.

   a. Decrease, decrease
   b. Increase, increase
   c. Increase, decrease
   d. Decrease, increase
   e. Increase, will not change

THINK IT THROUGH

1. Discuss the functions of the Federal Reserve System.

2. Discuss the three tools of monetary control and how they can be used to influence equilibrium interest rates.

3. The Fed can control the rate of growth in the monetary base reasonably well over an extended period of time, but it has more difficulty achieving growth rate targets for the money supply. Can you think of any reasons why?

4. Suppose that as a manager, you are trying to decide whether to borrow short-term or long-term funds for modernization of your facilities. If you expect interest rates to rise, you will borrow by taking long-term loans at today's low interest rate. If you expect interest rates to fall, you will avoid long-term loans, preferring to borrow short-term funds until interest rates fall. What would you do if you heard that the Fed just lowered the discount rate and announced that it had been actively purchasing securities for the last several weeks?

In Brief: Chapter Summary

1. Twelve 2. Six 3. Open Market 4. U.S. government securities 5.Federal Reserve notes 6. Monetary base 7. Discount 8. Increase 9. Decrease 10. Increase 11. Decrease 12. Sales 13. Sales to 14. Purchases from 15. Open market operations 16. Reduces 17. Rise 18. Fall 19. Increase 20. Reduces 21. Increases 22. Increases 23. Increases 24. Fall 25. Reduces 26. Increases 27. Reduce 28. More 29. Smaller 30. Larger 31. Larger 32. Smaller 33. Upward sloping

Vocabulary Review

1. Federal Open Market Committee 2. Monetary base 3. Open market operations 4. Discount loans 5. Money supply 6. Regional Federal Reserve Banks 7. Discount rate 8. Board of Governors of the Federal Reserve System

Skills Review

1. a. A b. A c. L d. L e. L f. L g. A h. A

2. a. 5 b. $1,000 billion c. 5.26 d. $1,052 billion

3. a.

Reserve Multiplier	Checkable Deposits
10	$1,000 billion
5	500 million
4	400 million

   b. Reduces, increases

4. a.

Federal Reserve

Assets	Liabilities and Net Worth
Loans to banks $10	Deposits of banks $10

Bank A

Assets		Liabilities and Net Worth
Reserve deposits	$10	Borrowings $10

   b. $10 million, $10 million c. $50 million d. Decreases, fall, decrease e. Increases, rise, increase

5. a.

Federal Reserve

Assets	Liabilities and Net Worth
Securities $25	Deposits of banks $25

Bank A

Assets	Liabilities and Net Worth
Reserve deposits $ 25	
Securities -25	

   b. Increases, $25 million; no change; increase, $25 million

c.   Increase, $25 million, increase, $125 million
d.   No e. Increase, increase

6.   a.   Federal Reserve

Assets   Liabilities and Net Worth

Securities $-20   Deposits of banks $-20

                          Bank A

Assets   Liabilities and Net Worth

Reserve deposits $-20
Securities   20

b.   Decrease, $20 million c. Decrease, $200 million d. Decrease, $200
     million, does not fall e. Decrease, decrease

7.   Decrease, increase; increase, decrease; positive, positively

8.   a.

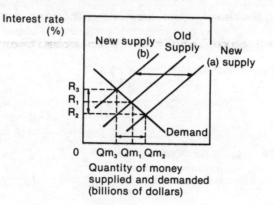

b.   Decrease
     Increase
c.

	Change in Monetary Base	Change in Excess Reserves	Change in Checkable Deposits
1.	0	−	−
2.	−	−	−
3.	+	+	+
4.	0	+	+
5.	−	−	−
6.	+	+	+

Self-Test for Mastery

1. d 2. d 3. b 4. d 5. b 6. d 7. a 8. c 9. d 10. c 11. a 12. d 13.
a 14. b 15. d 16. a 17. c

Think it Through

1.   In addition to regulating the money supply, the Fed is responsible for
maintaining the safety and solvency of the banking system, which it does
through bank regulation and oversight and acting as a lender of last resort.
The Fed also holds reserve deposits of member banks, supplies currency and coin
to banks, clears checks, makes loans to banks, aids the Treasury in the issue
of new government securities, and holds the Treasury deposits on which U.S.
government checks are written.

2.   The three tools of monetary control are the reserve ratio, the discount rate, and open market operations. If the Fed wants to expand the money supply, it can reduce the discount rate and the reserve ratio and purchase government securities. A policy designed to reduce the money stock might include increases in the reserve ratio and the discount rate and sales of government securities. In practice, the reserve ratio, while having a powerful impact on the supply of money, is not used as a device for regulation of the money supply. Open market operations together with support of the discount policy constitute the primary approach to monetary control.

3.   The Fed has more direct control over the growth of the monetary base because of the Fed's ability to buy and sell huge quantities of government securities. In contrast, the money multiplier is determined not only by the Fed via the reserve ratio, but also by the portfolio decisions of the public such as the banking system's propensity to hold excess reserves. The growth of the money supply depends on changes in both the monetary base and the money multiplier. So while the Fed can target the growth of the monetary base reasonably well over a period of several months, it is less successful in achieving its growth targets for the money stock.

4.   Both of the Fed's actions will expand the supply of money and reduce the interest rate. Because of this news, you expect interest rates to fall, which means you would be better off borrowing short-term funds and waiting until interest rates drop before you make long-term loan commitments.

18

Stabilization of the Economy Through Monetary Policy

CHAPTER CHALLENGES

After studying your text, attending class, and completing this chapter, you should be able to:

1. Discuss the mechanism through which monetary policy can affect interest rates.
2. Show how an expansionary monetary policy shifts the economy's aggregate demand curve and affects macroeconomic equilibrium.
3. Show how a contractionary monetary policy shifts the economy's aggregate demand curve and affects macroeconomic equilibrium.
4. Discuss the quantity theory of money and the possible long-term effects of monetary policy on the price level.
5. Discuss the basic ideas and implications of monetarism for monetary policy.
6. Evaluate some of the difficulties involved in choosing target goals for monetary policy.

IN BRIEF: CHAPTER SUMMARY

Fill in the blanks to summarize chapter content.

Monetary policy is used to influence the level of aggregate demand and macroeconomic equilibrium. The mechanism by which changes in the money supply influence aggregate demand is through changes in (1)_____ (prices, interest rates). Interest rates are (2)_____ (inversely, positively) related to the level of investment and other credit-sensitive expenditures. For instance, an increase in interest rates (3)_____ (reduces, increases) the level of investment which, in turn (4)_____ (reduces, increases) the level of aggregate demand and vice versa.

If the Fed wants to increase aggregate demand, it can engage in a/an (5)_____ (contractionary, expansionary) monetary policy. The Fed can expand the banking system's excess reserves. Excess reserves result in an increase in the stock of money, which reduces real interest rates and increases planned investment and aggregate demand. The effectiveness of such a policy depends on the willingness of the banking system to use the new excess reserves to make loans and on the sensitivity of investment and other expenditures to changes in the (6)_____ (interest rate, rate of inflation). If the increase in excess reserves is ultimately successful in increasing aggregate demand, real GNP and the price level increase if the economy is (7)_____ (above, below) potential real GNP. Expansionary monetary policy is useful as a tool for combating (8)_____ (recessionary, inflationary) GNP gaps and unemployment.

For the case of (9)_____ (recessionary, inflationary) GNP gaps, the Fed could withdraw reserves from the banking system. A decline in bank reserves will result in a/an (10)_____ (decrease, increase) in the real interest rate and a/an (11)_____ (decrease, increase) in planned investment and aggregate demand. As aggregate demand decreases, the price level and the level of real GNP will (12)_____ (rise, fall). A/An (13)_____ (contractionary, expansionary) monetary policy could be used to reduce inflation and bring the economy back to potential real GNP.

The long-run effect of monetary policy depends upon the demand for money, the growth of real GNP, and the growth of (14)_____ (the money stock, prices). If the income velocity of circulation of money, V, is defined as nominal GNP divided by the money stock, then the following identity emerges: (15)_____ (MQ = PV, MV = PQ). The stock of money times the income velocity of circulation equals the price level times real GNP. Velocity moves inversely with changes in the demand for money. But if velocity is constant and real GNP is assumed constant at its potential level, increases in the money stock result in (16)_____ (larger, proportionate) increases in the price level. This is the classical quantity theory of money. In the long run, the classical quantity theory of money implies a/an (17)_____ (vertical, upward sloping) aggregate supply curve at potential real GNP. An increase in the money stock increases aggregate demand (18)_____ (and results in an increase in both real GNP and the price level, but results in only an increase in the price level).

Monetarists and Keynesians believe that velocity is not constant, but the (19)_____ (monetarists, Keynesians) believe it is reasonably stable and changes in velocity are predictable. If changes in velocity are predictable, changes in the money supply can be used to influence nominal GNP. If the money stock is allowed to grow at the rate of growth of real GNP, then (20)_____ (some, no) inflation results. Inflation takes place when the money stock is allowed to grow at a rate (21)_____ (in excess of, less than) the growth rate of real GNP. Monetarists recommend constant growth of the money stock at a rate (22)_____ (equal to, less than) the economy's average growth rate of real GNP as a way to prevent inflation. Velocity has not always been stable or predictable, however. If the money supply increases at a rate faster than real GNP, inflation may not increase if velocity is (23)_____ (rising, falling).

A dilemma confronting the Fed is whether to use monetary policy to influence interest rates and aggregate demand in the short run or whether to concentrate on the long-run relationship between money growth and growth in real GNP. (24)_____ (Unfortunately, the Fed cannot, Fortunately, the Fed can) simultaneously achieve interest rate and money supply goals or targets. If real GNP or the price level increases, the demand for money will increase. In order to keep interest rates from rising, the Fed has to (25)_____ (decrease, increase) the money supply. If the goal is to keep the money supply constant in the face of an increase in money demand, then interest rates must rise. Thus controlling the interest rate means that the Fed effectively gives up control of the money stock and vice versa. This makes it (26)_____ (difficult, easy) for the Fed to achieve real GNP, employment, and inflation goals simultaneously. From the early 1940s to the mid-1970s, the Fed concentrated on controlling (27)_____ (the money stock, interest rates) as a means of stabilizing the economy. Beginning in late 1979, the Fed made an effort to concentrate on (28)_____ (the money stock, interest rates), but had to abandon the effort by mid-1982 because of the deepening recession.

VOCABULARY REVIEW

Write the key term from the list below next to its definition.

Key Terms

Stabilization policies
Monetary policy
Expansionary monetary policy
Contractionary monetary
  policy
Monetarism

Income velocity of
  circulation of money
Equation of exchange
Classical quantity theory
  of money

Definitions

1. _____: actions taken by central banks to influence money
supply or interest rates in an attempt to stabilize the economy.

2. _____: action by the Federal Reserve System to decrease
the monetary base or its rate of growth.

3. _____: an identity that shows the relationship between
nominal GNP, the money stock, and the income velocity of circulation of
money.

4. _____: a model of the long-run functioning of the
economy that maintains that over the long run, changes in the money stock
result in proportional changes in the price level.

5. _____: a theory of long-term macroeconomic equilibrium,
based on the equation of exchange, that assumes that shifts in velocity
are reasonably predictable.

6. _____: policies undertaken by governing authorities for
the purpose of maintaining full employment and a reasonably stable price
level.

7. _____: action by the Federal Reserve System to decrease
the monetary base or its rate of growth.

8. _____: the number of times per year on average a dollar
of the money stock is spent on final purchases.

SKILLS REVIEW

Concept: Monetary policy, interest rates, and aggregate demand

1.   The data below are for an economy. Using the data determine the market
     rate of interest, the level of planned investment, and the level of
     aggregate demand.

Interest Rate (%)	Supply of Loanable Funds	Demand for Loanable Funds	Planned Investment	Aggregate Demand
	($ billions)			($ billions)
14	$125	$75	$10	$2,010
13	115	80	20	2,020
12	105	85	30	2,030
11	100	90	40	2,040
10	95	95	50	2,050
9	85	100	60	2,060
8	75	105	70	2,070

a.   Equilibrium rate of interest = _____ %.

b.   Planned investment = $ _____ ; aggregate demand = $ _____ .

c.   The Fed engages in an expansionary monetary policy, and the supply of
     loanable funds increases by $15 billion at each interest rate. The
     new market rate of interest is _____ %, planned investment
     _____ to $ _____ , and aggregate demand _____ to
     $ _____ . The aggregate demand curve shifts to the
     _____ .

d.   Assume that the initial supply of loanable funds is given in the
     table above. The Fed engages in a contractionary monetary policy
     such that the supply of loanable funds decreases by $20 billion at
     each interest rate. The new interest rate is _____ %, planned
     investment _____ to $ _____ , and aggregate demand
     _____ to $ _____ . The aggregate demand curve shifts
     _____ .

e.   The figure below shows the aggregate demand curve for the economy
     described above. Find the point on the aggregate demand curve
     associated with part b. Now show what happens to the point for parts
     c and d. Draw new aggregate demand curves through the points
     parallel to ADo.

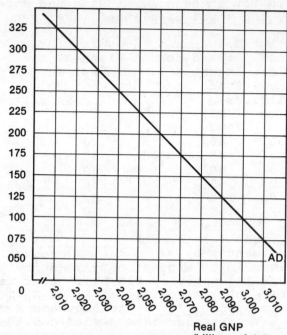

Price level
(base year = 100)

Real GNP
(billions of dollars)

Concept: Monetary policy and macroeconomic equilibrium

2.   Below is an aggregate demand and supply model of the economy.

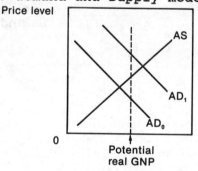

a.   Given aggregate demand ADo, the economy is experiencing an/a
     _____ (inflationary, recessionary) gap. In order to eliminate
     the gap, the Fed could _____ the money stock. This would
     _____ interest rates and _____ planned investment,
     causing the aggregate demand curve to shift _____.
b.   Given aggregate demand AD1, the economy is experiencing an/a
     _____ (inflationary, recessionary) gap. In order to eliminate
     the gap, the Fed could _____ the money stock. This would
     _____ interest rates and _____ planned investment, causing
     the aggregate demand curve to shift _____.
c.   For part a above, equilibrium real GNP will _____ and the
     equilibrium price level will _____. For part b above,

equilibrium real GNP will _____ and the equilibrium price level will _____.

3. The effectiveness of monetary policy depends upon:

    a. _____
    b. _____

4. Below are two investment demand schedules for an economy.

Interest Rate (%)	Planned Investment (I1)	Planned Investment (I2)
	($ billions)	
14	$250	$150
13	300	250
12	350	350
11	400	450
10	450	550
9	500	650
8	550	750

a. Which of the investment schedules above, I1 or I2, displays the greater sensitivity of investment expenditures to changes in the interest rate?

b. At an interest rate of 12% the level of planned investment is the same for both I1 and I2. Assume that the aggregate demand curve shown in the figure below is associated with a level of planned investment equal to $350 billion. On the figure, show the effect of a reduction in the interest rate from 12% to 9% on the aggregate demand curve for the case of investment schedule I1. (Assume that the aggregate demand curve shifts parallel to ADo.)

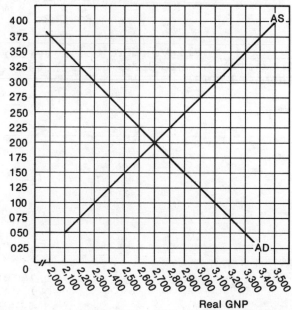

c. On the figure above, show the effect of an decrease in interest rates from 12% to 9% on the aggregate demand curve for the case of

255

investment schedule I2. (Assume that the aggregate demand curve shifts parallel to ADo.)
- d. Monetary policy is _____ effective if the investment schedule is I1 and is _____ effective if the investment schedule is I2.

Concept: Classical quantity theory of money; long-term effects of money

5. a. Assume that the current level of real GNP, Q, is $2 trillion, the implicit price deflator, P, is 200, and the stock of money, M, equals $500 billion. The velocity of circulation of money equals _____.

   b. According to the classical quantity theory of money, both _____ and _____ are assumed constant. If for part a above the money stock doubles, then according to the quantity theory of money the price level, P, will _____ to _____. But if velocity falls by half its value as the stock of money doubles, the price level will _____.

   c. Which of the two aggregate supply curves in the figure below is associated with the classical quantity theory of money and is based on the assumption of flexible wages and prices?_____ If monetary policy shifts the aggregate demand curve from ADo to AD1 along the aggregate supply curve, the price level will _____ and real GNP _____.

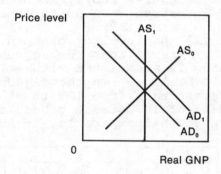

   d. The _____ believe that while velocity is not constant, it is at least predictable enough to use monetary policy to accurately influence nominal GNP.

Concept: Conflicting goals of monetary policy

6.   The figure below shows an economy's loanable funds market. Assume that
     the Fed wants to peg interest rates at their current level as given by the
     demand for loanable funds, Dlf-1. Assume that because of economic
     expansion, the demand for loanable funds shifts outward to Dlf-2.

     a.   What must the Fed do to prevent the interest rate from changing?
          Show this on the figure below. This monetary policy is
          _____ (expansionary, contractionary) and may result in
          _____ (more, less) inflation.

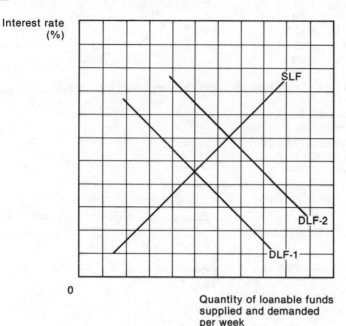

Interest rate
(%)

SLF

DLF-2

DLF-1

0

Quantity of loanable funds
supplied and demanded
per week

     b.   If the Fed decided to control the stock of money, interest rates
          would _____. Show this on the figure above.
     c.   The _____ (inability, ability) to simultaneously attain interest
          rate and money supply targets makes it _____ (easy, difficult)
          to reach macroeconomic goals such as full employment and stable
          prices.

SELF-TEST FOR MASTERY

Select the best answer.

1.   Policies undertaken by governing authorities for the purpose of
     maintaining full employment and a reasonably stable price level is the
     definition of which of the following?

     a.   Monetary policy
     b.   Stabilization policies
     c.   Contractionary monetary policy
     d.   Expansionary monetary policy

2. Action by the Federal Reserve System to increase the monetary base or its rate of growth is the definition for which of the following?

   a. Monetary policy
   b. Stabilization policies
   c. Contractionary monetary policy
   d. Expansionary monetary policy

3. An expansionary monetary policy _____ the monetary base, causing the real interest rate to _____ and planned investment to _____.

   a. Decreases, rise, fall
   b. Increases, rise, rise
   c. Decreases, fall, fall
   d. Increases, rise, fall
   e. Increases, fall, rise

4. Which of the following is true of contractionary monetary policy?

   a. The monetary base declines.
   b. Real interest rates increase.
   c. Planned investment falls.
   d. Aggregate demand falls.
   e. All of the above.

5. If the economy is experiencing an inflationary GNP gap, _____ monetary policy could be used to _____ aggregate demand and _____ the general price level.

   a. Contractionary, reduce, reduce
   b. Contractionary, increase, increase
   c. Contractionary, reduce, increase
   d. Expansionary, reduce, reduce
   e. Expansionary, increase, reduce

6. Monetary policy is more effective:

   a. The less willing bankers are to make loans.
   b. The more responsive credit-sensitive expenditures, including investment, are to changes in interest rates.
   c. The more willing bankers are to make loans with new excess reserves.
   d. A and c.
   e. B and c.

7. If the economy is experiencing a recessionary GNP gap, _____ monetary policy could be used to _____ aggregate demand and _____ real GNP.

   a. Contractionary, reduce, reduce
   b. Contractionary, increase, increase
   c. Contractionary, reduce, increase
   d. Expansionary, increase, reduce
   e. Expansionary, increase, increase

8. Which of the following is not true of the income velocity of circulation of money?

   a. Velocity is defined as nominal GNP/M1.
   b. Historically, velocity has proved to be constant.
   c. Velocity is inversely related to the demand for money.
   d. Changes in velocity influence nominal GNP.

9. If the price level, P, equals 1.50, real GNP is $3000 billion, and the stock of money equals $900 billion, the velocity of circulation of money equals:

    a. 4.
    b. 5.
    c. 6.
    d. 7.
    e. 8.

10. Which of the following is the equation of exchange?

    a. MP = VQ
    b. MT = Q/P
    c. MP = QT
    d. MV = PQ

11. Which of the following assumptions about the economy is central to the classical quantity theory of money?

    a. Wages and prices are rigid in the downward direction.
    b. Flexible wages and prices ensure that the economy will operate at full employment.
    c. Velocity is variable.
    d. Velocity is constant.
    e. B and d.

12. The classical quantity theory of money states that:

    a. Money is a medium of exchange necessary for the efficient functioning of the economy.
    b. Increases in the stock of money result in greater increases in the price level.
    c. Decreases in the stock of money increase the price level.
    d. Increases in the stock of money result in proportionate increases in the price level.

13. The classical quantity theory of money implies that an increase in aggregate demand:

    a. Will increase only real GNP.
    b. Will increase output, but not nominal GNP.
    c. Will increase only the price level.
    d. Will increase the price level, but will reduce nominal GNP.

14. Evidence indicates that:

    a. Velocity is unimportant.
    b. Velocity is constant.
    c. Velocity exhibits long-term trends.
    d. Velocity can increase one year, decrease the next, and increase the following year.
    e. C and d.

15. Monetarists argue that changes in the stock of money can have predictable impacts on _____ GNP assuming that _____ is reasonably stable and predictable.

    a. Real, prices
    b. Real, costs
    c. Nominal, velocity
    d. Nominal, income

16. Which of the following groups is associated with the policy recommendation that the money stock should grow only at the rate of growth in real GNP?

    a. Monetarists
    b. Keynesians
    c. Classical quantity theorists
    d. Republicans and Democrats

17. If the Fed pegs the interest rate at its current level and the demand for money increases, what must the Fed do to prevent the interest rate from changing?

    a. Increase the interest rate on nonfinancial assets.
    b. Decrease the money stock.
    c. Decrease money demand.
    d. Increase the money stock.

18. An inflationary expansion of the economy increases the demand for money. If the Fed has a policy to peg the interest rate, what is the likely consequence of its policy response?

    a. The economy will immediately fall into a depression.
    b. Inflation will fall.
    c. Inflation will rise.
    d. Unemployment will rise and inflation will fall.

19. Which of the following is true of monetary policy?

    a. From the 1940s to the present the Fed has concentrated on attaining monetary targets.
    b. From the 1940s to the 1970s the Fed emphasized interest rate stability.
    c. From late 1979 to late 1982 the Fed pegged the interest rate.
    d. The Fed has always simultaneously targeted both interest rates and the money stock.

THINK IT THROUGH

1. When the Fed increased the money supply after mid-1982, monetarists warned of impending inflation. Instead the U.S. economy has experienced stable inflation for several years. Can you think of any reasons why?

2. Discuss why monetary policy might be ineffective in a severe recession.

3. Explain how a policy to peg interest rates can cause the business cycle to exhibit more volatility.

POP QUIZ   Read the news brief at the end of this chapter and answer the
                questions below.

   1.   What action did the Fed take and for what purpose? Discuss.
   2.   Among other goals, the Fed is trying to prevent increases in
inflation while at the same time it is also trying to maintain the
international value of the dollar within a given range. What problems are
confronted in trying to attain these goals simultaneously?

CHAPTER ANSWERS

In Brief: Chapter Summary

1. Interest rates 2. Inversely 3. Reduces 4. Reduces 5. Expansionary 6.
Interest rate 7. Below 8. Recessionary 9. Inflationary 10. Increase 11.
Decrease 12. Fall 13. Contractionary 14. The money stock 15. MV = PQ 16.
Proportionate 17. Vertical 18. But results in only an increase in the price
level 19. Monetarists 20. No 21. In excess of 22. Equal to 23. Falling
24. Unfortunately, the Fed cannot 25. Increase 26. Difficult 27. Interest
rates 28. The money stock

Vocabulary Review

1.   Monetary policy 2. Contractionary monetary policy 3. Equation of
exchange 4. Classical quantity theory of money 5. Monetarism 6.
Stabilization policies 7. Expansionary monetary policy 8. Income velocity of
circulation of money

Skills Review

1.   a. 10 b. $50 billion, $2,050 billion c. 9%, increases, $60 billion,
      increases, $2,060 billion; right d. 12%, decreases, $30 billion,
      decreases, $2,030; left

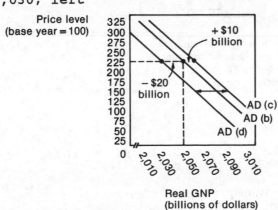

2.   a.   Recessionary; increase; decrease, increase, right
      b.   Inflationary; decrease; increase, decrease, left
      c.   Increase, increase; decrease, decrease

3.   a.   Willingness of bankers to make loans with the newly created excess
            reserves
      b.   Sensitivity of investment and other expenditures to changes in the
            interest rate

4. a. I2
    b.

Price level
(base year = 100)

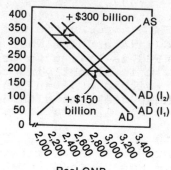

    c. On figure above
    d. Less, more

5. a. 8
    b. Velocity, real GNP; increase, 400; not change
    c. AS1; increase, will not change
    d. Monetarists

6. a. The Fed must increase the monetary base sufficiently to increase the
        stock of money equal to the increase in the demand for money.
        Expansionary, more

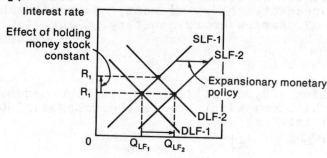

    b. Rise. On figure above.
    c. Inability, difficult

Self-Test for Mastery

1. b 2. d 3. e 4. e 5. a 6. e 7. e 8. b 9. b 10. d 11. e 12. d 13.
c 14. e 15. c 16. a 17. d 18. c 19. b

Think it Through

1.   The monetarists' warnings of inflation were based on the assumption that
velocity was reasonably predictable and on the noticeable increase in the rate
of growth in the money stock. According to the equation of exchange, if
velocity is stable or at least predictable, increases in the money stock in
excess of increases in real GNP will result in a rising price level. But
velocity unexpectedly fell at times in the early to mid-1980s, offsetting the
effect of increases in the money stock on nominal GNP.   The deregulation of the
banking industry and the introduction of financial innovations have been part
of the reason for the greater volatility of velocity in the 1980s.

2.   In a severe recession, bankruptcies and the consequent loan losses might cause bankers to withhold excess reserves from the loanable funds market because of the default risks associated with loans. Investment prospects would not be expected to be very bright in a recession with firms operating with substantial excess capacity. Firms will not likely borrow to expand capacity if they are operating with excess capacity. In a severe recession or depression, an increase in the monetary base may not increase the money stock enough to reduce interest rates. And if interest rates did fall, there is no assurance that firms would borrow and spend the funds. Therefore there is a chance that aggregate demand would be little affected by an expansionary monetary policy.

3.   Suppose that the Fed has a policy to keep interest rates constant. In an economic expansion, the demand for money rises relative to the supply of money, putting upward pressure on market rates of interest. In order to keep interest rates from rising, the Fed has to increase the stock of money. This accelerates the expansion and may even result in worsening inflation. If the economy is declining and the demand for money is falling relative to the stock of money, the Fed must reduce the money supply in order to keep interest rates unchanged. But this results in further economic decline and unemployment. A policy to peg the interest rate over the business cycle will increase the instability of the economy.

Pop Quiz

1.   The Fed increased the discount rate, confirming that it is willing to slow the economy rather than risk an upsurge in inflation. The board of governors was worried that the economy's growth would be too vigorous to maintain the inflation rate at its present level. The Department of Commerce reported that hourly earnings increased at a 6% annual rate, supporting the view of those believing the economy's growth might ignite inflation. Other indications of strong growth include a high capacity utilization rate and continued increases in employment (or decreases in unemployment).

2.   In the chapter, Hyman noted that it is difficult if not impossible to achieve interest rate and money supply targets simultaneously. Likewise, if the Fed chooses to pursue domestic target goals, it may have to give up attempts to achieve international trade and finance goals. Increasing the discount rate will slow the economy and reduce the threat of inflation, but it will also increase interest rates. As domestic interest rates rise relative to foreign interest rates, foreigners purchase more U.S. financial assets. This causes the dollar to appreciate relative to foreign currencies, making U.S. goods and services less price competitive abroad. Exports would likely fall relative to imports, causing the balance of trade to worsen. As a result, attempts to reduce or prevent inflation domestically may result in an eventual deterioration of the balance of international trade.

Higher Interest

Raising Discount Rate, Fed Puts Inflation War Ahead of Dollar Policy

---

Action Is Likely to Push Up Greenback Even Further, Despite 7-Nation Accord

---

Bush Campaign Could Suffer

By ALAN MURRAY
And WALTER S. MOSSBERG
Staff Reporters of THE WALL STREET JOURNAL

WASHINGTON — Defying election-year pressures and a rising dollar, the Federal Reserve Board is raising interest rates decisively to head off a resurgence of inflation.

In a surprise step, the central bank increased its discount rate yesterday to 6.5% from 6%. Even more important, Fed officials made it clear in interviews that they plan to push up other short-term interest rates as well. The key federal-funds rate, for example, will move above the 8% level in coming days, officials said, up from about 7¾% in recent weeks. Bank prime rates, mortgage rates and other consumer-interest rates are likely to follow.

The Fed acted despite the dollar's recent strength in foreign-exchange markets. Higher interest rates, which make U.S. investments more attractive to foreign buyers, are likely to push the greenback to even loftier heights—perhaps breaking through the secret trading ranges that the major industrial nations have set to promote exchange-rate stability. In recent days, the U.S. and other governments have been battling to keep the dollar from climbing too sharply against the West German mark; they want to keep the U.S. trade deficit declining.

Domestic Considerations First

The increase in the discount rate—the rate the Fed charges on loans to financial institutions—proves once again that, when push comes to shove, U.S. officials put concern about the domestic economy above concern about a stable dollar. "The decision reflects the intent of the Federal Reserve to reduce inflationary pressures," the central bank said in announcing the increase.

"First things first," a senior Fed official explained yesterday. "You use monetary policy for domestic purposes, to fight inflation. That's the first priority."

Moreover, the push for higher interest rates, coming just a few days before the Republican convention, diminishes fears that Fed Chairman Alan Greenspan and his fellow Republican board members would shrink from fighting inflation in an election year.

"The election appears to be very far from their minds," says Scott Pardee, a former high Fed official and now vice chairman of Yamaichi International (America) Inc., a Japanese securities firm. Mr. Pardee believes that it was time for the Fed to tighten to head off potential difficulties: "The main problem they have is an economy that is strong, but not booming, and inflation that is troublesome, although not out of hand."

Markets' Reaction

Short-term interest rates and the dollar both rose after the Fed's announcement. Stock prices skidded on fears that higher rates will slow the economy. Bond prices plunged. (See story on page 3.)

Although the Fed's action yesterday isn't likely to slow the economy significantly before the November presidential election, higher rates could amplify the uncertainty that many voters already feel about the nation's economic health, thus hurting Vice President George Bush. Political-economic analysts note that in September 1980 the Fed, then led by Paul Volcker, raised the discount rate, helping wreck President Carter's re-election bid.

The timing of the Fed's move is awkward for the Reagan administration, too. The Treasury Department is going through a transition, with Secretary James Baker departing next week to take over Mr. Bush's election campaign and investment banker Nicholas Brady awaiting Senate confirmation as Mr. Baker's replacement. The move took many Treasury officials by surprise; Mr. Baker himself had said emphatically on NBC's "Meet the Press" Sunday that he didn't think the Fed had indicated any plan to raise rates.

Costly to Treasury

Moreover, the action came on the same day the Treasury was beginning its quarterly refunding operations, its offerings of new securities to replace maturing issues. As a result, it forced the government to pay higher interest rates on the securities it sells. The average yield on the three-year notes sold yesterday was 8.77%, the highest in three years.

White House spokesman Marlin Fitzwater, reading a statement approved by Secretary Baker, said that the administration is "disappointed" by the Fed's move but that "we understand there's a sound reason for it." He added that "we think the Federal Reserve has done a good job . . . the Fed's on the right course."

House Minority Leader Robert Michel of Illinois expressed some discomfort with the Fed's decision. "I don't see the signs of inflation out there," he said. But he noted that the impact of the Fed move won't be entirely negative for his party because price stability has been a Reagan "hallmark" that Republicans will stress at their convention next week.

For the Fed, the action resolved a battle that has been brewing for weeks between the presidents of the system's regional banks and the members of the Fed's board of governors. Worried by signs of strong economic growth, many of the presidents have argued that the Fed needs to raise rates. But some of the governors have resisted such suggestions, and the dispute was threatening to explode at next week's meeting of the policy-making Federal Open Market Committee, which is composed of the Reserve Board members and five Reserve Bank presidents.

The governors apparently were moved to act, however, when they discovered at their regular Monday meeting that nine of the 12 regional banks were requesting a discount-rate rise, up from only six last week. Late Monday, Chairman Greenspan called a board meeting for yesterday morning, and all six governors (one board seat is vacant) agreed to support the rate increase. They also decided to announce it in the morning, to give investors time to react before the Treasury refunding.

The rise in the discount rate brought it to its highest level since July 1986. The Fed's expected new level of just over 8% for the federal funds rate—the fee banks charge on loans to each other—would boost that rate to its high since early 1986.

U.S. officials emphasize that the Fed's move doesn't signal a defection from the general effort by the Group of Seven leading industrial nations to stabilize the dollar within a secret range of exchange rates. In addition to citing the matter of priorities, they explain that the G-7 exchange-rate system is flexible, allowing for short-term deviations and even unannounced changes in the exchange-rate ranges if economic fundamentals shift.

But the Fed's action marked the second time in less than a year that American monetary policy makers have felt compelled to meet a domestic-policy challenge at the expense of international dollar policy. Last October, in the wake of the stock-market crash, the Fed slashed interest rates to stave off a recession, even though the move drove the dollar down below levels the G-7 thought desirable. In yesterday's case, as in October, the U.S. informed its economic partners in advance of the move and, officials say, received general support for it.

A Tactical Retreat

It has been widely assumed that the upper end of the secret range is about 1.90 marks and 140 yen to the dollar, though the governments have never confirmed this. The G-7 central banks had been fighting in recent days to keep the dollar from piercing the 1.90-mark ceiling, by selling greenbacks in currency markets. But the Fed's decision pushed the dollar firmly above 1.90 marks, and the governments beat a tactical retreat.

"With this move by the Fed, we expect the dollar to stay firm for a while," says Fred Scala, a senior currency trader at Manufacturers Hanover Trust Co. in New

York. "I expect we'll see new highs every day because the foreign-exchange market has become so interest-rate sensitive."

The officials indicate that the G-7 governments would probably avoid drastic exchange-rate actions for now and wait to see how far the dollar rises against the mark—and how long it stays high—before mounting any huge intervention campaign or changing joint exchange-rate policies.

They say other coming events—including next week's scheduled release of U.S. trade data—could moderate the dollar's rise. And they indicate that the G-7 might wait until its next scheduled meeting, around Sept. 22, before formally reconsidering whether its secret range still meshes with the fundamental positions of the world's major economies.

The lower, more stable dollar that has resulted from the G-7 effort has helped produce the desired boom in U.S. exports. Yesterday, officials said they weren't sure how much damage to the trade improvement a further surge in the greenback would cause just now. They noted that the dollar's surge, both before and after the Fed action, has been mainly against the German mark. The dollar's value against the Japanese yen has remained comfortably within the supposed ceiling of 140 yen. The officials said that if the dollar's climb remains more moderate in terms of the yen, it could have less detrimental effect on the trade balance than an overall surge.

Fed Vice Chairman Manuel Johnson and several other governors who watch financial-market indicators of inflation, rather than focus on the pace of economic growth, have tried to play down worries of inflation in recent weeks. A rising dollar, a strong bond market and stable commodity prices suggested to them that inflation fears were under control.

Employment Report Cited

But concern about inflation stepped up Friday when the Labor Department announced that employment increased strongly in July and that hourly earnings rose at a 6% annual pace. That added to the belief of many district Fed presidents that the economy couldn't continue to grow so rapidly without sparking inflation.

"The evidence suggests the economy is continuing to grow in a 3.5% to 4% range," Kansas City Fed President Roger Guffey says. "Given the strong employment numbers that have been posted recently and the high capacity utilization rates, that all adds up in my mind to the idea that inflationary pressures are quite likely to increase."

On Monday, Chairman Greenspan, who has worked to reconcile the two opposing camps, apparently was able to convince all five of his fellow governors that the time for action had come. Even Governor Martha Seger, who has dissented on many of the Fed's votes for a tighter policy, supported the move.

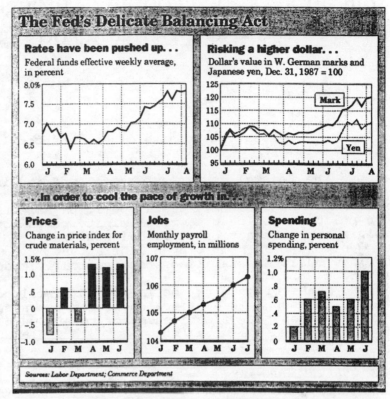

The Fed's Delicate Balancing Act

Rates have been pushed up...
Federal funds effective weekly average, in percent

Risking a higher dollar...
Dollar's value in W. German marks and Japanese yen, Dec. 31, 1987 = 100

...in order to cool the pace of growth in...

Prices
Change in price index for crude materials, percent

Jobs
Monthly payroll employment, in millions

Spending
Change in personal spending, percent

Sources: Labor Department; Commerce Department

In its statement, the Fed first mentioned the need to curb "inflationary pressures" and then added that "the action was also taken in light of the growing spread of market interest rates over the discount rate." The Fed hadn't changed the discount rate since last September, but it has been steadily pushing up other short-term interest rates since late March.

The increase was initially requested by the boards of all the Fed district banks except those in Chicago, Minneapolis and Dallas. Late yesterday, the Chicago and Minneapolis banks also requested a discount-rate increase.

Asked about the Fed's move yesterday, Lawrence Summers, a Harvard economist and an adviser to Democratic presidential candidate Michael Dukakis, said, "It just illustrates that the Federal Reserve is in an extraordinarily difficult position as long as we have so strong an economy coinciding with such large budget deficits."

The Fed's move puts the German government, too, in a difficult position.

For weeks, capital has been surging out of Germany. Much of it has gone into dollar-denominated holdings, helping to lift the dollar against the mark. That trend is partly due to higher U.S. interest rates, but U.S. officials and market participants also attribute it to investors' growing perception that Germany's economy is too stagnant and regulated to attract much investment. Germany's growth rate has been hovering around 2%—far below that of the

U.S. and Japan—partly because its government has been too worried about inflation to favor much stimulus.

Now, the German government and the independent central bank, the Bundesbank, face a cruel choice. They can raise interest rates to try to maintain the differential with U.S. rates and thus bolster the mark a bit. But such an increase, following a flurry of others recently, might slow German growth even further and cause the capital outflow to continue or even speed up. That might weaken the mark so much as to more than offset the bolstering effect of an interest-rate rise.

"As soon as the Bundesbank hikes rates again, it will start running the risk of choking off economic growth," says Ulrich Ramm, the chief economist of Commerzbank AG in Frankfurt. "At this point, the Bundesbank ought to wait. The higher the dollar rises, the sooner it can fall."

The Bundesbank's next scheduled opportunity to alter its key interest rates will come Aug. 25, when its policy-setting Central Bank Council returns from a four-month break. The Bundesbank yesterday left unchanged at 4.25% the rate it charges on its one-month securities-repurchase agreements, the bank's favored tool for steering German money-market rates.

Elsewhere in Europe, the effects will be much smaller. The Bank of England raised its own base rates by 0.5 percentage point Monday but insisted yesterday that its action and the Fed's weren't coordinated.

19

Stabilization of the Economy Through Fiscal Policy: Effects on Aggregate Demand and Aggregate Supply

CHAPTER CHALLENGES

After studying your text, attending class, and completing this chapter, you should be able to:

1. Discuss the federal government budget and its impact on aggregate demand in the economy.
2. Explain how expansionary fiscal policies affect the economy and show how such policies can be used to eliminate recessionary GNP gaps.
3. Explain how contractionary fiscal policies affect the economy and show how such policies can help prevent inflation.
4. Show how built-in stabilizers automatically moderate shifts in aggregate demand.
5. Discuss means of gauging the impact of fiscal policy on the economy.
6. Explain how supply-side fiscal policies can affect the economy in the long run and assess the effectiveness of recent supply-side policies.

IN BRIEF: CHAPTER SUMMARY

Fill in the blanks to summarize chapter content.

The government can influence the level of aggregate demand in both the short run and the long run through the use of fiscal policy. A budget (1)_____ (surplus, deficit) exists when government purchases exceed tax revenues. Budget (2)_____ (surpluses, deficits) occur when tax revenues exceed government purchases. Budget deficits have an/a (3)_____ (expansionary, contractionary) impact on aggregate demand, whereas budget surpluses have an/a (4)_____ (expansionary, contractionary) impact.

If the economy is experiencing a recessionary GNP gap, the government can increase real GNP by pursuing an expansionary fiscal policy. Specifically, the government can (5)_____ (decrease, increase) government purchases, increase transfer payments to individuals and organizations, or (6)_____ (decrease, increase) taxes. If the economy is in the horizontal segment of the aggregate supply curve, an expansionary fiscal policy will increase real GNP (7)_____ (without igniting, and cause) inflation. The extent of fiscal stimulus can be determined by dividing the recessionary GNP gap by the multiplier.

Tax cuts have a similar effect on aggregate demand. A reduction in taxes (8)_____ (will, will not) increase aggregate demand as much as an equivalent increase in government spending because the marginal propensities to consume and import reduce the amount of new income from the tax cut available for expenditure. If government spending is financed by an equal increase in taxes, the net effect is (9)_____ (expansionary, negative) because the government spending multiplier exceeds the net tax multiplier. The most expansionary fiscal policy is an increase in government spending

(10)_____ (financed with higher taxes, that increases the budget deficit).

If the economy has an inflationary GNP gap, the price level can be reduced by a contractionary fiscal policy. The government can (11)_____ (reduce, increase) its expenditures, (12)_____ (decrease, increase) transfers, or (13)_____ (decrease, increase) taxes. Real GNP falls toward its potential level as the price level falls. If, however, the government expands the economy when there is an inflationary GNP gap, inflation, which is already a problem, becomes worse.

Several problems are associated with the implementation of fiscal policy. For one, it is unlikely that the political process will produce the correct economic stabilization legislation. Politicians look to the next election and recognize the political problems inherent in raising taxes or cutting programs that benefit their constituencies. While it is politically much (14)_____ (more difficult, easier) to cut taxes or increase government purchases in a recession, it is much (15)_____ (more difficult, easier) to raise taxes or cut government purchases in an inflationary period.

Economic forecasting is necessary in implementing fiscal policy. Policy makers need to know where the economy is headed in order to determine the proper amount of stimulus or contraction needed. If forecasts are in error, fiscal policy (16)_____ (will, will not) likely close the recessionary or inflationary GNP gap. Lags in fiscal policy implementation also add to the difficulty of closing recessionary and inflationary gaps. The time lags include the recognition lag, the administrative lag, and the operational lag. We do not know if we have entered an expansion or a recession until weeks or even months after the occurrence. This is the (17)_____ (operational, administrative, recognition) lag. The (18)_____ (operational, administrative, recognition) lag is the length of time it takes the government to devise a policy response. And finally, the (19)_____ (operational, administrative, recognition) lag is the length of time the policy response takes to change real GNP, the price level, and the level of unemployment. Because the lengths of these lags are not known with certainty, fiscal policy may be ill timed and as a result may not close the inflationary or recessionary GNP gap.

Fortunately, the government budget still has a stabilizing impact on the economy through its automatic stabilizers--a form of (20)_____ (discretionary, nondiscretionary) fiscal policy. These include income taxes and transfer payments. The transfers that vary over the business cycle are entitlement programs such as unemployment insurance, cash assistance welfare benefits, (21)_____ (in-kind assistance, private pension benefits), and Social Security pension payments. As the economy falls into a recession, income tax revenues decline and transfers increase automatically. This (22)_____ (increases aggregate demand more than, prevents the level of aggregate demand from falling as much as) it would have otherwise. An economic expansion increases tax revenues and reduces transfer payments, which aids in restraining aggregate demand. This (23)_____ (reduces, increases) the threat of inflation. In order to determine if discretionary fiscal policy is stimulative or contractionary, it is necessary to hold constant the effect of the automatic stabilizers. This is done with the concept of the (24)_____ (balanced budget, high-employment deficit), in which government spending and revenues are compared assuming the economy is operating over the year at the natural rate of unemployment.

In addition to demand-side effects, fiscal policies can also have supply-side effects over the long run. A cut in tax rates, it is argued, will increase the after-tax returns to work, saving, and investment. If the number of labor hours increases and the levels of saving and investment increase, the

(25)_____ (aggregate supply curve will shift rightward, the aggregate demand curve will shift leftward). Evidence suggests that these effects (26)_____ (are, are not) very large, particularly in the short run. In the short run, a cut in tax rates will increase aggregate demand more than aggregate supply, implying the possibility of (27)_____ (unemployment, inflation) if the economy is on the upward-sloping portion of its aggregate supply curve. To prevent tax cuts from causing inflation and to allow sufficient time for them to have supply-side effects on the aggregate supply curve, aggregate demand will have to be restrained somewhat through reduced government spending. In addition to cuts in tax rates, legislation allowing individual retirement accounts may increase saving, and accelerated depreciation allowances and investment tax credits may (28)_____ (increase, decrease) capital formation, both of which could shift the aggregate supply curve (29)_____ (leftward, rightward).

VOCABULARY REVIEW

Write the key term from the list below next to its definition.

Key Terms

Fiscal policy   Automatic stabilizers
Government budget   High-employment deficit (or surplus)
Expansionary fiscal   Supply-side fiscal policies
  policy   Accelerated depreciation allowances
Contractionary
  fiscal policy

Definitions

1. _____: the use of government spending and taxation for the specific purpose of stabilizing the economy.

2. _____: features of the federal budget that automatically adjust net taxes to stabilize aggregate demand as the economy expands and contracts.

3. _____: generous deductions from pretax business income that are allowed when firms acquire new equipment or new purchases.

4. _____: a policy under which the government acts to restrain aggregate demand by decreasing spending or increasing taxes, or both.

5. _____: seek to influence long-run economic growth in real GNP through government subsidies and tax collections.

6. _____: a policy under which the government acts to increase aggregate demand by increasing spending or decreasing taxes, or both.

7. _____: gives the budget deficit (or surplus) that would prevail if the natural rate of unemployment were achieved.

8. _____: a plan for spending funds and raising revenues through taxation, fees, and other means, and borrowing funds if necessary.

SKILLS REVIEW

Concept: **Impact of the federal budget on aggregate demand; fiscal policies to close recessionary and inflationary GNP gaps**

1. Assume that the economy in the figure below is currently at its potential level of real GNP.

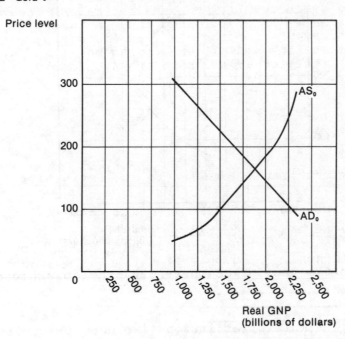

a. Identify the equilibrium price level and level of real GNP on the figure.
b. Assume a decrease in autonomous spending reduces aggregate purchases by \$125 billion. If the multiplier is 2, the aggregate demand curve will shift _____ by \$_____. Show the new AD curve and label it AD1.
c. The economy is now experiencing a/an _____ gap. Real GNP _____ potential GNP, and the unemployment rate _____ than the natural rate of unemployment.
d. If the government wanted to reduce unemployment by closing the recessionary gap, it would have to _____ government spending by \$_____.
e. Alternatively the government could close the recessionary gap by _____ taxes and/or _____ transfer payments.
f. What would be the effect if the government pursued an expansionary fiscal policy given the initial aggregate demand curve, ADo?

269

2. Assume the economy in the figure below is presently suffering from an inflationary GNP gap.

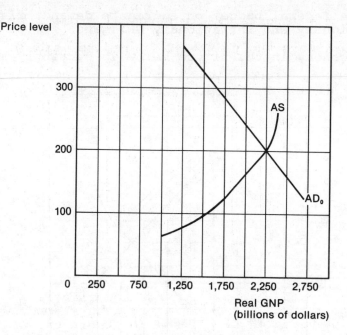

a. In order to close the inflationary gap, the government could:
    (1) _____
    (2) _____
    (3) _____

b. If the economy's multiplier is 2.5 (includes price-level effects) and the decline in government spending necessary to move the economy back to its potential level of real GNP is $200 billion, potential real GNP is short of the current inflationary level of real GNP by $_____. A/An _____ in government spending of $_____ will close the inflationary gap.

c. Show on the figure above the effect of a contractionary fiscal policy. Be sure to identify the changes in the price level and real GNP.

3. List three problems associated with the implementation of fiscal policy.

    a. _____
    b. _____
    c. _____

4. Advanced Question Given the following equations, find the change in government spending necessary to close a recessionary GNP gap of $100 billion. The recessionary gap could alternatively be closed by what change in the tax rate?

$$Y = C + Ip + G + NE \qquad \text{where } A = \$300$$
$$C = A + (MPC)DI \qquad\qquad Ip = \$400$$
$$DI = Y - T \qquad\qquad\qquad G = \$500$$
$$T = tY \qquad\qquad\qquad\quad E = \$200$$
$$Ip = Io \qquad\qquad\qquad\quad MPC = .9$$
$$G = Go \qquad\qquad\qquad\quad t = .3$$
$$NE = E - M \qquad\qquad\quad MPI = .15$$
$$M = (MPI)Y$$

C = consumption, Y = real GNP, Ip = planned investment, G = government purchases, NE = net exports, A = autonomous consumption, DI = disposable income, MPC = marginal propensity to consume, T = net taxes, t = net tax rate, E = exports, M = imports, MPI = marginal propensity to import

Concept: Built-in stabilizers and shifts in aggregate demand

5.   Assume that the economy represented in the figure below currently has a level of aggregate demand as shown by the AD curve, ADo.

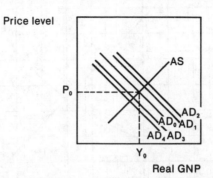

a.   As an economy expands, taxes _____ and transfers _____. An increase in aggregate demand caused by a given increase in autonomous purchases is represented by AD1 and AD2 where one of the AD curves is associated with an economy having built-in stabilizers and the other is not. Which AD curve, AD1 or AD2, is consistent with the existence of built-in stabilizers? _____
b.   As an economy contracts, taxes _____ and transfers _____. A given reduction in autonomous purchases shifts the aggregate demand curve leftward from ADo. AD3 and AD4 result from the same decline in autonomous spending, but one of the curves is for an economy with automatic stabilizers and the other curve is not. Which of the two aggregate demand curves, AD3 or AD4, is consistent with built-in stabilizers? _____
c.   Built-in stabilizers _____ the fluctuations in aggregate demand and real GNP for given fluctuations in autonomous spending.

Concept: Supply-side fiscal policy

6.   Show on the figure below the supply-side effect of a cut in tax rates. Be
      sure to identify the changes in real GNP and the price level.

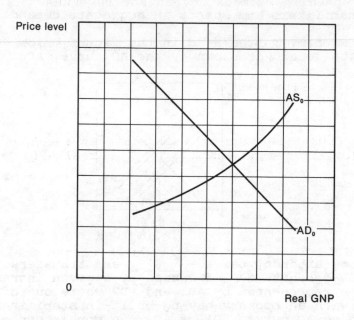

a.   A cut in tax rates will _____ the after-tax returns to work,
      saving, and investment and is expected to _____ the levels of
      hours worked, saving, and investment.
b.   If the aggregate supply curve shifts _____, the price level will
      fall and the level of real GNP will _____.
c.   Evidence indicates that the short-run effect on the aggregate supply
      curve of cuts in tax rates will be _____ relative to shifts in
      the aggregate demand curve.
d.   If the economy is at its potential level of real GNP when tax rates
      are reduced, the price level will likely _____ unless the
      government _____ government purchases.

SELF-TEST FOR MASTERY

Select the best answer.

1.   The use of government spending and taxation for the purpose of stabilizing
      the economy is called:

      a.   Budget policy.
      b.   Monetary policy.
      c.   Fiscal policy.
      d.   Trade policy.

2. A budget deficit exits when:

   a. Tax revenue exceeds government spending.
   b. Government spending equals government revenues.
   c. Government spending exceeds government revenues.
   d. The public debt decreases.

3. An increase in the budget deficit _____ aggregate _____.

   a. Increases, demand
   b. Increases, supply
   c. Decreases, demand
   d. Decreases, supply

4. An increase in a budget surplus or a decrease in a budget deficit
   _____ aggregate demand and _____ real GNP.

   a. Increases, reduces
   b. Increases, decreases
   c. Decreases, increases
   d. Decreases, reduces

5. A recessionary GNP gap can be closed by which of the following?

   a. An increase in government spending
   b. A decrease in taxes
   c. An increase in transfer payments
   d. All of the above

6. If the marginal respending rate (MRR) is .6 and the current level of
   equilibrium real GNP is short of the desired level of real GNP by $250
   billion, by how much will the government have to increase aggregate
   demand? (Assume that the economy is in the flat portion of the AS curve.)

   a. $40 billion
   b. $60 billion
   c. $80 billion
   d. $100 billion
   e. $120 billion

7. Which of the following fiscal policies is the most stimulative in the
   short run?

   a. Increases in government spending financed by borrowing (incurring a
      deficit)
   b. Increases in government spending financed by taxation
   c. Equal decreases in taxes and government spending
   d. Increases in transfers financed by taxation

8. When the price level is responsive to changes in aggregate demand, the
   multiplier will be _____ the multiplier presented in the text
   chapter.

   a. Greater than
   b. Less than
   c. Equal to
   d. Twice the size of

9. Which of the following policies should be used to close an inflationary GNP gap?

   a. Increases in government spending
   b. Tax cuts
   c. Increases in transfer payments
   d. An increase in taxes

10. Which lag in the implementation of fiscal policy is due to the length of time that it takes fiscal policy to have the desired impact on the economy?

    a. Recognition lag
    b. Administrative lag
    c. Operational lag
    d. Cyclical lag

11. Automatic stabilizers:

    a. Are a form of nondiscretionary fiscal policy.
    b. Include income taxes and cash assistance to the poor.
    c. Include in-kind assistance and Social Security benefits.
    d. A and b.
    e. All of the above.

12. As the economy expands, tax revenues _____ and transfer payments _____, causing the economy to expand _____ than it would in the absence of these built-in stabilizers.

    a. Fall, rise, more
    b. Fall, fall, less
    c. Rise, fall, more
    d. Rise, fall, less
    e. Rise, rise, more

13. Built-in stabilizers result in _____ fluctuations in aggregate demand for given autonomous changes in spending than as would be the case for an economy in which built-in stabilizers did not exist.

    a. Greater
    b. More severe
    c. Smaller
    d. The same

14. Which of the following budget concepts measures the policy stance of discretionary fiscal policy--that is, whether it is expansionary or contractionary?

    a. Balanced budget
    b. Budget deficit
    c. Potential output budget
    d. High-employment deficit (or surplus)

15. A reduction in tax rates _____ the after-tax returns to work, saving, and investment, which in the long run may _____ aggregate supply.

    a. Reduces, increase
    b. Reduces, decrease
    c. Increases, decrease
    d. Increases, increase

16. Proponents of supply-side fiscal policies argue that a cut in tax rates will:

    a. Increase the number of hours worked.
    b. Increase the level of saving.
    c. Increase the level of investment.
    d. Increase potential real GNP.
    e. All of the above.

17. Evidence indicates that a cut in tax rates in the short run will likely increase _____ more than _____, causing the price level to _____ unless government reduces _____.

    a. Aggregate demand, aggregate supply, rise, government spending
    b. Aggregate supply, aggregate demand, fall, transfers to the poor
    c. Aggregate supply, aggregate demand, rise, tax rates
    d. Aggregate demand, aggregate supply, fall, its borrowing
    e. None of the above

THINK IT THROUGH

1. If the current unemployment rate exceeds the natural rate of unemployment and the current government budget is in balance, the high-employment budget is in (balance/deficit/surplus). What are the effects on the economy?

2. Conflicts such as World War II and the Vietnam War created domestic economic expansion. Explain. How does this relate to the ease or difficulty of implementing fiscal policy?

3. Discuss the case for and against supply-side fiscal policies.

POP QUIZ   Read the news brief at the end of this chapter and answer the questions below.

1. Some people argue that an increase in taxes will not reduce the federal budget deficit because higher taxes invite lawmakers to increase spending. Discuss Herbert Stein's response to this assertion.

2. Historically, why have deficits increased?

3. What assumptions are being made by the administration in projecting a decline in the deficit to $23 billion by 1993? Are any of these assumptions inconsistent with the administration's argument that tax increases will simply fuel spending rather than reduce the deficit?

CHAPTER ANSWERS

In Brief: Chapter Summary

1. Deficit 2. Surpluses 3. Expansionary 4. Contractionary 5. Increase 6. Decrease 7. Without igniting 8. Will not 9. Expansionary 10. That increases the budget deficit 11. Reduce 12. Decrease 13. Increase 14. Easier 15.

More difficult 16. Will not 17. Recognition 18. Administrative 19.
Operational 20. Nondiscretionary 21. In-kind assistance 22. Prevents the
level of aggregate demand from falling as much as 23. Reduces 24. High-
employment deficit 25. Aggregate supply will shift rightward 26. Are not 27.
Inflation 28. Increase 29. Rightward

Vocabulary Review

1. Fiscal policy 2. Automatic stabilizers 3. Accelerated depreciation
allowances 4. Contractionary fiscal policy 5. Supply-side fiscal policies 6.
Expansionary fiscal policies 7. High-employment deficit (or surplus) 8.
Government budget

Skills Review

1. a.

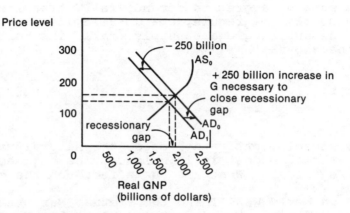

b. Leftward, $250 billion
c. Recessionary GNP gap, falls below, is higher
d. Increase, $125 billion
e. Reduce, increase
f. Real GNP would exceed potential real GNP and the unemployment rate
    would fall below its natural rate, putting upward pressure on the
    price level.

2. a. (1) Increase taxes (2) Reduce transfer payments (3) Reduce
        government spending
    b. $500 billion; decrease, $200 billion

    c.

3. a. Political problems b. Forecasting problems c. Timing problems

276

4. This particular model is analyzed in the appendix that presents a complete Keynesian model. For the equations and values given, the multiplier is 1.923. Thus if the policy goal is to expand real GNP by $100 billion, divide this amount by the multiplier to determine the necessary change in government spending. ($100 billion/1.923 = $52 billion.) Government spending must be increased by $52 billion in order to increase equilibrium real GNP by $100 billion and close the recessionary GNP gap.

Alternatively, the recessionary gap can be closed by a reduction in the tax rate. The first step is to find the tax rate multiplier (change in real GNP/change in the tax rate). Dividing the tax rate multiplier into the recessionary gap of $100 billion will give the necessary change in tax rates. For those students familiar will calculus, the tax rate multiplier can be found by solving the system of equations for the equilibrium level of real GNP, Y, and taking the partial derivative of Y with respect to the tax rate, t. The tax rate multiplier is as follows:

Tax rate multiplier = $-[MPC(Y)]/[1 - MPC + (MPC)t + MPI]$

For the values given, the tax rate multiplier equals -4659.75. Dividing this into $100 billion gives -.021. The tax rate must be reduced from 30% to 27.9% in order to close the recessionary gap.

5. a.   Increase, decrease; AD1
    b.   Decrease, increase; AD3
    c.   Moderate

6.

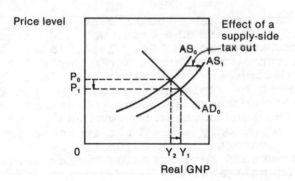

    a.   Increase, increase b. Rightward, Increase   c. Very small
    d.   Rise, reduces

Self-Test for Mastery

1. c 2. c 3. a 4. d 5. d 6. d 7. a 8. b 9. d 10. c 11. e 12. d 13. c 14. d 15. d 16. e 17. a

Think it Through

1.   If the current government budget is in balance but the economy is operating below potential real GNP, the high-employment budget would be in surplus. Thus discretionary fiscal policy would be contractionary if the economy expanded to its potential level of real GNP. Fiscal policy would act as a "drag" on the economy as it approached potential real GNP.

2.   During wars, U.S. government spending has far exceeded tax revenues. The increases in the deficit during the war years created domestic economic expansion. This is powerful evidence of the ability of government budget

deficits to expand the economy in the short run. But it also points to a difficulty in the implementation of fiscal policy. National defense and security, economic stabilization, and other goals of society compete with one another. Economic stabilization may require certain budget changes, whereas the provision of national defense may require completely different budget changes. Nevertheless, any budget change that alters a deficit or surplus will have short-run macroeconomic effects that may or may not be desirable with regard to economic stabilization.

3.   During periods of stagflation, the traditional discretionary fiscal policy of aggregate demand management is unlikely to reduce inflation and unemployment simultaneously. If fiscal policy could shift the economy's aggregate supply curve rightward in the short run, real output would increase and both the unemployment rate and price level (or rate of inflation) would fall. The argument for supply-side fiscal policies is that not only would the price level and unemployment fall, but the potential level of real GNP would increase, allowing higher future living standards. All of this is based upon the belief that a cut in tax rates will have large impacts on hours worked, saving, and investment, thus shifting the aggregate supply curve rightward. Few economists would dispute the argument that tax rate cuts increase to some extent hours worked, saving, and investment. But the empirical evidence suggests that the short-run impacts of a cut in tax rates will primarily affect the aggregate demand curve rather than the aggregate supply curve. If the economy is already suffering from inflation and tax rates are cut, there will be greater rather than less pressure for prices to rise.

Pop Quiz

1.   Herbert Stein argues that increased government spending is not the direct result of higher taxes. If that were the case, why didn't government expenditures fall when taxes were cut in 1948, 1954, 1963, 1969, 1971, 1978 and 1981? Taxes were raised during World War I, World War II, the Korean War, and the Vietnam War but not by as much as government spending. The budget experience of the 1980s cannot be explained in terms of the theory that increased revenues result in increased spending. From 1980 to 1986 government spending increased by 158% of the increase in revenues. From 1986 to 1988 government spending increased by only 47% of the increase in revenues. According to Stein, "...the proportions in which the revenue (from a tax increase) would be divided between more spending and a smaller deficit are not determined by an iron law of politics."

2.   Government expenditures and revenues matched each other fairly closely until roughly the Reagan administration. Past deficits typically increased only during recessions and wars, but not during periods of prosperity and peace.

3.   In fact, the only way that the government can reach its deficit goal by 1993 is by not spending all of the increased tax revenues resulting from growth. On the one hand, the official rhetoric is that taxes should not be increased to reduce the deficit because that will increase spending; but on the other hand, the administration's budget projection assumes just the opposite.

The New Parkinson's Law

By Herbert Stein

Thirty-one years ago we all laughed at a joke called Parkinson's Law, written by a British historian. The Law was that work expands to fill the time available. I call it a joke because, like the stories about the stingy Scotsman and the mean mother-in-law, it appealed to our sense of the ridiculous but was not true. In fact, Parkinson made little attempt to prove that his Law was a law aside from telling some cute anecdotes.

Today, a version of Parkinson's Law has become an important feature of policy talk, and possibly of policy, in America. Today's Law is that government expenditures rise to meet the revenue available. This is now the primary argument used to demonstrate that a tax increase will not reduce the deficit. It has supplanted the proposition that a tax increase will not raise the revenue.

The new Law is supposed to be a corollary of the proposition that politicians are shortsighted and venal. If they have more money, they will spend it. Of course, that applies only to the other politicians, the "bad" ones—the liberals, Democrats and congressmen—not to the "good" ones like us.

But even a moment's reflection raises serious questions about the Law. If expenditures are determined by revenue, where did the $2 trillion debt come from? And if "They" spend all the revenue that the tax system yields, where did the tax cuts of 1948, 1954, 1963, 1969, 1971, 1978 and 1981 come from? Something else seems to be going on besides spending all the revenue available.

Sequence Is Important

During most of our history, until approximately the Reagan administration, expenditures and revenue were fairly close together except in wars and recessions. But that does not show that the expenditures rose to equal the revenue. It also could have been true that the revenue usually rose to equal the expenditures, which were determined by something other than the available revenue. The sequence is important.

In this century there have been three main sources of revenue increases—tax increases during wars, revenue increases from the existing tax system due to growth and inflation (creep), and tax increases to fund Social Security.

Taxes were raised during World War I, World War II, the Korean War and the Vietnam War. In no case were taxes raised enough to cover the cost of the war. In no case did expenditures rise enough after the war to absorb the revenue that would have been available if the war taxes had been retained. We did not retain enough of the war taxes even to pay off the debt accumulated during the war.

Expenditures did not rise enough to equal the rise of revenue that was produced by economic growth and inflation since World War II. The tax cuts of 1948, 1963, 1969, 1971, 1978 and 1981 gave back much of that increased revenue. Expendi-

---

Board of Contributors

If expenditures are determined by revenue, where did the $2 trillion debt come from? And if "They" spend all the revenue that the tax system yields, where did the tax cuts come from?

---

tures did rise during that period, absolutely and relative to gross national product, but there is no clear evidence that the rise was governed by the increased revenue. It is at least equally likely that the amount of the revenue give-back during this period was governed by the actual and prospective expenditures.

The increases in the payroll tax for Social Security were clearly motivated by the desire to pay for benefits under actual or proposed legislation. It was not because there was a lot of money in the Social Security reserves that we got the benefit increases.

For the benefit of those who may be unconvinced by my thumbnail history, I refer to a statistical analysis done by Profs. George von Furstenberg, R. Jeffery Green and Jin-Ho Jeong, "Tax and Spend, or Spend and Tax?" that was published in The Review of Economics and Statistics, May 1986. Their conclusion was summarized as follows:

"Assertions about how changes on one side of the federal budget are processed on the other cover the range of possibilities. One such assertion, tax and spend, holds that spending can be moved with prior tax action both up and down. This implies that those who raised taxes invited more spending while those who lower taxes can subdue it. . . . The evidence assembled in this paper provided no support for the first assertion [the one just cited] which was tested with quarterly data for 1954-1982."

The recent behavior of the budget is impossible to explain on the theory that expenditures closely follow revenue. Between 1980 and 1986 the increase in expenditures was 158% of the increase in receipts. That was how we got the big deficit. Between 1986 and 1988 (Office of Management and Budget estimate) the rise in expenditures was 47% of the rise in revenue. That was how we got the big reduction of the deficit.

The Administration's Scenario

If it were literally true that expenditures rise to equal revenue, there would be no way to reduce the deficit. But people who say that the deficit cannot be reduced by raising taxes do not say that the deficit cannot be reduced at all. They claim to have a different way. But their way also depends on expenditures not rising as fast as revenue. For example, the administration's scenario for reducing the deficit to $23 billion by 1993 counts on revenue rising by $349 billion between 1988 and 1993 but expenditures rising by only 65% as much. That is, it counts on "Them," the other politicians, not spending all the revenue that is expected to come from economic growth.

None of this suggests that the revenue from a tax increase would be automatically and fully reflected in a reduction of the deficit. It means that the proportions in which the revenue would be divided between more spending and a smaller deficit are not determined by an iron law of politics. The proportions will be determined by a struggle between competing claimants and its outcome is not predetermined. The president is a powerful actor in that struggle. He should not believe himself incapable of affecting the result if he makes cutting the deficit a matter of high priority.

Mr. Stein, chairman of the Council of Economic Advisers under Presidents Nixon and Ford, is a senior fellow at the American Enterprise Institute.

20

The Federal Budget Deficit and the National Debt

CHAPTER CHALLENGES

After studying your text, attending class, and completing this chapter, you should be able to:

1. Discuss the advantages and disadvantages of an annually balanced federal budget.
2. Explain how the federal budget deficit's impact on interest rates can influence private investment, economic growth, and international trade.
3. Discuss the impact of the national debt on the well-being of current and future generations.
4. Discuss some of the problems involved in measuring the federal budget deficit and explain how the deficit has been reduced in recent years to comply with the Gramm-Rudman-Hollings Act.

IN BRIEF: CHAPTER SUMMARY

Fill in the blanks to summarize chapter content.

Until the 1930s, it was believed that it was necessary to balance the budget annually. Government outlays for the year had to be financed by an equal amount of government revenue. An annually balanced budget, (1)_____ (stabilizes rather than destabilizes, destabilizes rather than stabilizes) the business cycle. In recessions, tax revenue falls and transfer payments rise, producing a federal budget deficit where federal government outlays exceed government receipts. In order to balance the budget, (2)_____ (revenues, government outlays) must be increased or (3)_____ (revenues, government outlays) reduced. But this is contractionary and will make the recession worse. In expansions, federal government surpluses may arise where taxes and other government revenues rise above government outlays. But a balanced-budget policy requires decreases in taxes or increases in government outlays, both of which are (4)_____ (expansionary, contractionary) in an economic expansion.

Deficits can be financed in two ways if taxes are not increased. The deficit can be (5)_____ (financed by selling government securities to the public, monetized), which ultimately results in an increase in the money supply. Or the deficit can be (6)_____ (financed by selling government securities to the public, monetized). In the latter case, because the Fed does not intervene and buy an equivalent quantity of securities, the money supply does not increase. Deficits are expansionary, and the method of financing deficits may add to or retard that expansionary effect. With monetization, the increase in the money stock is (7)_____ (contractionary, expansionary). The aggregate demand curve will shift farther (8)_____ (leftward, rightward) when deficits are financed by monetization. When the government sells securities to the public, the demand for loanable funds increases, causing interest rates to (9)_____ (rise, fall). This causes some

(10)_____ (crowding out, crowding in) meaning that rising interest rates reduce the level of private borrowing below the level that would have prevailed if the government had not borrowed to finance budget deficits. Empirical evidence suggests that on average the crowding-out effect from government deficits is (11)_____ (large, small). On net, the expansionary effect of the deficit is still positive, (12)_____ (and larger than, but not as large as) the case of monetization. Both methods of financing are (13)_____ (more, less) expansionary, however, than increasing taxes to cover the deficit.

Deficits may also have an impact on international trade. If the financing of deficits results in higher U.S. interest rates relative to foreign rates of interest, foreigners will seek to (14)_____ (purchase, sell) the relatively higher-yielding U.S. financial assets such as U.S. government securities. But they first have to convert their foreign currencies into dollars in order to make the purchases. This increases the (15)_____ (supply of, demand for) dollars, causing the dollar's price to rise relative to those of foreign currencies. This in turn causes the relative prices of U.S. goods to (16)_____ (fall, rise) in foreign countries and the relative prices of imported goods in the United States to fall. Exports fall and imports rise, resulting in an/a (17)_____ (increase, decline) in aggregate demand. Deficits also affect international trade because deficits are expansionary and increases in the nation's disposable income cause imports to (18)_____ (fall, rise) relative to exports, causing net exports and aggregate demand to fall.

If crowding out is significant to the extent that interest rates are higher and investment spending is lower, U.S. businesses may not engage in enough development of new technology to remain competitive in world markets. A lower rate of capital growth (19)_____ (reduces, increases) the rate of growth of the economy and reduces future potential standards of living. But the government's use of resources is (20)_____ (always unproductive, not unproductive). The government subsidizes research and new technologies and encourages investment through government tax policies.

A deficit (21)_____ (reduces, adds to) the national debt, whereas a budget surplus (22)_____ (reduces, adds to) the national debt. The (23)_____ (net federal debt, national debt) is the dollar amount that the federal government owes to its creditors at a given point in time. The (24)_____ (net federal debt, national debt) is the credit extended to the federal government by those other than the Fed and government agencies. The national debt as a percentage of GNP fell from 89% in 1950 to 33% in 1980 (25)_____ (and has continued to fall to under 23%, but has risen since then to over 45%). In 1986, most of the net public debt, 84.3%, was (26)_____ (externally, internally) held by U.S. individuals, businesses, and state and local governments. The remainder of the net public debt, 15.7%, is (27)_____ (externally, internally) held by foreigners. This inflow of foreign saving acts to (28)_____ (offset to some extent, worsen) the crowding-out effect.

Two major burdens are associated with a large public debt. First, future generations will have to pay more taxes to pay interest on the debt. These additional taxes otherwise would have been used to provide additional government goods and services. Second, assuming a large crowding-out effect, a decline in investment (29)_____ (will not, will) impair the growth rate of the economy.

Several other aspects of the public debt merit consideration. Part of the national debt was incurred to acquire public capital assets. These assets have value and to some extent offset the national debt. It is prudent policy for governments to finance capital assets by borrowing, as is done in the private sector. Inflation affects the real value of the national debt. For instance, during periods of inflation and high interest rates, the real value of the national debt (30)_____ (rises, falls). The actual deficit overstates the real value of the deficit. This constitutes a transfer of purchasing power from the government's creditors to the government. During periods of low and stable inflation and low interest rates, the real value of the national debt is higher, in effect transferring purchasing power from the government to the holders of government securities. Here the actual deficit (31)_____ (understates, overstates) the real value of the deficit.

Deficits can be reduced by increasing taxes, government fees and charges and other receipts, by reducing government outlays, or by the sale of public assets. The sale of public assets to private business interests is known as (32)_____ (competitive bidding, privatization). The Reagan administration has been reluctant to reduce expenditures for Social Security benefits or national defense, which together make up 70% of federal government outlays. Another 15% is pledged to interest payments on the national debt. This leaves all other government programs representing only 15% of federal government outlays. It is politically very difficult to eliminate the deficit by cuts in that 15% of the budget alone. Because the Reagan administration resisted tax increases, the deficit continues to remain very large.

VOCABULARY REVIEW

Write the key term from the list below next to its definition.

Key Terms

Crowding-out effect   Internal debt
National debt   External debt
Net federal debt   Privatization

Definitions

1. _____: the portion of the national debt owed to citizens of other nations.

2. _____: the dollar amount that the federal government owes to its creditors at a given point in time.

3. _____: the process of selling government assets to private business interests.

4. _____: the portion of the national debt owed to those other than the Fed and government agencies.

5. _____: the portion of the national debt owed to the nation's own citizens.

6. _____: the reduction in private investment purchases caused by higher interest rates that result from borrowing by the government to cover its budget deficit.

SKILLS REVIEW

Concept: Annually balanced budget

1.   Assume that the economy shown in the figure below is at its potential
     level of real GNP and the federal budget policy is to balance the budget.

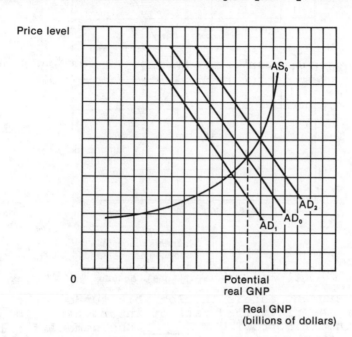

a.   Suppose the level of aggregate demand falls from ADo to AD1. As
     real GNP _____, tax revenues _____ and transfer payments
     _____, causing the budget to be in _____.
b.   Because of the balanced-budget policy, the government must
     _____ or _____, both of which shift the AD curve
     _____. Show this graphically on the figure above and identify
     the change in equilibrium real GNP.
c.   Assume that the economy is once again at its potential level of real
     GNP and aggregate demand increases to AD2. As real GNP _____,
     tax revenues _____ and transfers _____, causing the
     budget to be in _____.
d.   In order to balance the budget, the government must _____ or
     _____, both of which shift the AD curve _____. Show this
     graphically on the figure above and identify the change in
     equilibrium real GNP.
e.   Given initial changes in aggregate demand, a balanced-budget policy
     results in _____(larger, smaller) fluctuations in real GNP.

283

Concept: Deficits, interest rates, crowding out, and international trade

2. The figure below shows a loanable funds market for an economy.

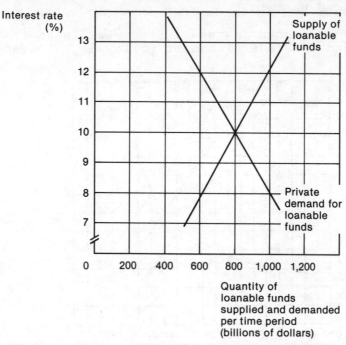

a. Suppose the government enters the loanable funds market to borrow $200 billion at the prevailing rate of interest to finance the deficit. Government borrowing _____ the demand for loanable funds by $200 billion at every interest rate. Show this on the figure above and identify the change in the interest rate. Interest rates _____ to _____%, causing investment spending and other credit-sensitive expenditures to _____ by $_____.

b. As investment spending _____, the economy's future rate of growth will be _____.

c. If the economy is in a deep recession, it is likely that investment spending is _____ to changes in interest rates. In a deep recession, crowding out is _____.

3. If deficits increase U.S. interest rates relative to foreign rates of interest:

a. Foreign demand for U.S. dollars _____ (increases, decreases).

b. The price of the U.S. dollar_____ (rises, falls) relative to the prices of foreign currencies.

c. U.S. goods and services become _____ (more, less) price competitive abroad.

d. Exports _____ (rise, fall) and imports _____ (rise, fall).

e. Net exports and aggregate demand _____ (increase, decrease).

f. Equilibrium real GNP _____ (increases, decreases).

Concept: Burden of the national debt, measuring and reducing the deficit

4. List and describe the two major burdens of the national debt.

a. _____
b. _____

5. a. During periods of high inflation and interest rates, the real value
        of the net federal debt _____ . The actual deficit _____
        the real deficit.
    b. During periods of low inflation and interest rates, the real value of
        the net federal debt _____ . The actual deficit _____
        the real deficit.

6. List three ways government can reduce the deficit.

    a. _____
    b. _____
    c. _____

SELF-TEST FOR MASTERY

Select the best answer.

1. In 1986, the federal budget deficit was $_____ and was equal to
    _____% of federal expenditures.

    a. $100 billion, 16%
    b. $100 million, 23%
    c. $200 million, 22%
    d. $220 billion, 22%

2. Which of the following prevails when federal government receipts for a
    year exceed government outlays?

    a. High-employment budget
    b. Balanced budget
    c. Federal budget deficit
    d. Federal government surplus

3. What was true of budget policy prior to the 1930s?

    a. The budget should be balanced annually.
    b. Recessions produced deficits, requiring a contractionary budget
        response.
    c. Expansions produced surpluses, requiring an expansionary budget
        response.
    d. The budget actually destabilized the economy.
    e. All of the above.

4. Of the ways listed below for financing or eliminating a deficit, which
    policy is the least expansionary?

    a. Tax financing
    b. Sale of government securities to the public
    c. Monetization
    d. None of the above

5. Of the ways listed below for financing or eliminating a deficit, which policy is the most expansionary?

   a. Tax financing
   b. Sale of government securities to the public
   c. Monetization
   d. Privatization

6. A deficit financed by monetization results in an aggregate demand curve:

   a. That lies to the left of the AD curve when deficits are financed by taxes.
   b. That lies to the left of the AD curve when deficits are financed by selling government securities to the public.
   c. That does not shift.
   d. That lies to the right of the AD curve when deficits are financed by selling government securities to the public.

7. If a deficit results in _____ interest rates and _____ private investment, there is said to be _____ .

   a. Higher, less, crowding out
   b. Higher, less, monetization
   c. Lower, more, crowding in
   d. Lower, less, crowding out
   e. B and c

8. Empirical studies suggest that the impact of federal budget deficits on interest rates:

   a. Is very large.
   b. Is large and has caused our international trade problems.
   c. Is small.
   d. Rises and falls with fluctuations in real GNP.

9. If the budget deficit causes _____ U.S. interest rates relative to foreign interest rates, imports will _____ and exports will _____ .

   a. Lower, rise, rise
   b. Higher, rise, fall
   c. Higher, rise, rise
   d. Higher, fall, fall
   e. Lower, fall, fall

10. An increase in the budget deficit will eventually _____ the nation's disposable income, which _____ imports and _____ aggregate demand below what it would be in the absence of international trade.

    a. Decrease, decreases, increases
    b. Increase, decreases, decreases
    c. Decrease, increases, decreases
    d. Increase, increases, decreases
    e. Decrease, decreases, decreases

11. Which of the following terms represents the credit extended to the federal government by those other than the Fed and government agencies?

    a. All private securities holders
    b. Government debt
    c. National debt
    d. Net federal debt

12. Which of the following terms is defined as the dollar amount that the federal government owes to its creditors at a given point in time?

    a. All private securities holders
    b. Government deficit
    c. National debt
    d. Net federal debt

13. Today the national debt as a percentage of GNP is over:

    a. 22%.
    b. 19%.
    c. 63%.
    d. 45%.

14. Most of the national debt is _____ held, which means that when the debt is repaid there is _____ in aggregate demand.

    a. Internally, a significant reduction
    b. Internally, no change
    c. Externally, no change
    d. Externally, a significant reduction
    e. Internally, an increase

15. The externally held debt was what percentage of the total net public debt in 1986?

    a. 12%
    b. 50%
    c. 84.3%
    d. 15.7%

16. During periods of high inflation and high interest rates, the actual deficit _____ the real deficit, resulting in a gain to _____ at the expense of _____.

    a. Overstates, the government's creditors, the government
    b. Overstates, the government, the government's creditors
    c. Understates, the government, the government's creditors
    d. Understates, the government's creditors, the government

17. Which of the following acts establishes deficit reduction targets?

    a. Deficit Reduction Act of 1981
    b. Tax Reform Act of 1986
    c. Monetary Decontrol Act of 1980
    d. PL 1492
    e. Gramm-Rudman-Hollings Act

18. Which of the following are reasons why the federal budget deficit has not been reduced significantly in the 1980s?

    a. The Reagan administration was unwilling to increase taxes to eliminate the deficit.
    b. The administration was reluctant to cut Social Security benefits and national defense spending, both of which together constitute 70% of federal government spending.
    c. An increasing portion, now 15%, of the federal government's outlays is pledged as interest payments to holders of the public debt.
    d. It has proved politically very difficult to eliminate the deficit

entirely by cutting the government programs that make up the remaining 15% of government outlays.

e.   All of the above.

THINK IT THROUGH

1.   If the economy is at its potential level of real GNP and the government budget deficit increases, which method of deficit financing would you favor and why? Would it be better to raise taxes or borrow?

2.   "A balanced-budget amendment is necessary to keep lawmakers fiscally responsible and to stabilize the economy." Do you agree? Explain.

3.   Discuss the implications for the relationship between the budget deficit and international trade given studies that suggest that government deficits do not have large crowding-out effects.

CHAPTER ANSWERS

In Brief: Chapter Summary

1. Destabilizes rather than stabilizes 2. Revenues 3. Government outlays 4. Expansionary 5. Monetized 6. Financed by selling government securities to the public 7. Expansionary 8. Rightward 9. Rise 10. Crowding out 11. Small 12. But not as large as 13. More 14. Purchase 15. Demand 16. Rise 17. Decline 18. Rise 19. Reduces 20. Not unproductive 21. Adds to 22. Reduces 23. National debt 24. Net federal debt 25. But has risen since then to over 45% 26. Internally 27. Externally 28. Offset to some extent 29. Will 30. Falls 31. Understates 32. Privatization

Vocabulary Review

1. External debt 2. National debt 3. Privatization 4. Net federal debt 5. Internal debt 6. Crowding-out effect

Skills Review

1.   a.   Falls, fall, rise, deficit
      b.   Increase taxes, reduce government outlays, leftward

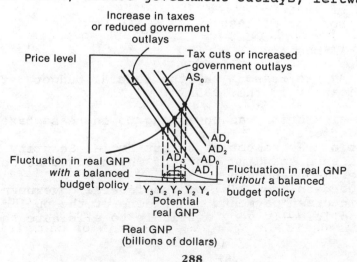

288

c.   Increases, rise, fall, surplus
d.   Reduce taxes, increase government outlays, rightward
e.   Larger

2.   a.   Increases, rise, 11%, fall, $100 billion

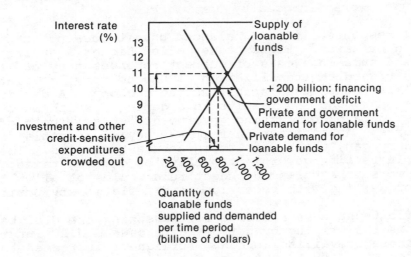

Quantity of
loanable funds
supplied and demanded
per time period
(billions of dollars)

b.   Falls, reduced
c.   Unresponsive, very small or nonexistent

3.   a.   Increases b. Rises c. Less d. Fall, rise e. Decrease f. Decreases

4.   a.   Future generations will have to pay more interest on the debt instead
         of receiving government goods and services in return for those taxes.
         If the percentage of the net federal debt externally held increases,
         the payment of interest results in an outflow of purchasing power
         from the United States, resulting in a lower level of aggregate
         demand than otherwise would be the case.
     b.   If the crowding-out effect is substantial, a growing federal debt
         will decrease private investment and reduce the growth rate of the
         private capital stock. This slows the growth of worker productivity
         and real GNP and results in lower living standards than would have
         been the case if investment spending had not been crowded out. The
         inflow of foreign saving resulting from the externally held debt,
         however, serves to moderate the crowding-out effect.

5.   a.   Falls; overstates b. increases; understates

6.   a.   Increase taxes, charges and fees b. Reduce government outlays
     c.   Sale of public assets

Self-Test for Mastery

1. d 2. d 3. e 4. a 5. c 6. d 7. a 8. c 9. b 10. d 11. d 12. c 13.
d 14. b 15. d 16. b 17. e 18. e

Think it Through

1.   If a deficit must be incurred at the level of potential real GNP, then the
least expansionary form of financing should be used to prevent excessive
overheating of the economy. A deficit will produce an inflationary GNP gap,
but it can be minimized by selling U.S. government securities to the public
rather than monetizing the deficit. At least the sale of securities to the

public will not add fuel to the fire by expanding the money stock. With monetization, in contrast, the money stock increases, resulting in a larger inflationary gap. At potential real GNP, it would be preferable to finance government outlays with tax increases. On net, there would still be an expansionary effect producing an inflationary gap, but the gap would be smaller than if the expenditures were financed by borrowing.

2.   Regarding fiscal responsibility, a balanced budget does not necessarily mean a cap on spending or taxes. Higher taxes allow higher spending, but if lawmakers want to spend sums in excess of current revenues they can simply increase taxes. With regard to stabilization of the economy, a balanced-budget policy would destabilize rather than stabilize the economy. A decline in real GNP produces a recessionary gap and results in a deficit, which must be eliminated by increasing taxes or cutting government outlays, both of which make the recession worse. An increase in real GNP beyond potential real GNP produces an inflationary gap, which results in a budget surplus. The surplus can be eliminated by increasing government outlays or cutting taxes, both of which make inflation worse. A balanced-budget rule would not allow the policy flexibility needed for dealing with recessions and inflationary periods.

3.   Large budget deficits have been blamed for worsening the U.S. balance of trade. The argument is that rising budget deficits caused U.S. interest rates to rise relative to those prevailing abroad. Foreigners increased their demand for U.S. dollars so that they could purchase U.S. financial assets such as government securities. The increase in the price of the dollar relative to the prices of foreign currencies reduced the price competitiveness of U.S. goods abroad and resulted in a reduction in net exports. This prevented aggregate demand and equilibrium real GNP from attaining a higher level. If empirical evidence shows that the impact of deficits on interest rates is small, then the high interest rates that were in part causing the deterioration of net exports must be due to factors other than federal budget deficits. The point is that theoretical cause-and-effect relationships may or may not have important quantitative impacts on the economy even though it is commonly believed by the public that those relationships are significant.

21

Tradeoffs Between Inflation and Unemployment and the Theory of Rational Expectations

CHAPTER CHALLENGES

After studying your text, attending class, and completing this chapter, you should be able to:

1. Discuss the historical tradeoff between annual inflation and unemployment in modern economies through the use of the Phillips curve.
2. Show how shifts in aggregate supply can affect the tradeoff between the goals of reducing inflation and reducing unemployment.
3. Understand how rational expectations of changes in the price level can affect the behavior of workers and investors and influence macroeconomic equilibrium.
4. Understand some of the difficulties of implementing stabilization policies and explain how rational expectations about the effect of stabilization policies might frustrate achievement of their goals.

IN BRIEF: CHAPTER SUMMARY

Fill in the blanks to summarize chapter content.

In the 1950s, A.W. Phillips investigated the relationship between the unemployment rate and the rate of change in wages for Great Britain. He discovered what appeared to be a very stable (1)_____ (direct, inverse) relationship between the unemployment rate and wage inflation. As the unemployment rate fell, the rate of wage inflation increased and vice versa. The Phillips curve was consistent with models of the economy that emphasized changes in aggregate (2)_____ (demand, supply) as the source of fluctuations in real GNP and the price level. Using data for the (3)_____ (1970s, 1960s), a stable Phillips curve (expressed as a relationship between the unemployment rate and the rate of change in prices) seemed to explain the unemployment-inflation experience of the United States. Policy makers believed that it was possible to choose the desired unemployment rate-inflation rate along the Phillips curve by using demand-management policies. The Phillips curve analysis assumes that the aggregate supply curve shifts rightward in an/a (4)_____ (erratic, predictable) manner. Further, it does not consider the role of inflation expectations.

In the 1970s and 1980s the Phillips curve for the United States has (5)_____ (not remained stable but has shifted due to, remained stable in part because of) supply-side shocks and changes in inflation expectations. For instance, the oil-price shocks of the early 1970s caused the aggregate supply curve to shift (6)_____ (leftward, rightward) more than the aggregate demand curve shifted (7)_____ (leftward, rightward) resulting in a rising price level at a time when the economy was experiencing increases in the rate of unemployment. Between 1978 and 1980, as unemployment rose from 6% to 7%, the rate of inflation rose from 8% to over 13% per year. These events directly (8)_____ (support, counter) the belief that the

Phillips curve is stable over the long run. Over short periods, such as 1986 and 1987, the Phillips curve tradeoff between inflation and the unemployment rate was present, but over the long run the Phillips curve shifts. Supply-side shocks that increase input prices increase the rate of inflation for given unemployment rates and shift the Phillips curve (9)_____ (downward, upward). Supply-side shocks that reduce input prices, such as the decline in oil prices in 1986, shift the Phillips curve (10)_____ (downward, upward).

There are two major competing theories of how we form expectations. One theory holds that we form expectations adaptively. Our expectations are dependent solely on past observations of the variable to be forecast. The other major theory, the theory of (11)_____ (aggregate expected demand, rational expectations), holds that individuals use all information, past and present, including relevant economic models, in their forecasts of economic variables. This theory assumes that the expected value of the forecast variable equals the actual future value of that variable. This doesn't mean that individuals forecast correctly all the time; rather it means that forecasting errors will not be systematically high or low in the long run.

If an increase in aggregate demand is anticipated, it is argued that rational individuals will use this information in forming inflation expectations. If labor, for instance, expects higher inflation as a result of an anticipated increase in aggregate demand, they will press for higher wages as a way of maintaining the real value or purchasing power of their wage income. If wages and other input prices rise at exactly the same rate as prices, real wages and real input prices will not change, (12)_____ (causing, and there is no reason for) employers to alter their current rates of employment and production. Thus the rational expectations theory holds that anticipated changes in aggregate demand, which include changes caused by fiscal and monetary policy, will be (13)_____ (completely, partially) offset by input suppliers as they react to anticipated changes in inflation. The aggregate supply curve shifts leftward by (14)_____ (the same amount as, less than) the aggregate demand curve shifts rightward. The price level increases, but real GNP and employment remain unchanged.

Increases in inflation expectations cause the Phillips curve to shift (15)_____ (downward, upward). If inflation expectations rise, labor and other input suppliers will renegotiate contracts, thus increasing unit production costs and causing firms to raise prices. Inflation rises at given levels of unemployment. The (16)_____ (Keynesian model, accelerationist hypothesis) argues that attempts by policy makers to reduce the rate of unemployment below the natural rate with expansionary fiscal or monetary policy will work only in the (17)_____ (long run, short run). In the (18)_____ (long run, short run), input suppliers will increase their inflation expectations and press for higher input prices when they discover that inflation is higher than expected. This causes the unemployment rate to return to its natural level.

Counter cyclical policy requires that policy makers first determine if macroeconomic problems are the result of demand-side or supply-side shocks. If they are due to demand-side shocks, the first problem of stabilization efforts is (19)_____ (to implement policy, forecasting shifts in aggregate demand). Second, the government must respond quickly to offset the undesired change in aggregate demand. Third, the extent to which monetary and fiscal policy should be used depends upon the predicted impacts of changes in the money supply or the government deficit. The ability of policy to offset an undesired change in aggregate demand depends to some extent on whether the policy change is anticipated or unanticipated. Policy will likely be (20)_____ (more, less) effective if it is unanticipated.

Some economists argue that policy makers often make errors that result in economic instability. They argue that policy exacerbates business cycle fluctuations and should not be used. They suggest that policy makers (21)_____ (use a policy rule such as a constant rate of money growth, always balance the budget) rather than use discretionary fiscal and monetary policy. Another view holds that stabilization policy has nevertheless (22)_____ (reduced, increased) the severity of economic fluctuations since the end of World War II. (23)_____ (Fiscal, Incomes) policies such as jawboning, wage-price guidelines, and wage-price controls have been used in addition to monetary and fiscal policy to control inflation. Wage-price controls are (24)_____ (frequently, rarely) used in peacetime because they distort the price system and contribute to the variability of inflation.

VOCABULARY REVIEW

Write the key term from the list below next to its definition.

Key Terms

Phillips curve	Policy rule
Disinflation	Incomes policies
Rational expectations	Wage-price guidelines
Accelerationist hypothesis	Wage-price controls

Definitions

1. _____: argues that attempts by policy makers to reduce the unemployment rate below the natural rate can succeed only in the short run.

2. _____: a preannounced government rule that will inform the public of future economic stabilization policies.

3. _____: refers to use by individuals of all available information, including any relevant economic models, in their forecasts of economic variables.

4. _____: policies that seek to curb inflation by directly influencing both prices and wages without reducing aggregate demand through the use of monetary or fiscal policy.

5. _____: a sharp reduction in the annual rate of inflation.

6. _____: rules established by government authorities that result in control of prices, wages, and their rate of increase.

7. _____: a curve showing the hypothesized inverse relationship between annual unemployment and annual inflation in a nation.

8. _____: standards established by government authorities that seek to keep wage and price increases within certain bounds over a period.

Concept: **Shifts in the aggregate supply curve and the inflation-unemployment tradeoff**

1.   The figure below shows an economy at its potential real GNP of $3,000 billion with a natural unemployment rate of 6%. The price level is 100, and the rate of inflation is zero.

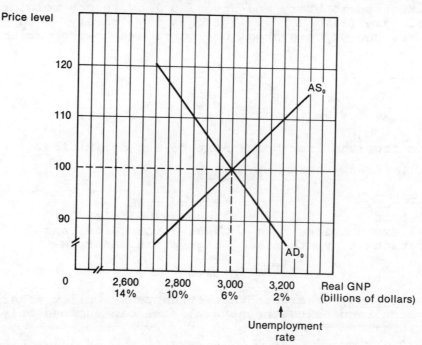

a.   Assume that autonomous increases in aggregate demand shift the AD curve by $100 billion at every price level. The aggregate demand curve shifts _____. Show this on the figure above and label the new AD curve AD1.

b.   Now assume that in addition to the increase in aggregate demand, a supply-side shock increases input prices, shifting the AS curve by $200 billion at every price level. The aggregate supply curve shifts _____. Show this on the figure above and label the new AS curve AS1.

c.   The price level has _____ from 100 to _____, resulting in a _____ % change in the price level. Real GNP _____ from $3,000 billion to $_____, and the unemployment rate _____ from 6% to _____ %.

d. On the figure below, find the point representing the initial rate of
    inflation, 0%, and initial rate of unemployment, 6% and label that
    point A. Now find the coordinate that represents the new rate of
    change in the price level and the new rate of unemployment from part
    c and label that point B.

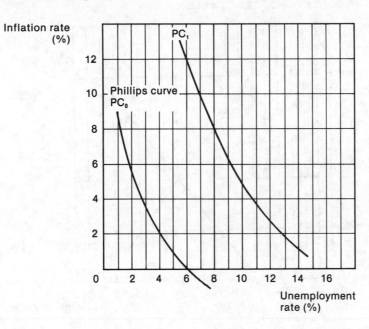

e. The Phillips curve shown in the figure above has shifted
    _____ from PC1 to _____. The inflation-
    unemployment tradeoff has _____ (worsened, improved).
    Adverse supply-side shocks that increase input prices shift the
    Phillips curve _____.

2. Given the level of aggregate demand, a favorable supply-side shock that
    decreases input prices will shift the aggregate _____ curve
    _____ and will shift the Phillips curve _____. The unemployment-
    inflation tradeoff _____ (worsens, improves).

Concept: Rational expectations, the AD-AS model, and implications for
          stabilization policy

3.   Suppose the economy shown in the figure below, like that in the first
     figure, is at potential real GNP where the natural rate of unemployment is
     attained with a zero rate of inflation.

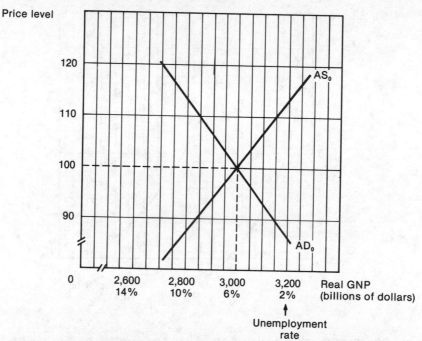

a.   Assume that an increase in the money supply that shifts the aggregate
     demand curve rightward by $150 billion at every price level is fully
     anticipated by the public. Show the new AD curve and label the curve
     AD1.   According to rational expectations theory, if the increase in
     aggregate demand is fully anticipated, input suppliers push for
     _____ input prices, causing the AS curve to shift _____ by
     $_____ billion. Show the new AS curve in the figure above and
     label it AS1. After the shifts in the AD and AS curves, the price
     level _____ from 100 to _____, resulting in a _____% change
     in the price level. Real GNP and the rate of unemployment
     _____.

b.   In the figure below, plot the initial rate of change in the price
     level and unemployment rate. Now plot the new rate of change in the
     price level and unemployment rate found in part a. Draw a line
     connecting the two points.

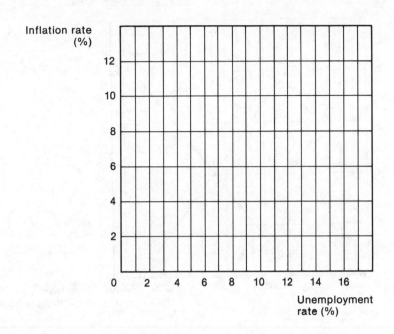

Inflation rate (%)

Unemployment rate (%)

c.   The proponents of the rational expectations theory view the Phillips
     curve as _____ (downward sloping, vertical). Anticipated
     increases in aggregate demand _____ real GNP and the unemployment
     rate, although the rate of inflation _____.
d.   According to the rational expectations theory, if changes in the
     federal budget deficit or the money supply are completely
     anticipated, fiscal and monetary policy are _____ (effective,
     ineffective) in altering real GNP and the rate of unemployment.

4.   List two criticisms of the rational expectations theory.

     a.   _____

     b.   _____

297

Concept: Accelerationist hypothesis and stabilization policy

5.   The economy shown in the figure below is currently operating at its
     potential level of real GNP with an inflation rate equal to zero.

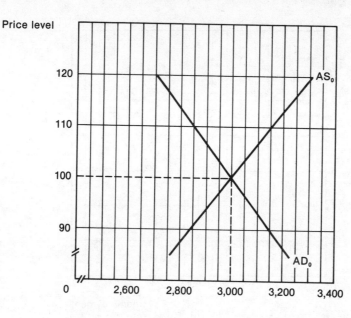

a.   Suppose policy makers want to reduce the unemployment rate below
     the natural rate of unemployment to 3% by using expansionary fiscal
     policy. Equilibrium real GNP must rise to $3150 billion in order to
     reduce the unemployment rate to 3%. Show the new aggregate demand
     curve in the figure above and label the AD curve AD1.

b.   The price level rises from 100 to _____, producing a _____%
     change in the price level. Workers and other input suppliers will
     eventually revise their expected rates of inflation from 0% to
     _____. As this happens, wages and other input prices _____,
     causing the aggregate _____ curve to shift _____ until real GNP
     equals $_____. Show the new aggregate supply curve and label
     the AS curve AS1.

c.   If government once again expands the economy in an effort to reduce
     the unemployment rate below the natural rate, real GNP will _____,
     the rate of unemployment will _____, and the price level will _____
     _____. The effects on real GNP and the unemployment rate _____
     in the long run as input suppliers react to the realization that
     actual inflation exceeds expected inflation. The price level
     is_____ in the long run.

d.   According to the accelerationist hypothesis, fiscal and monetary
     policy are able to affect real GNP and the unemployment rate in the
     _____, but not in the _____.

SELF-TEST FOR MASTERY

Select the best answer.

1. In the 1950s, A.W. Phillips investigated the relationship between:

    a. Wage and price inflation.
    b. Output and price changes.
    c. The unemployment rate and the rate of change in wages.
    d. The unemployment rate and the rate of change in prices.

2. The U.S. Phillips curve in the 1960s:

    a. Shifted erratically.
    b. Appeared to be stable.
    c. Shifted consistently upward.
    d. Shifted downward during the first half of the decade.

3. The Phillips curve tradeoff implies:

    a. That if the curve is stable, society must accept increases in inflation in exchange for decreases in unemployment.
    b. That if the curve is unstable, society must accept increases in inflation in exchange for decreases in unemployment.
    c. That if the curve is stable, society must accept increases in inflation in exchange for increases in unemployment.
    d. That if the curve is unstable, society must accept falling unemployment when inflation falls.

4. Which of the following can cause the Phillips curve to shift?

    a. An increase in inflation expectations
    b. A decrease in inflation expectations
    c. An adverse supply-side shock increasing input prices
    d. A favorable supply-side shock decreasing input prices
    e. All of the above

5. The oil-price shock of 1973 had the effect of shifting the aggregate supply curve _____ by _____ than the aggregate demand curve shifted _____. The outcome was stagflation.

    a. Rightward, less, leftward
    b. Rightward, less, rightward
    c. Leftward, less, leftward
    d. Leftward, less, rightward
    e. Leftward, more, rightward

6. The U.S. Phillips curve in the 1970s:

    a. Was stable.
    b. Shifted upward due to supply-side shocks and rising inflation expectations.
    c. Shifted downward due to supply-side shocks.
    d. Shifted downward in the first half of the decade and upward in the second half.

7. In the 1980s, the Phillips curve has shifted _____ in part because of _____ and _____ .

   a. Downward, declines in oil prices, falling inflation expectations
   b. Upward, increases in oil prices, rising inflation expectations
   c. Downward, rising wages, falling prices
   d. Upward, falling wages, rising prices
   e. None of the above

8. Which of the following terms represents a sharp reduction in the rate of inflation?

   a. Crawling inflation
   b. Deflation
   c. Hyperinflation
   d. Disinflation
   e. B and d

9. Which of the following theories of expectations holds that individuals form expectations by looking only to past values of the variable to be forecast?

   a. Rational expectations theory
   b. Certainty equivalent theory
   c. Expected value analysis
   d. Adaptive expectations theory

10. Which of the following theories of expectations holds that individuals use all information available in forming expectations?

   a. Rational expectations theory
   b. Certainty equivalent theory
   c. Expected value analysis
   d. Adaptive expectations theory

11. Rational expectations theory implies that anticipated changes in aggregate demand:

   a. Affect real GNP and the price level only in the long run.
   b. Will be completely offset by the actions of input suppliers as they react to their inflation expectations.
   c. Will always affect real but not nominal GNP.
   d. Will result in economic expansion over the long run.
   e. A and d.

12. Which of the following theories holds that efforts by policy makers to reduce the unemployment rate below the natural rate of unemployment will be successful only in the short run?

   a. Adaptive expectations theory
   b. Rational expectations theory
   c. New classical-RE model
   d. Accelerationist hypothesis

13. An increase in inflation expectations causes input suppliers to push for _____ input prices, which _____ unit production costs and prices. This results in a/an _____ shift in the Phillips curve.

   a. Higher, increase, downward
   b. Lower, decrease, downward
   c. Lower, increase, upward

d.   Higher, increase, upward
e.   Lower, decrease, upward

14.   The first problem of stabilization policy is to:

a.   Predict the impact of changes in the money stock or the
      government deficit on the economy.
b.   Quickly implement countercyclical policies.
c.   Predict shifts in aggregate demand.
d.   Follow a policy rule.

15.   The second problem of stabilization policy is to:

a.   Predict the impact of changes in the money stock or the
      government deficit on the economy.
b.   Quickly implement countercyclical policies.
c.   Predict shifts in aggregate demand.
d.   Follow a policy rule.

16.   The third problem of stabilization policy is to:

a.   Predict the impact of changes in the money stock or the
      government deficits on the economy.
b.   Quickly implement countercyclical policies.
c.   Predict shifts in aggregate demand.
d.   Follow a policy rule.

17.   Incomes policies have proved _____ in reducing wage and price
      inflation over the long run and as a result are used _____ during
      peacetime.

a.   Successful, frequently
b.   Unsuccessful, often
c.   Successful, infrequently
d.   Unsuccessful, only rarely

18.   Which of the following are examples of incomes policies?

a.   Jawboning
b.   Wage-price guidelines
c.   Wage-price controls
d.   Tax cuts
e.   A, b, and c

THINK IT THROUGH

1.   "At times during the 1970s and 1980s in the United States, the rate of
inflation and the rate of unemployment moved in the same direction. This is
evidence that the Phillips curve does not exist and policy makers need not pay
any attention to the tradeoff it implies." Analyze this statement.

2.   Identify the implication of rational expectations theory regarding the
ability of monetary and fiscal policy to affect real GNP and the rate of
unemployment. This policy implication depends upon several important
assumptions: (a) individuals form expectations rationally, (b) wages and prices
are flexible, and (c) all markets are competitive markets that constantly

clear--are in equilibrium. How might this policy implication change if wages and prices are in fact slow to adjust?

3. Use the accelerationist hypothesis to describe an inflationary process that begins with demand-pull inflation and is followed by cost-push inflation to be followed again by demand-pull inflation and so on. In other words, how can the accelerationist hypothesis be used to explain a wage-price spiral?

CHAPTER ANSWERS

In Brief: Chapter Summary

1. Inverse 2. Demand 3. 1960s 4. Predictable 5. Not remained stable, but has shifted due to 6. Leftward 7. Rightward 8. Counter 9. Upward 10. Downward 11. Rational expectations 12. And there is no reason for 13. Completely 14. The same amount as 15. Upward 16. Accelerationist hypothesis 17. Short run 18. Long run 19. Forecasting shifts in aggregate demand 20. More 21. Use a policy rule such as a constant rate of money growth 22. Reduced 23. Incomes 24. Rarely

Vocabulary Review

1. Accelerationist hypothesis 2. Policy rule 3. Rational expectations 4. Incomes policies 5. Disinflation 6. Wage-price controls 7. Phillips curve 8. Wage-price guidelines

Skills Review

1. a. Rightward

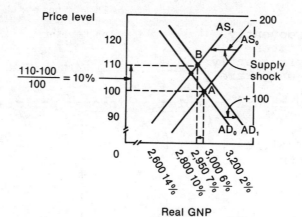

   b. Leftward
   c. Increased, 110, 10%; falls, $2,950 billion, rises, 7%

302

d.

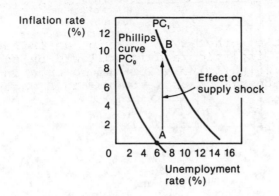

e.   Upward, PC1; worsened; upward

2.   Supply, rightward, downward; improves

3.   a.

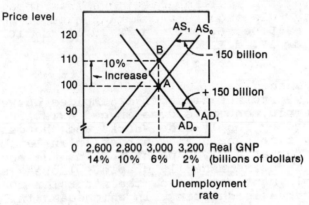

Higher, leftward, $150 billion; rises, 110, 10%; remain unchanged

b.

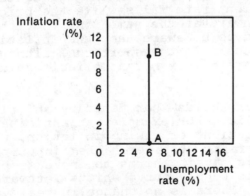

c.   Vertical; do not change the level of; increases
d.   Ineffective

4.   a.   Individuals do not have access to all information, nor do they make
          use of all available information.
     b.   Wages and other input prices are slow to adjust due to the existence
          of annual and multi-year contracts.

303

5. a.

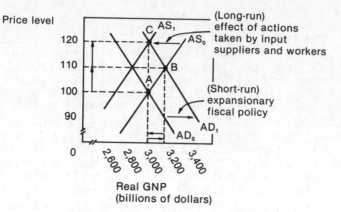

Price level

(Long-run) effect of actions taken by input suppliers and workers

(Short-run) expansionary fiscal policy

Real GNP
(billions of dollars)

b.   110, 10%; 10%; rise, supply, leftward, $3,000 billion
c.   Increase, decrease, rise; vanish, higher
d.   Short run, long run

Self-Test for Mastery

1. c 2. b 3. a 4. e 5. e 6. b 7. a 8. d 9. d 10. a 11. b 12. d 13. d 14. c 15. b 16. a 17. d 18. e

Think It Through

1.   The Phillips curve and the tradeoff it implies between the rate of inflation and the unemployment rate does indeed exist in the short run when the economy is not buffeted by supply-side shocks and changes in inflation expectations. Supply-side shocks and changes in inflation expectations shift the Phillips curve. But at a given point in time the economy operates on a Phillips curve that is not necessarily stable. Increases in aggregate demand that reduce the unemployment rate below the natural rate will cause inflation unless the Phillips curve is shifting, in which case inflation may increase or decrease as the unemployment rate falls. For instance, if an increase in aggregate demand is accompanied by a favorable supply-side shock that shifts the aggregate supply curve rightward more than the aggregate demand curve shifts rightward, the unemployment rate falls while the price level falls. The Phillips curve is shifting downward at the same time that the unemployment rate is falling. Policy makers need to be aware that the inflation-unemployment tradeoff will likely present itself in the short run, although it is likely to shift over the long run and therefore is not a reliable guide to the long-run tradeoff.

2.   Rational expectations theory holds that monetary and fiscal policy changes will be anticipated by the public. For example, an anticipated increase in the money stock will produce expectations of rising inflation, which will cause workers and other input suppliers to push for higher input prices. This increases unit production cost,s causing firms to increase prices at given levels of output. The aggregate supply curve shifts leftward as the aggregate demand curve shifts rightward. There is no change in real variables such as real GNP and the unemployment rate, only increases in the price level. Thus it is argued that anticipated monetary or fiscal policy will not be effective in altering real GNP or unemployment rates and should not be used. If, however, wages and other input prices are slow to adjust as they certainly are due to the existence of multi-period contracts, leftward shifts in the aggregate supply curve will lag behind the rightward shift in the aggregate demand curve, resulting in higher real GNP and a lower rate of unemployment in the short run. It is argued that the length of time it takes for complete adjustment may well be quite long, resulting in a "long" short run.

3.   Suppose policy makers want to reduce the unemployment rate below the
natural rate of unemployment. If the economy is at its potential level of real
GNP and expansionary monetary or fiscal policy is used, demand-pull inflation
results as real GNP rises and the unemployment rate falls. In time, input
suppliers will realize that actual inflation exceeds expected inflation and
will push for higher input prices, causing the aggregate supply curve to shift
leftward. Now the unemployment rate is rising and the rate of inflation is
worsening--cost-push inflation is occurring. But suppose policy makers persist
in their efforts to reduce the unemployment rate and once again use
expansionary policy. This causes inflation to worsen still further but reduces
the unemployment rate below the natural rate. As was the case previously,
workers and other input suppliers will eventually realize that actual inflation
is outpacing expected inflation, which will cause them to press for higher
input prices. Again the aggregate supply curve shifts leftward, returning the
unemployment rate to its natural level, but at still higher rates of inflation.
Activist demand-management policy that tries to keep the rate of unemployment
below the natural rate of unemployment will only succeed in creating a wage-
price spiral in the long run.

22

International Trade, Productivity, and the Economics of Less Developed Countries

CHAPTER CHALLENGES

After studying your text, attending class, and completing this chapter, you should be able to:

1. Understand the underlying basis for international trade and the gains in well-being possible from free trade with foreign nations.
2. Discuss the principle of comparative advantage and show how productivity changes in specific industries can affect their comparative advantage in international trade.
3. Discuss controversies regarding free trade vs. protection of U.S. industries from foreign competition in light of the basic theory of international trade.
4. Analyze the impact on the economy of tariffs, import quotas, and other trade restrictions.
5. Discuss some of the unique economic problems of less developed countries and the causes of low per capita income and slow economic growth in those nations.

IN BRIEF: CHAPTER SUMMARY

Fill in the blanks to summarize chapter content.

Nations engage in international trade because it is mutually beneficial for all trading nations to do so; otherwise they would not trade. Some nations may have a/an (1)_____ (comparative, absolute) advantage in producing goods, meaning that with a given complement of resources, one nation can produce more of an item than another nation with the same quantity of resources. But the presence of an absolute advantage in the production of an item does not indicate whether a nation should specialize in and export that good or whether the good should be imported. A country should specialize in and export those goods for which it has an/a (2)_____ (absolute, comparative) advantage and import those goods for which other countries have a comparative advantage. A nation has a comparative advantage in the production of a good relative to another nation if it produces the good at (3)_____ (lower, higher) opportunity cost than its trading partner.

Nations that trade on the basis of comparative advantage (4)_____ (gain at the expense of their rivals, mutually gain from trade). On an international scale, resources are used more efficiently as nations produce output based upon comparative advantages. World output, income, and living standards are (5)_____ (higher, lower) as a result of specialization and trade than would be the case in the absence of trade. All trading partners gain, although not equally. The distribution of the gains from trade is determined by the (6)_____ (foreign exchange rate, terms of trade)--the rate at which goods can be traded or exchanged for one another on international markets. A nation will be induced to trade goods for which it has a comparative advantage

306

for import goods if it can obtain the imported goods at prices below the domestic opportunity cost of production. The real terms of trade are determined by (7)_____ (government, world demand and supply). For trade incentives to exist, the terms of trade must be (8)_____ (below, above) the opportunity cost of producing each additional unit of the good a nation desires to import. When countries specialize in and export those goods for which they have a comparative advantage and import goods for which other nations have a comparative advantage, the consumption possibilities curve of each nation lies (9)_____ (outside, inside) the production possibilities curve.

Changes in productivity can affect a nation's competitiveness in international markets. If a nation experiences slower technological growth or lower levels of investment in human and physical capital relative to those of its trading partners, in time it may lose its (10)_____ (absolute, comparative) advantage in those industries where international competitiveness requires improvements in productivity. The nation that invests more heavily in things that enhance productivity will eventually (11)_____ (gain, lose) a comparative advantage relative to the lagging nation and will capture a share of the international market that it previously did not have. Productivity growth (growth in output per labor hour) in the United States from 1981-1985 was among the (12)_____ (highest, lowest) for industrialized nations at about (13)_____ (10%, 1%) per year. This has been cited as a reason for the decline in the competitiveness of some U.S. export industries. The primary cause of the low productivity growth is believed to be the low rate of annual (14)_____ (government, investment) spending as a percentage of domestic production relative to other nations, particularly Japan. Increased government regulation and (15)_____ (a liberal Congress, higher energy prices) have also been cited as factors contributing to the productivity decline of the 1970s.

As comparative advantage changes, nations losing the comparative advantage in a good no longer export that good. Industry sales and output fall, causing some workers with specialized skills to become unemployed and other suppliers of specialized inputs to experience a decline in income. Both the owners of the declining industry and its input suppliers are harmed. But this has to be balanced against the widespread gains to society when a nation produces on the basis of comparative advantage. Changes in comparative advantage are painful in the short run, but nations are better off in the long run by specializing in and exporting those goods for which they have a comparative advantage and trading for those goods for which they do not.

Several arguments, however, have been advanced for protecting domestic industries. It is argued that some industries may need to be protected from international competition to maintain production capacity (16)_____ (vital to national security, necessary to be self-sufficient). Protecting (17)_____ (large and established industries, new and emerging "infant" industries) from the rigors of international competition is considered a way of allowing an industry to grow in a sheltered environment until it attains sufficient economies of scale to compete internationally. Industries experiencing changes in comparative advantage can be spared some of the short run costs to specialized input suppliers and owners by receiving some protection from foreign rivals. Some industries are protected from what is viewed as unfair competition by foreign governments that subsidize their export industries. Arguments against free trade derive from changes in the (18)_____ (distribution of income that occur, efficiency with which goods are produced) as some industries fail and lose their comparative advantage.

Two methods of import protection are import tariffs and import quotas. A (19)_____ (quota, tariff) is a tax on an imported good. The intention is to reduce imports and increase the sales of domestic products. A tariff (20)_____ (raises, lowers) the price of the imported good to the consumer, (21)_____ (increases, reduces) the net price to the foreign producer, and generates tax revenue for the government. A/An (22)_____ (tariff, import quota) is a limit on the quantity of foreign goods that can be sold in a nation's domestic market. Like the tariff, an import quota (23)_____ (increases, reduces) the quantity of imported goods sold and (24)_____ (raises, lowers) the price to the consumer, but unlike a tariff, the import quota also (25)_____ (lowers, raises) the price received by the foreign producer. If the demand for the imported good is inelastic, the foreign producer (26)_____(is always worse off, may be better off) operating with a quota. Further, quotas raise no revenue for government. But protectionism invites retaliation from trading partners. If a nation's trading partners also impose import tariffs and quotas, all of the trading nations (27)_____ (lose, gain) because the level of international trade is lower and consumers in each country are paying higher prices than necessary.

(28)_____ [Newly industrialized countries, Less developed countries (LDCs)] have very low real per capita GNPs. This is because of (a) (29)_____ (high, low) rates of saving and capital accumulation, (b) poorly skilled and educated workers, (c) lagging technological know-how, (d) (30)_____ (high, low) population growth and unemployment, and (e) political instability and government policies that discourage production. These nations are dependent on foreign trade to acquire capital and technology necessary for increases in their standard of living. But unless they export enough to acquire the foreign exchange to purchase the imported goods, these nations will not be able to advance significantly without the help of gifts or loans from foreign nations.

VOCABULARY REVIEW

Write the key term from the list below next to its definition.

Key Terms

Specialization
Mutual gains from
   international trade
Absolute advantage
Comparative advantage
Real terms of trade

Consumption possibilities
   curve
Tariff
Import quota
Real per capita output
Less developed country
   (LDC)

Definitions

1. _____: shows combinations of two goods a nation can consume given its resources, technology, and international trade.

2. _____: the actual market exchange rate of one good for another in international trade.

3. _____: a tax on imported goods.

4. _____: a nation has a comparative advantage over a trading partner in the production of an item if it produces that item at lower opportunity cost per unit than its partner does.

5. _____ : a limit on the quantity of foreign goods that can be sold in a nation's domestic markets.

6. _____ : a nation has an absolute advantage over other nations in the production of an item if it can produce more of the item over a certain period with a given amount of resources than the other nations can.

7. _____ : a measure of output per person in a nation; calculated by dividing real GNP by population.

8. _____ : on average, citizens in all trading nations gain from exchanging goods in international markets.

9. _____ : a country whose real GNP per capita is generally much less than $1000 per year.

10. _____ : use of labor and other resources in a nation to produce the goods and services for which those resources are best adapted.

SKILLS REVIEW

Concept: Absolute vs. comparative advantage, terms of trade, gains from trade

1. The domestic production possibilities of two nations, nation A and nation B, for two goods, cases of wine and boxes of cheese, are shown below.

Production Possibilities

	Nation A	Nation B
Wine (cases)	1 million	600,000
Cheese (boxes)	500,000	400,000

a. Plot the production possibilities curve for each nation in a and b in the figure below.

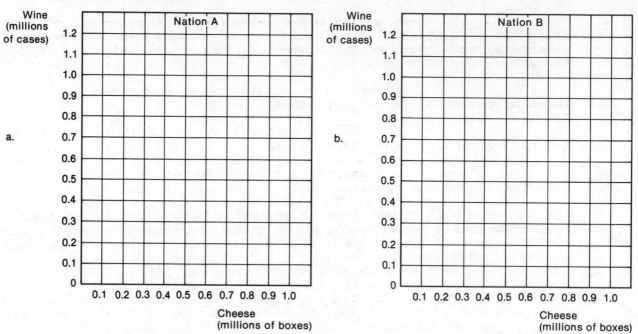

b. Assuming each nation has the same quantity of resources, 1000 workers, and both nations produce only wine, the number of cases of wine per worker in nation A of _____ cases _____ the number of cases of wine per worker of _____ cases in nation B. Similarly, if both nations produce only cheese, the number of boxes of cheese per worker in nation A of _____ boxes _____ the number of boxes of cheese per worker in nation B of _____ boxes. Nation A has a/an _____ advantage in the production of both wine and cheese. Nation A's production possibilities curve _____ nation B's production possibilities curve.

c. In nation A, the opportunity cost of producing a case of wine is _____ boxes of cheese and the opportunity cost of producing a box of cheese is _____ cases of wine. The slope of nation A's production possibilities curve is _____, which means that the opportunity cost of producing an additional box of cheese is _____ cases of wine.

d. In nation B, the opportunity cost of producing a case of wine is _____ boxes of cheese and the opportunity cost of producing a box of cheese is _____ cases of wine. The slope of nation B's production possibilities curve is _____, which means that the opportunity cost of producing an additional box of cheese is _____ cases of wine.

2. Regarding the problem above, nation A has a comparative advantage in the production of _____, whereas nation B has a comparative advantage in the production of _____. Nation A should specialize in and export _____ and should import _____. Nation B should specialize in and export _____ and should import _____. For nation A to be induced to trade for _____, it must give up less _____ than that implied by its domestic opportunity cost of _____. For nation B to be induced to trade for _____, it must give up less _____ than that implied by its domestic opportunity cost of _____. Trade will be mutually beneficial to both nations if 1 box of cheese trades for between

_____ and _____ cases of wine. Alternatively, trade will result if 1 case of wine trades for between _____ and _____ boxes of cheese.

3. a. Assume that the terms of trade for cheese are set exactly between the two quantities of wine you cited in question 2 above. Alternatively, assume that the terms of trade for wine are set exactly between the two quantities of cheese you cited above. What are the terms of trade?

     1 box of cheese = _____ cases of wine
     1 box of wine   = _____ boxes of cheese

    b. Given the terms of trade, in a and b in the figure above plot the consumption possibilities curve for each nation.

    c. If nation A specializes in wine and keeps 800,000 cases for its domestic consumption and trades 200,000 cases to nation B, how many boxes of cheese can it get in return? _____ boxes Given nation A's domestic opportunity cost of cheese of _____ cases of wine, it can domestically produce only _____ boxes of cheese by sacrificing 200,000 cases of wine. Trade results in a gain of _____ boxes of cheese over what was possible in the absence of trade.

    d. If nation B trades cheese for 200,000 cases of nation A's wine, how much cheese will it have to trade? _____ boxes of cheese. Given B's domestic opportunity cost of wine of _____ boxes of cheese, it can domestically produce 200,000 cases of wine only by sacrificing _____ boxes of cheese, but it only has to give up _____ boxes of cheese through international trade to acquire the same quantity of wine. Trade results in a gain of _____ boxes of cheese over what was possible in the absence of trade.

Concept: Protectionism, tariffs, and quotas

4. List four arguments in favor of protectionism.

    a. _____
    b. _____
    c. _____
    d. _____

5.   In a and b in the figure below are shown the domestic and import markets
     for shoes.

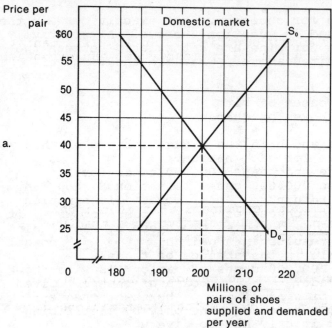

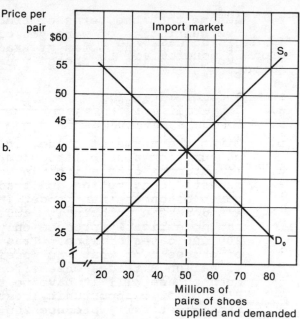

a.   Suppose that domestic shoe manufacturers and their input suppliers
     are able to win an import tariff of $10 per pair of imported shoes.
     Show the new import supply curve in b above. The $10 tariff causes
     the price to the consumer to _____ to $_____ and the net price
     to foreign shoe manufacturers to _____ to $_____. Sales of
     imported shoes _____ to _____ million pairs. The tariff has
     raised tax revenue of $_____. Show these effects in b.

b.   In a, assume that the decline in import sales causes an increase in
     domestic shoe demand by an equal amount at each price level. The
     domestic demand for shoes shifts _____ by _____ million pairs
     of shoes. Domestic shoe prices _____ to $_____ and sales
     _____ to _____ million pairs.

c.   In effect, the tariff redistributes income from _____ and
     _____ to the owners and input suppliers of the protected
     domestic shoe industry.

d.   If an import quota had been used instead to achieve the lower level
     of import sales that you found in part a above, the price of
     imported shoes paid by the consumer and received by the foreign
     producer _____ to $_____. The domestic market price of shoes
     _____ to $_____, and sales _____ to _____ million
     pairs of shoes. In this case, the government receives _____ tax
     revenue and the foreign producer may experience a/an _____ in
     total revenue if the demand for imported shoes is sufficiently
     inelastic. Show the case of an import quota in b in the figure
     above.

SELF-TEST FOR MASTERY

Select the best answer.

1. If a nation has a/an _____ in the production of an item, it can produce more of the item with a given quantity of resources than can other nations.

    a. Special advantage
    b. Comparative advantage
    c. Absolute advantage
    d. Mutual gain

2. A nation's comparative advantage is determined by:

    a. The total cost of production.
    b. The quantity of resources required to produce a unit of output.
    c. The opportunity cost of producing an item relative to a trading partner's opportunity cost of producing the same item.
    d. Specialization in the production of all goods.

3. If nations trade on the basis of comparative advantage, a nation should specialize in and _____ those goods for which it has a comparative advantage and should _____ those goods for which other nations have a comparative advantage.

    a. Export, import
    b. Import, export
    c. Export, export
    d. Import, import

4. If nations trade on the basis of comparative advantage:

    a. A nation can gain only at the expense of trading partners.
    b. Exporting nations gain and importing nations lose.
    c. Importing nations gain and exporting nations lose.
    d. All trading partners mutually gain.

5. A nation will be induced to trade for imported goods if the nation can give up _____ goods through international trade for the imported item than implied by its domestic _____ cost of production.

    a. More, total
    b. More, opportunity
    c. Fewer, variable
    d. Fewer, opportunity

6. Which of the following refers to the rate at which goods are exchanged for one another in international markets?

    a. Exchange rate
    b. Terms of trade
    c. Specialization
    d. Opportunity cost
    e. None of the above

7. If nations trade on the basis of _____ advantage, the consumption possibilities curve lies _____ the production possibilities curve.

   a. Absolute, inside
   b. A unique, parallel to
   c. Comparative, parallel to
   d. Comparative, outside

8. When a nation's productivity growth lags behind that of its trading partners, in time it may:

   a. Lose its comparative advantage in some industries.
   b. Gain a comparative advantage as a result of the lag in productivity growth.
   c. Diversify with "infant" industries.
   d. Experience a reduction in the opportunity cost of producing the good.

9. Lagging productivity growth of a nation relative to its trading partners:

   a. Results in a loss of comparative advantage in some industries.
   b. Results in an increase in the opportunity cost of producing some goods relative to that of foreign rivals.
   c. Results in a loss of income to the owners and specialized input suppliers in the industries experiencing lagging productivity growth.
   d. All of the above.

10. The United States from 1981 to 1985 experienced an average rate of growth of _____% in its output per worker, which was among the _____ for industrialized nations.

    a. 1, lowest
    b. 3.5, lowest
    c. 10, highest
    d. 8, highest

11. Which of the following have been cited as reasons for the slow productivity growth in the United States in the 1970s?

    a. Average annual net investment of 6% of domestic production
    b. Increased government regulation to improve working conditions and the environment
    c. Rising energy prices
    d. All of the above
    e. None of the above

12. Which of the following is not an argument in favor of protectionism?

    a. National security
    b. Reducing structural unemployment
    c. Protecting infant industries
    d. Protecting U.S. industries against subsidized foreign producers
    e. Goal of self-sufficiency

13. Which of the following is a tax on an imported good?

    a. Income tax
    b. Import quota
    c. Rationing tax
    d. Tariff

14. A tariff does which of the following?

    a. Increases the price of the imported good to the consumer
    b. Decreases the net price received by the foreign producer
    c. Increases the price of the domestic good
    d. Redistributes income from domestic consumers and foreign producers to
        the protected industry
    e. All of the above

15. Which of the following places a limit on the quantity of a foreign good
    that can be imported into a domestic market?

    a. Import capacity limit
    b. Import quota
    c. Export quota
    d. Tariff

16. An import quota does which of the following?

    a. Increases the price of the imported good to the consumer
    b. Increases the price received by the foreign producer
    c. Increases the price of the domestic good
    d. Redistributes income from domestic consumers to the protected
        domestic exporter
    e. All of the above

17. Which of the following is a country whose real GNP per capita is generally
    less than $1000 per year?

    a. A newly industrialized country
    b. A less developed country
    c. An industrialized country
    d. A socialist state

18. Which of the following is not a reason for low per capita output in a
    country?

    a. Low rates of saving and investment
    b. Poorly skilled and educated workers
    c. High population growth and unemployment
    d. Lagging technology
    e. Socialism

THINK IT THROUGH

1. "In international trade, one nation's trade surplus (exports in excess of
imports) must be another nation's trade deficit (imports in excess of exports).
Therefore the mercantilists must be correct in saying that a nation should
encourage exports and discourage imports." Evaluate this statement.

2. The United States has lost its international competitiveness in some basic
industries, particularly those that produce standardized goods with large
economies of scale. Can you think of any reasons why?

3. If a nation employs protectionist measures such as tariffs or quotas and
trading partners retaliate in kind, discuss some likely consequences.

POP QUIZ　　　　Read the news brief at the end of this chapter and answer the questions below.

1.　In the first half of 1988, the U.S. trade deficit was $70 billion, but it narrowed from $84.45 billion in the first half of 1987. In June of 1988, the trade deficit widened to $12.54 billion from $9.76 billion the previous month. Discuss the changes in imports and exports for the month of June that produced this widening gap.

2.　How did the U.S. trade deficit change with major trading partners? In light of this chapter, discuss how the United States benefits from trade even though its deficit with several major trading partners widened in June of 1988.

CHAPTER ANSWERS

In Brief:　Chapter Summary

1. Absolute　2. Comparative　3. Lower　4. Mutually gain from trade　5. Higher
6. Terms of trade　7. World demand and supply　8. Below　9. Outside　10. Comparative　11. Gain　12. Lowest　13. 1%　14. Investment　15. Higher energy prices　16. Vital to national security　17. New and emerging "infant" industries　18. Distribution of income that occur　19. Tariff　20. Raises　21. Reduces　22. Import quota　23. Reduces　24. Raises　25. Raises　26. May be better off　27. Lose　28. Less developed countries (LDCs)　29. Low　30. High

Vocabulary Review

1. Consumption possibilities curve　2. Real terms of trade　3. Tariff　4. Comparative advantage　5. Import quota　6. Absolute advantage　7. Real per capita output　8. Mutual gains from international trade　9. Less developed countries (LDCs)　10. Specialization

Skills Review

1.　a.

Wine (millions of cases) — Nation A
Gain: 16,667 boxes of cheese
Consumption possibilities curve
Production possibilities curve
583,333
116,667
Cheese (millions of boxes)

Wine (millions of cases) — Nation B
Consumption possibilities curve
Production possibilities curve
Gane: 16,667 boxes of cheese
Possibilities curve
283,333
266,667
Cheese (millions of boxes)

b.　1,000, exceeds, 600; 500, exceeds, 400; absolute; lies farther from the origin than
c.　1/2, 2; -2, 2
d.　2/3, 1.5; -1.5, 1.5

2.　Wine, cheese; wine, cheese; cheese, wine; cheese, wine, cheese; wine, cheese, wine; 1.5, 2; 1/2, 2/3

316

3. a. 1.75 cases of wine, 7/12 box of cheese
    b. Shown on figure above
    c. 116,667; 2, 100,000; 16,667
    d. 116,667; 2/3, 133,333; 116,667; 16,667

4. a. National security
    b. Protect infant industries
    c. Reduce structural unemployment
    d. Protect U.S. industries against subsidized foreign producers

5. a.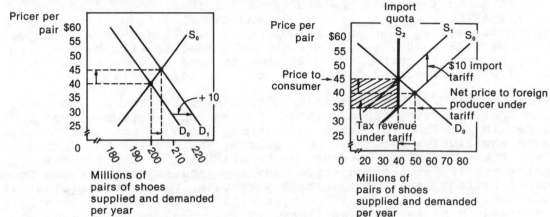

    Rise, $45, fall, $35; fall, 40; $400 million
    b. Rightward, 10; increase, $45, rise, 205
    c. Consumers, foreign producers
    d. Increase, $45; increases, $45, rise, 205; no, increase

Self-Test for Mastery

1. c 2. c 3. a 4. d 5. d 6. b 7. d 8. a 9. d 10. a 11. d 12. e 13. d 14. e 15. b 16. e 17. b 18. e

Think It Through

1. A nation's wealth is not defined in terms of the foreign currency (or gold during the mercantilist era) earned from trade surpluses, but by the total goods consumed by the nation in part as a result of international trade. A nation may run a trade deficit yet still consume more goods than if the nation engaged in no international trade. It is true that a trade deficit means a lower level of domestic aggregate demand and level of real GNP, but that level of real GNP may be higher than it would have been if the nation did not produce and trade on the basis of comparative advantage.

2. The United States has experienced lagging productivity growth in several of its heavy industries--those that produce standardized goods and whose firms realize substantial economies of scale. Other nations have had more rapid productivity growth in some of these industries, taking away the comparative advantage once enjoyed by the U.S. industries. New techniques of production were being introduced abroad at a time during which many U.S. plants were aging and becoming obsolete. U.S. firms were not investing enough in new plant and equipment and technology to maintain their relatively lower opportunity cost of production. Several foreign nations that have captured the comparative advantage from the United States have done so by investing a greater percentage of their domestic production in physical capital and technology. They also have an advantage in having a relatively less costly labor force.

3. If all trading nations are engaging in protectionist measures, all lose in that the volume of international trade will be lower, the level of world output

and living standards will be lower, and household real incomes will be lower because the prices of imported and domestic goods will be higher than in the absence of trade restrictions.

Pop Quiz

1. The U.S. trade deficit increased in June because imports for the month exceeded exports. Imports increased by 5.7% and included the following changes: imports of capital goods increased by 10%, imports of consumer goods increased 8%, auto imports increased 12.5%; however, food, feeds, and beverage imports fell 4%, oil imports fell 9.3%, and imported industrial supplies fell 2.8%. Exports fell by 2.4% and included the following changes: exports of capital goods fell by 6%, auto and auto parts exports fell by 7.3%, food, feeds, and beverage exports fell 7.2%, but exports of industrial supplies increased 3.2% and exports of consumer goods increased 2.4%.

2. Although the U.S. trade deficits with Canada and Taiwan increased, the U.S. trade deficits with Japan, Western Europe, and various oil-producing nations declined. The U.S. trade deficit implies a lower level of aggregate demand and equilibrium real GNP than would be the case if the United States did not have a trade deficit. However, by specializing in and exporting those goods for which it has a comparative advantage and importing those goods for which other nations have a comparative advantage, the United States may enjoy higher domestic standards of living even with a trade deficit than if the nation engaged in no international trade.

U.S. Trade Gap Widened in June To $12.54 Billion

Result, After 42-Month Low In May, Came as Imports Rose 5.7% to a Record

By David Wessel
Staff Reporter of The Wall Street Journal

WASHINGTON—The nation's merchandise trade deficit worsened in June, as a strong U.S. economy boosted imports to a record.

The Commerce Department put the deficit at $12.54 billion, substantially widened

---

Markets Rebound

Stock and bond markets and the U.S. dollar initially fell on the trade-gap news, but rebounded through the day. The Dow Jones Industrial Average rose 17.24 to 2021.51. Bonds wound up with small gains, as did the dollar, after a day of volatile trading. See related stories on pages 41, 26 and 33.

---

from the revised $9.76 billion reported for May. The May gap was a 42-month low.

Imports rose 5.7% to $39.35 billion in June as Americans bought more foreign-made capital goods, consumer products and autos. Exports fell by a modest 2.4% to $26.81 billion, but they remain well above year-earlier levels. The deficit worsened with all major trading partners.

Slow and Difficult

Although the U.S. trade picture still appears brighter than last year, the report underscores how slow and difficult the process of closing the trade gap will be. "The June deficit confirms . . . the willingness of the U.S. to consume more than we can actually afford," said James Howell, a Bank of Boston economist.

"Our economy is drawing a larger-than-expected quantity of goods into the coun-

try, and we're probably running into bottlenecks in getting goods out of the country," said James Cochrane, an economist with Texas Commerce Bancshares Inc. in Houston.

Surging imports suggest that the Federal Reserve Board, which already has pushed interest rates higher, is likely to force them still higher, economists said. "We're going to have to keep import demand slow and that means more of a lift for short-term interest rates," warned Robert Barbera, a Shearson Lehman Hutton Inc. economist.

Monthly trade figures can be misleading because they are volatile. Commerce Secretary C. William Verity insisted that the underlying trend in the U.S. trade position "remains favorable," noting that the trade deficit in the second quarter was narrower than those in each of the preceeding three quarters.

First Half

In the first half of this year, the U.S. trade deficit was $70 billion, narrowed from $84.45 billion in the first half of 1987. The trade figures are adjusted for usual seasonal fluctuations, but not for higher prices. If the effects of higher prices are removed, the improvement in the trade deficit is far more impressive, Mr. Verity said.

The Commerce Department said U.S. imports of capital goods rose 10% in June to $9.22 billion, a reflection of the continued U.S. boom in capital spending. Imports of consumer goods were up 8.5% to $8.68 billion. And auto imports rose 12.5% to $7.51 billion, mainly because of more imported Canadian cars.

Imports of food, feeds and beverages fell 4% in June to $2.08 billion, and imports of industrial supplies dropped 2.8% to $10.74 billion. Oil imports, which aren't adjusted for seasonal fluctuations, fell 9.3% to $3.57 billion, as both the volume of imports and the price declined.

On the export side, the Commerce Department said exports of capital goods dropped 6% in June to $8.69 billion. Ex-

ports of autos and parts fell 7.3% to $2.25 billion. And exports of foods, feeds and beverages declined 7.2% to $2.72 billion. But exports of industrial supplies were up 3.2% to $7.37 billion and consumer-goods exports rose 2.4% to $1.97 billion.

Major Partners

The trade deficit with major U.S. trading partners widened in June, but the deficits with Japan, Western Europe, the Organization of Petroleum Exporting Countries and the newly industrializing countries of Asia all were lower than in June 1987.

The trade deficit with Canada, America's largest trading partner, rose to $1.4 billion in June from $1.04 billion in May and was more than double its $530.5 million level in June 1987. An increase in imports of Canadian autos and parts accounted for much of the change. The auto industry's trade deficit with Canada widened to $826.1 million in June from $621 million in May and $226.9 million in June 1987.

But Commerce Department officials warned that for the past several months Canadian customs data—upon which the U.S. relies—have understated U.S. exports, forcing subsequent revisions in the department's reports. The figure for U.S. exports to Canada in May was revised up by $300 million.

The trade deficit with Taiwan widened a substantial 30% in June to $1.23 billion, and is now larger than the U.S. deficit with any single country except Japan and Canada. This occurred even though Taiwan bought $200 million of non-monetary gold in June, and $300 million in May, in what U.S. officials have described as a "gimmick" to shrink its reported trade surplus with the U.S. Taiwanese central-bank officials said in July they were suspending the gold purchases.

The seasonally adjusted trade deficit for May originally was estimated at $10.93 billion. Before seasonal adjustments, the Commerce Department said the trade deficit in June was $12.62 billion, up from $9.51 billion in May.

U.S. Merchandise Trade Deficits

(In billions of U.S. dollars, not seasonally adjusted)

	JUNE '88	MAY '88	JUNE '87
Japan	$4.40	$4.12	$5.35
Canada	1.40	1.04	0.53
Western Europe	1.91	1.20	2.93
NICs*	2.72	2.35	3.70

*Newly industrialized economies, including Singapore, Hong Kong, Taiwan, South Korea

Source: Commerce Department

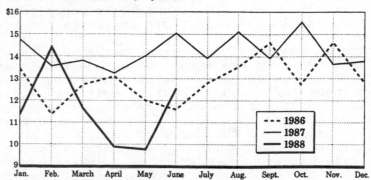

Tracking the Trade Deficit

(In billions of dollars, seasonally adjusted)

- - - 1986
— 1987
— 1988

Note: Monthly figures for 1986 aren't adjusted for undocumented exports to Canada

Source: Commerce Department

23

The Economics of Foreign Exchange and the Balance of International Trade

After studying your text, attending class, and completing this chapter, you should be able to:

1. Understand how international transactions between the United States and the rest of the world involve the exchange of dollars for units of foreign currency.
2. Use supply and demand analysis to show how exchange rates of one currency into another are established in foreign exchange markets.
3. Use aggregate supply and demand analysis to show the impact of changes in the real exchange rate of the dollar on macroeconomic equilibrium.
4. Explain the causes of currency appreciation and depreciation in foreign exchange markets and discuss the evolution of the current international monetary system.
5. Understand how a balance of trade deficit in the United States in a given year implies an increase in net foreign acquisition of U.S. financial and other assets in that year.

IN BRIEF: CHAPTER SUMMARY

Fill in the blanks to summarize chapter content.

International trade requires the exchange of currencies. The (1)_____ (foreign exchange rate is, terms of trade are) the price of one nation's monetary unit in terms of the monetary unit of another nation. The (2)_____ (stock market, foreign exchange market) is a market in which currencies are exchanged. Here the forces of supply and demand determine the rate at which any two currencies are exchanged.   For example, a U.S. importer wants to purchase foreign goods with dollars but foreign exporters want to be paid in their own currencies. An exchange of currency must take place. For a fee, the importer can use dollars to purchase a bank draft denominated in foreign currency from a U.S. bank. This constitutes (3)_____ (a demand for, an increase in the supply of) the foreign currency.

Equilibrium in the foreign exchange market occurs where the supply of and demand for a currency are equal--where the supply and demand curves for a currency intersect. If the price of a currency (expressed in terms of units of another currency) is higher than the equilibrium exchange rate, a (4)_____ (shortage, surplus) of the currency will cause a decline in the exchange rate. If the exchange rate is below the equilibrium exchange rate, a (5)_____ (shortage, surplus) of the currency results in an increase in the exchange rate.   Influences that shift the demand or supply curves will alter the exchange rate between two currencies. Several factors can affect the equilibrium exchange rate of the U.S. dollar: (a) foreign demand for U.S. exports, (b) U.S. demand for imports, (c) real interest rates in the United States relative to those in foreign nations, (d) profitability of direct investment in U.S. businesses and real estate relative to profitability of similar investments in foreign nations, (e) expectations of an increase in the price of the dollar in terms of foreign currency, and (f) the price level (6)_____ (established by the Bretton Woods agreement; in the United States) relative to the price levels in foreign nations.

If real interest rates in the United States rise relative to interest rates in Great Britain, for instance, the British will increase their (7)_____ (supply of, demand for) U.S. dollars in the foreign exchange markets in order to purchase higher-yielding U.S. financial assets. As the demand for dollars rises relative to the supply of dollars, the exchange rate of the dollar (8)_____ (falls, rises). The dollar will be exchanged for more British pounds than previously. Conversely, the British pound will be exchanged for (9)_____ (more, fewer) U.S. dollars. The dollar (10)_____ (depreciates, appreciates) and the pound (11)_____ (depreciates, appreciates). British goods valued in dollars fall in price, and U.S. goods valued in British pounds increase in price. As a result, U.S. goods exported to Great Britain become (12)_____ (more, less) price competitive with British domestic output. Likewise, in the United States, British imported goods become (13)_____ (more, less) expensive relative to U.S. domestic output.

A higher rate of interest in the United States increases the real exchange rate between the pound and dollar, causing U.S. exports to Britain to (14)_____ (rise, fall) and U.S. imports from Britain to rise. U.S. net exports (15)_____ (fall, rise), causing the aggregate demand curve to shift (16)_____ (rightward, leftward). But an appreciation of the dollar also reduces the dollar prices of imported raw materials and other inputs, which shifts the aggregate supply curve (17)_____ (rightward, leftward). It is expected that the change in aggregate demand is larger than the change in aggregate supply, causing equilibrium real GNP and the price level to (18)_____ (rise, fall).

Conversely, a depreciation of the dollar makes U.S. goods (19)_____ (more, less) price competitive abroad while increasing the relative prices of imports to the United States. U.S. exports (20)_____ (fall, rise) and imports (21)_____ (fall, rise), causing net exports to rise. An increase in net exports shifts the aggregate demand curve (22)_____ (rightward, leftward). The aggregate supply curve shifts leftward because the prices of imported inputs (23)_____ (decrease, increase). On net, the increase in aggregate demand will outweigh the decrease in aggregate supply, causing equilibrium real GNP and the price level to (24)_____ (fall, rise). These changes may take some time to develop. Empirical evidence indicates that it may take up to 2 years before changes in exchange rates significantly affect import prices. This, of course, depends upon the profit goals of foreign producers. If foreign producers wish to maintain prices in foreign markets, they may absorb most of the change in exchange rates as lower profits. If import prices remain unchanged relative to other prices, there is no reason for net exports to change.

The foreign exchange market described above is a free market often referred to as a (25)_____ (fixed, floating or flexible) exchange rate market. Prior to the 1930s, however, exchange rates were fixed within narrow limits. This was accomplished by the gold standard, under which currencies were convertible into (26)_____ (gold, the U.S. dollar) at fixed rates. This meant that each currency had (27)_____ (several exchange rates, a unique exchange rate) relative to every other currency. Exchange rates remained fixed as long as the gold price of each currency remained (28)_____ (flexible, unchanged). Nations concerned with domestic macroeconomic problems would often devalue their currency rather than allow an outflow of gold that would reduce the nation's money stock. Devaluation alters exchange rates, however. This system was replaced in 1944 by the (29)_____ (managed float, Bretton Woods system) in which the values of foreign currencies were tied to the U.S.

dollar rather than to gold. The United States abandoned its role as the guarantor of exchange rate stability when it chose to suspend convertibility of the dollar into gold in (30)_____ (1971, 1961). In 1973, the United States and other nations abandoned the fixed exchange rate system in favor of the (31)_____ (modified gold standard, flexible exchange rate system). Today the foreign exchange market is characterized as a managed float rather than a freely floating or flexible exchange rate system. The Federal Reserve System and foreign central banks intervene in the market to effect desirable changes in exchange rates.

The balance of payments for a nation shows the net exchange of the nation's currency for foreign currencies from all transactions between that nation and foreign nations in a given year. In the United States the balance of payments consists of the current account and the capital account. The (32)_____ (capital, current) account shows the effect of the volume of goods and services traded on international markets, including changes in investment income and other miscellaneous transactions. The balance (33)_____ (on the current account, of trade) represents the difference between the value of merchandise exports and imports. The balance (34)_____ (on the current account, of trade) is more comprehensive in that it measures U.S. net exports for the year, including transactions involving services, investment income, and transfers. As recently as 1981, the United States had a surplus in its current account balance but had a large merchandise trade deficit.

In 1985, the current account registered a (35)_____ (deficit, surplus) of over $117 billion. This means U.S. citizens supplied $117 billion more to foreigners than foreigners supplied in foreign currencies to Americans. A net outflow must be offset (financed). When the current account is in deficit, the United States must sell assets or borrow to finance the deficit. These transactions are shown in the (36)_____ (capital, current) account. As foreigners purchase U.S. financial and real assets at a rate greater than U.S. citizens purchase those assets abroad, the net inflow of dollars just offsets the current account deficit.

VOCABULARY REVIEW

Write the key term from the list below next to its definition.

Key Terms

Foreign exchange rate	Bretton Woods system
Foreign exchange market	International Monetary Fund (IMF)
Foreign exchange	Special drawing right (SDR)
Currency appreciation	International balance of payments
Currency depreciation	Balance of trade
Purchasing power parity	Managed float
Gold standard	Real exchange rate
Balance on current account of the balance of payments	Nominal exchange rate

Definition

1. _____: the price of a unit of one nation's currency in terms of a unit of a foreign currency.

2. _____: the price of one nation's monetary unit in terms of the monetary unit of another nation.

3. _____ :   the sacrifice of goods and services that foreign buyers must make when they use their own currency to purchase goods of the first nation worth one unit of that nation's currency.

4. _____ :   a market in which buyers and sellers of bank deposits denominated in the monetary units of many nations exchange their funds.

5. _____ :   an international monetary system that required that currencies be converted into gold at a fixed price.

6. _____ :   the money of one nation held by citizens of another nation either as currency or as deposits in banks.

7. _____ :   describes the current international monetary system, under which central banks affect supply of and demand for currencies in ways that influence equilibrium in foreign exchange markets.

8. _____ :   occurs when there is an increase in the number of units of one nation's currency that must be given up to purchase each unit of another nation's currency.

9. _____ :   established under the Bretton Woods agreement; set rules for the international monetary system to make loans to nations that lack international reserves of dollars.

10. _____ :   occurs when there is a decrease in the number of units of one nation's currency that must be given up to purchase each unit of another nation's currency.

11. _____ :   an international monetary system developed in 1944 and based on fixed exchange rates, with the value of foreign currencies tied to the U.S. dollar.

12. _____ :   a principle that states that the exchange rate between any two currencies tends to adjust to reflect changes in the price levels in the two nations.

13. _____ :   a paper substitute for gold that is created by the International Monetary Fund and is distributed to member nations to use as international reserves.

14. _____ :   a statement showing the net exchange rate of a nation's currency for foreign currencies from all transactions between that nation and foreign nations in a given year.

15. _____ :   the difference between the value of merchandise exported by a nation's firms and the nation's imports of foreign-produced goods.

16. _____ :   measures U.S. net exports for the year, including transactions involving services, investment income, and transfers.

SKILLS REVIEW

Concept: Foreign exchange rates and foreign exchange markets

1. The figure below represents a foreign exchange market for the U.S. dollar and the Canadian dollar.

Price (number of Canadian dollars)

Millions of U.S.
dollars per day

   a. Given demand curve Do and supply curve So, the equilibrium exchange rate between the Canadian and U.S. dollar is 1 U.S. dollar = _____ Canadian dollars or alternatively, 1 Canadian dollar = _____ U.S. dollars.

   b. A U.S. good valued at $1000 in U.S. dollars would cost _____ Canadian dollars. A Canadian good valued at 100 Canadian dollars would cost _____ U.S. dollars.

2. List six factors that influence the exchange rate of the dollar.

   a. _____
   b. _____
   c. _____
   d. _____
   e. _____
   f. _____

3. Referring to the figure above, suppose real interest rates in the United States rise relative to interest rates abroad, causing the demand for dollars to increase to Dl.

   a. What are the new exchange rates?

      (1) 1 U.S. dollar = _____ Canadian dollars
      (2) 1 Canadian dollar = _____ U.S. dollars

   b. The U.S. dollar has _____, and the Canadian dollar has _____.

   c. A U.S. good valued at 1000 U.S. dollars now costs _____ Canadian dollars. A Canadian good valued at 100 Canadian dollars now costs _____ U.S. dollars.

   d. U.S. goods become _____ price competitive in Canada, and Canadian goods become _____ price competitive in the United States.

4. Referring to the figure above, given the initial demand curve, Do, assume that U.S. firms increase their imports from Canada, causing the supply of U.S. dollars to shift to S1.

    a. What are the new exchange rates?

        (1) 1 U.S. dollar = _____ Canadian dollars
        (2) 1 Canadian dollar = _____ U.S. dollar
    b. The U.S. dollar has _____, and the Canadian dollar has
        _____.
    c. A U.S. good valued at 1000 U.S. dollars now costs _____ Canadian dollars. A Canadian good valued at 100 Canadian dollars now costs _____ U.S. dollars.
    d. U.S. goods become _____ price competitive in Canada, and Canadian goods become _____ price competitive in the United States.

Concept: **Changes in real exchange rates and equilibrium real GNP and the price level**

5. The figure below represents an economy.

Price level

Real GNP
(billions of dollars)

    a. A depreciation of the U.S. dollar relative to the Canadian dollar makes U.S. goods _____ price competitive in Canada and Canadian goods _____ price competitive in the United States. U.S. exports _____, imports _____, and net exports _____.
    b. Given the initial aggregate demand and supply curves, ADo and ASo, the change in net exports indicated above shifts the AD curve to _____ (AD1, AD2).
    c. The price of imported inputs in U.S. dollars _____, causing the AS curve to shift to _____ (AS1, AS2).
    d. Equilibrium real GNP _____ from Yo to _____.

6. Refer to the figure above in answering this question.

    a. An appreciation of the U.S. dollar relative to the Canadian dollar makes U.S. goods _____ price competitive in Canada and Canadian goods _____ price competitive in the United States. U.S. exports _____, imports _____, and net exports _____.
    b. Given the initial aggregate demand and supply curves, ADo and ASo, the change in net exports indicated in part a above shifts the AD curve to _____ (AD1, AD2).
    c. The prices of imported inputs in U.S. dollars _____, causing the AS curve to shift to _____ (AS1, AS2).
    d. Equilibrium real GNP _____ from Yo to _____.

Concept: International balance of payments

7.   Identify which of the following represent a <u>capital account</u> and which
      represent a <u>current account</u> transaction in the balance of payments and
      state whether the transaction results in an <u>inflow</u> or <u>outflow</u> of U.S.
      dollars.

      a.   U.S. exports of services increase.
      b.   Foreigners purchase U.S. Treasury bills.
      c.   Automobile imports into the United States decrease.
      d.   Transfers to foreigners increase.
      e.   U.S. firms purchase factories abroad.
      f.   Rich oil sheiks purchase Texas ranch land.
      g.   Hitachi receives income from its U.S. plants.
      h.   Foreigners increase imports of U.S. merchandise goods.
      i.   U.S. citizens purchase stock in foreign enterprises.

            Capital or Current   Inflow or Outflow?
                 Account?
      a.   _____   _____
      b.   _____   _____
      c.   _____   _____
      d.   _____   _____
      e.   _____   _____
      f.   _____   _____
      g.   _____   _____
      h.   _____   _____
      i.   _____   _____

SELF-TEST FOR MASTERY

Select the best answer.

1.   A market in which buyers and sellers of bank deposits denominated in the
      monetary units of many nations exchange their funds is known as:

      a.   The loanable funds market.
      b.   The money market.
      c.   The capital market.
      d.   The foreign exchange market.

2.   If the price of a dollar in terms of units of a foreign currency is above
      the equilibrium exchange rate, a _____ exists, which will put
      _____ pressure on the equilibrium exchange rate of the dollar.

      a.   Shortage, downward
      b.   Shortage, upward
      c.   Surplus, downward
      d.   Surplus, upward

3. If a $10,000 U.S.-made automobile is sold in France and the exchange rate
    between the dollar and the franc is $1 = 8 francs, the U.S. automobile
    sold in France will cost _____ francs.

    a. 20,000
    b. 40,000
    c. 60,000
    d. 80,000
    e. 100,000

4. The exchange rate between the dollar and the franc is $1 = 8 francs, and
    the price of a bottle of imported French wine is $5. If the exchange rate
    changes to $1 = 4 francs, the dollar price of the French wine _____ to
    $_____.

    a. Falls, $2.50
    b. Rises, $10
    c. Rises, $20
    d. Does not change

5. An increase in foreign demand for U.S. exports will _____ demand for
    the dollar, causing the dollar to _____.

    a. Decrease, appreciate
    b. Increase, depreciate
    c. Increase, appreciate
    d. Decrease, depreciate

6. An increase in U.S. demand for imports will _____ the _____
    U.S. dollars, causing the dollar to _____.

    a. Increase, demand for, appreciate
    b. Increase, supply of, appreciate
    c. Decrease, supply of, depreciate
    d. Decrease, demand for, appreciate
    e. Increase, supply of, depreciate

7. If real interest rates in the United States rise relative to interest
    rates abroad, the _____ dollars will _____, causing the dollar to
    _____.

    a. Demand for, increase, appreciate
    b. Demand for, increase, depreciate
    c. Supply of, decrease, depreciate
    d. Supply of, increase, appreciate

8. If the rate of inflation in the United States rises relative to the rate
    of inflation in foreign nations, U.S. exports _____ and imports
    _____, causing the demand for dollars to _____ and the supply of
    dollars to _____.

    a. Increase, decrease, rise, fall
    b. Decrease, increase, fall, rise
    c. Increase, increase, fall, fall
    d. Decrease, decrease, rise, rise

9. The price of a unit of one nation's currency in terms of a unit of a
    foreign currency is called:

    a. The nominal exchange rate.
    b. The real exchange rate.

c. Foreign exchange.
d. Purchasing power parity.
e. None of the above.

10. Empirical evidence suggests that:

   a. Import prices respond very quickly to changes in exchange rates.
   b. Net exports respond within a year to changes in the exchange rate of the dollar.
   c. Import prices are slow to respond to changes in exchange rates, taking up to 2 years to be affected.
   d. There is an immediate link between exchange rates and import prices.

11. An increase in the real exchange rate of the dollar causes aggregate demand to _____ and aggregate supply to _____, resulting in a/an _____ in real GNP.

   a. Decrease, decrease, decrease
   b. Increase, increase, increase
   c. Increase, decrease, decrease
   d. Increase, increase, decrease
   e. Decrease, increase, decrease

12. A depreciation of the dollar causes aggregate demand to _____ and aggregate supply to _____, resulting in a/an _____ in real GNP.

   a. Decrease, decrease, decrease
   b. Increase, increase, increase
   c. Increase, decrease, increase
   d. Increase, increase, decrease
   e. Decrease, increase, decrease

13. The Bretton Woods agreement:

   a. Represented a new international monetary system.
   b. Tied the value of foreign currencies not to gold but to the dollar.
   c. Was established in 1944.
   d. Also established the International Monetary Fund.
   e. All of the above.

14. The present international monetary system is best described as a:

   a. Fixed exchange rate system.
   b. Purchasing power parity system.
   c. Flexible exchange rate system.
   d. Managed float.

15. Which of the following summarizes the transactions involving the international exchange of goods and services, investment income, and other miscellaneous transactions?

   a. Balance of trade
   b. Statistical discrepancy
   c. Current account
   d. Capital account

16. Which of the following is the difference between the value of merchandise exported and merchandise imported?

    a.   Balance of trade
    b.   Balance on the current account
    c.   Budget balance
    d.   Balance of payments

17. Which of the following measures net exports for the year, including transactions involving services, investment income, and transfers?

    a.   Balance of trade
    b.   Balance on the current account
    c.   Budget balance
    d.   Balance of payments

18. When the current account is in deficit, the capital account must

    a.   Be balanced.
    b.   Be zero.
    c.   Not add to the deficit.
    d.   Have an equal and offsetting surplus.

THINK IT THROUGH

1.   How can the Fed, through domestic monetary policy, cause the U.S. dollar to depreciate?

2.   How can the Fed, through direct intervention in foreign exchange markets, cause the U.S. dollar to depreciate?

3.   If the U.S. dollar depreciates, what are the likely economic consequences?

POP QUIZ   Read the news brief at the end of this chapter and answer the questions below.

1.   Lindley Clark cites two reasons for the recent climb in the exchange rate of the U.S. dollar. What are they?

2.   According to the article, why would Japan, Britain, and West Germany be hesitant to intervene to slow the appreciation of the dollar?

CHAPTER ANSWERS

In Brief: Chapter Summary

1. Foreign exchange rate is 2. Foreign exchange market 3. A demand for 4. Surplus 5. Shortage 6. In the United States 7. Demand for 8. Rises 9. Fewer 10. Appreciates 11. Depreciates 12. Less 13. Less 14. Fall 15. Fall 16. Leftward 17. Rightward 18. Fall 19. More 20. Rise 21. Fall 22. Rightward 23. Increase 24. Rise 25. Floating or flexible 26. Gold 27. A unique exchange rate 28. Unchanged 29. Bretton Woods system 30. 1971 31.

Flexible exchange rate system 32. Current 33. Of trade 34. On the current account 35. Deficit 36. Capital

Vocabulary Review

1. Nominal exchange rate 2. Foreign exchange rate 3. Real exchange rate 4. Foreign exchange market 5. Gold standard 6. Foreign exchange 7. Managed float 8. Currency appreciation 9. International Monetary Fund (IMF) 10. Currency depreciation 11. Bretton Woods system 12. Purchasing power parity 13. Special drawing right (SDR) 14. International balance of payments 15. Balance of trade 16. Balance on the current account of the balance of payments

Skills Review

1. a. 1.5, 2/3
    b. 1,500, $66.67

2. a. Foreign demand for U.S. exports
    b. U.S. demand for imports
    c. Real interest rates in the United States relative to those in foreign nations
    d. Profitability of direct investment in U.S. businesses and real estate relative to profitability of similar investments in foreign nations
    e. Expectations of an increase in the price of the dollar in terms of foreign currency
    f. The price level in the United States relative to the price levels in foreign nations

3. a. 2, 1/2
    b. Appreciated, depreciated
    c. 2,000; 50
    d. Less, more

4. a. 1, 1
    b. Depreciated, appreciated
    c. 1,000; 100
    d. More, less

5. a. More, less; rise, fall, increase
    b. AD1
    c. Rises, AS2
    d. Increases, Y1

6. a. Less, more; fall, rise, decrease
    b. AD2
    c. Falls, AS1
    d. Decreases, Y4

7. a. Current, inflow
    b. Capital, inflow
    c. Current, outflow
    d. Current, outflow
    e. Capital, outflow
    f. Capital, inflow
    g. Current, outflow
    h. Current, inflow
    i. Capital, outflow

Self-Test for Mastery

1. d   2. c   3. d   4. b   5. c   6. e   7. a   8. b   9. a   10. c   11. e   12. c   13. e   14. d   15. c   16. a   17. b   18. d

Think It Through

1.   If the Fed pursues an expansionary monetary policy that reduces the real rate of interest in the United States relative to interest rates abroad, Americans will increase their demand for foreign currencies by supplying more dollars to the international foreign exchange markets in order to purchase higher-yielding foreign financial assets. The increase in the supply of dollars relative to demand will cause the dollar to depreciate. The expansionary monetary policy will also increase the nation's income, causing imports to increase. In order to increase imports, Americans must supply dollars to acquire foreign exchange to purchase the foreign goods. This too will cause the dollar to depreciate. If the expansionary monetary policy is also inflationary such that the rate of inflation in the United States rises relative to foreign rates of inflation, U.S. exports will fall and imports will rise. This will cause foreign demand for the dollar to fall and the supply of dollars to increase, also resulting in depreciation of the dollar.

2.   If the Fed wished to depreciate the dollar, it could purchase foreign currencies with its dollar holdings, causing the demand for foreign currencies to rise and the supply of dollars to increase. This in turn would cause the dollar to depreciate relative to the foreign currencies purchased by the Fed.

3.   If the dollar depreciates, U.S. goods become less costly in foreign currencies, increasing their price competitiveness in foreign markets. Likewise, foreign goods become more costly in dollars, decreasing their price competitiveness in the United States. U.S. imports of foreign goods decrease, and U.S. exports to foreign nations increase. The increase in net exports causes the aggregate demand curve to shift rightward. But foreign inputs now cost more in dollars. As production costs rise, the aggregate supply curve shifts leftward. On net, however, real GNP increases.

Pop Quiz

1.   According to the article, the dollar has appreciated because the U.S. downing of an Iranian airliner in the Persian Gulf raised fears of a possible international crisis. Money tends to flow to "safe-haven" currencies such as the dollar when there are mounting fears of international instability. It is noted that increases in U.S. exports and foreign investors' optimism regarding the inflation outlook in the United States were also responsible for the rise in the exchange rate of the dollar. Exports create a demand for the dollar, causing its exchange rate to rise. If foreign investors expect U.S. inflation to remain stable, they will be more likely to invest in U.S. dollar-denominated securities. This too creates a demand for the dollar, causing it to appreciate.

2.   All of these nations are enjoying strong economies. If they intervened in foreign exchange markets to prevent the appreciation of the dollar, they would have to purchase their own currencies with their dollar holdings. The increase in the supply of dollars keeps the dollar from appreciating, and the increased demand for foreign currencies prevents the foreign currencies from depreciating relative to the dollar. These actions, however, keep foreign currencies from depreciating and foreign export industries from becoming more price competitive in the United States. "Defending" the dollar against appreciation means that foreign nations sacrifice an increase in net exports and income.

331

The Outlook

Should the Dollar Find Its Own Market Level?

NEW YORK

Anyone who wonders why Japan hesitates to let the yen become an international currency should consider the continuing convolutions of the U.S. dollar. Not only the U.S. but most major countries want to manage the dollar to suit their own convenience. Japan may be an industrial giant, but it has no desire to subject the yen to that sort of nonsense.

The dollar has been climbing lately, at least temporarily reversing the drop that began in February 1985. Early last week, the dollar spurted on foreign markets for reasons entirely separate from U.S. economic management. The accidental U.S. downing of an Iranian passenger plane in the Persian Gulf, killing all 290 persons aboard, raised fears of a new international crisis. In an international crisis, investors seek a safe-haven currency, and the dollar still is perceived to be the best around.

The rise in the dollar stems in large part from the increase in U.S. exports, which has shrunk the merchandise trade deficit. The dollar's rise, moreover, lessens inflation fears, since it tends to make imports less expensive. An analysis by Lawrence H. Meyer & Associates of St. Louis notes that the rise leads foreign investors to become more optimistic about the dollar's future and thus more willing to buy dollar securities, helping to push the dollar higher. "A stronger dollar," the firm says, "hints that the dollar may have bottomed."

Jerry L. Jordan, chief economist of First Interstate Bank of Los Angeles, is convinced that the dollar "has seen its lows for this cycle." He says Federal Reserve Chairman Alan Greenspan "is building up credibility as an inflation-fighter. He hasn't quite moved into the spot Paul Volcker held as the second most powerful man in the U.S., but he's making progress."

Some analysts argue that the stronger dollar will end the upsurge of U.S. exports, just as the weaker dollar started it. A few contend that the dollar not only will have to fall but will have to drop sharply to continue the improvement in the U.S. trade balance. The fact is that no one can be absolutely certain what level of the dollar is needed to sustain exports—or just what the future level of the dollar will be. The dollar's current strength is based heavily on a foreign perception that the U.S. is beginning to get its house in order. Evidence to the contrary could send the dollar down.

All of this is happening, it should be noted, when neither the Federal Reserve nor any other major central bank has much appetite to push the dollar significantly lower or higher. The Fed prefers peace and quiet in presidential election years, so its preference presumably would be a dollar that stabilized at about the current level—at least, between now and November. So far, Fed Chairman Greenspan has commented only that he sees no reason for the dollar to go lower. The U.S. hope obviously is that the dollar now is low enough to permit continued strength in U.S. exports.

Some central banks have sold dollars in an effort to slow the gains of the U.S. currency, but others are hesitant. If the Bank of Japan sells dollars it soaks up yen, tending to weaken the Japanese economy, now in the midst of a consumer-fueled boom. Japan knows it may eventually have to tighten credit to cool off the boom, but presumably it would prefer to base the timing on its domestic needs, not on the buoyant dollar.

The British and West Germans also have strong economies, which could be weakened by new dollar sales. Some foreigners find the current situation strange. A German banker quoted in this newspaper last week said he found it hard to believe that Germany would have to defend its mark when it has a low inflation rate, high current account surpluses and a booming export economy.

For the present, market factors seem to be working in favor of the dollar. "The question is how foreign net demand for our assets will compare with our net demand for foreign goods," Mr. Jordan says. "Our net demand for foreign goods is going down,

while net foreign demand for our assets has picked up sharply." The U.S. is still bringing assets home from abroad, while foreigners continue to buy assets here.

One reason the outlook for sales of assets to foreigners is strong is that the inflation rates seem to be moving in our favor. The foreign perception is that U.S. inflation has stabilized, at a time when other major industrial countries are worrying about rising inflation.

Time will tell. The U.S. has found that a nation with an international currency can largely ignore inflation, trade deficits and budget deficits for a long time without disaster. But no one can ignore such fundamental factors forever.

For the near term, the Federal Reserve needs to continue to provide investors, foreign and domestic, assurance of its determination to prevent a surge of inflation, a task that is complicated by higher food prices stemming from the Midwest drought. It's unlikely that much reduction of the budget deficit will be forthcoming until after the election, if then, but it would be helpful if the presidential candidates gave more evidence that they appreciated the seriousness of the problem.

In the long run, the fundamental factors must prevail. But it's no wonder that Japan prefers to keep the yen out of the uncertainties that persist until the fundamentals assert themselves. What is surprising is that government officials don't remember that the exchange rate is a market price and thus decide to let the dollar find its own level.

—LINDLEY H. CLARK JR.

24

Economics and Ideology: Socialism vs. Capitalism

CHAPTER CHALLENGES

After studying your text, attending class, and completing this chapter, you should be able to:

1. Discuss the ideas of Karl Marx and the ideological underpinnings of socialism.
2. Discuss modern socialist economies, particularly that of the Soviet Union.
3. Explain central planning as a means of allocating resources in a command economy.
4. Discuss issues involved in evaluating economic performance in modern economies.

IN BRIEF: CHAPTER SUMMARY

Fill in the blanks to complete the chapter summary.

(1)_____ (Capitalism, Socialism) is associated with private ownership of resources, freedom of enterprise, and an economy in which markets allocate resources. (2)_____ (Capitalism, Socialism), in contrast, is associated with government ownership of productive resources and central planning. Prices and resource allocation are determined by central planners rather than by markets.

According to Karl Marx, only (3)_____ (labor, capital) produces value. Even capital is the past product of labor. Marx argued that capitalists hire labor at subsistence wages, generating a (4)_____ (marginal revenue product, surplus value)--the wages paid to labor are less than the value of the worker's production. Capitalists therefore exploit workers and will continue to do so until the working class revolts and establishes a socialist state. Most workers, however, earn incomes well above a subsistence level in market economies. Marx did not foresee the enormous gains made in (5)_____ (profits, labor productivity) as a result of technology and capital formation. Over time, the (6)_____ (supply of, demand for) labor has outpaced the (7)_____ (supply of, demand for) labor, resulting in increases in real wages. The working class has not revolted in a manner envisioned by Marx because of gains in real living standards and social policy designed to alleviate some of the failures of market systems.

The Soviet Union is a (8)_____ (market, command) economy in which resources are allocated by central planners who set production goals. The (9)_____ (Gosplan, Politburo) is the central planning board for the Soviet Union and drafts 5-year plans listing production goals for the economy. The government sets prices to ensure the satisfaction of the output goals. Prices of many goods have been kept artificially low as a way of subsidizing consumption. But when prices are set below the level that equates supply and demand, (10)_____ (surpluses, shortages) become a problem. Shortages can be eliminated with a (11)_____ (lump sum, turnover) tax if it is equal to the difference between the price that would equate supply and demand and the lower subsidized price. Shortages are reduced, but only from a reduction in quantity demanded. Quantity supplied remains fixed at the planners' production target.

As of January 1, 1988, the Soviet economy began to institute reforms such as putting (12)_____ (10%, 60%) of Soviet enterprises on a self-financing basis. These firms are required to earn a profit or they will be shut down. Managers (13)_____ (will be, will not be) able to decide what is to be produced and how to produce it. In fact, many prices will be determined by markets rather than by central planning. Even prior to these reforms, farmers were allowed to sell produce in markets from private plots. These plots are considerably more productive than collective farms in producing food, accounting for as much as (14)_____ (25%, 75%) of Soviet agricultural output. Economic incentives are also used to motivate Soviet labor and existed prior to the reforms instituted at the beginning of 1988. In 1987, private enterprise was legalized in 29 areas, primarily in crafts and services. These changes will be beneficial to the Soviet economy. Managers will no longer have incentives to just meet output targets or exceed those targets, but will now have incentives to minimize costs in order to generate profits. This will result in a (15)_____ (less, more) efficient use of resources.

Other socialist systems vary in the degree to which central planning and markets are relied upon to allocate resources. In (16)_____ (North Korea, Yugoslavia), for example, most businesses are state owned but worker managed. Profits from these firms are used for investment in the enterprise or are divided among the firm's workers. In other nations, such as Great Britain, some large industrial enterprises are publicly owned, but the remainder of the economy is organized as a market economy.

In evaluating capitalism and socialism, important considerations include: (a) the extent to which the pursuit of self-interest and market exchange of goods and services produce results that coincide with a general consensus regarding national goals, (b) the way an economic system distributes well-being among members of a society, (c) the achievement of technological efficiency, (d) freedom of choice and responsiveness to consumer demands, and (e) economic growth and fluctuations.

VOCABULARY REVIEW

Write the key term from the list below next to its definition.

Key Terms

Economic system
Socialism
Labor theory of value
Surplus value
Command economy
Centrally planned economy

Gosplan
Materials balance
Consumer sovereignty
Turnover tax
Indicative planning

Definitions

1. _____: an economy in which politically appointed committees plan production and manage the economy to achieve political goals.

2. _____: the central planning board for the Soviet Union.

3. _____: an economy in which resource allocation decisions are determined largely by the central planning authorities who set production goals.

4. _____: exists when the supply of each intermediate product equals its demand as an input in some other productive process.

5. _____: defined by Karl Marx as the difference between a worker's subsistence wage and the value of the worker's production over a period.

6. _____: the responsiveness of the market economy to changes in consumer demand.

7. _____: maintains that only labor can produce something worth paying for.

8. _____: a sales tax used to raise revenue for the government; often used in planned economies to eliminate shortages in consumer markets.

9. _____: an economic system that is usually associated with government ownership of resources and central planning to determine prices and resource use.

10. _____: a system in which government encourages voluntary compliance by industrial and labor interests to coordinate economic decisions so as to achieve politically determined objectives.

11. _____: an accepted way of organizing production, establishing rights to ownership and use of productive resources, and governing economic transactions in a society.

Concept: Production targets, shortages, the turnover tax, and black markets

A competitive market for a good is shown in the figure below.

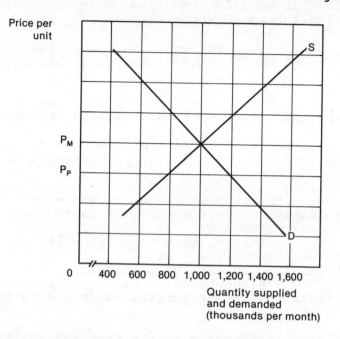

a.   Assume that this market economy now becomes a command economy in which central planners set production targets. Show the effect of a production target of 800,000 units where planners establish a price of Pp per unit. At the controlled price of Pp, there exists a _____ of _____ units.

b.   If the official government price is raised to the previous market level of Pm, there exists a _____ of _____ units.

c.   In order to eliminate the _____ and still maintain the production target of 800,000 units, a turnover tax equal to the difference between _____ and the _____ could be used. However, if a turnover tax is used in this manner, consumers in the command economy pay _____ prices and consume _____ output than they did previously in the market economy.

d.   Black markets will likely develop because some consumers will be willing to pay _____ prices than a government price like Pp in order to have additional units of the good. Even if a turnover tax eliminates shortages, black markets will likely still exist because the marginal cost of supplying an additional unit of a good will likely be _____ than the government price that eliminates shortages.

SELF-TEST FOR MASTERY

Select the best answer.

1. An economic system that is usually associated with government ownership of resources and central planning is known as:

    a. Capitalism.
    b. Fascism.
    c. Socialism.
    d. A market system.

2. Which of the following individuals argued that only workers create value?

    a. Adam Smith
    b. George Bush
    c. Karl Marx
    d. Karl Menninger

3. Marx argued that capitalists exploit workers by paying them a _____ in order to create _____.

    a. Subsistence wage, surplus value
    b. Wage equal to their marginal product, profits
    c. Portion of their profits, good will
    d. Wage less than their profit per worker, maximum growth for their enterprises

4. What main factor did Marx not foresee in making his prediction that workers would not rise above a subsistence standard of living?

    a. Population growth
    b. Growth in household consumption
    c. Growth in labor productivity
    d. Advances in technology
    e. C and d

5. The Soviet Union is an example of a:

    a. Market economy.
    b. Mixed-market system.
    c. Democratic socialist state.
    d. Command economy.

6. Which of the following is the Soviet Union's central planning board?

    a. Ministry of Industry
    b. Soviet Monetary Alliance
    c. <u>Perestroika</u>
    d. Gosplan

7. As of January 1, 1988, economic reforms were initiated in the Soviet Union. Which of the following is an economic reform?

    a. Requiring some soviet enterprises to earn a profit
    b. Allowing managers of some enterprises to decide what to produce and how to produce it
    c. Allowing many prices to be determined by markets
    d. All of the above

8. A turnover tax is:

    a. Used to reduce surpluses.
    b. Used to finance the Soviet economic reforms.
    c. Used to reduce shortages.
    d. The difference between the cost of a good and the price that equates supply and demand.

9. One advantage of a planned economy is that:

    a. It is more efficient.
    b. It responds more rapidly to changes in consumers' desires.
    c. It has achieved the highest living standards in the world.
    d. It can avoid fluctuations in aggregate demand and thus avoid the costs associated with business cycles.

10. Which of the following is true regarding private enterprise in the Soviet Union?

    a. The Soviet economic reforms have privatized collective farms.
    b. Private farm plots account for as much as 25% of the Soviet Union's total agricultural output.
    c. In 1987, private business was legalized in 29 areas.
    d. Most individuals engaged in private enterprise are in crafts or services.
    e. B, c, and d

11. In which of the following nations is a majority of enterprises state owned but worker managed?

    a. People's Republic of China
    b. France
    c. Yugoslavia
    d. Argentina

12. In which of the following nations is government ownership of or financial interest in large industrial enterprises common?

    a. United Kingdom
    b. France
    c. Italy
    d. All of the above
    e. A and c

13. Which of the following nations uses indicative planning--where private industry cooperates with the government to achieve political goals?

    a. Great Britain
    b. Yugoslavia
    c. Soviet Union
    d. United States
    e. France

14. In assessing the merits of capitalism vs. socialism, which of the following considerations are important?

    a.   The extent to which the pursuit of self-interest and market exchange of goods and services produce results that coincide with a general political consensus regarding national goals

    b.   The way an economic system distributes well-being among members of a society

    c.   The achievement of technological efficiency

    d.   Freedom of choice and responsiveness to consumer demands

    e.   All of the above

THINK IT THROUGH

1. Identify and briefly discuss some of the main differences between capitalism and socialism.

2. Several nations have returned state-owned enterprises to the private sector, whereas other socialist nations have instituted major market-based reforms. Can you think of any reasons why?

POP QUIZ   Read the news brief at the end of this chapter and answer the questions below.

1. Outline Angola's new economic plan. What is Angola's motivation for employing market-based reforms?

2. How do Angolans cope with the lack of product quantity and variety at state stores and a virtually worthless currency?

CHAPTER ANSWERS

In Brief: Chapter Summary

1. Capitalism 2. Socialism 3. Labor 4. Surplus value 5. Labor productivity
6. Demand for 7. Supply of 8. Command 9. Gosplan 10. Shortages 11.
Turnover 12. 60% 13. Will be 14. 25% 15. More 16. Yugoslavia

Vocabulary Review

1. Centrally planned economy 2. Gosplan 3. Command economy 4. Materials
balance 5. Surplus value 6. Consumer sovereignty 7. Labor theory of value
8. Turnover tax 9. Socialism 10. Indicative planning 11. Economic system

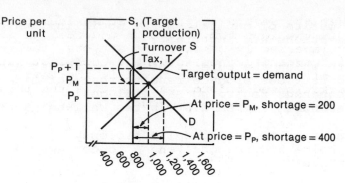

Price per unit

a.   Shortage, 400,000
b.   Shortage, 200,000
c.   Shortage, the subsidized price, price that would equate supply and demand; higher, less
d.   Higher, less

Self-Test for Mastery

1. c 2. c 3. a 4. e 5. d 6. d 7. d 8. c 9. d 10. e 11. c 12. d 13. e 14. e

Think It Through

1.   Capitalism relies on self-interest, private ownership, and markets to allocate resources. Socialism is distrustful of self-interest (the profit motive) and in the extreme case of a command economy, resources are allocated with extensive central planning. Capitalism rewards input suppliers on the basis of the quantity and productivity of inputs supplied. This is not necessarily so if markets are imperfectly competitive. A socialist state earns a profit from state-owned resources and redistributes it to workers in the form of wages and services. Modern mixed economies try to achieve equity in the distribution of income through transfer payments. In a competitive market economy, firms have an incentive to keep costs as low as possible, resulting in technological efficiency. Managers in socialist states often confront a much different set of costs and incentives, which reward managers not for minimizing costs, but for meeting production targets. In capitalist economies with competitive markets, consumers are sovereign. There is free choice in consumption, the employment of inputs, and the production of output. In a socialist state, individual freedoms are much less important than the achievement of political goals. A capitalist system is subject to recurrent ups and downs in real GNP and the rate of unemployment. The incidence of business cycles can be lessened considerably in command economies because aggregate demand is strictly controlled. If there are ups and downs in production, they are likely the result of supply-side shocks rather than fluctuations in aggregate demand.

2.   Competitive economies that rely on markets to allocate resources realize a higher level of technological efficiency than economies that rely on central planning. In a market system, self-interest coordinates decisions such that resources are allocated to their most productive employments. Workers are free to offer their labor services to the highest bidder. Entrepreneurs bring resources together to produce goods desired by consumers in hopes of earning a profit. Economic survival in a competitive economy requires technological

efficiency. Firms that are unable to produce at minimum possible unit costs
will exit the market in the long run. Even in the case of modern mixed
economies having many imperfectly competitive markets, the level of efficiency
is much higher than in command economies. Most socialist nations are
recognizing the power of incentives. As noted in the text, the Soviet Union is
embarking on major market-based reforms that require the pursuit of self-
interest in order to succeed.

Pop Quiz

1.   The economic plan Angola intends to implement is similar to those being
implemented in other socialist countries. The plan calls for autonomy for
managers and decentralization in decision making. It also involves returning
land to farmers and businesses to entrepreneurs in order to encourage private
sector production. Prices will be determined by the market, and wages will be
tied to labor productivity. Angola has turned to market incentives not because
of a radical ideological shift from Marxism, but because the war against Unita,
the rebel army supported by the United States and South Africa, is expensive
and requires an economy that can produce enough output to support the war
effort. Angola is using capitalism to defend Marxism!

2.   A thriving black market exists in Luanda, Angola. Here almost any good,
including imported goods, can be found and at prices well below the official
prices in state stores. The state stores have limited variety and encounter
shortages. The "official" prices are ridiculously high and bear no
relationship to market forces. In fact, either dollars or kwanzas are used to
purchase beer at state stores for $12 or 30,000 kwanzas. The beer is then
taken to the black market and sold for $15 in kwanzas, which can be traded for
other goods on the market. "Money is meaningless...Beer has meaning."
Angolans cope with scarcity in state stores and a worthless currency by having
an efficient black market that produces true market prices.

By Roger Thurow

Staff Reporter of THE WALL STREET JOURNAL

LUANDA, Angola—Capitalism literally has ended up on the scrap heap in this fervently Marxist country.

On the top of a hill overlooking this decaying port city, smack in the middle of a dump, a thriving black market coexists profitably with the garbage and flies. Vendors' prices are guided by the hand of Adam Smith rather than by state planners devoted to Karl Marx. The nearly worthless local currency is pegged to the price of beer. Anyone with the time to browse through this vast outdoor bazaar will find everything the socialist stores on the streets below are supposed to have, but don't.

The vendors first set up their stalls at the dump because it was a convenient open space. Now, garbage is taken only to the fringes of the market. Everyone, it seems, shops here: peasant farmers, factory workers, bureaucrats, soldiers, bankers, diplomats. Even state economists come looking for inspiration and ideas, as well as turnips and onions.

Destroyed by War

"We're studying this market, which is a very efficient market," says Victor Nunes, a Finance Ministry official responsible for overseeing Angola's ambitious economic adjustment program. "We have much to learn from it."

As Angola tries desperately to resuscitate its gasping socialist economy, it is taking a crash course in capitalism. A new economic plan, not coincidentally, is being launched at the same time Luanda is pushing for membership in the International Monetary Fund. The plan is similar to those being tinkered with in other rundown socialist countries: decentralizing economic decision-making, giving more autonomy to managers of businesses, encouraging the private sector, returning land to farmers and shops to entrepreneurs, harnessing prices to market forces and salaries to productivity, promoting foreign investment.

The catalyst for Angola's economic restructuring is the 13-year war against the rebel army known as Unita, which is supported by South Africa and the U.S. The war has devastated the economy, potentially one of the richest in Africa. More

mines than maize is planted in the countryside, much of which is controlled by the guerrillas. The industries of the big cities have ground to a halt from lack of material and spare parts. Skilled managers, always scarce here, are drafted as soldiers.

"We have come up with a slogan," says Dumilde das Chagas Simoes Rangel, Angola's trade minister. "Develop the economy to fight the war; fight the war to defend the economy."

Thus, if capitalism is what it takes to defend Marxism in Angola, so be it. "It is possible," says Mr. Nunes, "to construct socialism with rational economic means."

Like the free market. In the past, the state tried mightily to crush the illegal black markets, which account for the bulk of the country's economic activity. Today, however, the police on duty at the black markets are responsible for crowd control, not crowd dispersement. The state has decided to fight capitalism with capitalism, rather than with bulldozers and truncheons.

"We have to combat the parallel market with economic mechanisms," says Mr. Nunes, favoring the word "parallel" over "black."

At the moment, the black market is winning easily. Because of the deregulated prices and the more realistic exchange rate, many imported goods go directly from the port of Luanda to the unofficial markets, bypassing the state stores that stand forlorn and empty.

Empty Shelves

In downtown Luanda, a drugstore crumbling under a burned-out neon sign offers only a couple of packages of sinus pills and some dental floss. Its glass cabinets are empty, except for one that displays color posters of stomach ulcers. In contrast, the black market has a long row of vendors offering everything from antacids and aspirin to cough medicine and laxatives.

Also available on the black market: fruit, vegetables and fish; bubble gum, underwear and gin. Soap comes from Brazil, skin lightener from England, antihistamines from Switzerland, spaghetti from Bulgaria and soda pop from West Germany (though there is little from the U.S., which doesn't have diplomatic relations with Angola).

These are the things people want, not the bulky paraffin cookers or the industrial-type waffle irons ordered by the central planners and made here or in Russia. Even the name of the market reflects consumer choice: Roque Santeiro, the title of a popular Brazilian soap opera that is broadcast regularly in this former Portuguese colony.

'Money Is Meaningless'

Throughout Luanda, dollars and beer are the currencies of choice, favored over the local currency, the kwanza.

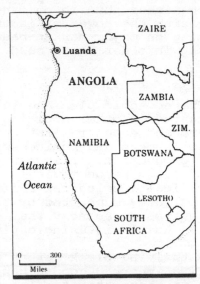

If anybody paid attention to the official rate of 30 kwanza to the dollar (nobody does), he would have to pay more than $60 for a packet of Marlboros or a can of orange pop. A heavy metal ashtray in the shape of a bug—its wings open up to collect the ashes—would cost more than $150 at a state store.

At the black market rate of 2,000 kwanza per dollar, the cigarettes and pop cost less than $1 each, and the ashtray is a steal at less than $3.

"Money is meaningless," says a budding economist who is wiling away Luanda's midnight-to-5 a.m. curfew by attending an all-night party. "Beer has meaning."

Imported Beer

He explains the two ways to get on the beer standard. If you have dollars, you simply head to one of the government-run hard-currency shops and buy a case of imported beer—Heineken, Beck's, Stella Artois—for $12. (Dollars aren't hard to get in Angola, at least for those in the middle class, who often travel abroad.)

But those who have only kwanza can get in on the deal, too. Typically, workers draw, as part of their salaries, coupons that can be redeemed at grocery stores run by their employers. These stores also have plenty of imported beer.

Having acquired a case of beer, you head to the neighborhood black market and cash in the 24 cans for 30,000 kwanza. (Recently, Stella Artois has been devalued to 15,000 kwanza because of unsubstantiated rumors here that it causes impotence.) This is worth $15 at the black-market rate and $1,000 at the official rate. Suddenly, you are rich, and you can load up on vegetables, fish, soap and clothes or even a plane ticket to Lisbon. The latter costs roughly two cases of beer.

Rich Food and Chic Clothes

The black marketeer, in turn, sells the

individual cans of beer for a nice profit: at 2,000 kwanza a can, he will collect 48,000 kwanza for a case. Everybody's happy.

"It works quite nicely," says the student economist at the all-night party. Because he hopes to work one day for the Bank of Angola, he agrees to speak on the condition he won't be identified. "You can get anything you want in Angola."

The party, attended by Luanda's young jet set, is proof of that. A feast unimaginable to all but a few Angolans is spread over several tables: lobster, prawns, beef, pork, chicken, cakes, pies and pastries. The bar is stocked with liquor from around the world, and the women are dressed in outfits from Lisbon, Paris and Rome.

The student giggles, somewhat embarrassed by these riches. "On the surface, Luanda looks miserable," he says. "But things aren't always as they seem."